Günter Scholze-Mertens

NEUE ENGLISCHE GRAMMATIK

Classic Edition

dnf-Verlag

NEUE ENGLISCHE GRAMMATIK, Classic Edition

von

Günter Scholze-Mertens

unter der Leitung
der Verlagsredaktion Sprachen, dnf-Verlag DAS NEUE FACHBUCH GmbH.

ISBN 978-3-89831-314-8

2. Auflage 02 | 10

© dnf-Verlag DAS NEUE FACHBUCH GmbH, Nürtingen 2010.

Alle Rechte vorbehalten. Reproduktionen, Speicherung in Datenverarbeitungs-
anlagen, Wiedergabe auf elektronischen, fotomechanischen oder ähnlichen
Wegen nur mit der ausdrücklichen Genehmigung des Verlages.

Vorwort

Die **Neue Englische Grammatik, Classic Edition** ist ein **lehrbuchunabhängiges** und ausführliches Lern- und Nachschlagewerk zur englischen Grammatik. Sie richtet sich an Studenten, fortgeschrittene Selbstlerner, Schüler und fortgeschrittene Volkshochschüler.

Besonderer Wert wurde auf einen **übersichtlichen Aufbau** gelegt, denn Übersichtlichkeit erleichtert das Lernen erheblich. So wurde stets darauf geachtet, dass die Einsparung von ein paar wenigen Seiten im Endeffekt nicht auf Kosten der Übersichtlichkeit ging.

Jeder Regel und ihrer Erklärung sind die entsprechenden **Beispiele** gegenübergestellt. So ist die Anwendung der Regel unmittelbar anhand der Beispiele nachvollziehbar. Die **deutsche Übersetzung** ist überall dort angegeben, wo Verständnisschwierigkeiten auftreten können.
Durch die Gegenüberstellung von Sachverhalten in **Tabellen** sind Unterschiede bzw. Parallelen sofort zu erkennen und leichter zu verstehen.
Komplexe Sachverhalte sind in ansprechend gestalteten **Übersichten** zusammengefasst. Diese kann man sich somit besser einprägen und verstehen.
Zu jedem Sachverhalt ist am rechten bzw. linken Seitenrand das entsprechende **Stichwort** gegeben. Man muss sich so nur das Stichwort merken und dieses dann mit dem entsprechenden Sachverhalt assoziieren.
Inhaltlich zusammengehörende Sachverhalte sind zusammen abgehandelt. Es konnte daher auf Querverweise und Fußnoten verzichtet und die damit verbundene Sucherei verhindert werden.
Alles Wesentliche ist farbig hervorgehoben. Auf **Fehlerquellen und Besonderheiten** wird durch ein Ausrufezeichen mit der entsprechenden Erklärung aufmerksam gemacht.

Umfangreiche **Übungen** am Ende eines Kapitels bieten ausführliche Möglichkeiten zu überprüfen, ob man das Gelernte verstanden hat. Zu jedem Übungssatz sind zwei Kontrollfelder zum Ankreuzen gegeben, die den Überblick über den eigenen Kenntnisstand ermöglichen. Ein Lösungsteil am Schluss des Buches stellt die **Lösungen zu jedem einzelnen Übungssatz** dar.

Alle **grammatischen Fachausdrücke mit** ihrer **englischen Bedeutung** und nicht zuletzt dem entsprechenden **deutschen Begriff** (z. B. Tunwort) sind stets an Ort und Stelle und in einer ausführlichen Liste zum Nachschlagen erläutert.

Verfasser und Verlag

Inhaltsverzeichnis

Abkürzungen 9

Das Alphabet
Das Alphabet 10

Betonung und Aussprache
Die Betonung 11
Die Aussprache 13

Verbformen und Verbarten
Das Verb 27

Die Konjugation
Die Konjugation 29
Die Konjugation von to have 32
Die Konjugation von to be 34
Die Konjugation der regelmäßigen Verben 36
Die Konjugation der unregelmäßigen Verben 38
Kurzformen 40
Die Stammformen 41
Übungen zur Konjugation 48

Die Hilfsverben
To Be 52
To Have 52
To Do 54
Übungen zu den Hilfsverben 58

Die Modalverben
Die Modalverben 63
Übungen zu den Modalverben 83

Die reflexiven und reziproken Verben
Die reflexiven Verben 86
Die reziproken Verben 87
Die Konjugation reflexiver Verben 88
Übungen zu den reflexiven Verben 90

Das Verb und seine Ergänzungen
Das Verb und seine Ergänzungen 92
Übungen zu den Ergänzungen zum Verb 97

Übereinstimmung von Verb und Subjekt
Übereinstimmung von Verb und Subjekt 99

Die Zeiten
Die Zeiten 103
Übungen zu den Zeiten 110
Simple und Continuous Form 115

Übungen zur Simple und Continuous Form ... 119

Das Passiv
Das Passiv ... 123
Umwandlung aktiver Sätze in passive Sätze ... 126
Die Konjugation passiver Formen ... 128
Übungen zum Passiv ... 130

Die indirekte Rede
Die indirekte Rede ... 137
Die Zeitenfolge in der indirekten Rede ... 144
Übungen zur indirekten Rede ... 148

Der Konditional
Der Konditional ... 158
Die Zeitenfolge im Bedingungssatz ... 159
Übungen zum Konditional ... 162

Der Subjunctive
Der Subjunctive ... 165

Der Imperativ
Der Imperativ ... 167

Der Infinitiv
Der Infinitiv ... 168
Übungen zum Infinitiv ... 178

Das Gerund
Das Gerund ... 183
Übungen zum Gerund ... 189

Die Partizipien
Die Partizipien ... 194
Übungen zu den Partizipien ... 200

Das deutsche *lassen*
Das deutsche *lassen* ... 204
Übungen zum deutschen *lassen* ... 206

Der Artikel
Der Artikel ... 209
Der bestimmte und der unbestimmte Artikel ... 210
Übungen zum Artikel ... 224
Die Stellung des Artikels ... 228
Übungen zur Stellung des Artikels ... 229
Die Wiederholung des Artikels ... 230

Das Substantiv
Das Substantiv ... 231
Das Geschlecht des Substantivs ... 233
Übungen zum Geschlecht des Substantivs ... 237

Der Numerus des Substantivs	238
Pluralbildung zusammengesetzter Substantive	249
Übungen zum Numerus des Substantivs	250
Common und Possessive Case	252
Übungen zum Common und Possessive Case	257

Das Adjektiv

Das Adjektiv	259
Die Steigerung des Adjektivs	260
Übungen zur Steigerung des Adjektivs	264
Das Adjektiv mit einem Stützwort	265
Übungen zum Stützwort des Adjektivs	266
Die Stellung des Adjektivs	267
Der Vergleich	268
Übungen zum Vergleich	270

Das Adverb

Das Adverb	271
Übungen zur Bildung des Adverbs	273
Die Steigerung des Adverbs	274
Übungen zur Steigerung des Adverbs	277
Die Stellung des Adverbs	278
Übungen zur Stellung des Adverbs	283
Adverb oder Adjektiv	286
Übungen zum Adverb und Adjektiv	289

Das Zahlwort

Die Grundzahlen	290
Die Ordnungszahlen	292
Die Bruchzahlen	294
Die Vervielfältigungszahlwörter	295
Die Uhrzeit und weitere Zeitangaben	296

Das Pronomen

Das Pronomen	298
Das Personalpronomen	299
Übungen zum Personalpronomen	304
Das Reflexivpronomen	305
Übungen zum Reflexivpronomen	307
Die Reziprokpronomen	308
Übungen zu den Reziprokpronomen	309
Das Possessivpronomen	310
Übungen zum Possessivpronomen	312
Das Demonstrativpronomen	314
Übungen zum Demonstrativpronomen	317
Das Determinativpronomen	318
Übungen zum Determinativpronomen	321
Das Relativpronomen	323
Übungen zum Relativpronomen	327
Das Interrogativpronomen	329
Übungen zum Interrogativpronomen	332
Die Indefinitpronomen	335
Übungen zu den Indefinitpronomen	346

Die Konjunktion
Die Konjunktion — 352

Die Präposition
Die Präposition — 356
Übungen zur Präposition — 359

Der Satz
Der Satz — 362
Der Aussagesatz — 364
Der Fragesatz — 373
Question Tags — 376
Übungen zu den Question Tags — 377
Der Aufforderungssatz — 379
Der Ausrufesatz — 380
Der Nebensatz — 381

Die Rechtschreibung
Groß- und Kleinschreibung — 384
Besonderheiten bei der Schreibung — 386
Britische und amerikanische Schreibweise — 390

Die Zeichensetzung
Die Zeichensetzung — 392

Die Silbentrennung
Die Silbentrennung — 398

Präfixe und Suffixe
Präfixe — 400
Suffixe — 402

Fachausdrücke — 407

Lösungen zu den Übungen — 419

Index — 445

Abkürzungen

adv.	adverbial	Obj.	Objekt
a. m.	ante meridiem	Objektpron.	Objektpronomen
Adj.	Adjektiv	o.s.	oneself
Adv.	Adverb		
AE	amerikanisches Englisch	p. m.	post meridiem
		Part.	Partizip, participle
BE	britisches Englisch	Past P.	past perfect
Best.	Bestimmung	Past Perf.	past perfect
bzw.	beziehungsweise	Past T.	past tense
		Past T. C.	past tense continuous
Con.	conditional	Past T. S.	past tense simple
Con. P.	conditional perfect	Perf.	Perfekt, perfect
Cont. Form	continuous form	Pers.	Person
		Pl.	Plural
d. h.	das heißt	Plur.	Plural
dir.	direkt	pos. case	possessive case
		präd.	prädikativ
etc.	et cetera	prädikat.	prädikativ
etw.	etwas	Präp.	Präposition
		präp.	präpositional
fem.	feminin	Pres.	present
ff	fortfolgende	Pres. P.	present perfect
Fut.	Futur, future	Pres. Perf.	present perfect
Fut. P.	future perfect	Pres. T	present tense
Fut. T.	future tense	Pres. T. C.	present tense continuous
		Pres. T. S.	present tense simple
Gen.	Genus	Present T.	present tense
Ger.	gerund	Pron.	Pronomen
Imp.	Imperativ, imperative	s.o.	someone
Ind.	Indikativ, indicative	s.th.	something
ind.	indirekt	Sg.	Singular
indir.	indirekt	Sing.	Singular
indirek.	indirekt	St.form	Stammform
Inf.	Infinitiv, infinitive	Sub.	subjunctive
intr.	intransitiv	Subj.pron.	Subjektpronomen
		Subjektpron.	Subjektpronomen
jm.	jemandem		
jn.	jemanden	tr.	transitiv
Kon.	Konsonant	vern.	verneint
Konj.	Konjunktiv	vgl.	vergleiche
lat.	lateinisch	z. B.	zum Beispiel
mask.	maskulin		
Mod.	Modus		
neutr.	neutrum		
Nu.	Numerus		

Das Alphabet (The Alphabet)

Buchstabe	Aussprache	Britisches Englisch	Amerikanisches Englisch	International
a	[ei]	Andrew	Abel	Amsterdam
b	[bi:]	Benjamin	Baker	Baltimore
c	[si:]	Charlie	Charlie	Casablanca
d	[di:]	David	Dog	Danemark
e	[i:]	Edward	Easy	Edison
f	[ef]	Frederick	Fox	Florida
g	[dʒi:]	George	George	Gallipoli
h	[eitʃ]	Harry	How	Havana
i	[ai]	Isaac	Item	Italia
j	[dʒei]	Jack	Jig	Jerusalem
k	[kei]	King	King	Kilogramme
l	[el]	Lucy	Love	Liverpool
m	[em]	Mary	Mike	Madagaskar
n	[en]	Nellie	Nan	New York
o	[ou]	Oliver	Oboe	Oslo
p	[pi:]	Peter	Peter	Paris
q	[kju:]	Queenie	Queen	Québec
r	[a:r]	Robert	Roger	Roma
s	[es]	Sugar	Sugar	Santiago
t	[ti:]	Tommy	Tare	Tripoli
u	[ju:]	Uncle	Uncle	Uppsala
v	[vi:]	Victor	Victor	Valencia
w	[dʌblju:]	William	William	Washington
x	[eks]	Xmas	X	Xanthippe
y	[wai]	Yellow	Yoke	Yokohama
z	[zed] (BE) [zi:] (AE)	Zebra	Zebra	Zürich

Die obigen Zeichen der internationalen Lautschrift werden wie folgt ausgesprochen:
[:] kennzeichnet einen langgezogenen Laut,
[ʒ] stimmhaftes (weiches) -sch (wie zum Beispiel in *Genie*),
[ʃ] stimmloses (scharfes) -sch (ähnlich dem deutschen -sch),
[r] Zungenspitze wird an den Obergaumen gelegt
[ʌ] kurzes, offenes -a.

Die Betonung (Accentuation)

Zweisilbige Wörter

Die meisten zweisilbigen Wörter germanischen Ursprungs und einige romanische Lehnwörter werden auf der ersten Silbe betont.

- **ac**-cess
- **bal**-ance
- **em**-pire
- **na**-ture

erste Silbe

Einige zweisilbige Wörter werden auf der Endsilbe betont. Es handelt sich hier häufig um romanische Lehnwörter.

- ad-**dress**
- ad-**vice**
- con-**tent**

Endsilbe

Dreisilbige Wörter

Die meisten dreisilbigen Wörter werden auf der ersten Silbe betont.

- **ar**-ti-cle
- **prej**-u-dice

erste Silbe

Einige werden auf der mittleren Silbe betont. Hierzu gehören besonders die Zusammensetzungen mit **im-, in-** und **un-,** wenn das Grundwort auf der ersten Silbe betont wird.

- mu-**se**-um
- re-**pub**-lic
- im-**mor**-al (**mor**-al)
- in-**dig**-nant (**dig**-nant)
- un-**cer**-tain (**cer**-tain)

mittlere Silbe

Einige dreisilbige Wörter werden auf der Endsilbe betont.

- em-ploy-**ee**
- in-tro-**duce**

Endsilbe

Vier- und mehrsilbige Wörter

Vier- und mehrsilbige Wörter werden meist auf der drittletzten Silbe betont. Einige werden auch auf der ersten Silbe betont.

- con-**serv**-a-tive
- rep-re-**sent**-a-tive
- **nom**-i-na-tive
- **par**-ti-ci-ple

drittletzte Silbe

Fünfsilbige Wörter

Einige fünfsilbige Wörter werden auf der viertletzten Silbe betont.

- con-**stit**-u-en-cy
- im-**ag**-i-na-tive

viertletzte Silbe

Betonung und Aussprache

Verben auf -ish, Substantive und Adjektive auf -ic, -id und -it

zweitletzte Silbe — Verben auf -ish, Substantive und Adjektive auf -ic, -id und -it werden meist auf der zweitletzten Silbe betont.

- di-**min**-ish
- re-**pub**-lic
- **val**-id

Wörter auf -al, -an, -ance, -ant, -ar, -ate, -ence, -ent, -ive, -ment, -ous, -ty, -ute und -y

drittletzte Silbe — Wörter auf -al, -an, -ance, -ant, -ar, -ate, -ence, -ent, -ive, -ment, -ous, -ty, -ute und -y werden in der Regel auf der drittletzten Silbe betont.

- po-**lit**-i-cal
- sig-**nif**-i-cance
- **mar**-vel-(l)ous
- pos-si-**bil**-i-ty

Substantive auf -ary, -alty und -ony und Adjektive auf -ary

viertletzte Silbe — Substantive auf -ary, -alty und -ony und Adjektive auf -ary werden in der Regel auf der viertletzten Silbe betont.

- **ad**-ver-sar-y
- **com**-men-tar-y
- **cas**-u-al-ty

Verschiedene Betonung gleich geschriebener und stammverwandter Wörter

unterschiedliche Betonung — Eine Reihe Wörter, die unterschiedlichen Wortarten (Verben, Substantiven, Adjektiven etc.) zuzuordnen sind, werden zwar gleich geschrieben, jedoch unterschiedlich betont. Dasselbe gilt für einige stammverwandte Wörter.

- **ab**-sent (abwesend) — to ab-**sent** o.s. (fernbleiben)
- **in**-crease (Zunahme) — to in-**crease** (zunehmen)
- **dem**-o-crat (Demokrat) — dem-**oc**-ra-cy (Demokratie)
- cou-**ra**-geous (mutig) — **cour**-age (Mut)

Gleich starke Betonung zweier Wörter oder Silben (level stress)

gleich stark betonte Silben — Häufig stehen zwei gleich stark betonte Wörter oder Silben nebeneinander. Man spricht dann von level stress. Dies gilt bei thirteen bis nineteen, twenty-one etc., Wörtern mit einer betonten Vorsilbe (arch-, ex-, half-, mis-, non-, over-, pre-, re-, under-) und vielen Wortzusammensetzungen.

- **four**-**teen**
- **for**-ty-**four**
- **arch**-**bish**-op
- **down**-**stairs**

Betonung und Aussprache

Die Aussprache (Pronunciation)

Zwischen Aussprache und Schreibweise bestehen im Englischen erhebliche Unterschiede. Die folgenden Ausführungen sollen mithelfen von der Aussprache auf die richtige Schreibweise schließen zu können. Die Zeichen der internationalen Lautschrift (in eckigen Klammern) sind in den daneben stehenden Beschreibungen erläutert.

Die Vokale (The Vowels)

Die Vokale (Selbstlaute) sind Laute, bei deren Aussprache kein anderer Laut benötigt wird. Zu den Vokalen gehören a, e, i, o, u.

a	[ɑː] (BE)	Langes, dunkles -a (BE).	▪ after
	[æ] (AE)	Helles, offenes -ä (AE).	▪ task
	[ɔː]	Langes, offenes -o.	▪ ball ▪ false
	[ə]	Kurzer, unbetonter „Murmellaut", ähnlich dem kurzen deutschen -e.	▪ about ▪ countable ▪ menace
	[ei]	Einsilbig gesprochener Diphthong aus -e und -i.	▪ blame ▪ fame
	[æ]	Helles, offenes, nicht zu kurzes -ä.	▪ cat ▪ man
	[eə]	Halbgeschlossenes, halblanges -ä. In dieser Weise kommt das -a nur in Verbindung mit -r vor.	▪ bare ▪ care ▪ dare ▪ mare
e	[e]	Kurzes, halbgeschlossenes -e.	▪ bed ▪ get
	[ə]	Kurzer, unbetonter „Murmellaut", ähnlich dem kurzen deutschen -e.	▪ fired ▪ hired ▪ tired
	[iː]	Langes, dumpfes -i.	▪ be ▪ equal
	[-]	Das -e bleibt am Wortende und vor bzw. nach -l häufig stumm.	▪ conceive ▪ candle ▪ panel
i	[i]	Kurzes, offenes -i.	▪ mix ▪ stick

Betonung und Aussprache

	[iː]	Langes, dumpfes -i.	■ ant**i**que ■ techn**i**que
	[ai]	Einsilbig gesprochener Diphthong aus hellem -a und -i.	■ div**i**de ■ tr**i**be
o	[ɔ] (BE) [ɑ] (AE)	Kurzes, sehr offenes -o (BE). Kurzes, dunkles -a (AE).	■ c**o**st ■ h**o**t
	[ou]	Einsilbig gesprochener Diphthong aus -o und -u.	■ cl**o**se ■ n**o**te
	[ə]	Kurzer, unbetonter „Murmellaut", ähnlich dem kurzen deutschen -e.	■ c**o**mpete ■ d**o**mestic ■ **o**bedience
	[u]	Kurzes, halbgeschlossenes -u.	■ d**o** ■ w**o**man
	[o]	Kurzes, geschlossenes -o. Dieses -o ist relativ selten.	■ m**o**lest
u	[juː] [uː]	Langes, halbgeschlossenes -ju. In der modernen Sprache wird es besonders nach -d, -t, -th, -n und -s und im Amerikanischen wie ein langes, halbgeschlossenes -u ausgesprochen.	■ p**u**re ■ ref**u**ge ■ st**u**dent ■ pres**u**me
	[u]	Kurzes, halbgeschlossenes -u.	■ b**u**tcher ■ p**u**t
	[i]	Kurzes, offenes -i.	■ b**u**sy ■ b**u**siness
	[ʌ] (BE) [əː] (AE)	Kurzer, halboffener Laut zwischen -o und dunklem -a (BE). Langer, unbetonter „Murmellaut" (AE).	■ b**u**t ■ h**u**rry ■ h**u**sband

Neben den reinen Vokalen gibt es noch Verbindungen aus zwei Vokalen (Diphthonge) oder Vokal und Konsonant.

ai	[ei]	Einsilbig gesprochener Diphthong aus e- und -i.	■ **ai**m ■ det**ai**l

Betonung und Aussprache

	[eə]	Halbgeschlossenes, halb-langes -ä.	• air • hair
ance	[əns]	Auf den kurzen, unbetonten „Murmellaut", ähnlich dem kurzen deutschen -e, folgt -ns.	• brilliance • maintenance • substance
ant	[ənt]	Auf den kurzen, unbetonten „Murmellaut", ähnlich dem kurzen deutschen -e, folgt -nt.	• assistant • attendant • resistant
au	[ɔː]	Langes, offenes -o.	• auction • autobus
	[ɑː]	Langes, dunkles -a.	• aunt • draught
aw	[ɔː]	Langes, offenes -o.	• awful • law
ay	[ei]	Einsilbig gesprochener Diphthong aus -e und -i.	• may • say
	[ei], [i]	Einsilbig gesprochener Diphthong aus -e und –i, oder seltener, kurzes, offenes -i.	• Monday • Wednesday • Friday
ea	[iː]	Langes, dumpfes -i.	• clean • eagle
	[ɜː]	Langer, unbetonter „Murmellaut", jedoch bei gespreizten Lippen zur Vermeidung des ö-Lautes.	• earn • learn
	[eə]	Halbgeschlossenes, halb-langes -ä.	• bear • wear
	[e]	Kurzes, halbgeschlossenes -e.	• breakfast • heaven
	[ei]	Einsilbig gesprochener Diphthong aus -e und -i.	• break • steak

Betonung und Aussprache

ee	[iː]	Langes, dumpfes -i.	▪ m**ee**t ▪ n**ee**d
ei	[ei]	Einsilbig gesprochener Diphthong aus -e und -i.	▪ **ei**ght ▪ w**ei**ght
	[ai]	Einsilbig gesprochener Diphthong aus hellem -a und -i.	▪ h**ei**ght ▪ **ei**ther (AE: [iːðə])
ence ense	[ens]	Auf kurzes, geschlossenes -e folgt -ns.	▪ f**ence** ▪ int**ense**
ent	[ənt]	Auf den kurzen, unbetonten „Murmellaut", ähnlich dem kurzen deutschen -e, folgt -nt.	▪ appar**ent** ▪ confid**ent** ▪ oppon**ent**
eu	[ju(ː)] (BE) [u(ː)] (AE)	Kurzes (bzw. langes), halbgeschlossenes -ju (BE). Kurzes (bzw. langes), halbgeschlossenes -u (AE).	▪ **Eu**ropean ▪ **eu**phoria ▪ f**eu**dalism ▪ n**eu**tral
ew	[ju(ː)] (BE) [u(ː)] (AE)	Langes, halbgeschlossenes -ju (BE). Langes, halbgeschlossenes -u (AE).	▪ bl**ew** ▪ n**ew** Wichtige Ausnahme: ▪ s**ew** [soʊ] (nähen)
ey	[iː]	Langes, dumpfes -i.	▪ k**ey** ▪ mon**ey**
ia	[aiə]	Einsilbig gesprochener Diphthong aus hellem -a und -i und kurzem, unbetonten „Murmellaut", wie das kurze deutsche -e.	▪ b**ia**s ▪ d**ia**l ▪ l**ia**r
	[ə]	Kurzer, unbetonter „Murmellaut", ähnlich dem kurzen deutschen -e, das -i ist stumm.	▪ As**ia** ▪ parl**ia**ment
ie	[iː]	Langes, dumpfes -i.	▪ med**ie**val ▪ spec**ie**s
ience ient	[əns] [ənt]	Auf den kurzen, unbetonten „Murmellaut", ähnlich dem kurzen deutschen -e, folgt -ns bzw. -nt.	▪ suffic**iency** ▪ pat**ience** ▪ pat**ient** ▪ suffic**ient**

Betonung und Aussprache

ir	[əː]	Langer, unbetonter „Murmellaut", jedoch bei gespreizten Lippen zur Vermeidung des ö-Lautes.	▪ circuit ▪ first ▪ thirst
oa	[ou]	Einsilbig gesprochener Diphthong aus -o und -u.	▪ boat ▪ soap
	[ɔː]	Langes, offenes -o.	▪ coarse ▪ roar
oe	[uː]	Langes, halbgeschlossenes -u.	▪ canoe ▪ shoe
	[ou]	Einsilbig gesprochener Diphthong aus -o und -u.	▪ toe ▪ woe
oi	[ɔi]	Einsilbiger Diphthong aus kurzem, offenem -o und -i.	▪ foil ▪ oil
oo	[u] [uː]	Kurzes, halbgeschlossenes -u bzw. langes, halbgeschlossenes -u.	▪ foot ▪ root
	[ʌ]	Kurzer, halb offener Laut aus -o und dunklem -a.	▪ blood ▪ flood
	[ɔː]	Langes, offenes -o.	▪ door ▪ floor
ou	[u] [uː]	Kurzes, halbgeschlossenes -u bzw. langes, halbgeschlossenes -u.	▪ could ▪ should ▪ soup ▪ wound
	[au]	Einsilbig gesprochener Diphthong aus hellem -a und -u.	▪ doubt ▪ house
	[ʌ] (BE) [əː] (AE)	Kurzer, halb offener Laut zwischen -o und dunklem -a (BE). Langer, unbetonter „Murmellaut" (AE).	▪ courage ▪ touch
	[ɔː]	Langes, offenes -o.	▪ court ▪ pour

Betonung und Aussprache

	[ə]	Kurzer, unbetonter „Murmellaut", ähnlich dem kurzen deutschen -e.	• borough • endeavour • jealous
ow	[ou]	Einsilbig gesprochener Diphthong aus -o und -u.	• mow • own
	[au]	Einsilbig gesprochener Diphthong aus hellem -a und -u.	• brown • down
oy	[ɔi]	Einsilbig gesprochener Diphthong aus kurzem, offenem -o und -i.	• boy • joy • toy
ue	[juː] [uː]	Langes, halbgeschlossenes -ju bzw. langes, halbgeschlossenes -u.	• argue • blue
ui	[i]	Kurzes, offenes -i.	• biscuit • circuit
	[uː]	Langes, halbgeschlossenes -u.	• bruise • cruise
ur	[ɜː]	Langer, unbetonter „Murmellaut", jedoch bei gespreizten Lippen zur Vermeidung des ö-Lautes.	• burglar • surgeon • Thursday

Betonung und Aussprache

Das folgende Schaubild stellt die Aussprache der Vokale und Diphthonge und ihre Schreibweisen im Überblick dar.

	[ɑ] [ʌ]	[æ] [eə]	[ai]	[au]	[ə] [e] [ɜ]	[ei]	[i]	[ɔ]	[oi]	[ou]	[(j)u]
-a	after	cat			about	blame		ball			
-ai		air				aim					
-au	aunt							auction			
-aw								law			
-ay						say	Friday				
-e					tired		be				
					bed						
-ea		wear			learn	break	clean				
-ee							need				
-ei			height			eight					
-eu											neutral
-ew											new
-ey						obey	key				
-i			divide				mix				
-ie							species				
-ir					first						
-o					obey			cost		close	do
-oa								roar		boat	
-oe										toe	shoe
-oi									oil		
-oo	blood							door			root
-ou	touch			doubt				court			could
-ow				brown						own	
-oy									boy		
-u	but						busy				put
-ue											blue
-ui							biscuit				bruise
-ur					urge						

Die Konsonanten (The Consonants)

Die Konsonanten (Mitlaute) sind Laute, für deren Aussprache noch ein anderer Laut benötigt wird. Zu den Konsonanten zählen alle Laute außer den Vokalen.

b	[b]	Es wird wie das deutsche -b ausgesprochen.	▪ break ▪ snob
c	[s]	Vor -e und -i ist es ein stimmloses -s.	▪ ceiling ▪ species
	[ʃ]	Vor -e und -i ist es ein stimmloses -sch.	▪ special ▪ social
	[k]	Vor -a, -o und -u, vor Konsonant und am Wortende wird es wie -k ausgesprochen.	▪ conceive ▪ customer ▪ character ▪ plastic
ch	[tʃ]	Es ist vor allem am Wortanfang und am Wortende ein stimmloses -tsch.	▪ cheat ▪ church ▪ search
	[ʃ]	Es ist vor allem in der Wortmitte ein stimmloses -sch.	▪ machine ▪ parachute
	[k]	Es wird nach kurzem, betontem Vokal und häufig am Wortende wie -k ausgesprochen.	▪ epoch ▪ Loch Ness ▪ monarch ▪ technique
d	[d]	Es wird wie das deutsche -d ausgesprochen.	▪ devote ▪ predate
f	[f]	Es wird wie das deutsche -f ausgesprochen.	▪ fever ▪ fame
g	[g]	Vor -a, -o, -u und vor Konsonant wird es wie -g ausgesprochen.	▪ game ▪ govern ▪ grace
		Soll es vor -e, -i und -y wie -g ausgesprochen werden, wird nach dem -g ein -u eingefügt.	▪ colleague ▪ fatigue ▪ guest
		In germanischen Wörtern wird es vor -e, -i und -y wie -g ausgesprochen.	▪ get ▪ gift ▪ give

Betonung und Aussprache

	[dʒ]	In romanischen Wörtern ist es vor -e, -i und -y ein stimmhaftes -dsch.	• general • giant • gymnastic
		Soll es vor -a und -o wie stimmhaftes -dsch ausgesprochen werden, wird nach dem -g ein -e eingefügt.	• sergeant • geography • pigeon • surgeon
gua	[gɑː]	Verbindung aus -g und langem, dunklem -a. Das -u bleibt stumm.	• guard • guardian
gui	[gai]	Verbindung aus -g und einsilbig gesprochenem Diphthong aus hellem -a und -i. Das -u ist stumm.	• disguise • guide • guile • guise
	[gi]	Verbindung aus -g und kurzem, offenem -i. Das -u bleibt stumm.	• guilt • guinea • guitar

+	-a	-e	-i	-o	-u	Kon.
-g	[g]	[dʒ] [g]	[dʒ] [g]	[g]	[g]	[g]
-ge	[dʒ]		[dʒ]			
-gu	[g]	[g]	[g]			

gh	[-]	Verbindungen aus -g und -h bleiben meist stumm.	• height • sight
	[f]	Am Wortende wird es häufig wie das deutsche -f ausgesprochen.	• cough • enough • tough
gn	[n]	Das -g bleibt vor -n häufig stumm.	• gnaw • foreign
h	[h]	Es wird wie das deutsche -h ausgesprochen.	• hazard • height
	[-]	In vielen Fällen bleibt es stumm, besonders nach -g, -r, -w, in der Wortmitte und in einigen Fällen am Wortanfang.	• ghost • Rhine • wheel • exhaust • hour

Betonung und Aussprache

j	[dʒ]	Stimmhaftes -dsch.	• injure • jealous
k	[k]	Es wird wie das deutsche -k ausgesprochen.	• basket • kick
kn	[n]	Das -k bleibt am Wortanfang vor -n stumm.	• know • knot
l	[l]	Vor Vokalen ist es ein helles Vorderzungen-l, sonst ist es ein dunkles Hinterzungen-l.	• land • leg • table
lk lm	[k] [m]	Das -l bleibt vor -k und -m meist stumm.	• chalk • palm
m	[m]	Es wird wie das deutsche -m ausgesprochen.	• man • mother
n	[n]	Es wird wie das deutsche -n ausgesprochen.	• never • nothing
mn	[m]	Das -n bleibt nach -m meist stumm.	• autumn • column
ng	[ŋg]	Das -g in der Verbindung -ng ist deutlich hörbar.	• finger • hunger
	[ŋ]	Es wird wie das deutsche -ng nasaliert (durch die Nase) ausgesprochen.	• long • singer
p	[p]	Es wird wie das deutsche -p ausgesprochen.	• complete • prevent
pn ps pt	[n] [s] [t]	Das -p bleibt vor -n, -s und -t meist stumm. Die Verbindung -pt kommt selten vor.	• pneumatic • psychologist • ptomaine
ph	[f]	Es wird wie das deutsche -f ausgesprochen.	• alphabet • photograph
qu	[kw]	Es wird vor allem am Wortanfang wie -kw ausgesprochen.	• equal • quarrel
	[k]	In einigen Fällen wird es wie -k ausgesprochen.	• antique • liquor

Betonung und Aussprache

r	[r]	Es ist weder ein deutsches „Zäpfchen"-r, noch ein gerolltes -r. Bei der Aussprache wird die Zungenspitze lose an den vorderen Obergaumen gelegt. Im amerikanischen Englisch wird die Zungenspitze weiter hinten gegen den Obergaumen gedrückt. Im britischen Englisch wird es nur vor Vokalen und am Ende eines Wortes, nur wenn ein mit Vokal beginnendes Wort folgt, gesprochen. Im amerikanischen Englisch wird es auch am Wortende und vor Konsonant gesprochen.	• radio • right • propose • there‿is • where‿are • father [fɑːð ə] (BE) • farm (f ɑːm] (BE) • father [fɑːðər] (AE) • farm [fɑːrm] (AE)
s	[s]	Am Wortanfang ist es meist ein stimmloses -s entsprechend dem deutschen -ß.	• salt • skill
	[z]	Am Wortende wird es häufig stimmhaft ausgesprochen.	• abuse • news • use
	[ʃ]	Stimmloses -sch, vor allem in Verbindung mit -i.	• sure • permission
	[ʒ]	Stimmhaftes -sch, vor allem vor -i.	• lesion • illusion
sc	[s]	Stimmloses -s wie das deutsche -ß. Das -c ist, besonders vor -i, häufig stumm.	• discipline • science • scissors
	[sk]	Stimmloses -s entsprechend dem deutschen -ß. Das -c wird wie -k ausgesprochen.	• discretion • masculine • rascal
sch	[sk]	Stimmloses -s entsprechend dem deutschen -ß. Das -ch wird wie -k ausgesprochen.	• scheme • school Wichtige Ausnahme: • schedule [ʃedjuːl] (BE)

Betonung und Aussprache

sh	[ʃ]	Stimmloses -sch.	• fish • show
st	[s]	Das -t bleibt nach -s in einigen Fällen stumm.	• castle • whistle
t	[t]	Es wird wie das deutsche -t ausgesprochen.	• test • rest
	[ʃ]	In einigen Fällen ist es ein stimmloses -sch, vor allem in Verbindung mit -i.	• discretion • essential • potential
th	[θ]	Stimmloser Lispellaut, der durch Anlegen der Zungenspitze an die Rückwand der oberen Schneidezähne erzeugt wird.	• method • path • thin • thick
	[ð]	Stimmhafter Lispellaut.	• breathe • father
v	[v]	Stimmhafter w-Laut, ähnlich dem deutschen -w.	• fever • prevent
w	[w]	Kurzes, aus der Mundstellung für -u heraus gesprochenes -w, aber kein deutsches -w.	• swan • water
wr	[r]	Das -w bleibt vor -r am Wortanfang meist stumm.	• write • wrong
x	[ks]	Verbindung aus -k und stimmlosem -s.	• prefix • wax
	[gz]	Verbindung aus -g und stimmhaftem -s.	• exact • examine
	[kʃ]	Verbindung aus -k und stimmlosem -sch.	• luxury
xc	[ks]	Verbindung aus -k und stimmlosem -s.	• exceed • excite
y	[j]	Kurzes -j, vor allem am Wortanfang.	• yield • you

Betonung und Aussprache

	[ai]	Einsilbiger Diphthong aus hellem -a und -i.	▪ cry ▪ shy
	[i]	Kurzes, offenes -i. Dies ist vor allem am Wortende und in der Endung -ly der Fall.	▪ heavy ▪ levy ▪ faithfully ▪ truly
z	[z]	Stimmhaftes -s.	▪ seize ▪ zebra

Betonung und Aussprache

Das folgende Schaubild stellt die Aussprache der Konsonanten und ihre mögliche Schreibweise im Überblick dar. Dabei sind die Konsonanten aufgeführt, die gleich oder ähnlich ausgesprochen werden und daher verwechselt werden können.

	[f]	[g]	[k]	[n]	[s]	[ʃ] / [ʒ]	[tʃ] / [dʒ]	[sk]
-c			cost		centre	social		
-ch			epoch			machine	cheat	
-f	fever							
-g		game					general	
-gh	tough							
-gn				gnaw				
-gu		guest						
-j							injure	
-k			kick					
-kn				know				
-lk			chalk					
-n				no				
-ph	photo							
-pn				pneumatic				
-ps					psychic			
-qu			liquor					
-s					salt	sure		
-sc					science			discrete
-sch								school
-sh						fish		
-st					castle			
-t						discretion		

Das Verb (The Verb)

Das Verb ist ein unentbehrlicher Teil eines Satzes. Es drückt einen Zustand oder Vorgang, eine Tätigkeit oder Handlung aus (Zeitwort, Tätigkeitswort, Tunwort).

Finite Verbformen (Finite Verbs)

Finite Verben sind konjugierte Verbformen. Sie ändern ihre Form nach Person (1., 2. Person etc.), Zahl (Singular, Plural), Zeit (Präsens, Futur etc.) und Modus (Indikativ, Konjunktiv etc.).

- He **reads** a book.
  (indicative present tense, 3. Person Singular)
- We **worked** from 9 to 5 o'clock.
- She **looks** after the baby.
- It **looks** fine.

Infinite Verbformen (Infinite Verbs)

Infinite Verbformen sind nicht konjugierte Verbformen. Hierzu zählen Infinitiv, gerund, Partizipien.

- to buy
- buying
- bought

Transitive Verben (Transitive Verbs)

Transitive Verben sind Verben, die mit einem direkten Objekt stehen.

- I **read** a book.
- I can **see** your brother.

Intransitive Verben (Intransitive Verbs)

Intransitive Verben sind Verben, die ohne direktes Objekt stehen.

- I **am** ill.
- He will **arrive** this afternoon.

Vollverben (Full Verbs)

Vollverben bilden das Prädikat alleine. Hierzu zählen alle Verben außer den Hilfsverben to be, to have und to do und den Modalverben.

- I **read** a book.
- He **wrote** a letter.
- We **open** the door.

Hilfsverben (Auxiliary Verbs)

Hilfsverben sind Verben, die für die Bildung der zusammengesetzten Zeiten und des Passivs benötigt werden. Die Hilfsverben sind to be, to have und to do, das zur Bildung von Fragen und verneinten Sätzen dient.

- I **have** read a book.
- I **am** going home.
- The door **is** opened by the caretaker.
- I **do** not like him.
- **Did** you read this book?

Verbformen und Verbarten

Modalverben (Modal Auxiliary Verbs)

Modalverben sind Verben, die den Inhalt eines anderen Verbs abwandeln. Ihnen folgt stets ein Infinitiv.

- You **can** go to the cinema tonight.
- **May** I lead the way?
- He **must** go to school every day.

▪ can	kann	▪ should	sollte
▪ could	konnte; könnte	▪ ought to	sollte
▪ may	dürfen	▪ will	wollen
▪ might	durfte; dürfte	▪ would	würden
▪ must	müssen	▪ used to	pflegte zu
▪ need	brauchen	▪ dare	wagen
▪ shall	sollen		

Reflexive Verben (Reflexive Verbs)

Reflexive Verben werden von einem Reflexivpronomen (myself, yourself etc.) begleitet. Das Reflexivpronomen bezeichnet dieselbe Person oder Sache wie das Subjekt.

- I **wash myself.**
  (I und myself bezeichnen dieselbe Person.)
- This morning he **cut himself** while shaving.

Reziproke Verben (Reciprocal Verbs)

Reziproke Verben drücken die Gegenseitigkeit, Wechselbeziehung aus (einander, gegenseitig). Diese Verben werden mit den Pronomen one another bzw. each other verbunden.

- They **love one another**.
  (Sie lieben einander.)
- They **think of each other**.
  (Sie denken aneinander.)

Die Konjugation (Conjugation)

Konjugation (Beugung) bedeutet Abwandlung der Grundform (Infinitiv) des Verbs bezüglich Person und Zeit, d. h. der Infinitiv des Verbs, z. B. speak wird im present tense in der 3. Person Singular zu speaks.
Grundsätzlich werden im Englischen zur Konjugation eines Verbs 3 Stammformen benötigt, mit denen sämtliche Zeiten – wie im Folgenden dargestellt – gebildet werden können.
Man unterscheidet regelmäßige und unregelmäßige Verben. Die regelmäßigen Verben hängen in der 2. und 3. Stammform lediglich -ed an. Die 1. Stammform ist der Infinitiv. Die unregelmäßigen Verben haben in der 2. und 3. Stammform eigene Formen, die auf Seite 41ff dargestellt sind.

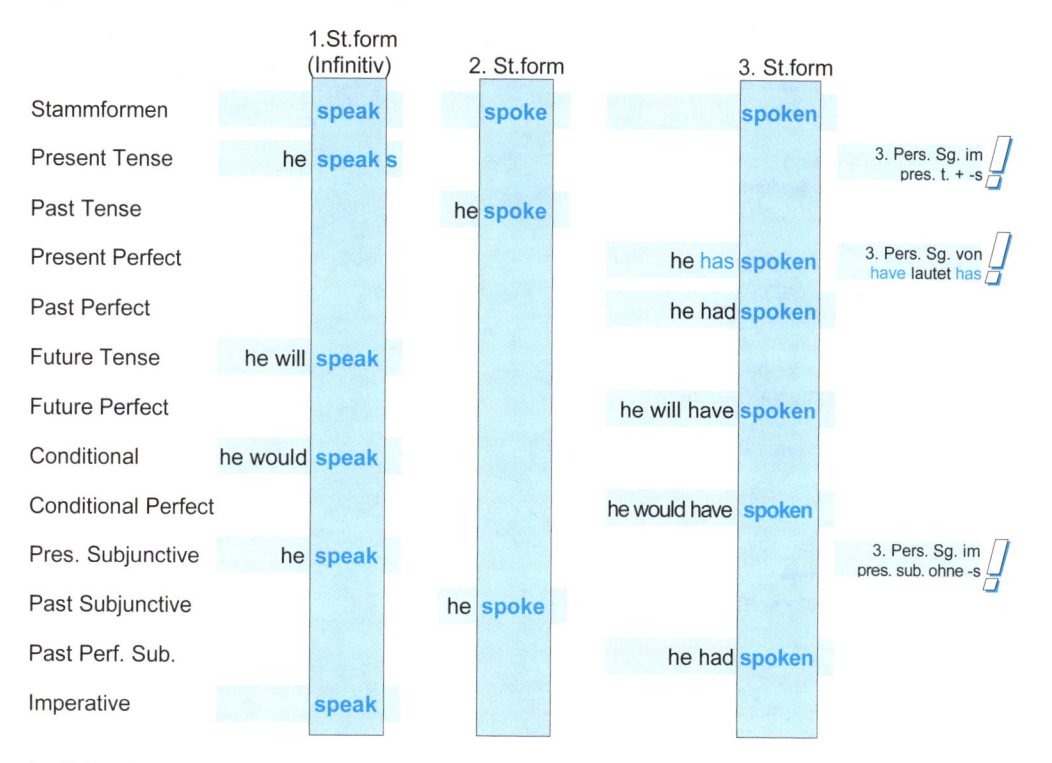

	1.St.form (Infinitiv)	2. St.form	3. St.form	
Stammformen	speak	spoke	spoken	
Present Tense	he speaks			3. Pers. Sg. im pres. t. + -s
Past Tense		he spoke		
Present Perfect			he has spoken	3. Pers. Sg. von have lautet has
Past Perfect			he had spoken	
Future Tense	he will speak			
Future Perfect			he will have spoken	
Conditional	he would speak			
Conditional Perfect			he would have spoken	
Pres. Subjunctive	he speak			3. Pers. Sg. im pres. sub. ohne -s
Past Subjunctive		he spoke		
Past Perf. Sub.			he had spoken	
Imperative	speak			

Im Folgenden ist die Konjugation von to have und to be sowie die Konjugation der regelmäßigen und unregelmäßigen Verben am Beispiel von to help und to eat dargestellt. Anhand dieser Beispielverben und mittels der Stammformen lässt sich jedes beliebige Verb konjugieren. Alle Verbendungen sind kursiv, Besonderheiten in den Verbformen sind blau gedruckt.

Bei der Bildung der einzelnen Verbformen sind zusätzlich noch einige Rechtschreibregeln zu beachten, die im Folgenden im Überblick dargestellt sind.

Die Konjugation

	Infinitiv	2. und 3. Stammform	3. Pers. Sing. Pres. Tense	-ing
Konsonant am Verbende Konsonant am Verbende verdoppelt sich vor -ed und -ing, wenn diesem ein einfacher, betonter (´) Vokal vorausgeht.	stóp	stópp ed	stop s	stópp ing
Endkonsonant wird nicht verdoppelt, wenn diesem ein unbetonter Vokal, zwei Vokale oder ein Konsonant vorausgehen.	cónquer look help	cónquer ed look ed help ed	cónquer s look s help s	cónquer ing look ing help ing
-l und -r am Verbende werden vor -ed und -ing verdoppelt. Im Amerikanischen wird das -l meist nicht verdoppelt.	quarrel quarrel prefer	quarrell ed quarrel ed preferr ed	quarrell s quarrell s prefer s	quarrell ing quarrel ing preferr ing
-l und -r werden nicht verdoppelt, wenn kein einfacher, sondern zwei Vokale vorausgehen.	sail repair	sail ed repair ed	sail s repair s	sail ing repair ing
Stummes -e am Verbende Stummes -e am Verbende entfällt vor -ed oder -ing.	live	liv- ed	live s	liv- ing
-ee am Verbende -ee am Verbende wird zu -e, vor Endungen, die mit -e beginnen.	agree	agre ed	agree s	agree ing
-ch, -sh, -ss, -x am Verbende Auf -ch, -sh, -ss, -x am Verbende folgt -es in der 3. Person Singular des present tense.	touch	touch ed	touch es	touch ing

Die Konjugation

	Infinitiv	2. und 3. Stammform	3. Pers. Sing. Pres. Tense	-ing
-o am Verbende Auf -o am Verbende folgt -es in der 3. Person Singular des present tense, wenn dem -o ein Konsonant vorausgeht.	do	did	does	doing
-ie am Verbende -ie am Verbende wird zu -y vor -ing und zu -i vor -ed.	die	died	dies	dying
-y am Verbende -y am Verbende wird bei vorausgehendem Konsonant zu -i bzw. -ie, wenn die Endung -ed bzw. -s angehängt wird. Vor -ing bleibt das -y erhalten.	cry	cried	cries	crying
-y bleibt erhalten, wenn dem -y ein Vokal vorausgeht.	enjoy	enjoyed	enjoys	enjoying

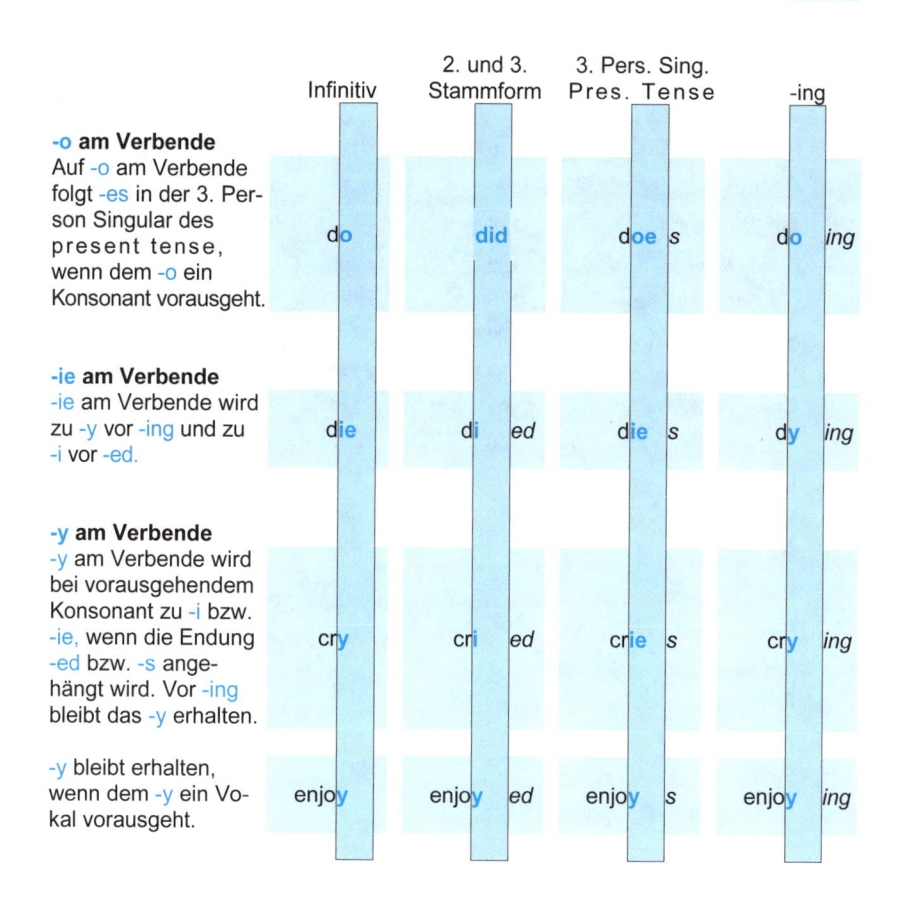

Die Konjugation

Die Konjugation von to have in der Simple Form

Mod.	Zeit		1. Person Singular			2. Person Singular			3. Person Singular	
	Pres.T.	I		have	you		have	he		has
	Past T.	I		had	you		had	he		had
Ind.	Pres.P.	I *have*		had	you *have*		had	he *has*		had
	Past P.	I *had*		had	you *had*		had	he *had*		had
	Fut. T.	I *will*		have	you *will*		have	he *will*		have
	Fut. P.	I *will have*		had	you *will have*		had	he *will have*		had
Con.	Con.	I *would*		have	you *would*		have	he *would*		have
	Con.P.	I *would have*		had	you *would have*		had	he *would have*		had
Sub.	Pres.	I		have	you		have	he		have
	Past	I		had	you		had	he		had
	Past.P.	I *had*		had	you *had*		had	he *had*		had
Imp.	Imp.			-			have			-
Inf.	Pres.			have						
	Perf.		*have*	had						
Part.	Pres.			hav*ing*						
	Past			had						
	Perf.		*having*	had						
Ger.	Pres.			hav*ing*						
	Perf.		*having*	had						

Die Konjugation von to have in der Continuous Form

Mod.	Zeit		1. Person Singular		2. Person Singular		3. Person Singular	
	Pres.T.	I	am hav*ing*	you	are hav*ing*	he	is hav*ing*
	Past T.	I	was hav*ing*	you	were hav*ing*	he	was hav*ing*
Ind.	Pres.P.	I *have*	been hav*ing*	you *have*	been hav*ing* he *has*		been hav*ing*
	Past P.	I *had*	been hav*ing*	you *had*	been hav*ing* he *had*		been hav*ing*
	Fut. T.	I *will*	be hav*ing*	you *will*	be hav*ing* he *will*		be hav*ing*
	Fut. P.	I *will have*	been hav*ing*	you *will have*	been hav*ing* he *will have*		been hav*ing*
Con.	Con.	I *would*	be hav*ing*	you *would*	be hav*ing* he *would*		be hav*ing*
	Con.P.	I *would have been having*		you *would have been having*		he *would have been hav*ing*	
Inf.	Pres.		be hav*ing*				
	Perf.		*have* been hav*ing*				

Die Zeiten future in the past bzw. future perfect in the past sind formgleich mit Will und would können in der 1. Person Singular und Plural durch shall und should ersetzt

Die Konjugation

	1. Person Plural			2. Person Plural			3. Person Plural		
we		have	you		have	they		have	3. Pers. Sg. im pres. t. + -s
we		had	you		had	they		had	
we	*have*	had	you	*have*	had	they	*have*	had	Hilfsverb in der 3. Pers. Sg. ist *has*
we	*had*	had	you	*had*	had	they	*had*	had	
we	*will*	have	you	*will*	have	they	*will*	have	
we	*will have*	had	you	*will have*	had	they	*will have*	had	
we	*would*	have	you	*would*	have	they	*would*	have	
we	*would have*	had	you	*would have*	had	they	*would have*	had	
we		have	you		have	they		have	3. Pers. Sg. im pres. sub. ohne -s
we		had	you		had	they		had	
we	*had*	had	you	*had*	had	they	*had*	had	
		-			have			-	

	1. Person Plural			2. Person Plural			3. Person Plural		
we		are hav*ing*	you		are hav*ing*	they		are hav*ing*	
we		were hav*ing*	you		were hav*ing*	they		were hav*ing*	
we	*have*	been hav*ing*	you *have*		been hav*ing*	they *have*		been hav*ing*	Hilfsverb in der 3. Pers. Sg. ist *has*
we	*had*	been hav*ing*	you *had*		been hav*ing*	they *had*		been hav*ing*	
we	*will*	be hav*ing*	you *will*		be hav*ing*	they *will*		be hav*ing*	
we	*will have*	been hav*ing*	you *will have*		been hav*ing*	they *will have*		been hav*ing*	
we	*would*	be hav*ing*	you *would*		be hav*ing*	they *would*		be hav*ing*	
we	*would have*	been hav*ing*	you *would have*		been hav*ing*	they *would have*		been hav*ing*	

dem conditional bzw. conditional perfect.
werden. In der modernen Sprache wird jedoch meist *will* und *would* verwendet.

Die Konjugation

Die Konjugation von to be in der Simple Form

Mod.	Zeit		1. Person Singular			2. Person Singular			3. Person Singular	
	Pres.T.	I		am	you		are	he		is
	Past T.	I		was	you		were	he		was
Ind.	Pres.P.	I have		been	you have		been	he has		been
	Past P.	I had		been	you had		been	he had		been
	Fut. T.	I will		be	you will		be	he will		be
	Fut. P.	I will have		been	you will have		been	he will have		been
Con.	Con.	I would		be	you would		be	he would		be
	Con.P.	I would have		been	you would have		been	he would have		been
Sub.	Pres.	I		be	you		be	he		be
	Past	I		were	you		were	he		were
	Past P.	I had		been	you had		been	he had		been
Imp.	Imp.			-			be			-
Inf.	Pres.			be						
	Perf.	have		been						
Part.	Pres.			being						
	Past			been						
	Perf.	having		been						
Ger.	Pres.			being						
	Perf.	having		been						

Die Konjugation von to be in der Continuous Form

Mod.	Zeit		1. Person Singular			2. Person Singular			3. Person Singular	
	Pres.T.	I	am	being	you	are	being	he	is	being
	Past T.	I	was	being	you	were	being	he	was	being
Ind.	Pres.P.	I have	been	being	you have	been	being	he has	been	being
	Past P.	I had	been	being	you had	been	being	he had	been	being
	Fut. T.	I will	be	being	you will	be	being	he will	be	being
	Fut. P.	I will have	been	being	you will have	been	being	he will have	been	being
Con.	Con.	I would	be	being	you would	be	being	he would	be	being
	Con.P.	I would have been being			you would have been being			he would have been being		
Inf.	Pres.		be	being						
	Perf.	have	been	being						

Die Zeiten future in the past bzw. future perfect in the past sind formgleich mit
Will und would können in der 1. Person Singular und Plural durch shall und should ersetzt

Die Konjugation

	1. Person Plural		2. Person Plural		3. Person Plural	
we		are	you	are	they	are
we		were	you	were	they	were
we have	been	you have	been	they have	been
we had	been	you had	been	they had	been
we will	be	you will	be	they will	be
we will have	been	you will have	been	they will have	been
we would	be	you would	be	they would	be
we would have	been	you would have	been	they would have	been
we	be	you	be	they	be
we	were	you	were	they	were
we had	been	you had	been	they had	been
	-		be		-

Hilfsverb in der 3. Pers. Sg. ist *has*

	1. Person Plural			2. Person Plural			3. Person Plural	
we		are	being	you	are	being	they	are	being
we		were	being	you	were	being	they	were	being
we have	been	being	you have	been	being	they have	been	being
we had	been	being	you had	been	being	they had	been	being
we will	be	being	you will	be	being	they will	be	being
we will have	been	being	you will have	been	being	they will have	been	being
we would	be	being	you would	be	being	they would	be	being
we would have	been	being	you would have	been	being	they would have	been	being

Hilfsverb in der 3. Pers. Sg. ist *has*

dem conditional bzw. conditional perfect.
werden. In der modernen Sprache wird jedoch meist *will* und *would* verwendet.

dnf 35

Die Konjugation

Die Konjugation der regelmäßigen Verben in der Simple Form

Mod.	Zeit	1. Person Singular		2. Person Singular		3. Person Singular	
	Pres.T. I		help	you	help	he	helps
	Past T. I		helped	you	helped	he	helped
Ind.	Pres.P. I *have*	helped	you *have*	helped	he *has*	helped
	Past P. I *had*	helped	you *had*	helped	he *had*	helped
	Fut. T. I *will*	help	you *will*	help	he *will*	help
	Fut. P. I *will have*	helped	you *will have*	helped	he *will have*	helped
Con.	Con. I *would*	help	you *would*	help	he *would*	help
	Con.P. I *would have*	helped	you *would have*	helped	he *would have*	helped
Sub.	Pres. I		help	you	help	he	help
	Past I		helped	you	helped	he	helped
	Past.P. I *had*	helped	you *had*	helped	he *had*	helped
Imp.	Imp.		-		help		-
Inf.	Pres.		help				
	Perf.	*have*	helped				
Part.	Pres.		helping				
	Past		helped				
	Perf.	*having*	helped				
Ger.	Pres.		helping				
	Perf.	*having*	helped				

Die Konjugation der regelmäßigen Verben in der Continuous

Mod.	Zeit	1. Person Singular		2. Person Singular		3. Person Singular	
	Pres.T. I	am	helping you	are	helping he	is	helping
	Past T. I	was	helping you	were	helping he	was	helping
Ind.	Pres.P. I *have*	been	helping you *have*	been	helping he *has*	been	helping
	Past P. I *had*	been	helping you *had*	been	helping he *had*	been	helping
	Fut. T. I *will*	be	helping you *will*	be	helping he *will*	be	helping
	Fut. P. I *will have*	been	helping you *will have*	been	helping he *will have*	been	helping
Con.	Con. I *would*	be	helping you *would*	be	helping he *would*	be	helping
	Con.P. I *would have been*	helping you *would have been*	helping he *would have been*	helping
Inf.	Pres.		be helping				
	Perf.	*have*	been helping				

Die Zeiten future in the past bzw. future perfect in the past sind formgleich mit
Will und would können in der 1. Person Singular und Plural durch shall und should ersetzt

Die Konjugation

	1. Person Plural		2. Person Plural		3. Person Plural		
we	help	you	help	they	help		3. Pers. Sg. im pres. t. + -s
we	helped	you	helped	they	helped		
we *have*	helped	you *have*	helped	they *have*	helped		Hilfsverb in der 3. Pers. Sg. ist *has*
we *had*	helped	you *had*	helped	they *had*	helped		
we *will*	help	you *will*	help	they *will*	help		
we *will have*	helped	you *will have*	helped	they *will have*	helped		
we *would*	help	you *would*	help	they *would*	help		
we *would have*	helped	you *would have*	helped	they *would have*	helped		
we	help	you	help	they	help		3. Pers. Sg. im pres. sub. ohne -s
we	helped	you	helped	they	helped		
we *had*	helped	you *had*	helped	they *had*	helped		
	–		help		–		

Form

	1. Person Plural		2. Person Plural		3. Person Plural		
we	*are* helping you		*are* helping they		*are* helping		
we	*were* helping you		*were* helping they		*were* helping		
we *have*	*been* helping you *have*		*been* helping they *have*		*been* helping		Hilfsverb in der 3. Pers. Sg. ist *has*
we *had*	*been* helping you *had*		*been* helping they *had*		*been* helping		
we *will*	*be* helping you *will*		*be* helping they *will*		*be* helping		
we *will have*	*been* helping you *will have*		*been* helping they *will have*		*been* helping		
we *would*	*be* helping you *would*		*be* helping they *would*		*be* helping		
we *would have*	*been* helping you *would have*		*been* helping they *would have*		*been* helping		

dem conditional bzw. conditional perfect.
werden. In der modernen Sprache wird jedoch meist *will* und *would* verwendet.

Die Konjugation

Die Konjugation der unregelmäßigen Verben in der Simple

Mod.	Zeit	1. Person Singular		2. Person Singular		3. Person Singular	
	Pres.T. I		eat	you	eat	he	eats
	Past T. I		ate	you	ate	he	ate
Ind.	Pres.P. I	have	eaten	you *have*	eaten	he *has*	eaten
	Past P. I	*had*	eaten	you *had*	eaten	he *had*	eaten
	Fut. T. I	*will*	eat	you *will*	eat	he *will*	eat
	Fut. P. I	*will have*	eaten	you *will have*	eaten	he *will have*	eaten
Con.	Con. I	*would*	eat	you *would*	eat	he *would*	eat
	Con.P. I	*would have*	eaten	you *would have*	eaten	he *would have*	eaten
Sub.	Pres. I		eat	you	eat	he	eat
	Past I		ate	you	ate	he	ate
	Past.P. I	*had*	eaten	you *had*	eaten	he *had*	eaten
Imp.	Imp.		-		eat		-
Inf.	Pres.		eat				
	Perf.	*have*	eaten				
Part.	Pres.		eat*ing*				
	Past		eaten				
	Perf.	*having*	eaten				
Ger.	Pres.		eat*ing*				
	Perf.	*having*	eaten				

Die Konjugation der unregelmäßigen Verben in der Continu

Mod.	Zeit	1. Person Singular		2. Person Singular		3. Person Singular	
	Pres.T. I	am	eat*ing* you	are	eat*ing* he	is	eat*ing*
	Past T. I	was	eat*ing* you	were	eat*ing* he	was	eat*ing*
Ind.	Pres.P. I *have*	been	eat*ing* you *have*	been	eat*ing* he *has*	been	eat*ing*
	Past P. I *had*	been	eat*ing* you *had*	been	eat*ing* he *had*	been	eat*ing*
	Fut. T. I *will*	be	eat*ing* you *will*	be	eat*ing* he *will*	be	eat*ing*
	Fut. P. I *will have*	been	eat*ing* you *will have*	been	eat*ing* he *will have*	been	eat*ing*
Con.	Con. I *would*	be	eat*ing* you *would*	be	eat*ing* he *would*	be	eat*ing*
	Con.P. I *would have been*	eat*ing*	you *would have been* eat*ing*		he *would have been* eat*ing*		
Inf.	Pres.	be	eat*ing*				
	Perf.	*have*	been eat*ing*				

Die Zeiten future in the past bzw. future perfect in the past sind formgleich mit
Will und would können in der 1. Person Singular und Plural durch shall und should ersetzt

Die Konjugation

Form

	1. Person Plural		2. Person Plural		3. Person Plural		
we		eat	you	eat	they	eat	3. Pers. Sg. im pres. t. + -s
we		ate	you	ate	they	ate	
we *have*		eaten	you *have*	eaten	they *have*	eaten	Hilfsverb in der 3. Pers. Sg. ist *has*
we *had*		eaten	you *had*	eaten	they *had*	eaten	
we *will*		eat	you *will*	eat	they *will*	eat	
we *will have*		eaten	you *will have*	eaten	they *will have*	eaten	
we *would*		eat	you *would*	eat	they *would*	eat	
we *would have*		eaten	you *would have*	eaten	they *would have*	eaten	
we		eat	you	eat	they	eat	3. Pers. Sg. im pres. sub. ohne -s
we		ate	you	ate	they	ate	
we *had*		eaten	you *had*	eaten	they *had*	eaten	
		-		eat		-	

ous Form

	1. Person Plural		2. Person Plural		3. Person Plural		
we	*are* eat*ing*	you	*are* eat*ing*	they	*are* eat*ing*		
we	*were* eat*ing*	you	*were* eat*ing*	they	*were* eat*ing*		
we *have*	*been* eat*ing*	you *have*	*been* eat*ing*	they *have*	*been* eat*ing*	Hilfsverb in der 3. Pers. Sg. ist *has*	
we *had*	*been* eat*ing*	you *had*	*been* eat*ing*	they *had*	*been* eat*ing*		
we *will*	*be* eat*ing*	you *will*	*be* eat*ing*	they *will*	*be* eat*ing*		
we *will have*	*been* eat*ing*	you *will have*	*been* eat*ing*	they *will have*	*been* eat*ing*		
we *would*	*be* eat*ing*	you *would*	*be* eat*ing*	they *would*	*be* eat*ing*		
we *would have*	*been* eat*ing*	you *would have*	*been* eat*ing*	they *would have*	*been* eat*ing*		

dem conditional bzw. conditional perfect.
werden. In der modernen Sprache wird jedoch meist will und would verwendet.

Die Konjugation

Kurzformen (Contractions)

Kurzformen von have

	have	have (vern.)	had	had (vern.)
I	've	haven't		
you	've	haven't		
he	's	hasn't		
we	've	haven't	'd	hadn't
you	've	haven't		
they	've	haven't		

Kurzformen von be und von do

	be	be (vern.)	was (vern.)	do (vern.)	did (vern.)
I	'm	'm not	wasn't	don't	
you	're	aren't	weren't	don't	
he	's	isn't	wasn't	doesn't	
we	're	aren't	weren't	don't	didn't
you	're	aren't	weren't	don't	
they	're	aren't	weren't	don't	

Kurzformen von will, shall, would

	will/shall	will (vern.)	shall (vern.)	would	would (vern.)
I					
you					
he					
we	'll	won't	shan't	'd	wouldn't
you					
they					

Andere Kurzformen

	be	will	shall	would	should
that	that's	that'll	that'll	that'd	that'd
this	-	this'll	this'll	this'd	this'd
there	there's	there'll	there'll	there'd	there'd
here	here's	here'll	here'll	here'd	here'd
who	who's	who'll	who'll	who'd	who'd
what	what's	what'll	what'll	what'd	what'd
where	where's	where'll	where'll	where'd	where'd
when	when's	when'll	when'll	when'd	when'd
how	how's	how'll	how'll	how'd	how'd

Die Konjugation

Die Stammformen (Principal Forms)

Die folgende Übersicht zeigt die Stammformen wichtiger unregelmäßiger Verben in alphabetischer Reihenfolge. Besonderheiten bei der Konjugation (besonders Verdoppelung des Endkonsonten vor -ing und Verbstämme, die vor -ing die Endung -e verlieren) sind blau dargestellt. Neben den drei Stammformen sind zusätzlich die Verbform der 3. Person Singular des present tense simple sowie das present participle, das zur Bildung der continuous form benötigt wird, aufgeführt (ing-Form).

1. St.form (Infinitiv)	2. St.form	3. St.form	3. Pers. Sg. Pres. Tense	-ing-Form	Bedeutung
Stammformen von to have, to be und to do					
have	had	had	has	having	haben
be	was	been	is	being	sein
do	did	done	does	doing	tun
Stammformen der regelmäßigen Verben (mit Besonderheiten in der Schreibung)					
help	helped	helped	helps	helping	helfen
cry	cried	cried	cries	crying	weinen, schreien
die	died	died	dies	dying	sterben
enjoy	enjoyed	enjoyed	enjoys	enjoying	genießen
love	loved	loved	loves	loving	lieben
stop	stopped	stopped	stops	stopping	aufhören
Stammformen der unregelmäßigen Verben					
abide	abided, abode	abided, abode	abides	abiding	bleiben
arise	arose	arisen	arises	arising	entstehen
awake	awoke	awoken	awakes	awaking	aufwecken
bear	bore	born	bears	bearing	gebären
bear	bore	borne	bears	bearing	(er)tragen
beat	beat	beaten	beats	beating	schlagen
become	became	become	becomes	becoming	werden
begin	began	begun	begins	beginning	beginnen
bend	bent	bent	bends	bending	biegen
bereave	bereft	bereft	bereaves	bereaving	berauben
beseech	besought, beseeched	besought, beseeched	beseeches	beseeching	ersuchen, anflehen
bestride	bestrode	bestridden	bestrides	bestriding	mit gespreizten Beinen stehen

3. St.form ohne Endung -e
3. St.form mit Endung -e

dnf 41

Die Konjugation

1. St.form (Infinitiv)	2. St.form	3. St.form	3. Pers. Sg. Pres. Tense	-ing-Form	Bedeutung
bet	bet, betted	bet, betted	bets	betting	wetten
bid	bade, bid	bidden, bid	bids	bidding	bieten
bide	bode, bided	bided	bides	biding	ab-, erwarten
bind	bound	bound	binds	binding	binden
bite	bit	bitten, bit	bites	biting	beißen
bleed	bled	bled	bleeds	bleeding	bluten
blend	blended, blent	blended, blent	blends	blending	vermischen
blow	blew	blown	blows	blowing	blasen
break	broke	broken	breaks	breaking	brechen
breed	bred	bred	breeds	breeding	züchten
bring	brought	brought	brings	bringing	bringen
build	built	built	builds	building	bauen
burn	burnt, burned	burnt, burned	burns	burning	brennen
burst	burst	burst	bursts	bursting	bersten
buy	bought	bought	buys	buying	kaufen
cast	cast	cast	casts	casting	werfen
catch	caught	caught	catches	catching	fangen
chide	chided, chid	chided, chid, chidden	chides	chiding	schelten, tadeln
choose	chose	chosen	chooses	choosing	(aus)wählen
cleave	cleft, clove, cleaved	cleft, cloven, cleaved	cleaves	cleaving	kleben (an); (zer)spalten
cling	clung	clung	clings	clinging	kleben, haften
clothe	clad, clothed	clad, clothed	clothes	clothing	kleiden
come	came	come	comes	coming	kommen
cost	cost	cost	costs	costing	kosten
creep	crept	crept	creeps	creeping	kriechen
crow	crew, crowed	crowed	crows	crowing	krähen
cut	cut	cut	cuts	cutting	schneiden
deal	dealt	dealt	deals	dealing	handeln

Die Konjugation

1. St.form (Infinitiv)	2. St.form	3. St.form	3. Pers. Sg. Pres. Tense	-ing-Form	Bedeutung	
dig	dug	dug	digs	digging	graben	
draw	drew	drawn	draws	drawing	ziehen; zeichnen	
dream	dreamt, dreamed	dreamt, dreamed	dreams	dreaming	träumen	
drink	drank	drunk	drinks	drinking	trinken	
drive	drove	driven	drives	driving	fahren	
dwell	dwelt	dwelt	dwells	dwelling	verweilen	
eat	ate	eaten	eats	eating	essen	
fall	fell	fallen	falls	falling	fallen	
feed	fed	fed	feeds	feeding	füttern	
feel	felt	felt	feels	feeling	fühlen	
fight	fought	fought	fights	fighting	kämpfen	
find	found	found	finds	finding	finden	
flee	fled	fled	flees	fleeing	fliehen	
fling	flung	flung	flings	flinging	werfen	
fly	flew	flown	flies	flying	fliegen	
forbid	forbade	forbidden	forbids	forbidding	verbieten	
forget	forgot	forgotten	forgets	forgetting	vergessen	vgl. get !
forgive	forgave	forgiven	forgives	forgiving	vergeben	
forsake	forsook	forsaken	forsakes	forsaking	im Stich lassen	
freeze	froze	frozen	freezes	freezing	gefrieren	
get	got	got	gets	getting	bekommen	vgl. forget !
gild	gilt, gilded	gilt, gilded	gilds	gilding	vergolden	
gird	girt, girded	girt, girded	girds	girding	umgürten	
give	gave	given	gives	giving	geben	
go	went	gone	goes	going	gehen	
grave	graved	graven, graved	graves	graving	(ein)meißeln	
grind	ground	ground	grinds	grinding	schleifen	
grow	grew	grown	grows	growing	wachsen	
hang	hung, hanged*	hung, hanged*	hangs	hanging	hängen	
hear	heard	heard	hears	hearing	hören	
heave	hove, heaved	hove, heaved	heaves	heaving	heben	

* He was hanged by the neck (er wurde aufgehängt).

Die Konjugation

1. St.form (Infinitiv)	2. St.form	3. St.form	3. Pers. Sg. Pres. Tense	-ing-Form	Bedeutung
hew	hewed	hewn, hewed	hews	hewing	hauen, hacken
hide	hid	hid, hidden	hides	hiding	verstecken
hit	hit	hit	hits	hitting	schlagen
hold	held	held	holds	holding	halten
hurt	hurt	hurt	hurts	hurting	verletzen, wehtun
keep	kept	kept	keeps	keeping	(be)halten
kneel	knelt, kneeled	knelt, kneeled	kneels	kneeling	knien
knit	knit, knitted	knit, knitted	knits	knitting	stricken
know	knew	known	knows	knowing	kennen, wissen
lade	laded	laden, laded	lades	lading	beladen
lay	laid	laid	lays	laying	legen
lead	led	led	leads	leading	führen, leiten
lean	leant, leaned	leant, leaned	leans	leaning	lehnen
leap	leapt, leaped	leapt, leaped	leaps	leaping	springen
learn	learnt, learned	learnt, learned	learns	learning	lernen
leave	left	left	leaves	leaving	verlassen
lend	lent	lent	lends	lending	leihen
let	let	let	lets	letting	lassen
lie	lay	lain	lies	lying	liegen
light	lit, lighted	lit, lighted	lights	lighting	anzünden
lose	lost	lost	loses	losing	verlieren
make	made	made	makes	making	machen
mean	meant	meant	means	meaning	meinen; bedeuten
meet	met	met	meets	meeting	treffen
mow	mowed	mown, mowed	mows	mowing	mähen
pay	paid	paid	pays	paying	bezahlen
put	put	put	puts	putting	setzen, stellen
read [ri:d]	read [red]	read [red]	reads	reading	lesen
rend	rent	rent	rends	rending	zerreißen

! Aussprache

Die Konjugation

1. St.form (Infinitiv)	2. St.form	3. St.form	3. Pers. Sg. Pres. Tense	-ing-Form	Bedeutung
rid	rid	rid	rids	ridding	befreien
ride	rode	ridden	rides	riding	reiten
ring	rang	rung	rings	ringing	klingeln
rise	rose	risen	rises	rising	sich erheben
rive	rived	riven, rived	rives	riving	spalten
run	ran	run	runs	running	rennen
saw	sawed	sawn, sawed	saws	sawing	sägen
say	said	said	says	saying	sagen
see	saw	seen	sees	seeing	sehen
seek	sought	sought	seeks	seeking	suchen
sell	sold	sold	sells	selling	verkaufen
send	sent	sent	sends	sending	schicken
set	set	set	sets	setting	setzen, stellen
sew	sewed	sewn, sewed	sews	sewing	nähen
shake	shook	shaken	shakes	shaking	schütteln
shear	sheared	shorn, sheared	shears	shearing	scheren
shed	shed	shed	sheds	shedding	verschütten
shine	shone	shone	shines	shining	scheinen
shoot	shot	shot	shoots	shooting	schießen
show	showed	shown	shows	showing	zeigen
shred	shred, shredded	shred, shredded	shreds	shredding	zerschnitzeln
shrink	shrank	shrunk	shrinks	shrinking	einlaufen
shrive	shrove	shriven	shrives	shriving	von Sünden lossprechen
shut	shut	shut	shuts	shutting	schließen
sing	sang	sung	sings	singing	singen
sink	sank	sunk	sinks	sinking	sinken
sit	sat	sat	sits	sitting	sitzen
slay	slew	slain	slays	slaying	erschlagen
sleep	slept	slept	sleeps	sleeping	schlafen
slide	slid	slid	slides	sliding	gleiten
sling	slung	slung	slings	slinging	schlingen

Die Konjugation

1. St.form (Infinitiv)	2. St.form	3. St.form	3. Pers. Sg. Pres. Tense	-ing-Form	Bedeutung
slink	slunk	slunk	slinks	slinking	schleichen
smell	smelt, smelled	smelt, smelled	smells	smelling	riechen
slit	slit	slit	slits	slitting	aufschlitzen
smite	smote	smitten, smote	smites	smiting	befallen, heimsuchen
sow	sowed	sown, sowed	sows	sowing	säen
speak	spoke	spoken	speaks	speaking	sprechen
speed	sped, speeded	sped, speeded	speeds	speeding	beschleunigen
spell	spelt, spelled	spelt, spelled	spells	spelling	buchstabieren
spend	spent	spent	spends	spending	ausgeben; verbringen
spill	spilt, spilled	spilt, spilled	spills	spilling	verschütten
spin	spun	spun	spins	spinning	spinnen
spit	spat	spat	spits	spitting	spucken
split	split	split	splits	splitting	spalten
spread	spread	spread	spreads	spreading	verbreiten
spring	sprung, sprang	sprung	springs	springing	springen
stand	stood	stood	stands	standing	stehen
steal	stole	stolen	steals	stealing	stehlen
stick	stuck	stuck	sticks	sticking	stecken
sting	stung	stung	stings	stinging	stechen
stink	stank, stunk	stunk	stinks	stinking	stinken
strew	strewed	strewn, strewed	strews	strewing	verstreuen
stride	strode	strided, stridden	strides	striding	schreiten
strike	struck	struck	strikes	striking	schlagen
string	strung	strung	strings	stringing	verschnüren
strive	strove	striven	strives	striving	bestrebt sein
swear	swore	sworn	swears	swearing	schwören; fluchen
sweat	sweat, sweated	sweat, sweated	sweats	sweating	schwitzen

Die Konjugation

1. St.form (Infinitiv)	2. St.form	3. St.form	3. Pers. Sg. Pres. Tense	-ing-Form	Bedeutung
sweep	swept	swept	sweeps	sweeping	kehren
swell	swelled	swollen	swells	swelling	anschwellen
swim	swam	swum	swims	swimming	schwimmen
swing	swung	swung	swings	swinging	schwingen
take	took	taken	takes	taking	nehmen
teach	taught	taught	teaches	teaching	lehren
tear	tore	torn	tears	tearing	zerreißen
tell	told	told	tells	telling	erzählen
think	thought	thought	thinks	thinking	denken
thrive	throve, thrived	thriven, thrived	thrives	thriving	gedeihen
throw	threw	thrown	throws	throwing	werfen
thrust	thrust	thrust	thrusts	thrusting	stoßen
tread	trod	trod, trodden	treads	treading	treten
understand	understood	understood	understands	understanding	verstehen
wake	waked (tr.), woke (tr, intr.)	waked (tr.), woken (tr., intr.)	wakes	waking	aufwachen
wear	wore	worn	wears	wearing	tragen (Kleidung)
weave	wove	woven	weaves	weaving	weben
weep	wept	wept	weeps	weeping	weinen
wet	wet, wetted	wet	wets	wetting	nass machen
win	won	won	wins	winning	gewinnen
wind	wound	wound	winds	winding	winden
wring	wrung	wrung	wrings	wringing	(aus)wringen
write	wrote	written	writes	writing	schreiben

Die Konjugation

Übungen zur Konjugation

1. Fügen Sie die fehlenden Verbformen ein und benutzen Sie das angege-

	Infinitive	Present T.	Past Tense	Pres. Perf.	Past Perf.
1.			he had		
2.		I am			
3.					
4.					
5.					
6.					
7.					
8.					
9.					he had put
10.					he had heard
11.		I mean			
12.			he met		
13.		I keep			
14.			he got		
15.			he forgot		
16.					
17.					
18.					
19.			he ran		
20.					

Die Konjugation

bene Personalpronomen.

	Future I	Future II	Con. I	Con. II	Cont. Form	richtig	falsch
	he will do						
	he will help						
	he will love						
			he would stop				
	he will cry						
	he will die						
	he will sit						
			he would say				
	he will begin						
			he would make				

Die Konjugation

	Infinitive	Present T.	Past Tense	Pres. Perf.	Past Perf.
21.					he had come
22.					
23.		you think			
24.					
25.					
26.		I stand			
27.					
28.					
29.					he had told
30.					
31.		we show			
32.					he had known
33.					
34.					
35.		he lies			
36.		I lay			
37.			he fell		
38.					
39.					

Die entsprechenden Lösungen befinden sich auf Seite 420ff.

Die Konjugation

	Future I	Future II	Con. I	Con. II	Cont. Form		
he will find							
he will buy							
he will take							
he will write							
he will speak							
			he would eat				
			he would see				
he will go							
			he would choose				
he will lose						richtig	falsch

Die Hilfsverben

Die Hilfsverben (Auxiliary Verbs)

Zu den Hilfsverben zählen to have, to be, die bei der Bildung der Zeiten und des Passivs verwendet werden und to do, das bei der Bildung verneinter und fragender Sätze und bei der Bildung von Befehlssätzen benötigt wird.
To have, to be und to do können sowohl als Hilfsverben als auch als Vollverben verwendet werden.

To Be

continuous form	Als Hilfsverb dient es zur Bildung der continuous form in allen Zeiten.	• He **is** reading a book. • He has **been** reading a book.
Passiv	Als Hilfsverb dient es zur Bildung des Passivs.	• The door **is** opened by the caretaker. • The little boy **was being** carried by Peter.
sich befinden, existieren	Als Vollverb in der Bedeutung *sich befinden, existieren, vorhanden sein*.	• **Are** there any books on the table? • He **was** in the dining-room.
to be about to, to be on the point of	Zum Ausdruck der sehr nahen Zukunft, eines unmittelbar bevorstehenden Ereignisses steht to be about to + infinitive oder to be on the point of + gerund.	• We **were about to** leave/**were on the point of leaving** when he came. (Wir **waren gerade dabei** zu gehen, als er kam.)
to be to	Zum Ausdruck von Befehlen, Aufforderungen, die der Sprecher wiedergibt oder zum Ausdruck strenger oder wiederholt ausgesprochener Befehle steht to be + to als Ersatz für das Modalverb shall.	• You **are to** go at once. (Du **sollst** sofort gehen.) • He says that we **are to** read this text.
	Zum Ausdruck von zweifelnden Fragen als Ersatz für die Modalverben shall, should steht to be + to.	• How **is** he **to** know what she will do? (Wie **soll** er wissen, was sie tun wird?)
	Zum Ausdruck der Absicht, des Plans als Ersatz für die Modalverben will und would. Diese Konstruktion ist ein beliebtes Stilmittel in der Zeitungssprache.	• She **is to** go on holiday next week. • The House of Commons **is to** pass this bill to the House of Lords.

To Have

zusammengesetzte Zeiten	Als Hilfsverb dient es zur Bildung der zusammengesetzten Zeiten.	• I **have** read a book. • I **have** been reading a book.

Die Hilfsverben

In der Bedeutung *(veran)lassen* steht have + Objekt + past participle. Es ist dann Vollverb und wird als solches im verneinten und fragenden Satz mit to do umschrieben.
In dieser Bedeutung kann auch to get stehen.

- I **had** my car washed.
  (Ich **ließ** meinen Wagen waschen.)
- I didn't **have** my car washed.
- At the moment I **am having** my car washed.
- I **got** my car washed.

veranlassen als Vollverb steht to have im verneinten und fragenden Satz mit to do

To have kann in der Bedeutung *essen, trinken, einnehmen* stehen. Es ist dann Vollverb und wird als solches im verneinten und fragenden Satz mit to do umschrieben.

- We **had** breakfast at 6 o'clock.
  (Wir **frühstückten** um 6 Uhr.)
- We didn't **have** breakfast at 6 o'clock.

essen, trinken

To have kann in der Bedeutung *besitzen* stehen. Es ist dann Vollverb und wird dann im verneinten und fragenden Satz mit to do umschrieben.

- He **has** a big house.
- He doesn't **have** a big house.
- He **has** a lot of money.

besitzen

To have kann in der Bedeutung *empfangen, aufnehmen* stehen. Es ist dann Vollverb und wird als solches im verneinten und fragenden Satz mit to do umschrieben.

- We **have** a lot of guests tonight.
- We don't **have** a lot of guests tonight.
- Would you **have** us next holiday?

empfangen

Zum Ausdruck einer durch Dritte auferlegten Verpflichtung oder Notwendigkeit steht to have (got) to als Ersatz für das Modalverb must.
In der Umgangssprache wird to have got to bevorzugt. In kurzen Antworten kann es ohne Vollverb stehen.

- I **have (got) to** go now.
  (Ich **muss** jetzt gehen.)
- Why are you reading this text? I **have (got) to** (read it).

Notwendigkeit, Verpflichtung

Zum Ausdruck gewohnheitsmäßiger Handlungen.
Bei bestimmten Gewohnheiten wird to have got bevorzugt.
Konstruktionen mit to have werden - besonders im Amerikanischen - mit to do umschrieben. To have got wird im britischen Englisch bevorzugt.

- Do you always **have** so much time?
  (**Haben** Sie immer so viel Zeit?)
- **Have** you **got** time *now*?
  (**Haben** Sie *jetzt* Zeit?)

Gewohnheit

Die Hilfsverben

To Do

	Umschreibung mit to do	Keine Umschreibung mit to do
bejahter Aussagesatz	Soll das Vollverb im bejahten Aussagesatz besonders betont werden, kann es in den einfachen Zeiten mit to do umschrieben werden. Das Vollverb steht dabei im Infinitiv.	Im bejahten Aussagesatz wird das Vollverb in den einfachen Zeiten nicht mit to do umschrieben. (Die zusammengesetzten Zeiten, die continuous form und das Passiv werden mit to have und to be gebildet.)
	▪ I do tell him the truth. (Ich werde ihm jetzt aber die Wahrheit sagen.) ▪ I do intend to pass the exam. ▪ I did intend to pass the exam.	▪ I intend to pass the exam. ▪ I intended to pass the exam. ▪ I have intended to pass the exam. ▪ I am reading a book. ▪ The door was opened.
verneinter Aussagesatz ❗ to do, to have werden als Vollverb mit to do umschrieben	Ist das Prädikat des bejahten Satzes ein Vollverb, so muss dieses bei der Bildung des verneinten Satzes mit to do umschrieben werden. To do, to have können selbst Vollverben sein. Sie werden dann auch mit to do umschrieben. To be wird auch als Vollverb nicht mit to do umschrieben.	Ist im Prädikat des bejahten Satzes ein Hilfs- oder Modalverb enthalten, so wird dieses bei der Bildung des verneinten Satzes verneint.
	▪ I do not like reading books. (I like reading books.) (Ich lese nicht gern Bücher.) ▪ I don't do it. (I do it.) ▪ I didn't have lunch yet. (I had lunch already.) ▪ He was not in the dining-room. (He was in the dining-room.)	▪ I have not made this mistake. (I have made this mistake.) ▪ You must not go out before you have finished your homework. (You must go out before you have finished your homework.)
verneinende Bestimmung	Bei einer verneinenden oder einschränkenden Bestimmung am Satzanfang kann das Vollverb mit to do umschrieben werden, jedoch ohne not. Das Subjekt des Satzes tritt zwischen to do und Vollverb. Diese Art der Formulierung findet sich nur noch in der literarischen und veralteten Sprache.	Wird die Verneinung durch eine verneinende oder einschränkende Bestimmung ausgedrückt, so wird das Vollverb nicht mit to do umschrieben. Zur besonderen Hervorhebung kann die Umschreibung mit to do im present und past tense eingesetzt werden.
	▪ *In vain* did he come. (Er kam vergeblich.) ▪ *Never* did he come back.	▪ He came *in vain*. ▪ He *never* does drink hard liquor.

Die Hilfsverben

Umschreibung mit to do	Keine Umschreibung mit to do	
Ist das Prädikat des bejahten Satzes ein Vollverb, so muss dieses bei der Bildung des Fragesatzes mit to do umschrieben werden. To do und to have können selbst auch Vollverb sein. Sie werden dann auch mit to do umschrieben. To be wird auch als Vollverb nicht mit to do umschrieben.	Ist im Prädikat des bejahten Satzes ein Hilfs- oder Modalverb enthalten, so dient dieses zur Bildung des Fragesatzes.	Fragesatz ohne Fragewort to do, to have werden als Vollverb mit to do umschrieben
• **Do** you like reading books? (You like reading books.) (Liest du gern Bücher?) • **Did** he do it? (He did it.) • **Does** he have a car? (He has (possesses) a car.) • **Was** he in the dining-room? (He **was** in the dining-room.)	• **Has** Peter gone to school by bus? (Peter **has** gone to school by bus.) • **Can** you solve this problem? (You **can** solve this problem.)	
Ist das Fragewort nicht selbst Subjekt oder ein Teil dessen, d. h. der Satz enthält schon ein anderes Subjekt (he, Peter etc.), so wird das Vollverb mit to do umschrieben.	Ist das Fragewort selbst Subjekt oder ein Teil dessen, d. h. der Satz enthält kein anderes Subjekt (he, Peter etc.), so wird das Verb nicht mit to do umschrieben.	Fragesatz mit Fragewort
• *Whom* **did you** meet at the station? • *Where* **does** he go?	• *Who* **solved** this problem? • *Who* has **solved** this problem?	
	Fragesätze mit Fragewort, die ein Hilfs- oder Modalverb enthalten, werden nicht mit to do umschrieben, gleichgültig ob das Fragewort Subjekt des Satzes ist oder nicht.	
	• *Who* **is** this? • *Where* **can** you meet him?	
Verneinte Fragen mit und ohne Fragewort, die ein Vollverb enthalten, werden mit to do umschrieben.	Verneinte Fragen mit und ohne Fragewort, die ein Hilfs- oder Modalverb enthalten, werden nicht mit to do umschrieben.	verneinte Fragen
• **Didn't** you meet him at the station? • *To whom* **didn't** you deliver the message yet? • *Who* **didn't** solve this problem?	• **Haven't** you met him at the station? • *To whom* **haven't** you delivered the message yet? • *Who* **cannot** solve this problem?	
	In kurzen Antwortsätzen, in denen nicht das Verb, sondern der vorangehende Satzinhalt oder ein anderes	kurze Antworten

Die Hilfsverben

	Umschreibung mit to do	Keine Umschreibung mit to do
kurze Antworten mit yes oder no, so, nor und neither		Wort verneint wird, wird die Verneinung nur mit not gebildet. - Will he come by car? I think (he will) **not.** Kurze Antworten mit yes, no und so (auch), nor und neither (auch nicht), die auf Fragen mit Hilfs- oder Modalverb antworten, werden nicht mit to do umschrieben. In der Umgangssprache steht statt nor und neither häufig not ... either. - **Has** he gone? Yes, he **has.** (Ist er gegangen? Ja.) - **Can** you post this letter for me? No, I **cannot/can't.** - **Has** he already gone? Nor/neither **has** she. (Ist er bereits gegangen? Sie auch nicht.) - **Has** he already gone? She **hasn't** either.
	Kurze Antworten mit yes, no und so (auch), nor und neither (auch nicht), die auf Fragen mit Vollverb antworten, werden mit to do und nicht mit dem Vollverb gebildet. In der Umgangssprache steht statt nor und neither häufig not ... either. - Do you go home at six? Yes, I **do.** (Gehst du um 6 heim? Ja.) - Does he like reading? No, he **doesn't.** - Do you play the piano? So **do** I. (Spielst du Klavier? Ich auch.) - Does he like reading? Nor/neither **does** Mary. (Liest er gern? Mary auch nicht.) - Does he like reading? Mary **doesn't** either.	
bejahter Imperativ	Werden die Formen des Imperativs durch betontes to do umschrieben, so wird ein damit zum Ausdruck gebrachter Befehl in eine dringende Bitte umgewandelt. - **Do** inform me as soon as possible. (Informiere mich doch bitte so bald wie möglich.)	Die Formen des Imperativs werden ohne to do gebildet. - **Inform** me as soon as possible. - **Come** in.
verneinter Imperativ	Der verneinte Imperativ wird stets mit to do umschrieben. - **Don't** inform him before I have told you to.	
Vergleichssatz mit Vollverb bzw. Hilfs- oder Modalverb *to do, to have werden als Vollverb mit to do umschrieben*	Der Vergleich wird mit to do gebildet, wenn der Vordersatz ein Vollverb enthält. Es ist zu beachten, dass to do und to have auch Vollverben sein können und dann im Vergleichssatz ebenfalls durch to do wieder aufgenommen werden.	Der Vergleich wird nicht mit to do gebildet, wenn der Vordersatz ein Hilfs- oder Modalverb enthält. Im Vergleichssatz wird dann das Hilfs- oder Modalverb wieder aufgenommen.

Die Hilfsverben

Umschreibung mit to do	Keine Umschreibung mit to do	
- He **went** as far *as* I **did**. (Er ging so weit *wie ich*.) - He **does** the same work *as* I **do**. - Peter **has** the same car *as* I **do**.	- She **has** talked as much as he **has**. (Sie hat so viel gesprochen *wie er*.) - He **isn't** as tall as I **am**. - She **can** work as hard as I **can**.	
Aussagen mit to have, die allgemeingültig sind, werden im verneinten und fragenden Satz mit to do umschrieben.	Aussagen mit to have, die nur für einen bestimmten Fall gelten, werden im verneinten und fragenden Satz nicht mit to do umschrieben. In der Umgangssprache wird hier häufig to have got verwendet.	Aussagen mit to have
- **Do** you *always* **have** your holiday in July?	- **Have you (got)** a holiday in July *this year*?	
In der Bedeutung *besitzen* kann to have im verneinten und fragenden Satz mit to do umschrieben werden.	In der Bedeutung *besitzen* kann to have im verneinten und fragenden Satz nicht mit to do umschrieben werden. In der Umgangssprache wird in dieser Bedeutung meist to have got eingesetzt.	to have in der Bedeutung *besitzen*
- He **doesn't** have a car. - **Does** he have a car?	- He **hasnt (got)** a car. - **Has** he **(got)** a car?	

Die Hilfsverben

Übungen zu den Hilfsverben

1. **Verneinen Sie die folgenden Sätze, die ein Vollverb enthalten. Beachten Sie dabei die Zeiten.**

   1. Barbara **likes** grapefruits.
   2. **Do** that!
   3. He **explained** why he thought Harry's idea all wrong.
   4. I certainly **do** think so.
   5. I **had** time to meet Bill and Claire.
   6. I'm quite sure Smith **did** the murder.
   7. It **makes** sense.
   8. Jack **obeyed** his father.
   9. **Say** that!
   10. They **sent** us a postcard.

   richtig   falsch

2. **Verneinen Sie die folgenden Sätze, die ein Hilfs- oder Modalverb enthalten. Beachten Sie dabei die Zeiten.**

   1. He **had left** a message to tell his father where he had gone.
   2. He **has forgotten** to ring me up.
   3. He **has had** time.
   4. I **am allowed** to tell you.
   5. I **am fond of** walking.
   6. My Dad said that he **would like** to drive a huge lorry.
   7. She **could remember** my name.
   8. The driver **had waited** for them.
   9. Their expectations **may have been** realistic.
   10. They **were** guilty of the crimes they were charged with.

   richtig   falsch

Die Hilfsverben

3. Verneinen Sie die folgenden Sätze.

1. They **show** their feelings so easily.
2. You **seem** to like my idea.
3. This problem **has been solved** satisfactorily.
4. We **are doing** very well.
5. You **are allowed** to smoke here.
6. You **have been** there.
7. You **were** very careful.
8. I **can tell** you where he was.
9. They **could hear** what the people were saying.
10. At 12 o'clock you **might be** there.

richtig   falsch

4. Formen Sie die folgenden Sätze, die ein Vollverb enthalten, in Fragesätze um. Beachten Sie dabei die Zeiten.

1. Drivers **have to** give way to ambulances.
2. Drivers **have to** have a licence.
3. He **did** it to her.
4. He **got** hurt.
5. He **knows** what you're doing.
6. He really **had** all the good qualities you thought he had.
7. He really **said** that.
8. He **sent** Tom a postcard.
9. She **got** many birthday presents.
10. She **wants** to go out this evening.
11. The translation **does** justice to the meaning of the original.
12. They **had** a good time.

Die Hilfsverben

13. They received the benefits to which they were entitled.
14. This little bag has to be weighed too.
15. Your brother likes dancing.

richtig falsch

5. Formen Sie die folgenden Sätze, die ein Hilfs- oder Modalverb enthalten, in Fragesätze um. Beachten Sie dabei die Zeiten.

1. He had been drinking.
2. He is getting on well at school.
3. He was seasick.
4. He was wanted for a serious crime.
5. He would do it.
6. I shall make some coffee.
7. It has stopped raining.
8. It is necessary to copy all this material.
9. Linda had gone.
10. She is hurt.
11. That would be wise.
12. The new rocket has been tested sufficiently.
13. They were friends of his.
14. We can go now.
15. We shall have lunch here.

richtig falsch

6. Formen Sie die folgenden Sätze in Fragesätze um. Verwenden Sie to do wo erforderlich und beachten Sie dabei die Zeiten.

1. Columbus discovered America.
2. He has asked Mr Miller to be present.

Die Hilfsverben

3. I wonder why Ken hasn't turned up yet. He might have had an accident.

4. Mike's business was a success.

5. She hadn't been invited.

6. The gang of eight or nine boys, aged around 18, have been caught.

7. The matter hasn't yet been put to the test.

8. The present owner hasn't got enough money to keep the place up.

9. They didn't pay any attention to it.

10. They serve a meal on the plane.

richtig   falsch

7. Formen Sie die folgenden Sätze, die ein Vollverb enthalten, in Fragesätze um und verwenden Sie das angegebene Fragewort. Beachten Sie dabei die Zeiten.

1. Bob **did** his homework after he came home from school. What ...

2. Columbus **discovered** America. Who ...

3. He **did** his homework very well. How ...

4. He **gave** her that lovely ring. Who ...

5. He **suspected** Mrs Smith of having been the thief. Whom ...

6. He usually **gets up** at 6 o'clock in the morning. When ...

7. His strange behaviour **irritated** her about him. What ...

8. Mr Clarke **left** the house first. Who ...

9. Sheila **married** Mr Winterbottom. Who ...

10. The boy in the blue jacket **broke** the window. Which of the boys ...

richtig   falsch

8. Formen Sie die folgenden Sätze, die ein Hilfs- oder Modalverb enthalten, in Fragesätze um und verwenden Sie das angegebene Fragewort. Beachten Sie die Zeiten.

Die Hilfsverben

1. A doctor **must be sent for** when somebody is ill. Who ...
2. He **can get** the book in the library. Where ...
3. He **had been arrested for** having stolen my car. What ...
4. He **has come back** to get his glasses. Why ...
5. He **was born** in 1900. When ...
6. He **was doing** his homework there. What ...
7. He **was promising** to come back early. What ...
8. He **will go to** the cinema next Sunday. Where ...
9. It is his bad behaviour she **is accusing** him **of**. What ...
10. Sheila **will be having** a sandwich for lunch. What ...

richtig falsch

9. Formen Sie die folgenden Sätze in Fragesätze um und verwenden Sie das angegebene Fragewort. Setzen Sie to do ein wo erforderlich und beachten Sie die Zeiten.

1. A lot of advances have been made in the last few years in computer technology. What ...
2. He does his homework in the afternoon. When ...
3. He has to be blamed for that. Who ...
4. His strange behaviour made her realize the situation. What ...
5. Mother needs a new dishwasher. What ...
6. People have to have their photograph in their passports. What ...
7. She could have acted otherwise. How ...
8. She helps him with his homework. Who ...
9. Someone has got the books. Who ...
10. She asked him to come to St. Paul's Cathedral. Where ...

richtig falsch

Die entsprechenden Lösungen befinden sich auf Seite 424ff.

Die Modalverben (Modal Auxiliary Verbs)

Die Modalverben wandeln den Inhalt eines anderen Verbs ab. Sie haben keinen Infinitiv und kein past participle und können somit auch keine zusammengesetzten Zeiten bilden. Sie müssen daher in den zusammengesetzten Zeiten durch sinnverwandte Ersatzverben ersetzt werden.
Die meisten Modalverben werden ohne to an den Infinitiv angeschlossen und in Fragesätzen und verneinten Sätzen nicht mit to do umschrieben. Die 3. Person Singular des present tense erhält kein -s.

Modalverb (Kurzform)	Verneinung (Kurzform)	Ersatzverb	Bedeutung (des Modalverbs)	
I can	I cannot (I can't)	to be able to to be allowed to to be permitted to	ich kann	cannot wird zusammengeschrieben
I could	I could not (I couldn't)	it will be possible to	ich konnte; ich könnte	
I may	I must not (I mustn't) (I may not) (I mayn't)	to be allowed to to be permitted to to be likely to Future Tense	ich darf	
I might	I might not (I mightn't)	Future in the Past	ich durfte; ich dürfte	
I must	I must not (ich darf nicht) (I mustn't)	to have (got) to to be compelled to to be forced to to be obliged to	ich muss	must not heißt nicht dürfen und keinesfalls nicht müssen
I need	I need not (I needn't)	to have (got) to	ich brauche	
I shall	I shall not (I shan't)	to be to to be supposed to to be said to to want s.o. to do to be allowed to to be permitted to to let to be going to	ich soll	
I should	I should not (I shouldn't)	to be to to be supposed to to be said to to want s.o. to do to be in the habit of to have the habit of	ich sollte	

Die Modalverben

Modalverb (Kurzform)	Verneinung (Kurzform)	Ersatzverb	Bedeutung (des Modalverbs)
I **ought to**	I **ought not** (I **oughtn't**)	to be supposed to to be said to	ich sollte
I **will** (I'**ll**)	I **will not** (I **won't**)	to be to to be going to to intend to to mean to to be willing to	ich will; (ich werde)
I **would** (I'**d**)	I **would not** (I **wouldn't**)	to want to to wish to to be in the habit of to have the habit of	ich wollte; (ich würde)
I **used to**	I **used not to** (I **usedn't to**)	to be in the habit of to have the habit of	ich pflegte zu
I **dare**	I **dare not** (I **daren't**)		ich wage

Die Modalverben

Can, could und ihre Ersatzverben

can	could	to be able to	
Zum Ausdruck der geistigen und körperlichen Fähigkeit. In der Bedeutung von *wissen, können* wird can + Vollverb oft durch to know ersetzt.	Zum Ausdruck vergangener geistiger und körperlicher Fähigkeiten. In der Bedeutung von *wusste, konnte* wird could + Vollverb oft durch knew ersetzt.	Zum Ausdruck der geistigen und körperlichen Fähigkeit, besonders bei einer ganz bestimmten einzelnen Handlung.	Fähigkeit
• **Can** you stand on your head? • I **can** speak English. • I **know** English quite well. (Ich **kann** ganz gut Englisch.)	• As a young man, he **could** dance all night. • I **could** speak English. • I **knew** English quite well. (Ich **konnte** ganz gut Englisch.)	• As a boy, I **was able to** climb any tree. • Although he was ill himself, he **was able to** help the others.	
Zum Ausdruck einer durch äußere Umstände gegebenen Möglichkeit.	Zum Ausdruck einer vergangenen Möglichkeit, die durch äußere Umstände gegeben war.	Zum Ausdruck einer durch äußere Umstände gegebenen Möglichkeit. Zum Ausdruck einer Möglichkeit, die in der Zukunft eintreten könnte, steht neben to be able to auch it will be possible to.	Möglichkeit
• This **can** be read everywhere. • Nowadays, England **can** be reached easily. • You **can't** be alone there for even five minutes. • **Can** this be true? • This **cannot** be true.	• This **could** be read everywhere. • I had no key, so I **couldn't** lock the door. • I **couldn't** go skiing last year because I was sick. • **Couldn't** you go on vacation last year?	• I know the town, so I **am able to** show them around. • **Were** you **able to** see him before he left? • If the new road is ready, it **will be possible to**/we **will be able to** take the car to town.	
can	could	to be allowed to, to be permitted to	
Zum Ausdruck der Erlaubnis wird can vor allem in der Umgangssprache verwendet.	Zum Ausdruck einer vergangenen Erlaubnis steht could vor allem in indirekter Rede, wenn das einleitende Verb in einer Zeit der Vergangenheit steht.	Zum Ausdruck der Erlaubnis zu ganz bestimmten Handlungen.	Erlaubnis

Die Modalverben

	can	could	to be allowed to, to be permitted to
	• You **can** go for a walk. • You **can** leave it on the table. • You **can** help her if you want to.	• *He said* we **could** park our car in front of his garage. • *David said* that we **could** borrow his videorecorder.	• We **were allowed to** stay *here*. • You **aren't allowed to** play *there*. • He **will not be allowed to** write to her.

	can	could
Bitte in Fragen	Zum Ausdruck einer höflichen Bitte, besonders in Fragen, wird can vor allem in der Umgangssprache verwendet.	Zum Ausdruck einer sehr höflichen Bitte, besonders in Fragen, wird could vor allem in der Umgangssprache verwendet. Es wird in dieser Bedeutung mit *könnte* übersetzt.
	• **Can** you help me? (*Können* Sie mir helfen?) • **Can** I have a word with Mr White? • **Can** you ring back later?	• **Could** you help me? (*Könnten* Sie mir helfen?) • **Could** I have a word with Mr White? • **Could** you ring back later?
Erstaunen, Ungeduld	In nachdrücklichen Fragen zum Ausdruck des Erstaunens, der Ungeduld.	In nachdrücklichen Fragen zum Ausdruck des Erstaunens, der Ungeduld.
	• What **can** that mean? • **Can** that be possible?	• What **could** that mean? • **Could** that be possible?
Bedingung	Zum Ausdruck der erfüllbaren Bedingung steht can in Verbindung mit dem **present tense** im Bedingungssatz.	Zum Ausdruck, dass die Erfüllung der Bedingung unwahrscheinlich ist, steht could in Verbindung mit dem **past tense** im Bedingungssatz. Zum Ausdruck, dass die Bedingung unerfüllt bleibt, steht could + **perfect infinitive** und **past perfect** im Bedingungssatz.
	• If I *study* harder, I **can** pass the exam.	• If I *studied* harder, I **could** pass the exam. • If I *had studied* harder, I **could** have passed the exam.

Die Modalverben

May, might und ihre Ersatzverben

may	might	to be allowed to, to be permitted to	
Zum Ausdruck der Erlaubnis zu gegenwärtigen Handlungen. May klingt relativ förmlich. Die Verneinung zu may ist must not (nicht dürfen). May not kann nur in Antworten auf Fragen mit may und in der Amtssprache stehen.	Zum Ausdruck der vergangenen Erlaubnis, vor allem in der indirekten Rede, wenn das einleitende Verb in einer Zeit der Vergangenheit steht. Might klingt relativ förmlich.	Zum Ausdruck einer offiziellen, allgemein gültigen Erlaubnis.	Erlaubnis
• You **may** take this book with you. (Du **darfst** dieses Buch mitnehmen.) • You **must not** take this book with you. (Du **darfst** dieses Buch **nicht** mitnehmen.) • **May** I take this book with me? No, you **may not**. • This lawn **may not** be walked on.	• You **might** take this book with you. (Du **durftest** dieses Buch mitnehmen.) • *They asked if* they **might** take this book with them. • *The salesman said* I **might** take the car for a test drive.	• They **were allowed to** smoke in this room. • She **is not allowed to** drive without her glasses. • You **are not permitted to** enter the building without a pass.	

may	might	to be likely to	
Zum Ausdruck der denkbaren Möglichkeit, der Wahrscheinlichkeit. In dieser Bedeutung kann may nur in bejahten Sätzen stehen. In verneinten und fragenden Sätzen steht can bzw. cannot (can't).	Zum Ausdruck der denkbaren Möglichkeit, der Wahrscheinlichkeit. Might kann in bejahten, verneinten und fragenden Sätzen stehen. Might ist schwächer als may und wird im Deutschen meist mit *könnte* übersetzt.	Zum Ausdruck der Wahrscheinlichkeit steht to be likely to besonders in Fragen und verneinten Sätzen, da may hier nicht verwendet werden kann.	Möglichkeit, Wahrscheinlichkeit
• He **may** be late. (Er **verspätet sich vielleicht**.) • This **may** be true. • **Can** this be true? • This **can't** be true.	• He **might** be late. (Er **könnte sich verspäten**.) • He **might** lose his way. • That **might not** be correct.	• **Are** we **likely to** meet him at the party? (Werden wir ihn **wohl** auf der Party **treffen**?) • This **is not likely to** happen.	
Zum Ausdruck vergangener Möglichkei-	Zum Ausdruck vergangener Möglichkei-	Handelt es sich um einen bereits vergan-	

dnf 67

Die Modalverben

	may	might	to be likely to
	ten, steht **may** + perfect infinitive. Im Deutschen wird dies häufig mit *könnte* oder dem Futur II übersetzt.	ten, steht **might** + perfect infinitive. Im Deutschen wird dies häufig mit *könnte* oder dem Futur II übersetzt.	genen Vorgang, steht **to be likely to** im past tense simple.
	- He **may** have taken it away. (Er hat es **vielleicht** weggenommen/**könnte** es weggenommen haben.) - He **may** just have left his office. (Er **wird** sein Büro schon **verlassen haben**.)	- He **might** have taken it away. (Er hat es **vielleicht** weggenommen/**könnte** es weggenommen haben.) - He **might** just **have left** his office. (Er **wird** sein Büro schon **verlassen haben**.)	- He **was** not very **likely to** win. (Es **war** nicht sehr **wahrscheinlich**, dass er gewinnt.) - He **was likely to** be home by six o'clock in the morning.

	may	might
Bedingung	Im Bedingungssatz, zum Ausdruck der Möglichkeit, wenn das Ergebnis unsicher ist. Im Bedingungssatz steht das *present tense*.	Im Bedingungssatz, zum Ausdruck der Möglichkeit, wenn das Ergebnis unsicher ist. Im Bedingungssatz steht das *present* oder *past tense*.
	- If he **sees** you, he **may** stop. - If you **pour** hot water into the glass, it **may** crack.	- If he **sees/saw** you, he **might** stop. - If you **pour/poured** hot water into the glass, it **might** crack.
Bitte in Fragen	Zum Ausdruck einer förmlichen Bitte, vor allem in Fragen.	Zum Ausdruck der förmlichen Bitte, vor allem in Fragen. Might ist höflicher als may. Might wird in dieser Bedeutung mit *dürfte, könnte* übersetzt. Wenn die Antwort auf eine Frage unsicher ist, steht might + Personalpronomen.
	- **May** I use your phone? (**Darf** ich Ihr Telefon benutzen?) - How **may** I help you? - **May** we please have four tickets to the concert?	- **Might** I use your phone? (**Dürfte** ich Ihr Telefon benutzen?) - You **might** post this letter for me. (Sie **könnten** diesen Brief für mich aufgeben.)

Die Modalverben

may	might	
In ungewissen Fragen, vor allem zum Ausdruck des Erstaunens. Diese Art der Formulierung ist jedoch selten.	Zum Ausdruck der ungewissen Frage, vor allem in der indirekten Rede, wenn das einleitende Verb in einer Zeit der Vergangenheit steht.	ungewisse Fragen
• Well, who **may** you be? (Wer **sind** Sie **denn**?)	• How old **might** she be? (Wie alt **mag** sie wohl sein?) • I wondered what he **might** say.	
	Zum Ausdruck der Aufforderung. Der Sprecher ist sicher, dass seine Aufforderung befolgt wird. Diese Art der Aufforderung klingt sehr vertraulich oder vorwurfsvoll.	Aufforderung
	• You **might** post this letter for me. (Du **könntest** diesen Brief für mich aufgeben.) • You **might** help me. (Du **könntest** mir **auch** helfen.)	
Im bejahten Satz, zum Ausdruck eines Vorschlags, einer Empfehlung, die man an andere Personen richtet, steht may häufig mit as well. Bezieht sich may auf die eigene Person, wird eine Absicht ausgedrückt. Im Deutschen wird dies mit dem Indikativ Präsens übersetzt.	Im bejahten Satz, zum Ausdruck eines Vorschlags, einer Empfehlung, die man an andere Personen richtet, steht might häufig mit as well. Might ist höflicher als may. Bezieht sich might auf die eigene Person, wird die Absicht ausgedrückt. Im Deutschen wird dies mit dem Konjunktiv II übersetzt.	Vorschlag, Empfehlung
• You **may** (as well) take the plane. (Sie **können** (ebenso gut) fliegen.) • I **may** (as well) take the plane.	• You **might** (as well) take the plane. (Sie **könnten** (ebenso gut)) fliegen.) • I **might** (as well) take the plane.	

Die Modalverben

	may	might	
Einräumug	Zum Ausdruck der Einräumung, besonders nach den Ausdrücken however, who-, what-, wherever etc. In diesem Zusammenhang kann may weggelassen werden.	Zum Ausdruck der Einräumung, besonders nach den Ausdrücken however, who-, what-, wherever etc. In diesem Zusammenhang kann might weggelassen werden.	
	▪ I promised him to buy the car whatever it **may** cost (costs). (... was immer es kosten mag.)	▪ I promised him to buy the car whatever it **might** cost (costs). (... was immer es kosten mag.)	
Hoffnung, Wunschgedanke	Zum Ausdruck der Hoffnung, des Wunschgedankens steht may + infinitive. Im Deutschen wird dies mit *möge* + Infinitiv (Konjunktiv I von *mögen*) oder dem Konjunktiv I des Vollverbs übersetzt.		
	▪ **May** God save the Queen. (Gott **möge** die Königin schützen./Gott **schütze** die Königin.) ▪ **May** she rest in peace. ▪ **May** you live a happy life. ▪ **May** he come back in good health.		

	may	might	Future Tense, Future in the Past
Furcht, Befürchtung	Zum Ausdruck der Furcht, Befürchtung vor allem nach den folgenden Ausdrücken, die, wenn sie mit may verbunden werden, im present tense stehen.	Zum Ausdruck der Furcht, Befürchtung vor allem nach den folgenden Ausdrücken, die, wenn sie mit might verbunden werden, im past tense stehen.	Zum Ausdruck der Furcht, Befürchtung steht das future tense für may, das future in the past für might, vor allem nach den folgenden Ausdrücken.
	▪ to be afraid ▪ to fear, for fear ▪ it is possible that ▪ there is a possibility	▪ to be afraid ▪ to fear, for fear ▪ it is possible that ▪ there is a possibility	▪ to be afraid ▪ to fear, for fear ▪ it is possible that ▪ there is a possibility

Die Modalverben

may	might	Future Tense, Future in the Past
• The President is afraid that the treaty may not be concluded. (Der Präsident befürchtet, dass der Vertrag nicht zu Stande kommt.)	• The President was afraid that the treaty might not be concluded. (Der Präsident befürchtete, dass der Vertrag nicht zu Stande kommen könnte.)	• The President is afraid that the treaty will not be concluded. • The President was afraid that the treaty would not be concluded.

Must, need und ihre Ersatzverben

must	need	to have (got) to	
Zum Ausdruck der Notwendigkeit, Verpflichtung wird es nur im present tense verwendet. In der indirekten Rede steht es auch im past tense, wenn das einleitende Verb in einer Zeit der Vergangenheit steht. Seine Form ändert es jedoch trotzdem nicht.	Zum Ausdruck der Notwendigkeit, Verpflichtung steht es als Modalverb vor allem im verneinten und fragenden Satz. Als Vollverb kann es in allen Zeiten stehen, die 3. Person Singular des present tense erhält ein -s, im verneinten und fragenden Satz wird es mit to do umschrieben und der Infinitiv wird mit to angeschlossen.	Zum Ausdruck einer durch Dritte auferlegten Notwendigkeit, Verpflichtung. Im verneinten und fragenden Satz wird to have to mit to do umschrieben. In der Umgangssprache wird to have got to bevorzugt.	Notwendigkeit, Verpflichtung
• Every child must go to school. • *He said that I must come and see him on my next visit to London.*	• Need you go now? • He needs the money. • He needed the money. • He has needed the money. • He needs to work for the money.	• Every child has (got) to go to school. • We have had to get up at five o'clock. • Do I have to do what he says?	
Zum Ausdruck der Notwendigkeit, Verpflichtung in ganz allgemeinen Fragen.	Zum Ausdruck der Notwendigkeit, Verpflichtung in Fragen, die die Hoffnung auf eine negative Antwort ausdrücken.	Zum Ausdruck einer durch Dritte auferlegten Notwendigkeit, Verpflichtung steht in Fragen do I have to, oder have I (got) to.	
• Mother, must I go? (Yes, you must.) (No, you need not.) • Must I do my homework immediately?	• Mother, need I go? (No, you need not.) • Need I do my homework immediately?	• Did you have to write an essay? • Has that man (got) to do all this work himself?	

Die Modalverben

	must	need	to have (got) to
Verbot, Nicht-Notwendigkeit	Must not drückt ein Verbot, den dringenden Rat, die Ermahnung etwas nicht zu tun aus. Must not bedeutet also *nicht dürfen* und keinesfalls *nicht müssen*.	Need not + infinitive ohne *to* heißt *nicht brauchen* und drückt aus, dass vom Sprecher aus keine Notwendigkeit, Verpflichtung zur Durchführung einer Handlung besteht.	Haven't got to heißt *nicht müssen* und drückt aus, dass vom Sprecher aus keine Notwendigkeit, Verpflichtung zur Durchführung einer Handlung besteht. Es steht dabei selten in der Vergangenheit.
⚠ must not heißt *nicht dürfen* und keinesfalls *nicht müssen*	• You **must not** go out in this rain. (Du **darfst** bei diesem Regen **nicht** rausgehen.) • You **must not** say such things.	• You **needn't** clean your room. • Everything is in order, so you **needn't** worry about anything.	• He **hasn't got to** clean his room. • He **hasn't got to** solve this problem all by himself.
		Don't/didn't need to drückt aus, dass von einem Dritten aus keine Notwendigkeit, Verpflichtung zur Durchführung einer Handlung besteht. Für die Vergangenheit steht häufig there was no need to.	
		• He **doesn't need to** clean his room. • He **didn't need to** clean his room. • **There was no need** (for him) to clean his room.	

	need	
unnötigerweise ausgeführte Handlungen	Zum Ausdruck von unnötigerweise ausgeführten Handlungen steht needn't + perfect infinitive.	
	• I **needn't** have written to him, because he never received my letters. (Ich **hätte** ihm **nicht schreiben brauchen,** weil er meine Briefe nie erhalten hat.)	

Die Modalverben

must
Zum Ausdruck der Vermutung, der Wahrscheinlichkeit, dass etwas sicher, kaum anders denkbar ist. Wird must verneint, wird es nicht mehr mit *nicht dürfen*, sondern mit dem Futur I bzw. Futur II übersetzt.

- He **must** be at home.
- He **must** have just left the office.
- He **must not** be at home now.
  (Er *wird* jetzt *nicht* zuhause sein.)
- She **must not** have received my letter.
  (Sie *wird* meinen Brief *nicht* bekommen haben.)

Vermutung

Shall, should, ought to und ihre Ersatzverben

should
Zum Ausdruck einer sittlichen, moralischen Verpflichtung (sollte eigentlich).
Bei unerfüllten Verpflichtungen steht should + perfect infinitive.

- I **should** take him to the airport.
- I **should** have paid this bill last week. Now I have to pay the fine.

ought to
Zum Ausdruck einer sittlichen, moralischen Verpflichtung. Es ist stärker als should.
Bei unerfüllten Verpflichtungen steht ought to + perfect infinitive.

- I **ought to** do this work at once.
- I **ought to** have paid this bill last week. Now I have to pay the fine.

to be supposed to
Zum Ausdruck der Verpflichtung.
Zum Ausdruck der unerfüllten Verpflichtung steht was (were) supposed to.

- Don't be so lazy. You **are supposed to** work hard.
- You **were supposed to** help him, but you didn't.

moralische Verpflichtung

should
Zum Ausdruck der Notwendigkeit, dass etwas wünschenswert, ratsam ist.

ought to
Zum Ausdruck der Notwendigkeit, dass etwas wünschenswert, ratsam ist.

Notwendigkeit

Die Modalverben

		should	ought to	
Erlaubnis, Versprechen		• You **should** clean your room immediately. • You **should not** have gone out last night.	• You **ought to** clean your room immediately. • You **ought not** to have gone out last night.	

	shall	to be allowed to, to be permitted to, to let
Erlaubnis, Versprechen	Zum Ausdruck der Erlaubnis, des Versprechens, das der Sprecher der 2. oder 3. Person gibt, wird **shall** im modernen Englisch selten verwendet.	Zum Ausdruck der Erlaubnis, des Versprechens, das der Sprecher gibt, steht **to be allowed/permitted to, to let**, vor allem im modernen Englisch anstelle von **shall**.
	• You **shall** go out tonight if you do your homework. • He **shall** receive a reward for his bravery.	• You **are allowed to** go out tonight. • You **are permitted to** do it again. • I will **let** you go out tonight.

	shall	should	to be to, to want s.o. to do s.th. to be supposed to
Aufforderung, Befehl	Zum Ausdruck der Aufforderung, des Befehls an die 2. und 3. Person wird **shall** im modernen Englisch selten verwendet.	Zum Ausdruck der Aufforderung, des Befehls des Sprechers selbst oder von Dritten, die der Sprecher wiedergibt.	Zum Ausdruck von Anweisungen, die der Sprecher selbst erteilt, steht **to want/don't want s. o. to do s. th.** Zum Ausdruck von Anweisungen, eines Dritten, die der Sprecher wiedergibt steht **to be to** oder **to be supposed to.** Zum Ausdruck strenger, wiederholt ausgesprochener Befehle, steht **to be to.** Zum Ausdruck, dass Anweisungen nicht befolgt worden sind, steht **was (were) supposed to.**
	• You **shall** not smoke in this room. • There **shall** be no talking during the test.	• You **should** meet him at the station. • You **should** not talk in such a loud voice.	• I **want you to** meet him at 6 o'clock. (Ich **möchte, dass** du ihn um 6 Uhr triffst.)

Die Modalverben

		to be to, to want s.o. to do s.th. to be supposed to	
shall	should	• You **are to** meet him at 6 o'clock at the station. • You **are supposed to** meet her at 6 o'clock. (Du **sollst** sie um 6 Uhr treffen.) • I have just told you several times that you **are to** stop talking. • You **were supposed to** meet her at 6 o'clock, but you didn't.	
should	ought to		Vorschlag, Empfehlung
Zum Ausdruck des Vorschlags, der Empfehlung. • You **should** invest in stock options.	Zum Ausdruck des Vorschlags, der Empfehlung. • You **ought to** come and see him tomorrow.		
shall	should	to be to, to be supposed to	Vereinbarung
In Fragen zum Ausdruck einer Vereinbarung mit der 1. und 3. Person Singular und Plural. Der Sprecher fragt nach dem Wunsch des Befragten. • **Shall** I come and see you tomorrow? • **Shall** we come and see you tomorrow? • **Shall** my brother come and see you tomorrow? • **Shall** the Browns come and see you tomorrow?	In Fragen zum Ausdruck einer Vereinbarung mit der 1. und 3. Person Singular und Plural. Der Sprecher fragt nach dem Wunsch des Befragten. • **Should** I come and see you tomorrow? • **Should** we come and see you tomorrow? • **Should** my brother come and see you tomorrow? • **Should** the Browns come and see you tomorrow?	Zum Ausdruck der Vereinbarung, die von einem Dritten getroffen worden ist und die der Sprecher wiedergibt. Zum Ausdruck nicht erfüllter Vereinbarungen der Vergangenheit steht was/were to bzw. was/were supposed to + (perfect) infinitive. • The conference **was to** take place in London. • You **are supposed to** meet her at 6 o'clock at the station. • She **was to** have met me by 3 p.m., but she never came. • You **were supposed to** meet her at 6 o'clock at the station, but you didn't.	

Die Modalverben

	shall	should	to be supposed to / to be said to
Vermutung, Annahme	Zum Ausdruck der Vermutung, der Annahme, der logischen Folge (müsste eigentlich, dürfte wohl). Shall ist stärker als should. • If you start now, you **shall** arrive in time. • Woody Allen's new film **shall** be very interesting.	Zum Ausdruck der Vermutung, der Annahme, der logischen Folge (müsste eigentlich, dürfte wohl). • If you start now, you **should** arrive in time. • Woody Allen's new film **should** be very interesting.	Zum Ausdruck der Vermutung, Annahme. To be supposed to steht vor allem in der Umgangssprache. • The President **is said to** be planning to retire from office tomorrow. (Der Präsident **soll** vorhaben, morgen zurückzutreten.) • The President **is supposed to** retire from office tomorrow.
	shall	should	to be to
zweifelnde Fragen	Zum Ausdruck zweifelnder Fragen. • How **shall** he know what she will do? • How **shall** we pay a bill like this?	Zum Ausdruck zweifelnder Fragen. • How **should** he know what she will do? • I wondered how I **should** help him.	Zum Ausdruck zweifelnder Fragen. • How **is** he **to** know what she will do? • He wondered when he **was to** see her again.
	should	Infinitive, Gerund, Subjunctive	
Entschlossenheit, Wille	Zum Ausdruck der Entschlossenheit, des festen Willens, Wunsches, vor allem nach den folgenden Verben und Ausdrücken. • to agree • to decide • to demand • it is desirable • to (be) determine(d) • it is important • to insist • to intend • it is/was necessary • to order • to provide • to require	In den Fällen, in denen der Nebensatz mit should durch das gerund, den infinitive oder subjunctive ersetzt werden kann, werden letztere bevorzugt. • to agree • to decide • to demand • it is desirable • to (be) determine(d) • it is important • to insist • to intend • it is/was necessary • to order • to provide • to require	

Die Modalverben

should

- to resolve
- to see to it
- to urge

- Education **should** be made free for everyone.
- I know that I **should** pass the exam next week.
- It is important that I **should** finish this work by next week.

Infinitive, Gerund, Subjunctive

- to resolve
- to see to it
- to urge

- He intends **to study** at Oxford University.
- I insist on **being asked** beforehand.
- It is necessary that matters **be** taken care of.

shall

Zum Ausdruck einer Drohung, die der Sprecher ausspricht, steht shall (not) (shan't) im modernen Englisch nur noch selten.

- You **shall** be punished if you come back home too late.
- You **shall not (shan't)** go out tonight if you haven't done your homework.

will

Zum Ausdruck einer Drohung, die der Sprecher ausspricht, steht will (not) (won't) vor allem im modernen Englisch statt shall.

- You **will** be punished if you come back home too late.
- You **will not (won't)** go out tonight if you haven't done your homework.

to be going to, to be allowed to, won't let

Zum Ausdruck einer Drohung, die der Sprecher ausspricht, steht to be going to, to be allowed to, won't let vor allem im modernen Englisch statt shall.

- You **are not going to** see your friend if you haven't done your homework.
- You **won't be allowed to** go out tonight if you haven't done your homework.
- I **won't let** you go out tonight if you haven't done your homework.

Drohung

should

Zum Ausdruck der subjektiven Empfindung, des persönlichen Urteils, vor allem nach den folgenden Ausdrücken. Der Sprecher möchte seine eigene Auffassung ausdrücken.

subjektive Empfindung

Die Modalverben

should

Im Deutschen steht der Indikativ Präsens.

- it is fitting
- it is funny
- it is inconceivable
- it is natural
- it is a pity
- it is proper
- I regret
- it is regrettable
- it is right
- it is a shame
- it is significant
- I am sorry
- it is strange
- I am surprised
- it is surprising
- it is unnatural
- it is wrong

- **It is regrettable** that he **shouldn´t** come and see us.
  (Es ist bedauernswert, dass er uns nicht **besuchen kommt**.)
- **It is natural** that he **should** want to study overseas.
- **I regret** that you **should** leave us so early.

Will, would, used to und ihre Ersatzverben

	will	would	to be to, to intend to, to be going to, to mean to
fester Wille, Entschlossenheit	Zum Ausdruck des festen Willens, der Entschlossenheit, vor allem in der 1. Person Singular und Plural. Vorangestellte Adverbien betonen die Entschlossenheit nachdrücklich.	Zum Ausdruck des festen Willens, der Entschlossenheit, vor allem in der 1. Person Singular und Plural. Vorangestellte Adverbien betonen die Entschlossenheit nachdrücklich.	Zum Ausdruck der Entschlossenheit, Absicht. To mean to steht dabei jedoch sehr selten im present tense. To be to ist ein beliebtes Stilmittel in der Zeitungssprache.

Die Modalverben

will	would	to be to, to intend to, to be going to, to mean to	
• I most certainly **will** tell him everything about it. • No matter what he says, I **will** not give in.	• He was very confused, but he **would** never show his feelings. • No matter what he said, he **would** not give in.	• I **am going to** tell him the truth. • I **intended to** tell him the truth. • The House of Commons **is to** pass this bill to the House of Lords.	

will	would	to want to, to wish to	
Zum Ausdruck des Wunsches, Willens (wollen, möchten) ist will selten und vorsichtig einzusetzen, da will meist die Zukunft (future tense) ausdrückt (werden).	Zum Ausdruck des Wunsches, Willens (wollen, möchten) ist would selten und sollte nur in den folgenden Wendungen in Verbindung mit dem subjunctive verwendet werden. • I would rather (ich möchte lieber) • I would sooner (ich möchte lieber) • I would as soon as (ich würde ebenso gerne)	Zum Ausdruck des Wunsches, Willens steht vorzugsweise to want to oder to wish to. To wish + subjunctive steht häufig anstelle von would.	Wunsch will als Modalverb *(wollen)* ist nicht zu verwechseln mit will im future t. *(werden)*
• As you **will**. (Wie Sie wünschen.) • I **will** go home. (Ich werde nach Hause gehen.)	• I **would** it were true. (Ich wünschte, es wäre wahr.) • I **would rather** stay at home.	• I **want/wish to** tell him everything about it. (Ich möchte ihm alles darüber erzählen.) • I **wish** it were true.	

will	would	to be willing to	
Zum Ausdruck der Bereitschaft.	Zum Ausdruck der Bereitschaft.	Zum Ausdruck der Bereitschaft.	Bereitschaft
• **Will** you take us to the cinema? • I've asked him to take us to the cinema, but he **won't**.	• He **would** take you to the cinema. • I've asked him to take us to the cinema, but he **wouldn't**.	• **Are** you **willing to** work harder? • **Were** you **willing to** accept his offer?	

will	would		
In Fragen zum Ausdruck einer Bitte. Die mit will formulierte Bitte	In Fragen zum Ausdruck einer Bitte. Die mit would formulierte		Bitte in Fragen

Die Modalverben

	will	would
	klingt relativ entschieden. Nach dem Imperativ kann *will you* an das Satzende gestellt werden. Diese Art der Bitte klingt vertraulich.	Bitte klingt relativ entschieden. *Would* ist höflicher als *will*. Im Deutschen wird dies mit *würden* übersetzt.

- **Will** you please give the money to your mother?
  (**Gibst** du das Geld bitte deiner Mutter?)
- Post this letter for me, **will you**?

- **Would** you please give the money to your mother?
  (**Würdest** du das Geld bitte deiner Mutter geben?)

	will
Vermutung, Erwartung	Zum Ausdruck der Vermutung, Annahme einer bestimmten Erwartung. Handelt es sich um einen bereits vergangenen Vorgang steht *will* + perfect infinitive. Im Deutschen steht hier oft Futur I bzw. Futur II.

- His new book **will be** a great success.
  (Sein neues Buch **wird wohl** ein großer Erfolg **(werden)**.)
- He **will** just **have left** the office.
  (Er **wird** das Büro schon **verlassen haben**.)

Erfahrungswerte	Zum Ausdruck bestimmter Erfahrungswerte. Im Deutschen wird dies oft durch ein Adverb wie *halt, nun einmal* übersetzt.

- Boys **will** be boys.
  (Jungs sind **halt** Jungs.)
- Accidents **will** happen.
  (Unfälle passieren **nun einmal**.)

Die Modalverben

would	used to	to be in the habit of, to have the habit of	
Zum Ausdruck vergangener Gewohnheiten, dass etwas immer wieder geschah.	Zum Ausdruck gewohnheitsmäßiger Handlungen. Used to bezeichnet gewohnheitsmäßige Handlungen der Vergangenheit. Used to kann im bejahten Satz nicht im present tense verwendet werden. Fragesätze und verneinte Sätze mit used to werden mit to do gebildet. Somit werden Person und Zeit durch to do angegeben, used to wird zu use to. Verneinte Sätze können auch ohne to do verwendet werden. Das Modalverb used to ist nicht zu verwechseln mit dem Vollverb to use (verwenden, gebrauchen).	Zum Ausdruck, dass etwas immer wieder geschieht, gewohnheitsmäßiger Handlungen. To be in the habit of und to have the habit of stehen mit nachfolgendem gerund.	Gewohnheit

used to + did wird zu use to

used to nicht verwechseln mit dem Vollverb to use |
| • Every evening, he **would** go for a walk. (Er pflegte jeden Abend spazieren zu gehen.)
• Every weekend, we **would** visit my grandmother in the country. (Jedes Wochenende besuchten wir meine Großmutter auf dem Land.) | • He **used to** go for a walk every evening. (Er pflegte jeden Abend spazieren zu gehen.)
• Didn't he **use to** play tennis?
• I didn't **use to** play tennis.
• I **used not to** like sports. | • She **has the habit of** going for a walk every evening.
• He **was in the habit of** going for a walk every evening. | |

Dare

Modalverb	Vollverb	
Als Modalverb kann es im bejahten Satz nur in I dare say (ich wage zu behaupten, dass; ich vermute) Als Modalverb kann es im bejahten Satz nur in I dare say (ich wage zu behaupten, dass; ich vermute)	Als Vollverb wird es im bejahten Satz mit to mit dem Infinitiv verbunden. Als Vollverb wird es im bejahten Satz mit to mit dem Infinitiv verbunden. Die 3. Person Singular	im bejahten Satz

Die Modalverben

	Modalverb	Vollverb
	verwendet werden.	erhält im **present tense** ein -s. Folgt auf dare ein direktes Objekt, heißt es *herausfordern*.
	■ **I dare say** he will not go.	■ Peter **dares** the boys to jump off the wall.
im verneinten Satz, im Fragesatz	Es steht im verneinten Satz und im Fragesatz nur im **present tense** und im **past tense** (meist nur in literarischer Sprache). Es steht beim Infinitiv ohne to, die 3. Person Singular im **present tense** erhält kein -s, und es wird nicht mit to do umschrieben.	Im verneinten Satz und im Fragesatz kann es an den Infinitiv mit und ohne to angeschlossen werden. In beiden Fällen muss es mit to do umschrieben werden.
	■ He **dare not/daren't** go. ■ **Dare** he come?	■ He doesn't **dare (to)** go. ■ Did he **dare (to)** come?

Die Modalverben

Übungen zu den Modalverben

1. Setzen Sie can, could oder ihr Ersatzverb to be able to ein.

1. ... you hear me?
2. I think I ... do it if I put my mind to it.
3. I want ... express my opinion freely.
4. I wished I ... swim as well as you can.
5. If ever I found out that you had told me a lie, I would never ... trust you again.
6. If I had a camera I ... take a picture of you.
7. If it goes on raining like this, we ...not have our picnic.
8. If only I ... do something useful.
9. It hurt terribly so I ... not walk.
10. It hurts terribly so I ...not walk.
11. Sheila and Susan ... not hear what the people were saying.
12. Since Mr Harrison has no money, he ...not buy a new car.
13. The doctor asked Gerald to open his mouth so that he ... have a good look at his teeth.
14. Don't use colloquialisms without ... (gerund) to pronounce them.
15. He earns less than enough to ... (infinitive) to keep his family at an acceptable standard.

richtig   falsch

2. Setzen Sie can, could, may oder might oder ihre Ersatzverben to be permitted oder to be allowed to ein.

1. He said that he ... not let you do it on your own.
2. I ...not let you through without a ticket.
3. In some states of the U.S.A. boys and girls ... drive a car at the age of sixteen.

Die Modalverben

4. The boss will have to read this before I ... let you put it in the shop window.

5. The fact that they ... not ... do it will in no way stop them.

6. The prisoner ... speak on his behalf.

7. We ... take as many sweets as we liked.

8. You ...not have any more money this month.

9. The patient ... only eat meat if the doctor approves.

10. He just called me three days ago and said I ... use his room if I cared to.

                                                                                          richtig   falsch

3. Setzen Sie must, need oder ihr Ersatzverb to have to ein.

1. ... drivers ... give way to ambulances?

2. He told them that they ... change trains.

3. He will, of course, know what ... be done.

4. She ... not have told him that.

5. The press ... not invade private rights or feelings.

6. There is no escaping the fact that the exercises ... be done.

7. There isn't much bread left. Someone ... go to the baker's.

8. We ... not tell him why.

9. We ... find a means of solving our problem.

10. You ... no longer consider yourself obligated to me in any way.

                                                                                           richtig   falsch

4. Setzen Sie should, ought to oder ihr Ersatzverb to be supposed to ein.

1. You ... have told me the truth.

2. You've kicked the cat. You ... be ashamed of yourself.

3. You ... stand to attention.

4. He ... be pardoned this time.

Die Modalverben

5. Such things ... not be spoken about in public.

6. You ... have known better than to believe all those lies.

7. She ... not have said that.

8. All the members of the Music Club ... come to last week's meeting.

9. Charles is a delicate boy whom one ... not laugh at all the time.

10. The United States Congress consists of two houses, which ... be equal in importance.

richtig   falsch

5. Setzen Sie should oder ihre Ersatzverben to be supposed to, to be to, to want s.o. to do s.th. ein.

1. When ... you ... go?

2. They always said I ... be careful.

3. You ... not have given the flowers so much water.

4. He ... us ... leave the room slowly and quietly.

5. Where do you ... me ... put the bag with the books?

6. In the eyes of the law one ... not make a distinction between one person and another.

7. I don't ... you ... be late.

8. Parliament alone ... decide which taxes ... be imposed.

9. He ... be addressed as captain.

10. He said what they ... do.

richtig   falsch

Die entsprechenden Lösungen befinden sich auf Seite 425.

Die reflexiven und reziproken Verben

Die reflexiven Verben (Reflexive Verbs)

Reflexive Verben werden von einem Reflexivpronomen (rückbezügliches Fürwort (myself, yourself etc.)) begleitet. Reflexivpronomen und Subjekt bezeichnen dieselbe Person. Bei Subjekten, die eine Sache bezeichnen wird das Verb in der Regel nicht reflexiv verwendet.
Im Englischen werden reflexive Verben viel weniger häufig verwendet als im Deutschen. Somit kann nicht jedes Verb, das im Deutschen reflexiv verwendet wird, auch im Englischen mit Reflexivpronomen stehen und umgekehrt.

> reflexive Verben im Deutschen sind im Englischen nicht automatisch reflexiv

Reflexiv gebrauchte Verben

Die folgenden Verben sind in der gegebenen Bedeutung stets reflexiv.

- to absent o.s. from — fernbleiben von
- to amuse o.s. — sich gut unterhalten
- to avail o.s. of — ergreifen (Gelegenheit)

- John **amused himself** at the party.
- Peter **prides himself** on his success.

- to confine o.s. to — sich beschränken auf
- to exert o.s. — sich bemühen
- to pride o.s. on — sich rühmen

Gelegentlich reflexiv gebrauchte Verben

Einige Verben werden sowohl reflexiv als auch nicht reflexiv verwendet. Häufig wird das Reflexivpronomen weggelassen, wenn eine Gewohnheit ausgedrückt wird. Das Verb steht mit Reflexivpronomen, wenn ausgedrückt werden soll, dass die Handlung bewusst ausgeführt wird.
Häufig haben die reflexiv verwendeten Verben eine andere Bedeutung als die nicht reflexiv verwendeten.

> Bedeutungsunterschied

- John **washed (himself)** and **dressed (himself)** for school.
- John **dressed himself** carefully for the ceremony.
- John **enjoyed** the party.
  (John **genoss** die Party.)
- John **enjoyed himself** at the party.
  (John **amüsierte sich** auf der Party.)
- **Behave yourself**.

to accustom o.s. to	sich gewöhnen an	to get accustomed to	sich gewöhnen an
to apply o.s. to	sich etw. widmen	to apply for	sich bewerben um
to behave o.s.	sich beherrschen	to behave	sich verhalten
to compose o.s.	sich sammeln	to compose	komponieren; bilden
to cut o.s.	sich schneiden	to cut	schneiden
to defend o.s.	sich verteidigen	to defend	verteidigen
to distinguish o.s.	sich auszeichnen	to distinguish	unterscheiden
to enjoy o.s.	sich gut unterhalten	to enjoy	genießen
to feel o.s.	sich fühlen	to feel	fühlen
to help o.s.	sich bedienen	to help	helfen
to hurt o.s.	sich verletzen	to hurt	verletzen, wehtun
to prepare o.s.	sich vorbereiten	to prepare	vorbereiten
to prove o.s.	sich erweisen	to prove	beweisen
to serve o.s.	sich bedienen	to serve	dienen
to submit o.s.	sich unterwerfen	to submit	unterwerfen
to surrender o.s.	sich ergeben	to surrender	übergeben, -lassen
to trouble o.s.	sich beunruhigen	to trouble	belästigen
to wash o.s.	sich waschen	to wash	waschen

Die reflexiven und reziproken Verben

Nicht reflexiv gebrauchte Verben

Viele Verben, die im Deutschen meist reflexiv sind, sind im Englischen nicht reflexiv.

- I can't buy the new car, because I can't **afford** it.
- He is a man who can be **relied upon**.

to afford	sich leisten
to amount to	sich belaufen auf
to approach	sich nähern
to boast of	sich rühmen
to bow to	sich verbeugen vor
to care about	sich kümmern um
to care for	sich sorgen um
to change	sich ändern
to complain of	sich beklagen über
to differ from	sich unterscheiden von
to diminish	sich verringern
to endeavour	sich bemühen
to fall in love with	sich verlieben in
to fancy	sich vorstellen
to happen	sich ereignen
to imagine	sich vorstellen/einbilden
to increase	sich vermehren
to improve	sich verbessern

to join	sich anschließen
to lie down	sich hinlegen
to look forward to	sich freuen auf
to meet	sich treffen
to move	sich bewegen
to realize	sich klarmachen
to recollect	sich erinnern
to recover	sich erholen
to refuse	sich weigern
to rejoice	sich freuen
to rely on	sich verlassen auf
to retire	sich zurückziehen
to rise	sich erheben
to sit down	sich setzen
to turn to	sich wenden an
to withdraw	sich zurückziehen
to wonder	sich fragen
to think s.th. over	sich etw. überlegen

Zur Vermeidung der Reflexivkonstruktion bedient sich das Englische gelegentlich folgender Ausdrücke:

to be
to get
to become   + past participle oder
to grow   Adjektiv oder Adverb

- After a few weeks, I **got accustomed to** the hard work in the field.
- At the conference, I **became acquainted with** Mr Chambers.
- Mary **is** very much **interested in** biology.
- Last year, she **got married to** Peter.

to get accustomed to	sich gewöhnen an
to become acquainted with	sich kennen lernen
to grow better	sich verbessern
to become cloudy	sich bewölken
to be contented with	sich begnügen mit
to get engaged to	sich verloben mit
to be glad of/about	sich freuen über

to be interested in	sich interessieren für
to get married to	sich verheiraten mit
to be mistaken	sich irren
to get rid of	sich entledigen
to grow stiff	sich versteifen
to grow worse	sich verschlechtern
to be satisfied with	sich zufriedengeben mit

Die reziproken Verben (Reciprocal Verbs)

Reziproke Verben drücken die Gegenseitigkeit, Wechselbeziehung aus (einander, gegenseitig). Diese Verben werden von den Pronomen each other bzw. one another begleitet, wobei each other vorzugsweise bei zwei Personen und one another bei mehreren Personen steht.

- We help **each other**.
- They think of **each other**.
- They heard **each other's** voice.
- They shook hands with **each other**.
- The neighbours help **one another**.
- They love **one another**.
- They care about **one another**.

Die refl exiven und reziproken Verben

Die Konjugation reflexiver Verben

Mod.	Zeit	1. Person Singular			2. Person Singular			3. Person Singular		
Ind.	Pres.T	I		cut myself	you		cut yourself	he		cuts himself
	Past T.	I		cut myself	you		cut yourself	he		cut himself
	Pres.P	I *have*		cut myself	you *have*		cut yourself	he *has*		cut himself
	Past P.	I *had*		cut myself	you *had*		cut yourself	he *had*		cut himself
	Fut. T.	I *will*		cut myself	you *will*		cut yourself	he *will*		cut himself
	Fut. P.	I *will have*		cut myself	you *will have*		cut yourself	he *will have*		cut himself
Con.	Con.	I *would*		cut myself	you *would*		cut yourself	he *would*		cut himself
	Con.P.	I *would have*	cut	myself	you *would have*	cut	yourself	he *would have*	cut	himself
Sub.	Pres.	I		cut myself	you		cut yourself	he		cut himself
	Past	I		cut myself	you		cut yourself	he		cut himself
	Past.P	I *had*		cut myself	you *had*		cut yourself	he *had*		cut himself
Imp.			-			cut yourself			-	

Inf.	Pres.		cut	oneself
	Perf.	have	cut	oneself
Part.	Pres.		cutting	oneself
	Past		cut	oneself
	Perf.	having	cut	oneself
Ger.	Pres.		cutting	oneself
	Perf.	having	cut	oneself

Beim weiblichen Personalpronomen (she) heißt das entsprechende Reflexivpronomen herself,

Die reflexiven und reziproken Verben

	1. Person Plural			2. Person Plural			3. Person Plural	
we		cut	ourselves	you	cut	yourselves	they	cut themselves
we		cut	ourselves	you	cut	yourselves	they	cut themselves
we *have*		cut	ourselves	you *have*	cut	yourselves	they *have*	cut themselves
we *had*		cut	ourselves	you *had*	cut	yourselves	they *had*	cut themselves
we *will*		cut	ourselves	you *will*	cut	yourselves	they *will*	cut themselves
we *will have*		cut	ourselves	you *will have*	cut	yourselves	they *will have*	cut themselves
we *would*		cut	ourselves	you *would*	cut	yourselves	they *would*	cut themselves
we *would have*		cut	ourselves	you *would have*	cut	yourselves	they *would have*	cut themselves
we		cut	ourselves	you	cut	yourselves	they	cut themselves
we		cut	ourselves	you	cut	yourselves	they	cut themselves
we *had*		cut	ourselves	you *had*	cut	yourselves	they *had*	cut themselves
		-			cut	yourselves		-

beim sächlichen Personalpronomen it heißt das entsprechende Reflexivpronomen itself.

Die reflexiven und reziproken Verben

Übungen zu den reflexiven Verben

1. Setzen Sie die entsprechenden Reflexivpronomen ein.

1. A selfish person thinks: first I must care for ..., let the others care for ...
2. Aren't you ashamed of ...?
3. Billy is a little too proud of ...
4. When Peggy looks in the mirror, she sees ...
5. We wrapped ... in blankets and huddled together to keep warm.
6. Look, some animal must have helped ... to the berries we picked.
7. England is only a part of the United Kingdom, which ... is a part of a big group of countries called the Commonwealth.
8. Someone who wants everything for ... is selfish.
9. Everybody had made ... comfortable, only Sue remained standing.
10. It was dreadful to find ... alone in such a place.

richtig   falsch

2. Setzen Sie das Reflexivpronomen oder den in Klammern gegebenen Ausdruck ein.

1. You can't please (ourselves, everybody).
2. Next time, we'll just please (ourselves; everybody).
3. John is only two years old. He can't wash (himself; your face).
4. You must wash (himself; your face).
5. Why do you defend (themselves; this criminal).
6. The Indians tried to defend (themselves; this criminal) against the enemy.
7. Luckily, the keepers were able to calm (yourself; the tigers).
8. Calm (yourself; the tigers) madam.
9. You must hide (yourself, messages).

Die reflexiven und reziproken Verben

10. There aren't many places to hide (yourself; messages).

11. She told me to show (themselves, her) my passport.

12. They dare not show (themselves; her) by day.

13. I will punish you if you don't behave (yourself; -) properly.

14. Behave (yourself, -)!

15. He lay back on the bed and tried to compose (himself; his next letter).

16. Tom began to compose (himself; his next letter) to them.

17. We hope you will enjoy (yourselves; the dish).

18. You boys enjoy (yourselves; the dish)!

19. Who helps (myself, you) with your homework?

20. He'd told me to help (myself, you) to his ties and jackets.

richtig   falsch

3. **Übersetzen Sie die Verben in Klammern im present tense simple oder der angegebenen Zeit.**

1. I can't (sich vorstellen) that he would ever agree to that.

2. I've got a few friends who (sich kümmern um) my safety.

3. She could not (sich erinnern an) my name.

4. He (sich fragen) (past tense simple) if he would find Sheila.

5. America (sich verändern) (present perfect simple) quite a lot since the first settlers arrived in the New World.

6. He (sich beklagen über) having too much to do.

7. Please fill up this form and then (sich anschließen) the queue.

8. We are (sich freuen auf) seeing you.

9. You can (sich verlassen auf) me to stand by you.

10. I cannot (sich leisten) a new car.

richtig   falsch

Die entsprechenden Lösungen befinden sich auf Seite 425ff.

Das Verb und seine Ergänzungen (The Verb and its Complements)

Die Verben können eine oder mehrere der folgenden Ergänzungen, d. h. Objekte oder prädikative Ergänzungen bei sich haben.
Es ist jedoch zu beachten, dass das englische Verb nicht dieselben Ergänzungen bzw. Objekte bei sich haben muss wie das deutsche Verb, d. h. ein Verb, das im Deutschen mit direktem Objekt steht, kann im Englischen mit indirektem Objekt stehen. Es empfiehlt sich daher jedes Verb gleich mit der entsprechenden Ergänzung zu lernen.

> deutsche Ergänzungen und englische stimmen nicht immer überein

Verben mit direktem Objekt (Verbs with a Direct Object)

Das direkte Objekt wird im Englischen stets ohne die Präposition *to* an das Verb angeschlossen.
Verben mit direktem Objekt heißen transitive Verben (transitive verbs).

> - He **allowed** me to stay until midnight.
> - He **answered** the question in a complicated way.
> - He slowly **approached** the unknown man.

to advise s.o.	jm. raten
to aid s.o.	jm. helfen
to allow s.o.	jm. erlauben
to answer s.o.	jm. antworten
to approach s.o.	sich jm. nähern
to assist s.o.	jm. helfen
to believe s.o.	jm. glauben
to command s.o.	jm. befehlen
to congratulate s.o.	jm. gratulieren
to contradict s.o.	jm. widersprechen
to flatter s.o.	jm. schmeicheln
to follow s.o.	jm. folgen
to forgive s.o.	jm. vergeben
to help s.o.	jm. helfen
to imitate s.o.	jn. nachahmen
to invade s.th.	in etw. eindringen
to join s.o.	sich jm. anschließen
to meet s.o.	jm. begegnen
to obey s.o.	jm. gehorchen
to oppose s.o.	sich jm. widersetzen
to order s.o.	jm. befehlen
to pardon s.o.	jm. verzeihen
to permit s.o.	jm. erlauben
to please s.o.	jm. gefallen
to recollect s.o.	sich an jn. erinnern
to remember s.o.	sich an jn. erinnern
to resemble s.o.	jm. gleichen
to resist s.o.	sich jm. widersetzen
to serve s.o.	jm. dienen, jn. bedienen
to succeed s.o.	jm. nachfolgen
to thank s.o.	jm. danken
to threaten s.o.	jm. drohen
to trust s.o.	jm. vertrauen

> Bedeutungsänderung

Einige Verben, die meist kein Objekt bei sich haben, können mit direktem Objekt verwendet werden. Sie ändern dann allerdings ihre Bedeutung oder werden mit *lassen* übersetzt. Diese Verben heißen faktitive (factitive) oder kausative Verben (causative verbs).

> - Her hair **grows** quickly.
>   (Ihr Haar **wächst** schnell.)
> - He **grows** rye and wheat.
>   (Er **baut** Roggen und Weizen **an**.)
> - He **returned** late in the night.
>   (Er **kam** spät in der Nacht **zurück**.)
> - I have to **return** the book tomorrow.
>   (Ich muss das Buch morgen **zurückgeben**.)

to dance	tanzen	to dance s.o.	jn. tanzen lassen
to descend	herabsteigen	to descend s.o.	jm. durch Erbschaft zufallen
to drop	fallen	to drop s.th.	etw. fallen lassen
to enter	eintreten	to enter s.th.	etw. eintragen

Das Verb und seine Ergänzungen

- to fail — scheitern
- to fly — fliegen
- to grow — wachsen
- to jump — springen
- to leap — springen
- to march — marschieren
- to mount — besteigen; reiten
- to pass — vorübergehen
- to race — rennen
- to return — zurückkehren
- to run — laufen
- to sink — sinken
- to stand — stehen
- to starve — verhungern
- to work — arbeiten

- to fail s.o. — jn. durchfallen lassen
- to fly s.th. — etw. fliegen lassen
- to grow s.th. — etw. anbauen
- to jump s.th. — etw. zum Springen bringen
- to leap s.th. — etw. springen lassen
- to march s.o. — jn. marschieren lassen
- to mount s.th. — beritten machen
- to pass s.th. — etw. reichen
- to race s.th. — etw. rennen lassen
- to return s.th. — etw. zurückgeben
- to run s.th. — etw. laufen lassen, leiten
- to sink s.th. — etw. versenken
- to stand s.th. — etw. aushalten
- to starve s.o. — jn. verhungern lassen
- to work s.o. — jn. arbeiten lassen

Verben mit indirektem Objekt (Verbs with an Indirect Object)

Das indirekte Objekt ist meist ein persönliches Objekt, also eine Person. Das indirekte Objekt kann mit und ohne die Präposition to an das Verb angeschlossen werden. Es steht mit to, wenn es besonders hervorgehoben werden soll, wenn es viel länger ist als das direkte Objekt oder wenn das direkte Objekt it oder them ist.
Die folgenden Verben müssen das indirekte Objekt jedoch immer mit der Präposition to anschließen. Das indirekte Objekt steht dann meist nach dem direkten Objekt.

- Mary **taught** John English.
- Mary **explained** the case to John.
- **Write** a letter to your cousin Jill who is very ill.
- I **explained** it to him.
- I **gave** them to John.
- I **introduced** John to my father.
- I **delivered** this letter to you, not to John.
- The teacher **demonstrated** to the pupils how to solve this problem.
- He **described** the case to me in detail.
- I **suggested** to him that he should leave her alone.

- to add s.th. to s.th. — etw. hinzufügen
- to address s.th. to s.o. — etw. an jn. richten
- to admit s.th. to s.o. — jm. etw. zugeben
- to allude to s.th. — auf etw. anspielen
- to announce s.th. to s.o. — jm. etw. ankündigen
- to ascribe s.th. to s.o. — jm. etw. zuschreiben
- to attribute s.th. to s.o. — jm. etw. zuschreiben
- to confide s.th. to s.o. — jm. etw. anvertrauen
- to declare s.th. to s.o. — jm. etw. erklären
- to deliver s.th. to s.o. — jm. etw. liefern
- to demonstrate s.th. to s.o. — jm. etw. demonstrieren
- to describe s.th. to s.o. — jm. etw. beschreiben
- to dictate s.th. to s.o. — jm. etw. diktieren
- to distribute s.th. to s.o. — jm. etw. austeilen
- to explain s.th. to s.o. — jm. etw. erklären
- to introduce s.th. to s.o. — jm. etw. vorstellen
- to mention s.th. to s.o. — bei jm. etw. erwähnen
- to prefer s.th. to s.th. — etw. vorziehen
- to propose s.th. to s.o. — jm. etw. vorschlagen
- to prove s.th. to s.o. — jm. etw. beweisen
- to read s.th. to s.o. — jm. etw. vorlesen
- to relate s.th. to s.o. — jm. etw. erzählen
- to repeat s.th. to s.o. — jm. etw. wiederholen
- to reply s.th. to s.o. — jm. etw. erwidern
- to say s.th. to s.o. — jm. etw. sagen
- to seem s.th. to s.o. — jm. scheinen
- to suggest s.th. to s.o. — jm. etw. vorschlagen

Verben mit präpositionalem Objekt (Verbs with a Prepositional Object)

Präpositionale Objekte werden mit einer Präposition an das Verb angeschlossen.
Es lassen sich keine allgemein gültigen Regeln dafür aufstellen, welche Präpositionen an welche Verben angeschlossen werden können. Es empfiehlt sich daher jedes Verb gleich mit seinen möglichen Präpositionen zu lernen.

- The criminal was **accused of** murder.
  (Der Verbrecher wurde **wegen** Mordes ange**klagt**.)
- He **asked** me **for** help.
  (Er **bat** mich **um** Hilfe.)
- He **congratulated** her **on** her great success.
  (Er **beglückwünschte** sie **zu** ihrem großen Erfolg.)

Verben mit adverbialen Bestimmungen (Verbs with Adverbial Elements)

Adverbiale Bestimmungen (Umstandsbestimmungen) geben die Zeit (adverbial elements of time), den Ort (adverbial elements of place), die Art und Weise (adverbial elements of manner), den Grund, die Ursache (adverbial elements of cause) an.

- We came back **last week.** (adverbiale Bestimmung der Zeit)
- We arrived **at the airport.** (adverbiale Bestimmung des Ortes)
- He **slowly** approached us. (adverbiale Bestimmung der Art und Weise (wie?))
- He was beside himself **with rage.**
  (adverbiale Bestimmung des Grundes, der Ursache)

Verben mit prädikativer Ergänzung (Verbs with a Predicative Complement)

Die prädikative Ergänzung kann ein Adjektiv oder Substantiv sein und bezieht sich entweder auf das Subjekt oder Objekt.

Verben der Ruhe

Prädikative Ergänzung zum Subjekt	Prädikative Ergänzung zum Objekt
Nach den Verben der Ruhe, besonders nach: ■ to be — sein ■ to keep — halten ■ to lie — liegen ■ to remain — bleiben ■ to sit — sitzen ■ to stand — stehen	Nach den Verben der Ruhe, des Innehaltens, besonders nach: ■ to keep — halten ■ to lie — liegen ■ to remain — bleiben ■ to sit — sitzen ■ to stand — stehen
■ He **stood silent** at the window. ■ He **lay quiet** in his bed.	■ He **kept** his eyes and ears **open.**

Das Verb und seine Ergänzungen

Prädikative Ergänzung zum Subjekt	Prädikative Ergänzung zum Objekt	
Nach den Verben des Werdens, der Bewegung.		Verben der Bewegung
▪ to become — werden ▪ to fall — fallen ▪ to get — bekommen ▪ to go — gehen ▪ to grow — werden ▪ to turn — werden		
• It is getting **dark**. • He became **Catholic**.		
Nach den Verben der Sinneswahrnehmung, besonders nach:	Nach den Verben der Sinneswahrnehmung, vor allem wenn eine Eigenschaft des Objekts beschrieben werden soll.	Verben der Sinneswahrnehmung
▪ to feel — fühlen ▪ to smell — riechen ▪ to sound — klingen ▪ to taste — kosten, probieren	▪ to feel — fühlen ▪ to smell — riechen ▪ to sound — klingen ▪ to taste — kosten, probieren	
• This morning I felt **awful**. • This cake tastes **good**. • This perfume smells **wonderful**.	• I feel him **breathing**. • I smell something **rotten**. • I feel it **necessary** to tell him all about it.	
Nach den Verben des Seins, Scheinens, äußeren Erscheinungsbilds.		Verben des Seins, Scheinens
▪ to appear — scheinen ▪ to be — sein ▪ to look — schauen ▪ to prove — beweisen ▪ to seem — scheinen ▪ to show — zeigen		
• He is very **intelligent**. • He looked **unhappy**. • She seemed very **sad**.		
In Passivsätzen nach den Verben des Ernennens, Erwählens und Dafürhaltens.	Nach den Verben des Ernennens, Erwählens und Dafürhaltens.	Verben des Ernennens, Dafürhaltens
▪ to acknowledge as — anerkennen als ▪ to appoint — ernennen ▪ to call — rufen ▪ to choose as/for — (aus)wählen als ▪ to consider as — ansehen als	▪ to acknowledge as — anerkennen als ▪ to appoint — ernennen ▪ to call — rufen ▪ to choose as — (aus)wählen als ▪ to consider as — ansehen als	

Das Verb und seine Ergänzungen

Prädikative Ergänzung zum Subjekt

to create	(er)schaffen
to crown	krönen
to declare	erklären
to elect	wählen
to look upon as	ansehen als
to make	machen
to name	nennen
to proclaim	proklamieren
to recognize as	ansehen als
to regard as	ansehen als
to think of as	halten für

- John F. Kennedy was elected President in 1960.
  (John F. Kennedy wurde 1960 zum Präsidenten gewählt.)
- He is considered an expert.

Prädikative Ergänzung zum Objekt

to create	(er)schaffen
to crown	krönen
to declare	erklären
to elect	wählen
to look upon as	ansehen als
to make	machen
to name	nennen
to proclaim	proklamieren
to recognize as	ansehen als
to regard as	ansehen als
to think of as	halten für

- The American people elected John F. Kennedy President of the United States.
- The pupils chose Mary as cheerleader.

Das Verb und seine Ergänzungen

Übungen zu den Ergänzungen zum Verb

1. Setzen Sie to ein wo nötig.

1. Can you give short answers ... all the questions?

2. Do you remember ... me?

3. Tom gave some milk ... the cat.

4. Tom gave ... the cat some milk.

5. I asked you to come here so that we can all thank ... Mr Smith.

6. It is necessary that we should help ... the poverty-stricken areas of the world.

7. Shall I send a messenger ... you?

8. Shall I send ... you a messenger?

9. Mrs Miller wrote a postcard ... the Barton family.

10. Sheila Donaldson told her story ... her friends.

11. On Christmas Day, 1066, William, now known as „the Conqueror", was crowned ... King of England in Westminster Abbey.

12. She handed the teapot ... her mother.

13. The prisoner refused to answer ... the judge's question.

14. Immigrants are only allowed to enter ... Britain if they had certificates to show that they have jobs waiting for them.

15. He just waved his hand ... me.

16. I don't believe ... those forgeries for one minute.

17. I see you do not trust ... me.

18. Some states allow ... local communities to impose their own speed limits.

19. Technical and business colleges offer further education ... the young workers in industry and commerce.

20. That's why I spoke ... you the other day.

Das Verb und seine Ergänzungen

21. I thought you might pass the message ... him.

22. You can't serve ... two masters and be in two places at the same time.

23. Generally, people readily accept the fact that obeying ... the law is necessary for the smooth running of national and neighbourhood affairs.

24. He resented the courtesy ... her.

25. How did Mrs Smith come to make this confession ... you?

richtig   falsch

Die entsprechenden Lösungen befinden sich auf Seite 426.

Übereinstimmung von Verb und Subjekt (Agreement of Verb and Subject)

Grundsätzlich richtet sich das Verb in Person und Zahl nach dem Subjekt, auf das es sich bezieht, d. h. steht das Subjekt z. B. in der 3. Person Singular, so steht das Verb ebenfalls in der 3. Person Singular.
Die folgenden Erläuterungen geben über Person und Zahl des Verbs Auskunft, wenn es sich auf ein bzw. mehrere Subjekte im Singular oder Plural bezieht.

Verb im Singular

Nach einem Subjekt im Singular.

- Peter **is** a nice boy.
- Mary **is** Peggy's best friend.
- This book **is** the most interesting book I've ever read.

Verb im Plural

Nach mehreren Subjekten im Singular. — *Subjekt(e) im Singular*

- Peter, John and Mary **are** very good friends.
- Awl, thread and last **are** the tools which are needed to make a shoe.

Nach einem bzw. mehreren Subjekten im Plural. — *Subjekt(e) im Plural*

- These houses **are** sold.
- These tables and these chairs **belong** together.

Einige Substantive, vor allem die, die Werkzeuge und Kleidungsstücke bezeichnen, die aus zwei Teilen bestehen, kommen nur im Plural vor. Das zugehörige Verb steht im Plural, auch wenn mit dem Substantiv nur eine Sache bezeichnet wird. — *Kleidungsstücke, Werkzeuge*

- ashes — Asche (im Ofen)
- binoculars — Fernglas
- breeches — enge Kniehose
- compasses — Zirkel
- contents — Inhalt
- earnings — Verdienst
- glasses — Brille
- goggles — Schutzbrille
- jeans — Jeanshose
- knickerbockers — Knickerbocker
- lungs — Lunge
- the Middle Ages — Mittelalter
- oats — Hafer
- outskirts — Randgebiet
- pants — Unterhose
- pincers — Kneifzange
- pliers — Kombizange

Übereinstimmung von Verb und Subjekt

Verb im Singular | Verb im Plural

Verb im Plural

- pyjamas — Pyjama
- premises — Grundstück
- riches — Reichtum
- scales — Waage
- scissors — Schere
- shears — Heckenschere
- shorts — kurze Hose
- spectacles — Brille
- stairs — Treppe
- surroundings — Umgebung
- suspenders (AE) — Hosenträger
- thanks — Dank
- tights — Strumpfhose
- tongs — Feuerzange
- trousers — lange Hose
- victuals — Lebensmittel

- These scissors **are** not sharp.
  (Diese Schere **ist** nicht scharf.)
- These trousers **are** torn.
  (Diese Hose **ist** zerrissen.)

Substantive mit Plural-s

Verb im Singular: Einige Substantive haben auch im Singular ein Plural-s. Sie stehen, wenn sie *eine* Sache bezeichnen, mit einem Verb im Singular.
The United States und the Netherlands stehen mit einem Verb im Singular.

- barracks — Kaserne
- gallows — der Galgen
- headquarters — Hauptquartier
- means — das Mittel
- news — Nachricht
- series — Serie
- species — Art
- works — Fabrik, Werk

Verb im Plural: Substantive auf -s stehen, wenn sie eine Sache im Plural bezeichnen, mit einem Verb im Plural.

- barracks — Kasernen
- gallows — die Galgen
- headquarters — Hauptquartiere
- means — die Mittel
- series — Serien
- species — Arten
- works — Fabriken, Werke

- This **is** bad news.
  (Das **ist** eine schlechte Nachricht.)
- The United States **is** called the country of unlimited opportunities.

- Many species of bird **are** migratory.
- Several television series **were** filmed in Chicago.

Substantive auf -ics

Verb im Singular: Namen von Wissenschaften auf -ics, Krankheiten und Spiele sind, trotz des Plural-s, Substantive im Singular und stehen folglich auch mit einem Verb im Singular.

- Mathematics **is** an exact science.
  (Die Mathematik **ist** eine exakte Wissenschaft.)

Verb im Plural: Die Namen praktischer Tätigkeiten auf -ics, vor allem die Namen von Sportarten, sind Substantive im Plural und stehen folglich mit einem Verb im Plural.

- Athletics **are** a very popular sport.
  (**Leichtathletik ist** eine sehr beliebte Sportart.)

Übereinstimmung von Verb und Subjekt

Verb im Singular	Verb im Plural	
- Measles **is** not a serious illness. (Masern **sind** keine ernstliche Krankheit.) - Darts **is** a very popular game. (Darts **ist** ein sehr beliebtes Spiel.)		
Substantive, die eine Gruppe von Personen bezeichnen, stehen mit einem Verb im Singular, wenn die Gruppe als Einheit angesehen wird.	Substantive, die eine Gruppe von Personen bezeichnen, stehen mit einem Verb im Plural, wenn die einzelnen Mitglieder gemeint sind.	Substantive, die eine Gruppe bezeichnen
- army — Armee - audience — Publikum - class — Klasse - company — Firma - couple — (Ehe)Paar - crew — Crew - crowd — Menge - enemy — Feind - family — Familie - government — Regierung - group — Gruppe - majority — Mehrheit - parliament — Parlament - party — Partei - police — Polizei - public — Öffentlichkeit - staff — Zeug - team — Team	- army — Armee - audience — Publikum - class — Klasse - company — Firma - couple — (Ehe)Paar - crew — Crew - crowd — Menge - enemy — Feind - family — Familie - government — Regierung - group — Gruppe - majority — Mehrheit - parliament — Parlament - party — Partei - police — Polizei - public — Öffentlichkeit - staff — Zeug - team — Team	
- The police **has** caught the criminal in the very act.	- There **are** many police in the town due to the football match.	
In der Bedeutung *Volk* kann people mit einem Verb im Singular stehen.	In der Bedeutung *Leute, Menschen* bezeichnet people den Plural und steht folglich auch mit einem Verb im Plural. Zur Bezeichnung mehrerer *Völker* erhält people ein Plural-s und steht ebenfalls mit einem Verb im Plural.	people
- The American people **is** said to be very rich. (Das amerikanische Volk **soll** sehr reich sein.) - The Chinese people **is** the most numerous people in the world.	- In this country people **are** very poor. (In diesem Land **sind** die Menschen sehr arm.) - Many different peoples **live** in America. (In Amerika **leben** viele verschiedene Völker.)	
Einige Substantive, vor allem Tiernamen, stehen, wenn sie nur ein Tier bezeichnen mit einem Verb im Singular.	Einige Substantive, vor allem Tiernamen, haben auch im Plural kein Plural-s. Diese Substantive stehen mit einem Verb im Plural.	Substantive in Singularform

Übereinstimmung von Verb und Subjekt

	Verb im Singular	Verb im Plural
	- antelope — Antilope - beaver — Biber - cod — Kabeljau - craft — Fahrzeug - deer — Hirsch, Reh - fish — Fisch - pike — Hecht - salmon — Lachs - sheep — Schaf - trout — Forelle	- antelope — Antilopen - beaver — Biber - cod — Kabeljau - craft — Fahrzeuge - deer — Hirsche Rehe - fish — Fische - pike — Hechte - salmon — Lachse - sheep — Schafe - trout — Forellen
	- This sheep **is** seriously ill. (Dieses Schaf **ist** ernstlich krank.) - This fish **is** my sister's favourite animal.	- These sheep **are** seriously ill. (Diese Schafe **sind** ernstlich krank.) - The fish in this river **are** endangered by environmental pollution.
Mengenausdrücke	Die folgenden Mengenausdrücke stehen mit einem Verb im Singular, wenn sie sich auf ein Substantiv im Singular beziehen. - a certain amount of — ein bestimmter Betrag von - a bit of — ein bisschen von - a good/great deal of — eine ganze Menge von - the number of — eine Anzahl von - a lot of, lots of — viele - part of — ein Teil von - plenty of — viele	Die folgenden Mengenausdrücke stehen mit einem Verb im Plural, wenn sie sich auf ein Substantiv im Plural beziehen. - a few (of) — einige von - a good many (of) — eine ganze Menge von - a number of — eine Anzahl von - a lot of, lots of — viele - part of — ein Teil von - plenty of — viele
	- A certain amount of money **has** been spent on this future project. - Plenty of beer **was** sold at the concert.	- A number of students **have** passed the exam. - Plenty of pupils **have** assembled in the auditorium.
Bruchzahlen	Nach den Bruchzahlen, wenn der Zähler 1 ist.	Nach den Bruchzahlen, wenn der Zähler größer 1 ist.
	- One third of the students **has** passed the exam.	- Two thirds of the students **have** passed the exam.
Prozentzahlen		Nach den Prozentzahlen. - 75 % of the students **have** passed the exam.
neutrales it, this	Nach neutralem it und this steht to be im Singular, auch wenn das nachfolgende Substantiv oder Pronomen im Plural steht. - Who rang the bell? It **is** the Maxwells. - Is that you Peter? No, it **is** us.	

Die Zeiten (The Tenses)

Mit Hilfe der Zeiten werden bestimmte Vorgänge oder Zustände der Vergangenheit, Gegenwart oder Zukunft zugeordnet.

Einfache Zeiten (Non-Compound Tenses)

Die einfachen Zeiten werden ohne Hilfsverb gebildet.

- I go to school.
- I went to school.

Zusammengesetzte Zeiten (Compound Tenses)

Die zusammengesetzten Zeiten werden mit Hilfsverb gebildet.

- I have lived in London.
- I will have lived in London.

Es ist zu beachten, dass die deutschen Zeiten nicht einfach ins Englische übertragen werden können, d. h. wenn im Deutschen z. B. das Präsens steht, ist dies im Englischen nicht automatisch mit dem present tense zu übersetzen. Die Auswahl der Zeiten im Englischen ist danach zu treffen, welcher Sachverhalt (z. B. Vorgang, der in die Gegenwart reicht etc.) ausgedrückt werden soll.

deutsche Zeit entspricht nicht automatisch der englischen Zeit

Present Tense Simple

Zum Ausdruck von Vorgängen, die in der Gegenwart stattfinden, von allgemein gültigen Tatsachen.

- Bob reads a book.
  (Bob liest ein Buch.)

Gegenwart

Past Tense

Zum Ausdruck von Vorgängen, die in der Vergangenheit stattfanden und in ihr völlig abgeschlossen sind.
Das past tense steht bei den folgenden Zeitangaben, die auf einen völlig abgeschlossenen Vorgang hinweisen.

Present Perfect

Zum Ausdruck, dass ein Vorgang, der in der Vergangenheit begonnen hat bis in die Gegenwart hineinreicht oder in der Gegenwart (ohne Unterbrechung) noch andauert. Im letzteren Fall wird meist das present perfect continuous verwendet, außer bei den Verben, die nicht in der continuous form

Vergangenheit

Die Zeiten

Past Tense	Present Perfect
	stehen. Dies wird im Deutschen durch das Präsens und häufig durch das Adverb *schon* übersetzt. Das **present perfect** steht häufig mit den folgenden Zeitangaben, die auf einen bis zur Gegenwart reichenden Zeitraum hinweisen.
▪ (two years) ago vor (2 Jahren) ▪ the other day neulich ▪ formerly früher ▪ in 1963 1963 ▪ last night, year etc. gestern Nacht, letztes Jahr ▪ at that moment in diesem Moment ▪ once einmal ▪ long since seit langem ▪ then dann ▪ at that time zu jener Zeit ▪ when wann ▪ yesterday gestern	▪ in my life in meinem Leben ▪ just gerade, jetzt ▪ meanwhile mittlerweile ▪ ever since seither ▪ since then seither ▪ so far bisher ▪ these days in diesen Tagen ▪ these last five days in den letzten fünf Tagen ▪ up till/to now bis jetzt ▪ up to the present bis jetzt ▪ (not) yet noch (nicht) ▪ as yet bis jetzt
▪ The train **arrived** at 10 o'clock. ▪ Last year, I **spent** my holidays in France.	▪ I **have lived** in London for 10 years. (Ich **lebe (schon)** seit 10 Jahren in London *(und ich lebe immer noch da).*)
Bei einigen Zeitangaben kann sowohl das **past tense** als auch das **present perfect** verwendet werden. Das **past tense** muss stehen, wenn der Vorgang als völlig abgeschlossen gilt.	Bei einigen Zeitangaben kann das **past tense** oder **present perfect** stehen. Das **present perfect** muss stehen, wenn der Vorgang bis in die Gegenwart hineinreicht bzw. andauert.

Die Zeiten

Past Tense

- **already** — schon
- **always** — immer
- **for two weeks** — seit 2 Wochen
- **ever** — jemals
- **lately** — kürzlich
- **never** — niemals
- **recently** — kürzlich
- **since** — seit
- **a short time ago** — vor kurzem
- **this week** — diese Woche
- **today** — heute

For bezeichnet einen Zeitraum und kann weggelassen werden, since bezeichnet einen Zeitpunkt und kann nicht weggelassen werden.

- This morning, Peter **went** to school by bus. *(Der Morgen ist vorbei, es ist nachmittags.)*
- We **were** there **(for)** an hour. *(Wir **waren** eine Stunde lang dort (und sind nicht mehr dort).)*

In Verbindung mit einer Zeitbestimmung, die eindeutig auf die Vergangenheit weist, muss jedoch das past tense stehen.

- I **opened** the window ten minutes ago.

Present Perfect

- **already** — schon
- **always** — immer
- **for two weeks** — seit 2 Wochen
- **ever** — jemals
- **lately** — kürzlich
- **never** — niemals
- **recently** — kürzlich
- **since** — seit
- **a short time ago** — vor kurzem
- **this week** — diese Woche
- **today** — heute

For bezeichnet einen Zeitraum und kann weggelassen werden, since bezeichnet einen Zeitpunkt und kann nicht weggelassen werden.

- This morning, Peter **has gone** to school by bus. *(Der Morgen ist noch nicht vorbei.)*
- We **have been** here **(for)** an hour. *(Wir **sind** seit einer Stunde hier (und wir sind immer noch hier)).*

Zum Ausdruck von Vorgängen, die in der Vergangenheit abgeschlossen sind, deren Ergebnis oder Folge für die Gegenwart noch gilt.

- I **have opened** the window (and it is still open).

Past Perfect

Zum Ausdruck der Vorvergangenheit, d. h. eines Vorgangs, der beendet war, bevor ein anderer einsetzte. Es wird von der Vergangenheit zurückgeblickt.

Past Tense

Das past perfect kann nur mit dem past tense stehen. Demnach steht der Vorgang, der nach dem Vorgang der Vorvergangenheit einsetzt im past tense.

Vorvergangenheit

Die Zeiten

Past Perfect
I had waited for 3 hours before the train finally arrived.
(Ich **hatte** 3 Stunden **gewartet**, bevor der Zug endlich ankam.
(Das Warten fand vor der Ankunft des Zuges statt.)

Past Tense
I had waited for 3 hours before the train finally **arrived.**

Zukunft
(von der Gegenwart aus gesehen)

will heißt nicht *wollen*, sondern *werden*

Future Tense
Zum Ausdruck von Vorgängen, die von der Gegenwart aus gesehen in der Zukunft liegen.
Im Deutschen wird hier häufig das Präsens verwendet.
Das *future tense*, das mit *will* + *infinitive* gebildet wird, ist nicht zu übersetzen mit dem deutschen Verb *wollen* (to want). Zum Ausdruck der Zukunft steht *will* immer in der Bedeutung *werden*.
In Verbindung mit den Verben *to go* und *to come* steht statt des *present tense continuous* häufig das *future continuous*.
Das *future tense* steht besonders mit den folgenden Ausdrücken, die auf die Zukunft weisen.

- to be afraid — fürchten
- to assume — annehmen
- to believe — glauben
- I dare say — ich wage zu behaupten
- to doubt — zweifeln
- to expect — erwarten
- to hope — hoffen
- to know — wissen
- to promise — versprechen
- to suppose — vermuten
- to be sure — sicher sein

going to
Zum Ausdruck von Vorgängen, die von der Gegenwart aus gesehen in der Zukunft liegen.
Die *going-to-*Form wird vor allem in der Umgangssprache zum Ausdruck der nahen Zukunft verwendet, für Vorgänge, die unmittelbar bevorstehen und die sehr wahrscheinlich sind.
In der gehobenen Sprache stehen *to go* und *to come* nicht in der *going-to-*Form.
Zum Ausdruck der nahen Zukunft wird häufig auch *to be about to, to be on the point of* + *gerund* (gerade dabei sein etw. zu tun) verwendet.

Present Tense
Zum Ausdruck von Vorgängen, die von der Gegenwart aus gesehen in der nahen Zukunft liegen.
Dabei steht es vor allem in Verbindung mit Zeitbestimmungen, die auf die Zukunft weisen (until, before etc.).
Bei den Verben der Bewegung (to go, to come, to arrive, to leave etc.) steht häufig das *present tense continuous.*

Die Zeiten

Future Tense

- to feel sure — sicher sein
- to think — denken
- to wonder — sich fragen
- maybe — vielleicht
- perhaps — vielleicht
- possibly — möglicherweise
- probably — wahrscheinlich
- surely — sicherlich
- undoubtedly — zweifellos

- In future, he **will work** much harder.
  (In Zukunft **wird** er viel härter **arbeiten**.)
- I think Manchester United **will win** 2:0.
- She **will** probably **be** elected to the Senate in November.
- How long **will** you **be staying**?
- We **won't be coming** to dinner.

going to

- I **am going to start** tomorrow morning.
  (Ich **werde** morgen früh **losfahren**.)
- I **was about to leave** the house when the telephone rang.
- I **was on the point of leaving** the house when the telephone rang.

Present Tense

- We **land** in Dublin at 4 p.m.
- I'll come and see you before you **leave**.
- **Are** you **doing** anything tonight? I **am going** to the theatre (tonight).

Future Perfect

Zum Ausdruck von Vorgängen, die an einem Zeitpunkt der Zukunft abgeschlossen sein werden.
Das future perfect steht meist mit Zeitangaben.
Neben dem Futur II, wird im Deutschen häufig auch das Perfekt verwendet.

- Next May, he **will have lived** in London for 10 years.
  (Nächsten Mai **wird** er 10 Jahre in London **gelebt haben**.
  Nächsten Mai **hat** er 10 Jahre in London **gelebt**.)

Future in the Past

Zum Ausdruck von Vorgängen, die von einem Zeitpunkt der Vergangenheit aus gesehen noch nicht geschehen waren, also noch in der Zukunft lagen.
Das future in the past hat dieselbe Form wie das conditional, das in Bedingungssätzen steht.

- The manager informed his secretary that he **would be** in the office on Monday.

Future Perfect in the Past

Zum Ausdruck von Vorgängen, die von einem Zeitpunkt der Vergangenheit aus gesehen an einem Zeitpunkt in der Zukunft abgeschlossen sein werden.
Das future perfect in the past hat dieselbe Form wie das conditional perfect, das in Bedingungssätzen steht.

- He thought that he **would have finished** his work by Monday.

Zukunft (von der Vergangenheit aus gesehen)

Die Zeiten

	Present Tense	Past Tense	
spannende Erzählungen, Beschreibungen	In lebhaften, spannenden Erzählungen, in Beschreibungen von Theaterstücken und Sportreportagen.	Zeitform in Erzählungen, in denen aufeinanderfolgende Vorgänge der Vergangenheit ausgedürckt werden.	
	▪ The curtain **rises**. The phone **rings**. Juliet **picks** it **up** and **listens**.	▪ Suddenly, there **was** a knock at the door. The girl **stopped** playing. He **came in**.	
	Present Perfect Simple	Future Tense	Present Tense Continuous
Zeitungssprache, Bericht	In den Medien zur Einführung eines Vorgangs, der dann im past tense weiter beschrieben wird.	In den Medien bei förmlichen Verkündigungen. Statt des future tense kann auch die going-to-Form stehen.	Zum Ausdruck förmlicher Verkündigungen im Gespräch.
	▪ 30 thousand pounds worth of jewellery **has been stolen**. The thieves **broke into** the shop Saturday night and ...	▪ The President **will announce** his resignation on Saturday. ▪ The President **is going to announce** his resignation on Saturday.	▪ The President **is announcing** his resignation on Saturday.

Neben der oben aufgeführten zeitlichen Verwendung der Zeiten können durch sie auch nicht zeitliche Sachverhalte zum Ausdruck kommen.

	Present Tense Simple	Past Tense Simple
Tatsachen	Zum Ausdruck allgemein gültiger Tatsachen.	Zum Ausdruck geschichtlicher Tatsachen.
	▪ The earth **revolves** round the sun. ▪ Water **consists** of hydrogen and oxygen.	▪ In 1952, Elizabeth II **was crowned** Queen of Great Britain.
	Future Continuous	going to
Erwartung, Vermutung, Wahrscheinlichkeit	Zum Ausdruck, dass man erwartet, dass etwas geschieht. Der Vorgang erstreckt sich meist über die gesamte Zeitspanne.	Zum Ausdruck der hohen Wahrscheinlichkeit, der Zuversicht oder dass man vermutet, dass etwas geschieht.
	▪ He **will be working** there up to 4 o'clock. (Er wird dort wohl bis 4 Uhr arbeiten.)	▪ She **is going to graduate** in June.

Die Zeiten

Fragen, Bitten

Future Tense

Zum Ausdruck höflicher Fragen und Bitten.

- **Will** you **join** me for dinner?
- **Will** you **have** a cigarette?

Future Continuous

Zum Ausdruck besonders höflicher Fragen, Bitten.

- How long **will** you **be staying**?
- **Will** you **be needing** anything?

Past Tense Continuous

In Fragen darüber, wie eine bestimmte Zeit verbracht wurde. Das past tense simple würde hier unhöflich klingen. So formulierte Fragen können auch ausdrücken, dass etwas Unrechtes geschah.
Mit dem past tense simple kann dies nicht ausgedrückt werden.

- What **were** you **doing** before you came here?
- What **were** you **telling** him about me?

Aufforderung; Feststellung

Future Tense Simple

Zum Ausdruck der Aufforderung, des Befehls.

- You **will work** in this room.
(Sie **arbeiten** in diesem Raum!)

Future Tense Continuous

Zum Ausdruck einer bloßen Feststellung.

- You **will be working** in this room.
(Sie **arbeiten** in diesem Raum.)

Gewohnheit

Present Tense

Zum Ausdruck gewohnheitsmäßiger, immer wiederkehrender Vorgänge und Handlungen.

- Every morning, I **go** to school by bus.
- We always **have** dinner at 7 o'clock.

Past Tense

Zum Ausdruck vergangener Gewohnheiten.

- He never **drank** alcohol.
- I always **bought** „The Times".

Future Tense

Zum Ausdruck wiederkehrender Vorgänge, von denen angenommen wird, dass dies in Zukunft auch so ist.

- Christmas **will come** again.
- I **will see** you tomorrow.

Absicht

going to

Zum Ausdruck der Absicht, der ein Plan zugrunde liegt.

- I **am not going to** accept your impertinent behaviour any longer.
- He **was going to** spend his holiday in Germany but he didn't.

Future Tense

Zum Ausdruck der Absicht, der kein Plan zugrunde liegt.

- I **will help** you with your homework if you like.
- She **will be** there as soon as possible.

Die Zeiten

Übungen zu den Zeiten

1. **Setzen Sie die Verben in Klammern ins present tense simple.**

    1. What is Linda doing there? (cry) Peter.
    2. Sport (play) a big role in English school life.
    3. The United States (lie) across the Pole to the North.
    4. When a forest (catch) fire, the air is soon polluted.
    5. My children never (wash) behind their ears.
    6. The Bristish Museum (possess) the finest collection of Greek and Roman art in the world.
    7. The concentration of newspapers (reach) its most extreme form in Britain.
    8. The English legal system (enjoy) a good reputation for fairness.
    9. What (distinguish) them most clearly is their dress.
    10. The Department of Education and Science (establish) standards to which schools ought to conform.

    richtig   falsch

2. **Setzen Sie die Verben in Klammern ins past tense simple.**

    1. The animals Sheila (enjoy) most of all were the elephants.
    2. Mr Miller (hate) the thought of listening to his aunt's gibberish.
    3. Julia (burst) into the room.
    4. I (send) Tom to buy some stamps.
    5. She (bury) her face in her hands, then jumped up and ran away.
    6. Tom turned the radio to a station that (play) dance music.
    7. This short story bears a resemblance to a story I (read) some weeks ago.
    8. He (control) himself by a tremendous effort.

Die Zeiten

9. I **(study)** him quietly without appearing to do so.

10. He **(obey)** an instinct that he did not know he **(possess)**.

richtig falsch

3. Setzen Sie die Verben in Klammern ins present perfect simple.

1. He **(drop)** a vase.

2. He **(hit)** his head on the doorway of the cabin.

3. Australia **(build)** an atomic reactor and is building another.

4. All rulers in all ages **(try)** to impose their view of the world upon their followers.

5. The injured **(die)** from their wounds.

6. He **(have)** time.

7. His name **(slip)** my memory for the moment.

8. Many great industrialists **(put)** large amounts of money into this project.

9. The American way of speaking **(develop)** independently of England.

10. Barbecues, espresso cafés and salami-bars **(spring)** up in the cities.

richtig falsch

4. Setzen Sie die Verben in Klammern ins past perfect simple.

1. He was a happy-go-lucky fellow and everyone **(like)** him.

2. He could not remember why he **(stop)** swimming.

3. This was the first time he **(travel)** so far west, and already he regretted it.

4. When Bob came home, his mother wanted to know what **(happen)**.

5. Ralph cried out as though he **(hurt)** himself.

6. I wondered whether he **(make)** friends with him.

7. The children hurried off to tell the others what they **(see)**.

Die Zeiten

8. He had a house in Rome, and I (stay) with him for several weeks.

9. She was looking at herself proudly in the mirror when she saw that she (forget) her brooch.

10. His father opened the door after he (get) his stick ready.

richtig   falsch

5. Setzen Sie die Verben in Klammern ins future tense simple.

1. This time I (teach) you a lesson.

2. London (continue) to be a world centre of finance.

3. It is time to adopt strategies for action that (produce) quick and visible progress.

4. I feel sure that she (let) me know.

5. I (give) you the money on condition that you spend it sensibly.

6. He (live) to be ninety, he is so strong.

7. We made the final arrangements for what it is hoped (prove) a successful demonstration.

8. Some universities (admit) any students provided that they have passed through all of the high-school courses.

9. He is not obliged to give way, but his reputation (suffer) if he obstinately refuses to do so.

10. A drowning man (catch) at a straw.

richtig   falsch

6. Setzen Sie die Verben in Klammern ins future perfect simple.

1. I (finish) by 10 o'clock.

2. It is likely that by 2050, all real knowledge of this language (disappear).

3. In twelve months she (forget) all about it.

4. If a state is choosing a senator the two parties in that state (choose) their candidates at a primary election some months before.

Die Zeiten

5. If you have listened carefully to the announcer at the beginning of the film, you **(hear)** that the programme is sponsored by I.T.S. richtig falsch

7. Setzen Sie die Verben in Klammern ins past tense simple oder ins present perfect simple.

1. I **(know)** him all his life.

2. In twenty years I **(never, change)** my mind about this.

3. Mary wants to know where we **(spend)** our last holidays.

4. Nearly all of the early settlers **(leave)** Europe for the New World to enjoy a free life.

5. Thank you very much for your last letter, I'm sorry that I **(not, reply)** for so long.

6. The King of Spain **(prepare)** a huge fleet, called the Armada, for the invasion of England.

7. These pictures show how much North America **(change)** since the Pilgrim Fathers **(arrive)** there.

8. For more than two hundred years, the need for cheap labour in the South **(make)** slave trading profitable to traders.

9. I **(marry)** (passive voice) and have had two children.

10. William the Conqueror who **(rule)** England for a long time never **(learn)** to speak the language of the people. richtig falsch

8. Setzen Sie die Verben in Klammern ins past tense simple oder ins past perfect simple.

1. The burglar **(come)** in through a window which someone **(leave)** open.

2. He **(meet)** her once or twice when he **(be)** in London.

3. She **(name)** a place where they **(can)** meet after work.

4. The children **(burst)** into laughter because Bob **(tell)** a funny story.

5. I **(give)** him an account of all that **(happen)** that evening.

6. He **(put)** on the pair of brown leather gloves he **(stick)** into his overcoat jacket.

Die Zeiten

7. He (not know) what (make) him pour out this stream of rubbish.

8. I (just, finish) trying on my new suit when I (find) that I (forget) my brooch.

9. He (move) a little to one side, so that he (have) a better view of the things on the table.

10. I (hear) that Phillip (have) a conversation with a girl that afternoon.

richtig   falsch

9. Setzen Sie die Verben in Klammern ins future tense simple, present tense simple, ins present tense continuous oder verwenden Sie to be going to.

1. You (come) back in a few minutes?

2. Father says I can't buy a motor-cycle until I (be) 18.

3. He (play) tennis this afternoon.

4. I (fly) to Paris this evening.

5. I expect we (make) a lot of mistakes when we write our first letter in English.

6. I hope you (enjoy) the rest of your stay in England.

7. I'm sure you (like) it.

8. The day (come) when you (believe) me.

9. The train (leave) at 8 a.m. From which platform?

10. We (move) to our new house in January.

richtig   falsch

Die entsprechenden Lösungen befinden sich auf Seite 426ff.

Die Zeiten

Simple (Ordinary) Form und Continuous (Progressive) Form

Die continuous oder progressive form (Verlaufsform) ist eine Besonderheit der englischen Sprache. Grundsätzlich können alle Zeiten in der simple oder continuous form verwendet werden. Die Wahl der richtigen Form hängt davon ab, welcher der folgenden Sachverhalte ausgedrückt wird.

Simple Form	Continuous Form	
Zum Ausdruck, dass ein Vorgang zu einem bestimmten Zeitpunkt nicht mehr andauert, unterbrochen ist.	Zum Ausdruck des ununterbrochenen Verlaufs, der Kontinuität, der allmählichen Entwicklung, dass ein Vorgang zu einem bestimmten Zeitpunkt noch andauert (gerade).	Unterbrechung; Verlauf, Kontinuität
▪ Bob **leaves** the house for school at 7 a.m. (Bob **verlässt** das Haus um 7 Uhr, um in die Schule zu gehen.)	▪ He **is washing** his hair. (Er **wäscht sich gerade** das Haar.) ▪ It **was getting** dark.	
Zum Ausdruck von Vorgängen, die von Dauer sind. Verben, die eine Dauer ausdrücken, stehen in der simple form.	Zum Ausdruck von Vorgängen, die von vorübergehender Dauer sind. Einigen Verben, die normalerweise in der simple form stehen, wird, wenn sie in der continuous form stehen, besonderer Nachdruck verliehen.	Vorgänge von Dauer; von vorübergehender Dauer
▪ to appear — erscheinen ▪ to contain — enthalten ▪ to consist of — bestehen aus ▪ to deserve — verdienen (Lob etc.) ▪ to exist — existieren ▪ to keep (on doing) — weitermachen (zu tun) ▪ to prefer — bevorzugen ▪ to resemble — ähneln ▪ to seem — scheinen ▪ to suffice — genügen		
▪ He **is** a really nice boy. ▪ I **enjoy** this kind of book.	▪ Bob **is doing** his homework. ▪ I **am** just **enjoying** this nice weather.	
Zum Ausdruck von Vorgängen, die nur einen Augenblick dauern. Dies ist besonders bei den folgenden Verben der Fall.	Manche Verben, die normalerweise in der simple form stehen, können auch in der continuous form verwendet werden. Sie ändern dann jedoch ihre Bedeutung.	Augenblickshandlungen Bedeutungsänderung !
▪ to arrive — ankommen ▪ to enter — eintreten ▪ to notice — wahrnehmen	▪ to arrive — gelangen zu ▪ to enter — einlaufen ▪ to notice — zur Kenntnis nehmen	

Die Zeiten

	Simple Form	Continuous Form
	- to recognize — erkennen - to switch on/off — ein-/ausschalten - to turn on/off — ein-/ausschalten - to understand — verstehen	
	- Suddenly, a man with a mask **entered** the shop. (Plötzlich **betrat** ein maskierter Mann den Laden.) - Pat **switched off** the light.	- The ship **was entering** the harbour at 6 o'clock in the morning. (Das Schiff **lief** um 6 Uhr morgens in den Hafen **ein**.)
aufeinander folgende; gleichzeitig verlaufende Vorgänge;	Zum Ausdruck aufeinander folgender Vorgänge.	Zum Ausdruck gleichzeitig, parallel verlaufender Vorgänge.
	- We **came** into the room, **sat down**, and **began** to write.	- My brother **was reading**, while I **was doing** my homework.
neu eintretende; noch andauernde Vorgänge	Zum Ausdruck eines neu eintretenden Vorgangs während ein anderer noch andauert. Der neu eintretende Vorgang steht dabei in der simple form.	Zum Ausdruck eines noch andauernden Vorgangs während ein anderer neu eintritt. Der noch andauernde Vorgang steht dabei in der continuous form.
	- While she was washing her hair, the telephone **rang**.	- While she **was washing** her hair, the telephone rang.
gewohnheitsmäßige Vorgänge	Zum Ausdruck gewohnheitsmäßiger, immer wiederkehrender Vorgänge.	
	- Every morning, I **go** to school. - Christmas **comes** but once a year.	
beabsichtigte; zufällige Handlung	Zum Ausdruck einer beabsichtigten Handlung, der kein Plan zugrunde liegt, die also vorher nicht überlegt wurde.	Zum Ausdruck einer nicht beabsichtigten, eher zufälligen Handlung.
	- I always **do** the washing-up right after dinner.	- I **was talking** to Tom the other day.
objektive Feststellung; Vorwurf, Tadel	Zum Ausdruck einer objektiven Feststellung vor allem in Verbindung mit den folgenden Adverbien: - always — immer - constantly — ständig - continually — laufend	Zum Ausdruck des Vorwurfs, Tadels vor allem in Verbindung mit den folgenden Adverbien: - always — immer - constantly — ständig - continually — laufend
	- Tom always **goes** away for the weekend. (Tom **geht** jedes Wochenende weg.)	- The teacher **is** always **picking** on me. (Der Lehrer **hackt** immer auf mir **herum**.)

Die Zeiten

Simple Form	Continuous Form	
Zum Ausdruck eines Besitzverhältnisses bzw. des Zustands stehen to have bzw. to be in der simple form.	Wenn es kein Besitzverhältnis ausdrückt, kann to have in der continuous form stehen. Zum Ausdruck, dass etwas vorübergehend, ausnahmsweise so ist, kann to be in der continuous form stehen.	to be, to have
▪ I **have** Bob's book. (Ich **habe (besitze)** Bobs Buch.) ▪ The children **were** quiet.	▪ I **am having** a bath. (Ich **nehme gerade** ein Bad.) ▪ The children **are being** very quiet today.	
Verben des Denkens und Meinens stehen normalerwiese in der simple form. ▪ to agree — zustimmen ▪ to believe — glauben ▪ to doubt — zweifeln ▪ to expect — erwarten ▪ to feel (= think) — denken ▪ to forget — vergessen ▪ to hope — hoffen ▪ to know — wissen, kennen ▪ to mean — meinen; bedeuten ▪ to mind — einwenden ▪ to recall — erinnern ▪ to recollect — erinnern ▪ to remember — erinnern ▪ to seem — scheinen ▪ to suppose — vermuten ▪ to think — denken ▪ to trust (= believe) — glauben ▪ to understand — verstehen	Einigen Verben des Denkens und Meinens wird, wenn sie in der continuous form stehen, besonderer Nachdruck verliehen.	Verben des Denkens, Meinens
▪ I **feel** that he will fail. (Ich **denke**, er wird scheitern.) ▪ How do you **feel** today?	▪ He **is forgetting** everything today. (Er **vergisst** heute **aber auch** alles.) ▪ How **are** you **feeling** today?	
Die Verben der Sinneswahrnehmung stehen normalerweise in der simple form. ▪ to hear — hören ▪ to realize — erkennen ▪ to see — sehen ▪ to taste — schmecken	Die Verben der Sinneswahrnehmung können in übertragener oder nachdrücklicher Bedeutung auch in der continuous form verwendet werden. ▪ to hear — Vorlesungen hören ▪ to see — jn. begleiten ▪ to see about/to — sich kümmern um ▪ to taste — kosten, probieren	Verben der Sinneswahrnehmung

Die Zeiten

	Simple Form	Continuous Form
	- I **hear** the music. (Ich **höre** die Musik.) - I **see** smoke. - She **realized** that she had forgotten her keys. - I **taste** a little sage in your turkey stuffing.	- I **am hearing** it clearly now. (Nun **höre** ich es **tatsächlich** ganz deutlich.) - I **was hearing** lectures at Oxford University. (Ich **hörte** an der Oxford Universität **Vorlesungen**.)
Verben des persönlichen Empfindens	Verben, die ein persönliches Empfinden, ein Gefühl, einen Wunsch ausdrücken, stehen normalerweise in der simple form.	Verben, die ein persönliches Empfinden, ein Gefühl, einen Wunsch ausdrücken, können in übertragener oder nachdrücklicher Bedeutung auch in der continuous form verwendet werden.
	- to adore — anbeten, vergöttern - to care — sorgen für - to desire — wünschen - to dislike — nicht mögen - to forgive — vergeben - to hate — hassen - to like — mögen - to love — lieben - to mind (don't mind) — merken; Acht geben - to prefer — bevorzugen - to refuse — ablehnen - to want — wollen - to wish — wünschen	- to dread — fürchten - to feel — fühlen - to forget — vergessen - to hate — hassen - to hope — hoffen - to like (= enjoy) — gefallen - to love (= enjoy) — gefallen
	- I **wish** it were true. - I **prefer** red to blue. - I **want** you to do your homework immediately. - I was invited to Peter's party but I **refused**.	- I **am hoping** that I shall see him. (Ich **hoffe doch,** dass ich ihn sehe.) - How I **am hating** this dress. (**Wie** ich dieses Kleid **doch hasse.**) - **Are** you **liking** the new book? (**Gefällt** Ihnen **denn** das neue Buch?)
Verben des Besitzens	Verben, die ein Besitzverhältnis ausdrücken, stehen meist nur in der simple form.	
	- to belong — gehören - to own — besitzen - to possess — besitzen	
	- His parents **own** this big house. - He **possesses** two cars.	

Die Zeiten

Übungen zur Simple und Continuous Form

1. Setzen Sie die Verben in Klammern ins present tense continuous.

1. He **(carry)** two bags and a carpet.
2. What you **(say)** may be English, but it sounds like Double Dutch.
3. Philip and Tom **(lie)** in the sand.
4. No one **(blame)** you.
5. A burglar **(slip)** into the house.
6. What **(happen)** to them?
7. How can you be sure that he **(obey)** you.
8. He **(live)** beyond his means.
9. Time **(get)** short, and we ought to start soon.
10. Time **(run)** out for the old man.

richtig   falsch

2. Setzen Sie die Verben in Klammern ins past tense continuous.

1. I told Mr Stevens that Tom **(stay)** at the inn.
2. The sick and wounded **(die)** like flies.
3. Mary **(lie)** in the sun too long. Of course she got sunburnt.
4. I wondered why Bob **(listen)** at the door when you came out.
5. The donkey that the peasant and his wife **(ride)** on was rather old.
6. I wondered whether she had been out, for she **(breathe)** hard as though she had been running.
7. The tennis player **(play)** safely, depending upon his opponent to make a fault.
8. The facts **(fit)** into place.
9. His disappearance **(stir up)** a great deal of excitement in the press.

Die Zeiten

10. It **(get)** dark, so we pushed the van off the road and decided to stay there for the night.   richtig   falsch

3. Setzen Sie die Verben in Klammern ins **present perfect continuous**.

1. He **(write)** all the morning.
2. Tremendous changes **(take place)** particularly since 1945.
3. In the past few years prices **(rise)** sharply.
4. For many years the federal government **(promote)** industrial development by building up the economic infrastructure.
5. The judge is helped by two Justices of the Peace who **(sit)** beside him throughout the proceedings.   richtig   falsch

4. Setzen Sie die Verben in Klammern ins **past perfect continuous**.

1. I didn't know where Daniel **(go)**.
2. She sent the white sweater with the red stripes that she **(knit)** for Peter.
3. He **(worry)** about it on and off all day.
4. He **(tap)** a message for more than three hours out into the storm and darkness: S.O.S.
5. In a moment the two men who **(lie)** on their beds had disappeared.   richtig   falsch

5. Setzen Sie die Verben in Klammern in die **simple oder continuous form im past tense**.

1. The water **(rise)** fast, and the passengers **(get)** very nervous.
2. Quickly he **(jump)** to the side and **(try)** to grab his son.
3. For several months they **(work)** every evening and every weekend.
4. Bob wrote to Mr Winters that he **(stay)** with Tom for a few days.
5. He **(stay)** at the hotel all the time.

Die Zeiten

6. Some **(play)** cards, others **(sit)** around talking, others **(drink)** at the bar when the news came.

7. Tom Stevenson **(ask)** the visitors to sit down round the table and then **(try)** to answer some of their questions.

8. Mr Johnson **(lead)** Tom to the living-room where Peter **(play)** cards with his mother.

9. Mr Winterbottom **(leave)** the house at eight o'clock every morning and **(return)** at six o'clock in the evening.

10. Will you have the goodness to explain what on earth you **(talk)** (present tense) about?

11. Everyone **(wait)** for the winner of the Marathon to run in through the gates.

12. When she **(hear)** that she **(change)** colour.

13. They **(have)** a geography lesson and Mrs Summers, the geography mistress, **(talk)** about all the things England gets from the Commonwealth countries.

14. He **(feel)** himself beginning to sweat, and he **(try)** to relax.

15. He **(reach)** out for the book, which **(lie)** on the floor, and **(sit up)** against the bedhead.

16. Look, the two gentlemen **(talk)** (present tense) of taking lessons in knife-throwing.

17. He **(continue)** to apply the battery current to the carbon lamp filament from time to time.

18. It was gin that **(sink)** him into stupor every night and gin that **(revive)** him every morning.

19. The lamps **(light)** in the hotel. (passive voice)

20. I **(steer),** and instead of watching where we **(go)**, I **(look)** at the big factories along the road.

richtig   falsch

6. Setzen Sie die Verben in Klammern in die simple oder continuous form. Beachten Sie dabei die Zeit.

1. Look, John **(repair)** his bicycle.

2. I **(fly)** to New York this afternoon.

Die Zeiten

3. One evening Jack (walk) along the shore all by himself when he saw a ship.

4. Max is still in bed. He (sleep) long enough, it's time to wake him up.

5. This is the book she (speak) of all the time.

6. He (not know) how long she (look) at him.

7. He (love) me as a child (love) his father.

8. At the age of twenty-three Robert (marry) and (start) his own business as a butcher.

9. The world population (grow) at a rate that will double by the year 2050.

10. Lucky for me, I got a job and was made a spot welder and that's what I (do) ever since.   richtig   falsch

Die entsprechenden Lösungen befinden sich auf Seite 427.

Das Passiv (The Passive Voice)

Im Passiv vollzieht sich ein Vorgang am Subjekt, d. h. das Subjekt des Satzes ist nicht selbst der Handelnde, sondern der „Leidende" (Leideform).
Im Aktiv (active voice) ist das Subjekt selbst der Handelnde, es führt eine Handlung selbst aus (Tätigkeitsform, Tatform).

Das Passiv wird aus to be + past participle gebildet, d. h. steht das Prädikat des Aktivsatzes zum Beispiel im present tense simple, so steht to be im Passivsatz ebenfalls im present tense simple und das past participle des Vollverbs wird hinzugefügt.
Der Urheber oder die Ursache der Handlung (by-agent) wird mit by angefügt. Er wird weggelassen, wenn er bzw. sie unbekannt oder irrelevant ist.
Das Objekt des Aktivsatzes wird zum Subjekt des Passivsatzes.

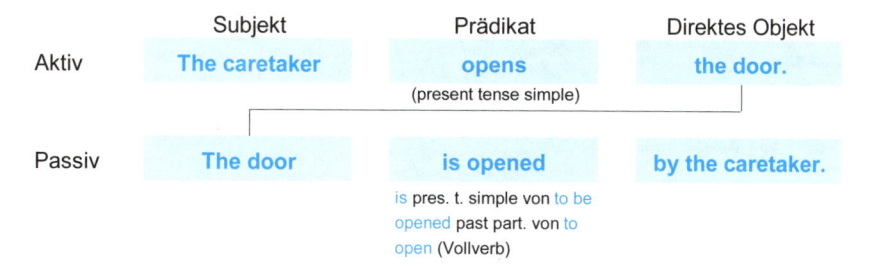

	Subjekt	Prädikat	Direktes Objekt
Aktiv	The caretaker	opens (present tense simple)	the door.
Passiv	The door	is opened	by the caretaker.

is pres. t. simple von to be
opened past part. von to open (Vollverb)

In Aktivsätzen, in denen ein direktes Objekt und ein indirektes Objekt + to enthalten ist, kann immer nur das direkte Objekt zum Subjekt des Passivsatzes werden.

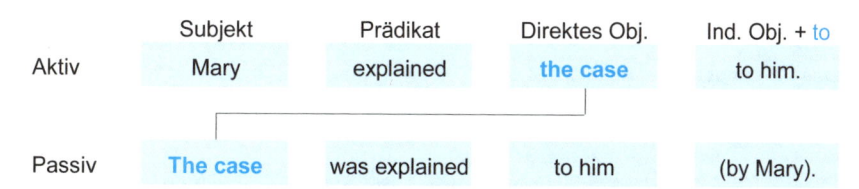

	Subjekt	Prädikat	Direktes Obj.	Ind. Obj. + to
Aktiv	Mary	explained	the case	to him.
Passiv	The case	was explained	to him	(by Mary).

In Aktivsätzen, in denen ein direktes Objekt und ein indirektes Objekt ohne to enthalten ist, wird meist das indirekte Objekt zum Subjekt des Passivsatzes. Gelegentlich, besonders in der Schriftsprache, kann auch das direkte Objekt zum Subjekt des Passivsatzes werden, das indirekte Objekt wird dann mit to angeschlossen.

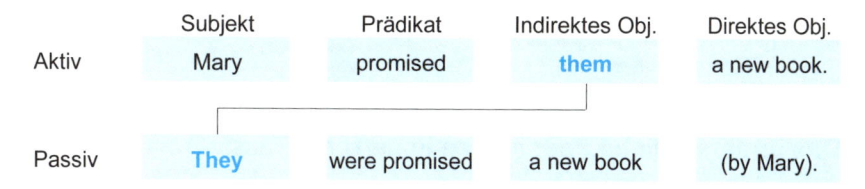

	Subjekt	Prädikat	Indirektes Obj.	Direktes Obj.
Aktiv	Mary	promised	them	a new book.
Passiv	They	were promised	a new book	(by Mary).

Das Passiv

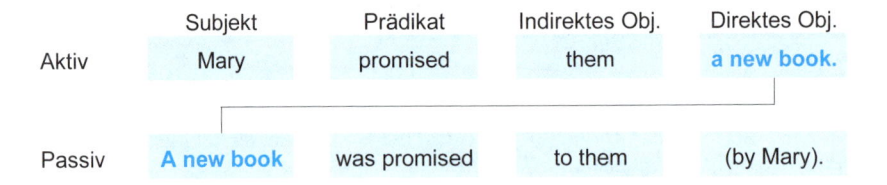

	Subjekt	Prädikat	Indirektes Obj.	Direktes Obj.
Aktiv	Mary	promised	them	a new book.

	Subjekt	Prädikat		
Passiv	A new book	was promised	to them	(by Mary).

In Aktivsätzen mit einem präpositionalen Objekt muss die mit dem Verb verbundene Präposition auch im Passivsatz erhalten bleiben.

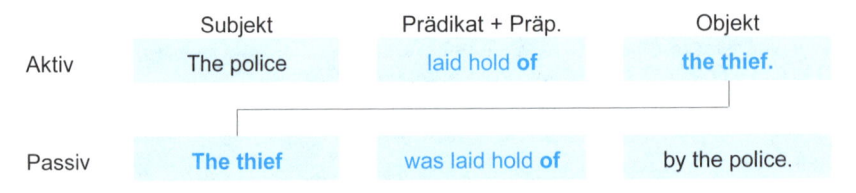

	Subjekt	Prädikat + Präp.	Objekt
Aktiv	The police	laid hold of	the thief.
Passiv	The thief	was laid hold of	by the police.

Die Umwandlung von Aktivsätzen in Passivsätze in allen Zeiten ist auf den Seiten 126 – 127 dargestellt.

Das Zustandspassiv

Das Zustandspassiv bezeichnet einen Zustand und wird im Deutschen mit *sein* gebildet (sein-Passiv).

- The window **is opened**.
  (Das Fenster ist geöffnet.)

Das Vorgangspassiv

Das Vorgangspassiv bezeichnet einen Vorgang und wird im Deutschen mit *werden* gebildet (werden-Passiv).

- The window **is opened** by the caretaker.
  (Das Fenster wird vom Hausmeister geöffnet.)

Im Gegensatz zum Deutschen haben Vorgangs- und Zustandspassiv die gleiche Form. Um welches Passiv es sich handelt, wird meist aus dem Zusammenhang deutlich.
Um Verwechslungen zwischen dem Vorgangs- und Zustandspassiv zu vermeiden, kann das Vorgangspassiv mit to get oder der continuous form, jedoch nur im present und past tense gebildet werden.

- The window **is opened**.
  (Das Fenster wird/ist geöffnet.)
- The window **got broken**.
  (Das Fenster ging kaputt.)
- The window **is being opened**.
  (Das Fenster wird geöffnet.)

Das unpersönliche Passiv (The Impersonal Passive)

Das unpersönliche Passiv ist selten und kann nur verwendet werden, wenn it einen folgenden Subjektsatz einleitet.

> - It is to be hoped that she will recover soon.
> (Es ist zu hoffen, dass sie sich bald erholt.)

Der Infinitiv des Passivs (The Passive Infinitive)

Die passive Form des Infinitivs steht nach there is, there was, nach den Adjektiven hard, easy, difficult, nice, pleasant, nach to be und to remain. Nach there is, there was und den Adjektiven kann auch der aktive Infinitiv stehen.

> - This house is to be sold immediately.
> (Das Haus ist sofort zu verkaufen.)
> - A lot of things remained to be done.
> - There was no time to be lost.
> (Es war keine Zeit zu verlieren.)
> - *There was* no time to lose. (active inf.)
> - This text is easy to learn.

Das Passiv kann in allen Zeiten der **simple form** gebildet werden. In der **continuous form** ist das Passiv nur im **present tense** und im **past tense** gebräuchlich.

In der folgenden Tabelle ist die Umwandlung eines Aktivsatzes in den entsprechenden Passivsatz durch alle Zeiten anhand der 3. Person Singular dargestellt. Zu jedem Satz ist die deutsche Übersetzung gegeben, wobei Normalschrift das Vorgangspassiv und Kursivschrift das Zustandspassiv bezeichnet. Die Konjugation der passiven Formen in sämtlichen Personen ist im Anschluss dargestellt.

Das Passiv

Umwandlung aktiver Sätze in passive Sätze

Mod.	Zeit		Aktiv		
		The caretaker	opens	the door.	
	Pres. T. S.	Der Hausmeister	öffnet	die Tür.	
		The caretaker	is opening	the door.	
	Pres. T. C.	Der Hausmeister	öffnet	die Tür.	
		The caretaker	opened	the door.	
	Past T. S.	Der Hausmeister	öffnete	die Tür.	
Ind.	Past T. C.	The caretaker	was opening	the door.	
		Der Hausmeister	öffnete	die Tür.	
		The caretaker	has opened	the door.	
	Pres. P.	Der Hausmeister	hat	die Tür	geöffnet.
		The caretaker	had opened	the door.	
	Past P.	Der Hausmeister	hatte	die Tür	geöffnet.
		The caretaker	will open	the door.	
	Fut. T.	Der Hausmeister	wird	die Tür	öffnen.
		The caretaker	will have opened	the door.	
	Fut. P.	Der Hausmeister	wird	die Tür	geöffnet haben.
		The caretaker	would open	the door.	
	Con.	Der Hausmeister	würde	die Tür	öffnen.
Con.		The caretaker	would have opened	the door.	
	Con. P.	Der Hausmeister	würde	die Tür	geöffnet haben.
		The caretaker	open	the door.	
	Pres.	Der Hausmeister	öffne	die Tür.	
Sub.	Past	The caretaker	opened	the door.	
		Der Hausmeister	öffnete	die Tür.	
		The caretaker	had opened	the door.	
	Past P.	Der Hausmeister	hätte	die Tür	geöffnet.

Das Passiv

Passiv

The door **is opened** by the caretaker.	Die Tür wird vom Hausmeister geöffnet. *Die Tür ist vom Hausmeister geöffnet.*
The door **is being opened** by the caretaker.	Die Tür wird vom Hausmeister geöffnet.
The door **was opened** by the caretaker.	Die Tür wurde vom Hausmeister geöffnet. *Die Tür war vom Hausmeister geöffnet.*
The door **was being opened** by the caretaker.	Die Tür wurde vom Hausmeister geöffnet.
The door **has been opened** by the caretaker.	Die Tür ist vom Hausmeister geöffnet worden. *Die Tür ist vom Hausmeister geöffnet gewesen.*
The door **had been opened** by the caretaker.	Die Tür war vom Hausmeister geöffnet worden. *Die Tür war vom Hausmeister geöffnet gewesen.*
The door **will be opened** by the caretaker.	Die Tür wird vom Hausmeister geöffnet werden. *Die Tür wird vom Hausmeister geöffnet sein.*
The door **will have been opened** by the caretaker.	Die Tür wird vom Hausmeister geöffnet worden sein. *Die Tür wird vom Hausmeister geöffnet gewesen sein.*
The door **would be opened** by the caretaker.	Die Tür würde vom Hausmeister geöffnet werden. *Die Tür würde vom Hausmeister geöffnet sein.*
The door **would have been opened** by the caretaker.	Die Tür würde vom Hausmeister geöffnet worden sein. *Die Tür würde vom Hausmeister geöffnet gewesen sein.*
The door **be opened** by the caretaker.	Die Tür werde vom Hausmeister geöffnet. *Die Tür sei vom Hausmeister geöffnet.*
The door **were opened** by the caretaker.	Die Tür würde vom Hausmeister geöffnet. *Die Tür wäre vom Hausmeister geöffnet.*
The door **had been opened** by the caretaker.	Die Tür wäre vom Hausmeister geöffnet worden. *Die Tür wäre vom Hausmeister geöffnet gewesen.*

Das Passiv

Die Konjugation passiver Formen in der Simple Form

Mod.	Zeit	1. Person Singular	2. Person Singular	3. Person Singular
	Pres.T.	am loved	are loved	is loved
	Past T.	was loved	were loved	was loved
Ind.	Pres.P.	*have* been loved	*have* been loved	*has* been loved
	Past P.	*had* been loved	*had* been loved	*had* been loved
	Fut.T.	*will* be loved	*will* be loved	*will* be loved
	Fut.P.	*will have been* loved	*will have been* loved	*will have been* loved
Con.	Con.	*would* be loved	*would* be loved	*would* be loved
	Con.P.	*would have been* loved	*would have been* loved	*would have been* loved
Sub.	Pres.	be loved	be loved	be loved
	Past	were loved	were loved	were loved
	Past P.	*had* been loved	*had* been loved	*had* been loved
Imp.		-	be loved	-
Inf.	Pres.	be loved		
	Perf.	*have* been loved		
Part.	Pres.	*being* loved		
	Past	-		
	Perf.	*having* been loved		
Ger.	Pres.	*being* loved		
	Perf.	*having* been loved		

Die Konjugation passiver Formen in der Continuous Form

Mod.	Zeit	1. Person Singular	2. Person Singular	3. Person Singular
Ind.	Pres.T.	*am* being loved	*are* being loved	*is* being loved
	Past T.	*was* being loved	*were* being loved	*was* being loved

Die Personalpronomen wurden aus Gründen der Übersichtlichkeit weggelassen.

Das Passiv

1. Person Plural			2. Person Plural			3. Person Plural		
	are	loved		*are*	loved		*are*	loved
	were	loved		*were*	loved		*were*	loved
have	*been*	loved	*have*	*been*	loved	*have*	*been*	loved
had	*been*	loved	*had*	*been*	loved	*had*	*been*	loved
will	*be*	loved	*will*	*be*	loved	*will*	*be*	loved
will have	*been*	loved	*will have*	*been*	loved	*will have*	*been*	loved
would	*be*	loved	*would*	*be*	loved	*would*	*be*	loved
would have been		loved	*would have been*		loved	*would have been*		loved
	be	loved		*be*	loved		*be*	loved
	were	loved		*were*	loved		*were*	loved
had	*been*	loved	*had*	*been*	loved	*had*	*been*	loved
		-		*be*	loved			-

Hilfsverb in der 3. Pers. Sg. ist *has*

1. Person Plural			2. Person Plural			3. Person Plural		
are	*being*	loved	*are*	*being*	loved	*are*	*being*	loved
were	*being*	loved	*were*	*being*	loved	*were*	*being*	loved

Das Passiv

Übungen zum Passiv

1. Setzen Sie die Verben in Klammern ins Passiv im present tense simple.

1. We know that your time (occupy) by affairs of the highest importance.
2. The city (lay out) rectangularly in twelve long avenues running north and south.
3. The automobile alone (estimate) to cause 60 % of America's total air pollution.
4. Once the Government has decided to introduce a bill, one minister (put) in charge of it.
5. At the age of 11 all Primary School pupils (send) to the same Comprehensive School.
6. The Queen's consent and approval (require) before a minister can take up office.
7. Doctors (bind) by the Hippocratic oath to preserve life at all costs.
8. More and more houses (build) nowadays with solar systems.
9. These people (bear) with an instinct for riding.
10. The costs of our school system (bear) mainly by state funds.

richtig   falsch

2. Setzen Sie die Verben in Klammern ins Passiv im past tense simple.

1. The harvests (destroy) by floods.
2. A reward (promise) to anyone who could write a good article for the school magazine.
3. Hawaii became the 50th state when it (admit) to the United States in 1959.
4. The man (hit) by Mr Green's car outside a zebra crossing.
5. A few days after the end of the war, Abraham Lincoln (shoot) by a fanatic Southerner while attending a theatre in Washington.

Das Passiv

6. The man who (hurt) died soon after.

7. He (leave) standing by himself.

8. Where she (take)? I think she (take) to the hospital.

9. The plan (work out, thoroughly and carefully) but within a year it (judge) to have been a failure.

10. The news (receive) in a silence of incomprehension and disbelief.

                                                                          richtig   falsch

3. Setzen Sie die Verben in Klammern ins Passiv im present perfect simple.

1. Several reforms (carry) out in recent years.

2. Enough (say) on that question.

3. About ten million new immigrants (admit) in the past fifty years.

4. Since 1958 the financial position of students (improve) by the provision of loans by the Federal government.

5. New schools (build) as part of the efforts to raise the standard of education throughout the country.

6. Most of what he (tell) is lies.

7. Millions of pounds (spend) on the preparation of middle-term and long-term plans.

8. England (divide) into counties for more than 1,000 years.

9. Rising material prosperity (accompany, often) by a decline in religious observance.

10. Central government funds (use) to contribute to local transport subsidies.

                                                                          richtig   falsch

4. Setzen Sie die Verben in Klammern ins Passiv im past perfect simple.

1. Two men sat in the dining-room, where coffee (serve) to them.

2. Every day the teacher asked if the homework (do).

3. After the steam-engine (invent) and a lot of factories (build) our air became more and more polluted.

Das Passiv

4. The present palace buildings were erected between 1840 and 1852, to replace older buildings which **(destroy)** by fire.

5. The doctor **(send)** for before she was taken to hospital.

6. Nothing **(see)** of him for nearly six months.

7. All the drawers were pulled out, the floor was strewn with scattered garments and the wardrobe **(empty)** of his best suits.

8. The House of Lords includes about 300 life peers. Most of these life peerages **(confer)** on the advice of Labour Prime Ministers.

9. Thinking she **(take)** ill, I hurried to see her.

10. The newspaper said that no crimes **(commit)** against him.

richtig   falsch

5. Setzen Sie die Verben in Klammern ins Passiv im future tense simple.

1. Much of the programme **(carry out)**.

2. Some candidates **(propose)** at the convention.

3. The next economic summit **(hold)** in Japan in the summer next year.

4. I only hope that nobody **(hurt)**.

5. Extensive alterations **(require)**.

6. As a general reporter she **(send)** on a large number of jobs.

7. Each of you **(give)** a brochure.

8. There you **(meet)** by a friend.

9. You **(make)** royally welcome.

10. If you don't learn the language you **(cut off)** from the people.

richtig   falsch

6. Setzen Sie die Verben in Klammern ins Passiv im present tense continuous.

1. A new airport **(build)** outside the town.

2. English **(teach)** in the library this morning.

Das Passiv

3. In the US, land **(urbanize)** at the rate of 3,000 acres a day.

4. Mr Stevenson has just left home and **(drive)** to his office.

5. English **(speak)** all over the world.

richtig   falsch

7. Setzen Sie die Verben in Klammern ins Passiv im past tense continuous.

1. A terrible hurricane was raging and the ship **(toss)** about.

2. I could scarcely understand what **(say)**.

3. The strange thing is that I didn't know I **(look for)**.

4. He stood aside while the bags **(bring)**.

5. He **(wait for)** in the garden.

richtig   falsch

8. Setzen Sie die folgenden Sätze mit einem Objekt ins Passiv.

1. The whole team obeyed the trainer's orders without any protest.

2. Several first-class orchestras regularly give concerts in London.

3. The afternoon train will take him there on Wednesday.

4. Clerks advise the Justices of the Peace on points of law.

5. They planned new industrial estates around the city.

6. We told Susan to come too, and she was the first to arrive.

7. We will do everything to make your flight comfortable.

8. They had set the table on the terrace for three.

9. We will find radioactive pollutants on the earth's surface for generations.

10. Her sister will join her.

11. We are making great efforts to ensure that poor people are helped.

12. Do not enter the studio, we are filming a play for today's programme.

Das Passiv

13. Bob had the feeling that somebody was following him.

14. If I hadn't fled and changed my name, they would have put me into prison.

15. A friend will meet you there.

richtig   falsch

9. Setzen Sie die folgenden Sätze mit zwei Objekten ins Passiv.

1. Someone addressed the letter to Mr Harrison.

2. He recommended me another doctor.

3. Here they offer the homeless warm food and dry beds.

4. On Christmas Day, 1066, they crowned William the Conqueror King of England in Westminster Abbey.

5. There they will give you all the instructions you need.

6. They allow him five pounds pocket money a week.

7. They announced the event to everybody.

8. They considered him a prudent man.

9. They granted her a small pension.

10. They made George Washington the first President of the United States of America.

11. They promised a reward to anyone who would write a good article for the school magazine.

12. They saved him a lot of trouble.

13. They shall ask us several questions.

14. They showed him all the books.

15. They will appoint him director general.

16. A top-level expert explained the computer to us.

17. At the airport passengers can buy duty-free cigarettes and during the flight the attendants may serve them dinner or a snack.

18. At today's press conference at the Yard they handed the journalists photographs of the stolen paintings.

Das Passiv

19. I hope they will spare him this ordeal.

20. In general they give the Bachelor's degree to students who pass examinations at the end of three or four years of study.

richtig   falsch

10. Setzen Sie die folgenden Sätze ins Passiv.

1. An expert has dealt with this question.

2. We have not heard of him since.

3. They have always laughed at him.

4. They listened to him with pleasure.

5. When Mrs Brown came home from hospital, she found that they had looked after the cat.

6. They looked upon him as a wise man.

7. They arrived at the solution by chance.

8. People have often discriminated against people because of race, religion, or colour.

9. Have they come to any decision?

10. Nothing seems to have been disarranged and nobody has interfered with the drawers.

11. Somebody has sat on my hat.

12. Somebody has slept in the bed.

13. They forgot their quarrels on seeing that somebody infringed upon their rights.

14. Amongst all this terrible poverty there were a few big beautiful houses in which rich men lived.

15. Oxford abounds in beauty, but it is a hidden beauty that you must seek for.

richtig   falsch

11. Setzen Sie die folgenden Sätze ins Aktiv.

1. English is spoken by more than 800 million people.

2. Bob checked in at the hotel Miramare which had been recommended to him by some Americans.

Das Passiv

3. That part of the road was closed for resurfacing.
4. Several reforms have been carried through in recent years.
5. He had run away at seventeen but had been brought back.
6. My business will be finished in a few hours.
7. He was given another 1,500 dollars.
8. The matter had been dealt with long ago.
9. Boys and girls of 16 needn't be looked after all the time.
10. Disposable dishware is used for everyday occasions.
11. The court is presided over by a judge, but the decision on guilt or innocence is made by a jury.
12. The public were warned of the dangers of drinking.
13. We are being followed.
14. Something was being done.
15. Some women with small children would like to work, if the children could be cared for during the mothers' working hours.
16. It was hoped that the Health Service would improve health in general.
17. It is a shame that he should have been treated like that.
18. The simple tasks are being turned over to the machines.
19. What is being done about the situation?
20. I don't want to be seen off.

richtig falsch

Die entsprechenden Lösungen befinden sich auf Seite 427ff.

Die indirekte Rede (Reported Speech)

In der indirekten Rede werden Aussagen einer Person A durch eine Person B an eine dritte Person C weitergegeben.

Die erlebte Rede (substitutionary narration, interior monologue) ist ein Stilmittel der literarischen Sprache, mit der ein Text abwechslungsreich gestaltet werden kann. Es wird dadurch die dauernde Wiederholung einleitender Verben des Sagens und Denkens sowie der Konjunktion that der indirekten Rede vermieden. Die Zeitenfolge in der erlebten Rede entspricht der Zeitenfolge der indirekten Rede.

In der indirekten Rede sind, neben der unten aufgeführten Veränderung der Zeiten, noch folgende Veränderungen bei Pronomen, Adverbien etc. vorzunehmen.

Direkte Rede	Indirekte Rede	
Die direkte Rede wird durch Doppelpunkt oder Komma eingeleitet und in Anführungszeichen gesetzt.	Die indirekte Rede wird nicht durch Komma oder Doppelpunkt und Anführungszeichen gekennzeichnet. Sie wird durch ein Verb des Sagens, Denkens oder Meinens (to say, to answer, to reply, to explain, to state etc.) und nachfolgendes that, das weggelassen werden kann, eingeleitet. Vor that steht kein Komma.	Einleitung kein Komma vor that
▪ He says: «I will go now.»	▪ He says (that) he will go at once.	
Die Modalverben ändern sich wie in nebenstehender Spalte aufgeführt. can could	Die in nebenstehender Spalte aufgeführten Modalverben ändern sich in der indirekten Rede wie folgt. could could	Modalverben can could
▪ He said: «We can go now.» ▪ He said: «We could go now.»	▪ He said (that) they could go at once. ▪ He said (that) they could go at once.	
may might	might might	may might
▪ He said: «May I lead the way?» ▪ He said: «You might take this book with you.»	▪ He asked if he might lead the way. ▪ He said: «You might take this book with you.»	
must	must zum Ausdruck einer ständig geltenden Notwendigkeit.	must
▪ He said: «You must stay at home after 8 o'clock.»	▪ He said (that) he must stay at home after 8 o'clock.	

Die indirekte Rede

Direkte Rede	Indirekte Rede
must	had to, (didn't have to) zum Ausdruck der (Nicht)Notwendigkeit im Augenblick des Sprechens.
• He said: «I **must** go immediately.»	• He said (that) he **had to** go immediately.
must	would have to, wouldn't have to zum Ausdruck einer für die Zukunft geltenden (Nicht)Notwendigkeit.
• He said: «I **must** go next week.»	• He said (that) he **would have to** go the following week.
must not	must not zum Ausdruck eines ständig geltenden Verbots.
• He said: «You **must not** leave the house after 8 o'clock.»	• He said (that) I **must not** leave the house after 8 o'clock.
must not	was/were not to zum Ausdruck eines nicht ständig geltenden Verbots.
• He said: «You **must not** go out now.»	• He said (that) I **was not to** go out then.
need not	need not zum Ausdruck der ständig geltenden Nicht-Notwendigkeit.
• He said: «You **need not** stay at school after 2 o'clock.»	• He said (that) I **need not** stay at school after 2 o'clock.
need not	didn't have to zum Ausdruck der Nicht-Notwendigkeit im Augenblick des Sprechens.
• He said: «You **need not** go immediately.»	• He said (that) I **didn't have to** go immediately.
need	wouldn't have to zum Ausdruck einer für die Zukunft geltenden Nicht-Notwendigkeit.
• He said: «When you are 18, you **need not** come home at 10 o'clock.»	• He said (that) when I am 18, I **wouldn't have to** stay at home after 10 o'clock.

Die indirekte Rede

Direkte Rede	Indirekte Rede	
shall should ought to	should should ought to	shall should ought to
▪ He said: «I shall go home now.» ▪ He said: «I should go home now.» ▪ He said: «I ought to go home now.»	▪ He said (that) he should go home at once. ▪ He said (that) he should go home at once. ▪ He said (that) he ought to go home at once.	
will would used to	would would used to	will would used to
▪ He said: «I will go home now.» ▪ He said: «I would go home now.» ▪ He said: «I always used to go home at 8 o'clock.»	▪ He said (that) he would go home at once. ▪ He said (that) he would go home at once. ▪ He said (that) he always used to go home at 8 o'clock.	
dare	dare	dare
▪ He said: «I dare not come after our violent quarrel.»	▪ He said (that) he dare not come after their violent quarrel.	
Bei der Änderung der Personenangaben hängt es letztendlich davon ab, wer eine Aussage an wen weitergibt. Im Allgemeinen werden die folgenden Personenangaben wie in nebenstehender Spalte aufgeführt, geändert. Den Sprecher betreffende den Angesprochenen betreffende, eine dritte Person betreffende Angaben.	Die in nebenstehender Spalte aufgeführten Personenangaben ändern sich zumeist wie folgt: 1. Person (der Sprecher gibt seine eigenen Worte wieder) 2. Person 3. Person	Personenangaben
▪ I said: «I will pass the exam in any case.» ▪ He said: «You must stay in bed.» ▪ You said: «He must go home.	▪ I said (that) I would pass the exam in any case. ▪ He said (that) you must stay in bed. ▪ You said (that) he must go home.	
Die folgenden Demonstrativpronomen ändern sich wie in nebenstehender Spalte aufgeführt. this in Verbindung mit einer Zeitangabe	Die in nebenstehender Spalte aufgeführten Demonstrativpronomen ändern sich wie folgt. that	Demonstrativpronomen this

Die indirekte Rede

	Direkte Rede	Indirekte Rede
	He said: «She is coming **this** week.»	He said (that) she was coming **that** week.
	this in der Funktion eines attributiven Demonstrativpronomens.	**the**
	He said: «I bought **this present** for her.»	He said (that) he had bought **the present** for her.
	this in der Funktion eines substantivischen Demonstrativpronomens.	**it**
	He said: «We will see **this** tomorrow.»	He said (that) they would see **it** tomorrow.
	this one wenn es eine bestimmte Auswahl von Dingen bezeichnet.	**the one**
	He said: «Which one will you choose?» She replied: «**This one** on the table.»	He asked which one she would choose. She replied (that) she would choose **the one** on the table.
that	**that** in der Funktion eines attributiven Demonstrativpronomens.	**the**
	He said: «I bought **that present** for her.»	He said (that) he had bought **the present** for her.
these	**these** in der Funktion eines attributiven Demonstrativpronomens.	**those, the**
	He said: «I bought **these presents** for her.»	He said (that) he had bought **those presents** for her.
	these in der Funktion eines substantivischen Demonstrativpronomens.	**they, them**
	He came back with two books and said: «I found **these** lying on the table in Sam's room.»	He came back with two books and said (that) he had found **them** lying on the table in Sam's room.
	these ones wenn es eine bestimmte Auswahl von Dingen bezeichnet.	**the ones**
	He asked: «Which ones will you choose?» She answered: «**These ones** on the table.»	He asked her which ones she would choose. She answered (that) she would choose **the ones** on the table.

Die indirekte Rede

	Direkte Rede	Indirekte Rede	
	Die folgenden Adverbien und adverbialen Bestimmungen ändern sich wie in nebenstehender Spalte aufgeführt.	Die in nebenstehender Spalte aufgeführten Adverbien und adverbialen Bestimmungen ändern sich wie folgt. Adverbiale Bestimmungen der Zeit, die am gleichen Tag wiedergegeben werden, bleiben unverändert.	Adverbien und adverbiale Bestimmungen
	today yesterday the day before yesterday tomorrow the day after tomorrow next week/month/year last week/month/year ago now here	that day the day before/the previous day two days before the next/following day in two days' time the following week/month/year the week before/the previous week before then/ at once there	
▪	He said: «I saw her two years *ago*.»	He said (that) he had seen her two years *before*.	
▪	He said: «I met her at the station, *yesterday*.»	He said (that) he had met her at the station *the day before*.	
	Fragesätze in der direkten Rede (direkte Fragesätze) werden mit Fragezeichen abgeschlossen.	Fragesätze in der indirekten Rede (indirekte Fragesätze) werden mit Punkt abgeschlossen und mit einem Verb wie *to ask, to inquire, to wonder, to want to know* etc. eingeleitet. Soll die befragte Person erwähnt werden, kann nur *to ask* verwendet werden.	Fragesätze
▪	He said: «Mary, what have you done in my room?»	He *asked Mary* what she had done in his room.	
	Direkte Fragesätze mit Fragewort werden durch Inversion von Subjekt und Prädikat gebildet, d. h. das Subjekt tritt hinter das Verb.	In indirekten Fragesätzen mit Fragewort wird das Fragewort wiederholt, die Wortstellung entspricht der des Aussagesatzes.	Fragen mit Fragewort
▪	He said: «*What has she done* in my room?»	He wondered *what she had done* in his room.	
	Entscheidungsfragen, sie erwarten eine Ja-/Nein-Antwort, werden durch Inversion von Subjekt und Prädikat gebildet, d. h. das Subjekt tritt hinter das Prädikat bzw. Hilfsverb.	Indirekte Entscheidungsfragen werden mit *whether* oder *if* eingeleitet, wobei *whether* zutreffender ist als *if*, *if* jedoch, vor allem in der Umgangssprache, häufiger ist. Die Wortstellung entspricht der des Aussagesatzes.	Entscheidungsfragen

Die indirekte Rede

	Direkte Rede	Indirekte Rede
Fragesätze mit will, shall	▪ He asked: «Have you done your homework?»	▪ He asked whether/if he had done his homework.
	Will, shall ändern sich in Fragesätzen wie in nebenstehender Spalte dargestellt. will wenn nach einem zukünftigen Vorgang gefragt wird.	Will, shall ändern sich in Fragesätzen wie folgt. would
	▪ He wondered: «Will I see her again?»	▪ He wondered whether/if he would see her again.
	shall wenn der Fragende erfahren möchte, ob er eine Anweisung ausführen soll.	should
	▪ He asked: «Shall I meet you at the station?»	▪ He asked whether/if he should meet him at the station.
Befehl, Aufforderung	Befehle werden in direkter Rede, im Gegensatz zum Deutschen, nicht mit Ausrufezeichen, sondern durch Punkt abgeschlossen.	Befehlssätze werden in indirekter Rede ebenfalls mit Punkt abgeschlossen und mit Verben wie to tell, to order, to warn (not to), to remind, to advise, to recommend, to beg, to invite, to urge, to ask (auffordern) etc. eingeleitet. Es ist zu beachten, dass indirekte Befehle nach to say nur durch should + infinitve ohne to wiedergegeben werden können. Nach to demand wird der present subjunctive verwendet. Eine andere Möglichkeit einen indirekten Befehl auszudrücken, stellt to + infinitive dar, vor allem wenn der Einführungssatz in einer Zeit der Gegenwart steht.
	▪ He said: «Buy the book.» ▪ He demanded: «Buy the book.» ▪ He said: «Buy the book.» ▪ He says/said: «Buy the book.»	▪ He said (that) I should buy the book. ▪ He told me that I should buy the book. ▪ He demanded that he buy the book. ▪ He told me to buy the book. ▪ He says/said (that) I am/was to buy the book.
Antworten mit yes und no	Antworten mit yes und no werden wie in nebenstehender Spalte aufgeführt wiedergegeben.	In Antworten mit yes und no wird, wenn sie ein Vollverb enthalten, dieses mit to do umschrieben. Ent-

Die indirekte Rede

Direkte Rede	Indirekte Rede
	halten sie ein Hilfs- oder Modalverb, so wird das Hilfs- bzw. das Modalverb wieder aufgenommen.
- He said: «Do you want to drive to Seattle?» She said: «Yes/No.» - He said: «Have you done your homework?» She said: «Yes/No.» - She said: «Can you see Big Ben?» He said: «Yes/No.»	- He asked whether/if she wanted to drive to Seattle and she said (that) she did/didn't. - He asked whether/if she had done her homework and she said (that) she had/hadn't. - She asked whether/if he could see Big Ben and he said (that) he could/couldn't.
	Ausrufesätze der direkten Rede werden in der indirekten Rede zu Aussagesätzen.
- He cried out: «What a terrible noise!»	- He said that it was a terrible noise.
	Des Weiteren werden nebenstehende Ausrufe und Ausdrücke zu folgenden Aussagen verändert.
- He said: «Thank you.» - He said: «Curse the wind.» - He said: «Good morning.» - He said: «Happy Easter.» - He said: «Congratulations.» - He said: «Liar.» - He said: «Damn.»	- He thanked me. - He cursed the wind. - He wished me a good morning. - He wished me a happy Easter. - He congratulated me. - He called me a liar. - He swore.

Ausrufesätze

Die indirekte Rede

Die Zeitenfolge in der indirekten Rede

keine Änderung der Zeit bei Einführungssätzen in der Gegenwart

Bei der Umwandlung der direkten Rede in die indirekte Rede ändert sich ihre Zeit nur, wenn der Einführungssatz in einer Zeit der Vergangenheit (z. B. past tense, past perfect) steht. Steht der Einführungssatz in einer Zeit der Gegenwart (z. B. present tense, present perfect, future tense), wird in der indirekten Rede dieselbe Zeit verwendet wie in der direkten Rede.

Im Gegensatz zum Englischen, wo der Modus keine Rolle spielt, kann im Deutschen sowohl der Indikativ als auch der Konjunktiv stehen.
Der Indikativ kann stehen, wenn die indirekte Rede mit *dass* eingeleitet wird. Er wird meist in der Umgangssprache verwendet.
Der Konjunktiv kann grundsätzlich immer verwendet werden, er muss jedoch stehen, wenn die einleitende Konjunktion *dass* fehlt. Er ist der Modus der gehobenen und geschriebenen Sprache.

In der indirekten Rede können im Deutschen immer Konjunktiv I und II verwendet werden. Normalerweise wird der Konjunktiv I verwendet.
Der Konjunktiv II wird eigentlich nur verwendet, wenn Konjunktiv I und Indikativ dieselbe Form haben und somit eine Unterscheidung nicht möglich ist.
Auch bei der Verwendung des Indikativs kann die Zeit der direkten Rede in der indirekten Rede beibehalten werden.

Außer der Verwendung von Indikativ, Konjunktiv I und Konjunktiv II besteht die Möglichkeit der Umschreibung mit der so genannten *würde-Form*. Diese Form wird häufig in der Umgangssprache verwendet und in der geschriebenen und gehobenen Sprache, wenn der Konjunktiv ungebräuchlich ist oder geziert klingen würde (z. B. beföhle, befähle).

Zu jedem Beispielsatz ist in der folgenden Tabelle die entsprechende deutsche Übersetzung gegeben, wobei in der jeweils 1. Zeile die Übersetzung mit dem Indikativ, in der jeweils 2. Zeile die Übersetzung mit dem Konjunktiv I, in der jeweils 3. Zeile die Übersetzung mit dem Konjunktiv II und in der jeweils 4. Zeile gegebenenfalls die Übersetzung mit der würde-Form gegeben ist. Bei Abweichungen ist der Modus in Klammern angegeben.

Die indirekte Rede

Direkte Rede	Einführung in der Vergangenheit	Indirekte Rede
Present Tense Simple/Continuous		**Past Tense Simple/Continuous**
«I **buy** a book.»		He said (that) he **bought** a book.
«I **am buying** a book.»		He said (that) he **was buying** a book.
«Ich **kaufe** ein Buch.»	Er sagte,	dass er ein Buch **kauft**.
	Er sagte,	er **kaufe** ein Buch.
	Er sagte,	er **kaufte** ein Buch.
	Er sagte,	er **würde** ein Buch **kaufen**.
Present Tense Simple		**Present Tense Simple ***
«The earth **revolves** round the sun.»		He said (that) the earth **revolves** round the sun.
«Die Erde **dreht** sich um die Sonne.»	Er sagte,	dass sich die Erde um die Sonne **dreht**.
	Er sagte,	die Erde **drehe** sich um die Sonne.
	Er sagte,	die Erde **drehte** sich um die Sonne.
	Er sagte,	die Erde **würde** sich um die Sonne **drehen**.
Past Tense Simple/Continuous		**Past Perfect Simple/Continuous**
«I **bought** a book.»		He said (that) he **had bought** a book.
«I **was buying** a book.»		He said (that) he **had been buying** a book.
«Ich **kaufte** ein Buch.»	Er sagte,	dass er ein Buch **kaufte**.
	Er sagte,	er **habe** ein Buch **gekauft**.
	Er sagte,	er **hätte** ein Buch **gekauft**.
Present Perfect Simple/Continuous		**Past Perfect Simple/Continuous**
«I **have bought** a book.»		He said (that) he **had bought** a book.
«I **have been buying** a book.»		He said (that) he **had been buying** a book.
«Ich **habe** ein Buch **gekauft**.»	Er sagte,	dass er ein Buch **gekauft hat**.
	Er sagte,	er **habe** ein Buch **gekauft**.
	Er sagte,	er **hätte** ein Buch **gekauft**.
Past Perfect Simple/Continuous		**Past Perfect Simple/Continuous**
«I **had bought** a book.»		He said (that) he **had bought** a book.
«I **had been buying** a book.»		He said (that) he **had been buying** a book.
«Ich **hatte** ein Buch **gekauft**.»	Er sagte,	dass er ein Buch **gekauft hatte**.
	Er sagte,	er **habe** ein Buch **gekauft**.
	Er sagte,	er **hätte** ein Buch **gekauft**.
Future Tense Simple/Continuous		**Conditional Simple/Continuous**
«I **will buy** a book.»		He said (that) he **would buy** a book.
«I **will be buying** a book.»		He said (that) he **would be buying** a book.
«Ich **werde** ein Buch **kaufen**.»	Er sagte,	dass er ein Buch **kaufen wird**.
	Er sagte,	er **werde** ein Buch **kaufen**.
	Er sagte,	er **würde** ein Buch **kaufen**.

* Zum Ausdruck allgemein gültiger Tatsachen findet keine Umwandlung statt.

Die indirekte Rede

Direkte Rede	Einführung in der Vergangenheit	Indirekte Rede
Future Perfect Simple/Continuous		**Conditional Perfect Simple/Continuous**
«I will have bought a book.»		He said (that) he would have bought a book.
«I will have been buying a book.»		He said (that) he would have been buying a book.
«Ich werde ein Buch gekauft haben.»	Er sagte,	dass er ein Buch gekauft haben wird.
	Er sagte,	er werde ein Buch gekauft haben.
	Er sagte,	er würde ein Buch gekauft haben.
	Er sagte,	er würde ein Buch gekauft haben.
Conditional Simple/Continuous		**Conditional Simple/Continuous**
«I would buy a book.»		He said (that) he would buy a book.
«I would be buying a book.»		He said (that) he would be buying a book.
«Ich würde ein Buch kaufen.»	Er sagte,	dass er ein Buch kaufen würde.
	Er sagte,	er würde ein Buch kaufen.
Conditional Perfect Simple/Continuous		**Conditional Perfect Simple/Continuous**
«I would have bought a book.»		He said (that) he would have bought a book.
«I would have been buying a book.»		He said (that) he would have been buying a book.
«Ich würde ein Buch gekauft haben.»	Er sagte,	dass er ein Buch gekauft haben würde.
	Er sagte,	er würde ein Buch gekauft haben.
Present Subjunctive		**should + Infinitiv ohne to**
«God save the Queen.»		He said (that) God should save the Queen.
«Gott schütze die Königin.»	Er sagte,	Gott schütze die Königin. (Konj. I)
	Er sagte,	Gott möge die Königin schützen. (Konj. I)
Past Subjunctive		**Past Subjunctive**
«I wish I knew.»		He said (that) he wished he knew.
«Ich wünschte, ich wüsste es.»	Er sagte,	er wünschte, er wüsste es.
Imperative (affirmative)		**should + Infinitiv ohne to**
«Buy the book.»		He said (that) I should buy the book.
«Kauf das Buch!»	Er sagte,	ich möge/möchte das Buch kaufen. *1
	Er sagte,	ich soll(e)/sollte das Buch kaufen. *2
	Er sagte,	ich hätte das Buch zu kaufen. *3
Imperative (affirmative)		**Objekt + Infinitiv + to**
«Buy the book.»		He told me to buy the book.
«Kauf das Buch!»	Er sagte,	ich möge/möchte das Buch kaufen. *1
	Er sagte,	ich soll(e)/sollte das Buch kaufen. *2
	Er sagte,	ich hätte das Buch zu kaufen. *3

*1 Konjunktiv I und II zum Ausdruck der Bitte,
*2 Konjunktiv I und II zum Ausdruck der Aufforderung,
*3 Konjunktiv II zum Ausdruck des Befehls.

Die indirekte Rede

	Einführung in der	
Direkte Rede	Vergangenheit	**Indirekte Rede**
Imperative (affirmative)		**Present Subjunctive**

«**Buy** the book.»   He demanded he **buy** the book.
                     (that)
«**Kauf** das Buch!»   Er verlangte,   er **möge/möchte** das Buch **kaufen.** *1
                       Er verlangte,   er **soll(e)/sollte** das Buch **kaufen.** *2
                       Er verlangte,   er **hätte** das Buch **zu kaufen.** *3

	Vergangenheit	
Imperative (affirmative)		**to be to** + Infinitiv

«**Buy** the book.»   He says (that) I **am to buy** the book.
                     He said (that) I **was to buy** the book.
«**Kauf** das Buch!»   Er sagte,   ich **möge/möchte** das Buch **kaufen.** *1
                       Er sagte,   ich **soll(e)/sollte** das Buch **kaufen.** *2
                       Er sagte,   ich **hätte** das Buch **zu kaufen.** *3

Imperative (negative)		**Objekt** + **not** + **Infinitiv**

«**Don't talk** boys.»   He told   the boys **not to talk.**
«**Sprecht nicht,** Jungs!»   Er sagte,   die Jungen **mögen/möchten** nicht sprechen. *1
                              Er sagte,   die Jungen **sollen/sollten** nicht sprechen. *2
                              Er sagte,   die Jungen **hätten** nicht zu sprechen. *3

---

*1 Konjunktiv I und II zum Ausdruck der Bitte,
*2 Konjunktiv I und II zum Ausdruck der Aufforderung,
*3 Konjunktiv II zum Ausdruck des Befehls.

Die indirekte Rede

Übungen zur indirekten Rede

1. **Ändern Sie die Verben im present tense in die richtige Zeit in indirekter Rede.**

   1. He muttered: «My name **is** Roger.»
      He muttered that his name ... Roger.

   2. Mother remarked; «We **need** a new car.»
      Mother remarked that they ... a new car.

   3. They said: «The army **doesn't need** any female nurses.»
      They said that the army ... any female nurses.

   4. David's friends thought: «The apple-tarts his mother **makes are** the best.»
      David's friends thought that the apple-tarts his mother ... the best.

   5. The announcer said: «Most of the audience **is going** to the bar for a drink.»
      The announcer said that most of the audience ... to the bar for a drink.

   6. One evening my wife reported: «My hairdresser **swears** that fresh lobster or shrimp or crabmeat **is** non-fattening.»
      One evening my wife reported that her hairdresser ... that fresh lobster or shrimp or crabmeat ... non-fattening.

   7. The Supreme Court ordered: «The southern educational authorities **are to integrate** their schools with all deliberate speed.»
      The Supreme Court ordered that the southern educational authorities ... their schools with all deliberate speed.

   8. He said: « They **are to** do.»
      He said that they ... do.

   9. He said: « If anything **happens** to me I **want** you to have these documents.»
      He said that if anything ... to him he ... me to have these documents.

   10. Peter said: «In summer I **do not use** the room, because I **like** to save it as a change of scene for the winter.»
       Peter said that in summer he ... the room, because he ... to save it as a change of scene for the winter.

   richtig   falsch

2. **Ändern Sie die Verben im past tense in die korrekte Zeit in indirekter Rede.**

Die indirekte Rede

1. The boy said: «I **didn't do** anything wrong.»
   The boy said that he ... anything wrong.

2. He claimed: «I **was** an expert.»
   He claimed that he ... an expert.

3. Some people complained: «There **was not** enough hard learning in the schools.»
   Some people complained that there ... enough learning in the schools.

4. He protested: «I **was** still quite wide awake.»
   He protested that he ... still ... quite wide awake.

5. He said: «Miles apparently **had** a few drinks.»
   He said that Miles apparently ... a few drinks.

6. I said: «Mr Stevens **died** of a disease of the stomach, made worse by the habit of drinking strong spirits to excess.»
   I said that Mr Stevens ... of a disease of the stomach, made worse by the habit of drinking strong spirits to excess.

7. Our teacher said: « While Isaac Newton **was** in his orchard he **saw** an apple fall to the ground, and this **gave** him the idea that the Earth must have been pulling at the apple.»
   Our teacher said that while Isaac Newton ... in his orchard he ... an apple fall to the ground, and this ... him the idea that the Earth must have been pulling at the apple.

8. He said: «Prior to the IMF meeting I **had** discussions with colleagues of the EC in Venice.»
   He said that prior to the IMF meeting he ... discussions with colleagues of the EC in Venice.

9. He said: «It **took** 96 weeks to build a factory in Britain and France.»
   He said that it ... 96 weeks to build a factory in Britain and France.

10. He said: «I **understood** your opinion.»
    He said that he ... my opinion.

richtig   falsch

3. **Ändern Sie die Verben im present perfect in die richtige Zeit in indirekter Rede.**

1. You said: «He **has** just **left** the city.»
   You said that he ... just ... the city.

2. She exclaimed: «I **have torn** my coat.»
   She exclaimed that she ... her coat.

Die indirekte Rede

3. He confessed: «For years I **have been** a member of an underground organization.»
   He confessed that for years he ... a member of an underground organization.

4. I said: «The Mayor **hasn't found** any of our ideas good enough yet.»
   I said that the Mayor ... any of our ideas good enough yet.

5. People said: «Mr Rush **has been** a very cautious man all his life.»
   People said that Mr Rush ... a very cautious man all his life.

6. He admitted: «This year's crop in Russia **has been** even worse than in previous years.»
   He admitted that this year's crop in Russia ... even worse than in previous years.

7. The computer explained: «I **have been given** the wrong license number by one of my human operators.»
   The computer explained that it ... the wrong license number by one of its human operators.

8. He said: «Nigeria, an OPEC member **has had** particular trouble selling oil recently.»
   He said that Nigeria, an OPEC member ... particular trouble selling oil recently.

9. The papers said: «Atkinson **has** just **been requested** by the police to answer questions.»
   The papers said that Atkinson ... just ... by the police to answer questions.

10. She said: «We **have done** our homework.»
    She said that they ... their homework.

    richtig   falsch

4. Ändern Sie die Verben im past perfect in die korrekte Zeit in indirekter Rede.

1. The document said: «The fingerprints really **had guaranteed** his innocence.»
   The document said that the fingerprints really ... his innocence.

2. He said: «$ 50,0000 **had been collected** as a present for her.»
   He said that $ 50,000 ... as a present for her.

3. He said: «The last communication from William Atkinson **had been** his letter to the Bank of Paris.»
   He said that the last communication from William Atkinson ... his letter to the Bank of Paris.

Die indirekte Rede

4. He confessed: «I **had been** a spy in the pay of an Eastasian government.»
He confessed that he ... a spy in the pay of an Eastasian government.

5. The Indians said: «Our people **had been killed,** our lands settled on, and our game wantonly destroyed.»
The Indians said that their people ..., their lands settled on, and their game wantonly destroyed.

6. She said: «It was extraordinary that I **had failed** to find out.»
She said that it had been extraordinary that she ... to find out.

7. He claimed: «I **had seen** a piece of paper which proved them innocent.»
He claimed that he ... a piece of paper which had proved them innocent.

8. He said: «Only two of the boys were bad, the others **had been led astray** by them.»
He said that only two of the boys were bad, the others ... by them.

9. She said: «My sufferings **had been** more than anyone should be asked to bear.»
She said that her sufferings ... more than anyone should be asked to bear.

10. They said: «We **had beaten** the record!»
They said that they ... the record.

richtig   falsch

5. Setzen Sie die Verben im future tense, future perfect tense oder im conditional I in die korrekte Zeit in indirekter Rede.

1. He remarked: «I **will be** absent tomorrow.»
He remarked that he ... absent the next day.

2. She replied: «I **will make** preparations at once.»
She replied that she ... preparations at once.

3. I said: «I **won't drink** any wine with my dinner.»
I said that I ... any wine with my dinner.

4. I thought: «That night **will** never **end.**»
I thought that that night ... never ....

5. She thought: «I **will have come** back by then.»
She thought that she ... back by then.

Die indirekte Rede

6. My Dad said: «I **wouldn't like** to drive such a huge lorry, I prefer my taxi.»
My Dad said that he ... to drive such a huge lorry, he preferred his taxi.

7. The inspector said: «I **would like** to examine the study.»
The inspector said that he ... to examine the study.

8. My father exclaimed: «This **will be** a good way to spend the holidays.»
My father exclaimed that this ... a good way to spend the holidays.

9. He swore: «I **will have** my revenge.»
He swore that he ... his revenge.

10. He said: «The supervisory board **will have** his full approval.»
He said that the supervisory board ... his full approval.

richtig   falsch

6. Setzen Sie die folgenden Modalverben in die indirekte Rede.

1. My wife complained: «I **can't find** my passport anywhere.»
My wife complained that she ... her passport anywhere.

2. He said: «I **couldn't do** it.»
He said that he ... it.

3. People said: «There **may be** intelligent beings on Mars.»
People said that there ... intelligent beings on Mars.

4. She said: «You **might have** flunked.»
She said that you ... flunked.

5. He suggested: «We **ought to** go.
He suggested that they ... go.

6. The doctor explained: «I **might be** called away to attend a patient.
The doctor explained that he ... called away to attend a patient.

7. He said: «All of us **must be** educated to equip us for life.»
He said that all of us ... educated to equip us for life.

8. The Constitution said: «No person **shall be** deprived of his life, liberty or property.»
The Constitution said that no person ... deprived of his life, liberty or property.

9. He said: «You **have to** make a report within twenty-four hours.»
He said that I ... make a report within twenty-four hours.

10. The Chancellor said: «If the nation **were to** work harder, wage increases **would be** fully justified.»
The Chancellor said that if the nation ... work harder, wage increases ... fully justified.

richtig falsch

7. Setzen Sie die folgenden Personalpronomen in die indirekte Rede.

1. I said: «**I/we** don't like that guy.»
I said that ... didn't like that guy.

2. I said: «**He/they** has/have one of those new electric cleaners.»
I said that ... had one of those new electric cleaners.

3. I said: «**You** were driving carefully.»
I said that ... had been driving carefully.

4. You said: «**I/we** don't advise you to try that.»
You said that ... didn't advise me/us to try that.

5. You said: «**He/they** lives/live in an ivory tower.»
You said that ... lived in an ivory tower.

6. You said: «**You** have to set the table.»
You said that ... had to set the table.

7. He said: «**I/we** will receive the Blairs out of doors.»
He said that ... would receive the Blairs out of doors.

8. He said: «**He/they** spoke the truth.»
He said that ... had spoken the truth.

9. He said: «**You** should go.»
He said that ... should go.

10. We said: «**We** are too highly specialised.»
We said that ... were too highly specialised.

11. We said: «**He/they** will find a solution.»
We said that ... would find a solution.

12. We said: «**You** will develop a better computer system.»
We said that ... would develop a better computer system.

13. They said: «**We** will see her soon.»
They said that ... would see her soon.

14. They said: «**They/he** will solve the crime problem.»
They said that ... would solve the crime problem.

Die indirekte Rede

15. They said: «**You** waste your money on idle luxury.»
    They said that ... wasted your money on idle luxury.

    richtig   falsch

8. Setzen Sie die folgenden Orts- und Zeitangaben in die indirekte Rede.

1. I said: «I have seen her **today**.»
   I said that I had seen her ....

2. I said: «He visited him at some time **yesterday**.»
   I said that he had visited him at some time ....

3. I said: «He visited him at some time **the day before yesterday**.»
   I said that he had visited him at some time ....

4. He remarked: «I will be absent **tomorrow**.»
   He remarked that he would be absent ....

5. Peter regretted: «I cannot come to your party **next week**.»
   Peter regretted that he could not come to my party ....

6. Peter regretted: «I could not come to your party **last week**.»
   Peter regretted that he could not come to my party ....

7. He said: I took my examination two years **ago**.
   He said that he had taken his examination two years ....

8. I said: «George and I will leave **now**.»
   I said that George and I would leave ....

9. The carrier remarked: «**Here** is a letter with stamps from Madrid.»
   The carrier remarked that ... was a letter with stamps from Madrid.

10. She said: «Standing **here tonight** just reminds me of **then**.»
    She said that standing ... ... just reminded her of ... .

    richtig   falsch

9. Setzen Sie die folgenden Sätze in die indirekte Rede.

1. I said: «I think he is wrong.»

2. He said: «Andrew Johnson is innocent.»

3. You said: « She doesn't admit anything.»

4. They said: «This will have only negative consequences.»

5. The Speaker said: «It is time to go on to the next question.»

Die indirekte Rede

6. The doctors said: «He has been dead at least twelve hours.»

7. We said: «The burglar entered the garden from the back.»

8. He said: «There was no risk of an accident.»

9. The captain said: «It was no use arguing with the angry crew.»

10. They said: «We will arrange to have a conference to settle the matter.»

11. He told us: «He will receive the Burtons on Sunday out of doors and give them tea in the garden.»

12. He said: «Between them, these two moves will lay a basis for future cooperation.»

13. They said: «Man's lot cannot be further improved by more material progress.»

14. She said: «There should be a redistribution of the male and female roles in society.»

15. I said: «Before taking a decision he ought to make thorough enquiries.»

richtig   falsch

10. Setzen Sie die folgenden Fragesätze ohne Fragewort in die indirekte Rede.

1. I wanted to ask you: «Have you got any razor blades?»

2. He asked: «Could you bring Carol over for a drink around 5 o'clock?»

3. Our teacher asked us: «Would you like to form a pen-club?»

4. I wondered: «Will he make it?»

5. I wondered: «Shall I ever have time to see London?»

6. I wondered: «Would you like to come to our house and see the President from our balcony?»

7. The Clerk read the indictment and asked the prisoner: «Are you guilty or not guilty?»

8. A group of scientists put their heads together to decide: «Do animals think or not?»

9. He wondered: «Will I ever get married?»

Die indirekte Rede

10. He wondered: «Is there a microphone hidden nearby?»

11. I wondered: «Is there anything I have left undone?»

12. My wife asked me: «Did you happen to see my passport lying about?»

13. At the end of every debate the Speaker put the question: «Will you accept the motion that has been debated or not?»

14. The Government decided to put to the people the question: «Should Britain remain within the E.C. or not?»

15. The shop keeper asked: «Is there anything I can do for you?»

richtig   falsch

11. Setzen Sie die folgenden Fragesätze mit Fragewort in die indirekte Rede.

1. I wondered: «Why hasn't Mike turned up yet?»

2. I wondered: «How often does the old lady leave her house?»

3. I wondered: «Why doesn't he come?»

4. I wondered: «What are Gerald and Caroline doing?»

5. I wondered: «Whose dog is this?»

6. He wondered: «What had they done to the woman in the yard?»

7. The king wondered: «What might I give the queen for her birthday?»

8. They asked: «What did people do with their leisure before there was television?»

9. Now that he has been in America for three years, I asked him: «What was your first impression?»

10. The theft made him ask again: «What happens to stolen paintings?»

11. She used to ask herself: «How should a teacher try to gain the positive interest of unco-operative pupils?»

12. The police were wondering: «Where the hell does he go to?»

13. As he was watching a gang of workmen putting in long pipes, he began to wonder: «What is this all about?»

Die indirekte Rede

14. I wondered: «Why did he have that idea?»

15. I was always asking him: «How do you spend your time?»

richtig   falsch

12. Setzen Sie die folgenden Befehle in die indirekte Rede.

1. He demanded: «Write neatly.»

2. He suggested: «Try the examination again.»

3. The officer demanded: «Lower the flag.«

4. They were told: «Lie on the grass and don't look up at any cost.»

5. They told me: «Go to the information desk.»

6. I told them: «Don't forget to lock the door.»

7. His wife told him: «Don't drive too fast.»

8. His mother told them: «Don't be greedy.»

9. My father said: «Let's go up to the restaurant to have a good look at the planes taking off.»

10. I told him: «Don't worry about having failed.»

richtig   falsch

Die entsprechenden Lösungen befinden sich auf Seite 429ff.

Der Konditional (The Conditional)

Der Konditional drückt eine Bedingung, Voraussetzung aus. Konditional- oder Bedingungssätze (conditional clauses, if-clauses) sind Nebensätze, die die Bedingung ausdrücken. Konditionalsätze werden durch Konjunktionen wie if (not), unless, but for, if only, suppose, supposing, provided (that), on condition that, in case, so/as long as eingeleitet. Die am häufigsten verwendete Konjunktion ist if.

Bedingung, if, if not, unless, but for	If (not) (wenn (nicht)) ist die Konjunktion, die am häufigsten in Bedingungssätzen steht. Steht if vor einem Hilfsverb (were, had, should), kann das Hilfsverb vor das Subjekt treten, if entfällt dann. Wird statt if not die Konjunktion unless (wenn nicht) verwendet, darf das folgende Verb nicht verneint werden. Im Sinne von if it were not, if it had not been for (wenn nicht ... gewesen wäre) kann auch but for verwendet werden.	• **If** I were rich, I would buy a big house. • **If** the train isn't late, we will arrive in time. • **Should you** need some information, don't hesitate to contact us. (**If** you should need ...) • **Unless** the train **is** late, we will arrive in time. • **But for** the storm, we should have arrived earlier.
auf unless folgende Verben sind nicht verneint		
Hoffnung, Bedauern, if only	If only (wenn nur) + present tense steht zum Ausdruck der Hoffnung, if only + past tense oder past perfect drückt das Bedauern aus.	• **If only** he **comes** in time, we will catch the train. • **If only** he **came/had come** in time, we would catch/would have caught the train.
Vorschlag, suppose, supposing	Suppose, supposing (angenommen, dass) drücken die Vermutung, den Vorschlag aus.	• **Supposing** you pass the exam, what will you do then? • **Suppose** you try again?
Erlaubnis, Provided (that), on condition that, in case, so/as long as	Provided (that), on condition that, so/as long as (vorausgesetzt, dass), in case (wenn, falls) drücken die Erlaubnis aus.	• You can go out tonight **provided (that)/on condition that** you do your homework now. • You can go now **so long as** somebody is in the office.

Der Konditional

Die Zeitenfolge im Bedingungssatz

Die Zeiten im Bedingungssatz sind im Englischen danach zu wählen, ob eine Bedingung möglich, erfüllbar oder unwahrscheinlich ist oder unerfüllt bleibt.
Zu jedem Beispielsatz ist in der folgenden Tabelle jeweils die deutsche Übersetzung und der entsprechende Modus angegeben.
Bis auf die am Ende dieses Kapitels dargestellten Sachverhalte gilt grundsätzlich: im if-Satz kein will, would, shall oder should!

> im if-Satz kein will, would, shall, should

Hauptsatz (principal clause)		Bedingungssatz (if-clause)

Realis (Real Present): die Bedingung ist erfüllbar, möglich (Typ I)

Future Tense		Present Tense
I will be happy Ich bin glücklich, (Indikativ Präsens)	if wenn	you come. ihr kommt. (Indikativ Präsens)

Irrealis der Gegenwart (Unreal Present): die Erfüllung der Bedingung ist unwahrscheinlich (Typ II)

Conditional		Past Tense
I would be happy Ich wäre glücklich, (Konjunktiv II Präteritum)	if wenn	you came. ihr kämt. (Konjunktiv II Präteritum)

Statt des oft ungebräuchlichen deutschen Konjunktiv II Präteritum bei Vollverben, steht hier oft die Umschreibung mit der *würde*-Form.

Conditional		Past Tense
He would pass the exam Er würde die Prüfung bestehen, (Er bestünde die Prüfung,	if wenn wenn	he studied harder. er mehr lernen würde. er mehr lernte.)

Irrealis der Vergangenheit (Past Unreality): die Bedingung bleibt unerfüllt (Typ III)

Conditional Perfect		Past Perfect
I would have been happy Ich wäre glücklich gewesen, (Konjunktiv II Plusquamperfekt)	if wenn	you had come. ihr gekommen wärt. (Konjunktiv II Plusquamperfekt)

Der Konditional

Neben den oben aufgeführten 3 Hauptgruppen können, je nach dem Sinn des Satzes, auch andere Zeiten stehen.

Die Bedingung ist erfüllbar, möglich

Hauptsatz (principal clause)		Bedingungssatz (if-clause)
Present Tense		Present Tense
We do not go for a walk	if	it rains.
Past Tense		Past Tense
Why didn't you come	if	you knew that he was ill.
Future Tense		Present Perfect
You will pass the exam	if	you have studied carefully.
can, could, may, might		Present Tense
You can, could pass the exam	if	you study carefully.
You may, might pass the exam	if	you study carefully.

Die Erfüllung der Bedingung ist unwahrscheinlich

Hauptsatz (principal clause)		Bedingungssatz (if-clause)
Present Tense		Present Tense
We do not go for a walk	if	it rains.
Conditional		Past Subjunctive/Past Tense*
That would be a catastrophe	if	it were/was true.
could, might		Past Tense
We could, might go home	if	the teacher was ill.

Die Bedingung bleibt unerfüllt

Hauptsatz (principal clause)		Bedingungssatz (if-clause)
Conditional		Past Perfect
He would be a rich man now	if	he had taken my advice.
Conditional Perfect		Past Perfect
He would have been rich	if	he had taken my advice.

*In der 1. und 3. Person Singular von to be wird zum Ausdruck der unwahrscheinlichen Bedingung in der gehobenen Sprache der past subjunctive (were) verwendet. In der Umgangssprache steht häufig das past tense (was).

Der Konditional

Hauptsatz (principal clause)		Bedingungssatz (if-clause)
could, might + Perfect Infinitive		Past Perfect
I **could, might have come** earlier	if	it **had been** necessary.

Bitte, Aufforderung

Enthält der Hauptsatz eine Bitte, Aufforderung und der Bedingungssatz drückt aus, dass ein Ereignis zufällig eintreten könnte, so steht im Bedingungssatz should.

Hauptsatz (principal clause)		Bedingungssatz (if-clause)
Present Tense		should
You **can tell** her that	if	you **should** see her today.
Future Tense		should
You **will meet** me at the bar	if	you **should** be there at 8 o'clock.
Imperative		should
Tell him to meet me at 8 o'clock	if	he **should** call.

Annahme, Vermutung

Hauptsatz (principal clause)		Bedingungssatz (if-clause)
Conditional		should, were to
He **would tell** him the truth	if	he **were to/should** see him today.

Der Konditional

Übungen zum Konditional

1. Setzen Sie die Verben in Klammern in die richtige Form (Typ I).

1. He (kill) me if I do that again.
2. Before the end of this century, if current trends continue, China (have) over a billion people.
3. A solution of the crisis (not be found) unless we look for it.
4. What (you, do) if someone talks to you in Chinese?
5. What will you do if your neighhour (pull) your hair?
6. I will punish him if he (not behave) properly.
7. They will get wet if it (rain).
8. If you will act the fool, I (can't) help it.
9. You (can) ask Jane, if you like. She will tell you.
10. If the Opposition (not like) a bill they will vote against it.
11. You (soon, be able to) swim if you practise hard.
12. If things continue on their present course, there (be) 600 million people living on the edge of survival.
13. What (be) the consequences if his advice is widely followed?
14. It (be) very simple for you to reach me if I am needed.
15. If he is sent to prison - he who loves the freedom of the open air - I (not answer) for what might happen to him.

richtig   falsch

2. Setzen Sie die Verben in Klammern in die richtige Form (Typ II).

1. You would catch the train if you (leave) earlier.
2. He would come if you (call).
3. If men (be) more reasonable, there would be no more war.
4. If she (have) Simon back, she would just explode with happiness.
5. It would be just as well if I (not mention) it to anybody.

Der Konditional

6. He (come) if you waited.

7. That's a beautiful mahogany bed, or at least it (be) if you could get the bugs out of it.

8. What would you do if a bee (sting) you?

9. If you (can) choose, would you prefer to live then or now?

10. He felt he would faint if he (stay) one minute longer in the dimly lighted foyer.

11. If I (be) you, I would say nothing about it.

12. If the workers (not give) (passive voice) decent wages, they would leave the factories to settle in the West.

13. If the powers of rulers were carefully defined and limited in legal terms they (not use) (passive voice) oppressively.

14. What places do you think he (be likely to) go if he wanted to hide out?

15. If I (have) a few hundred pounds spare, I would invest them.

richtig   falsch

3. Setzen Sie die Verben in Klammern in die richtige Form (Typ III).

1. If she had opened the door, the burglars (run away) or (catch) her.

2. If she had not missed her brooch, she (not go back) to the school building.

3. If Peggy (not try) on her new suit, she would not have found out about the missing brooch.

4. If the men (not carry) out the TV set and the other things, Sheila would not have thought they were burglars.

5. I would not have done anything to her if she (not hit) me.

6. Bob would have fallen from the raft if we (not hold) him.

7. About how long (take, Mr Palmer) to get home, if all had gone well?

8. He (be) in a position to procure the job for you, if he only had wanted to.

9. If you had done as I told you, you (have) more success.

Der Konditional

10. If they had opened the window, they **(have)** fresh air.

11. They would have done better if they **(buy)** something else.

12. It would have made no difference if it **(be)** the other way about.

13. If he **(can move)** he would have stretched out a hand.

14. What (he; **say)** if it had been possible for him to set his scattered thoughts in order.

15. If Mike had not been surrounded by experienced nurses, he (most certainly, **die)** in no time.   richtig   falsch

4. Setzen Sie die Verben in Klammern in die richtige Form.

1. If it **(rain)** this afternoon, it **(be)** too wet to play the match tomorrow.

2. It **(be)** impossible for me to finish my work if you **(not cease)** this chatter.

3. Most of the women with small children **(like)** to work, if the children **(can be)** cared for during the mothers' working hours.

4. What subjects (you; **choose)** to take if you **(be)** an American High School student?

5. If the burglars **(not go back)** to the house, the police **(not catch)** them.

6. If he **(know)** English was so difficult, he (never; **take)** it up.

7. The world's supplies of oil **(be exhausted)** fairly soon unless they **(be preserved)**.

8. If present trends **(continue)**, immigration **(add)** at least 35 million people to the current U.S. population by the year 2010.

9. If I **(be)** in Parliament I **(spend)** more money on hospitals.

10. If our planetary eco-system **(be to)** recover, then countries like Britain **(have to be)** the first to give up environmental pollutants.   richtig   falsch

Die entsprechenden Lösungen befinden sich auf Seite 432.

Der Subjunctive (The Subjunctive)

Die Modi (moods) drücken aus, ob in einer Aussage persönliche Empfindungen, Auffassungen des Sprechers oder ob eine Tatsache, Wirklichkeit zum Ausdruck kommt. Diese Wirklichkeit muss nicht objektiv, sie kann auch subjektiv sein, d. h. für den Sprecher gilt diese Wirklichkeit als sicher oder erwiesen.
Zu den Modi gehören indicative und subjunctive.
Der Indikativ oder die Wirklichkeitsform stellt einen Vorgang oder Zustand als tatsächlich oder wirklich dar. Durch ihn kommen also Tatsachen zum Ausdruck.
Der subjunctive oder die Möglichkeitsform stellt einen Vorgang oder Zustand als erwünscht, vorgestellt oder von einem anderen nur behauptet dar.
Der subjunctive wird im Englischen weniger häufig verwendet. Er steht vor allem in einigen festen Wendungen und gelegentlich in gehobener Sprache. Statt des subjunctive werden meist Modalverben wie may, might etc. verwendet.
Das Englische kennt drei verschiedene Formen beim subjunctive, den present subjunctive, den past subjunctive und den past perfect subjunctive.
Es ist zu beachten, dass die 3. Person Singular des present subjunctive kein -s erhält (die 3. Person Singular des present tense erhält ein -s).

> 3. Person Singular erhält kein Endungs-s

Der Present Subjunctive

Zum Ausdruck des Wunschgedankens, der Hoffnung.

- God **bless** you.
- God **save** the Queen.

Wunschgedanke, Hoffnung

Zum Ausdruck des Befehls, der Aufforderung, vor allem nach den folgenden Verben und Ausdrücken.
Der present subjunctive steht auch bei einem Hauptsatz im past tense und wird meist mit that angeschlossen.
In der Umgangssprache wird der present subjunctive häufig durch should + infinitive oder to + infinitive ersetzt.

- We **recommend that** he **move** into the advanced class.
- I **insisted that** she **call** me as soon a she arrived.
- She **proposed that** the meeting **be** adjourned.
- She proposed that the meeting **should be** adjourned.
- She proposed **to adjourn** the meeting.

Befehl, Aufforderung

- it is advisable — es ist ratsam
- to ask — fragen; bitten
- to command — befehlen
- it is crucial — es ist entscheidend
- to demand — verlangen, erfordern
- it is essential — es ist wesentlich
- it is important — es ist wichtig
- to insist — bestehen (auf)

- it is necessary — es ist notwendig
- to order — befehlen
- to prefer — bevorzugen
- to propose — vorschlagen
- to recommend — empfehlen
- to request — bitten; verlangen
- to suggest — vorschlagen
- it is vital — es ist lebenswichtig

Zum Ausdruck der nachdrücklichen Feststellung, Meinung nach it is/was + Adjektiv. Dies gilt besonders bei den folgenden Adjektiven.

- It is advisable that he **work** more carefully.
- It was important that everyone **send in** a membership card.

Meinung, Feststellung

Der Subjunctive

Bedingnung	In Bedingungssätzen steht der present subjunctive häufig in literarischer Sprache.	• If this **be** error, and upon me proved. (William Shakespeare)
Einräumung	In Einräumungssätzen steht der present subjunctive häufig in literarischer Sprache.	• Though the heart **be** still as loving. (Byron)

Der Past Subjunctive

unerfüllbarer Wunsch	Zum Ausdruck unerfüllbarer Wünsche, des Wunschgedankens der Gegenwart. Der past subjunctive steht vor allem nach to wish, das auch im past tense stehen kann.	• I wish it **were** true. • I wish I **knew**. • I wish I **were** you. • I wished it **were** true. • I wished I **knew**.
unerfüllbare Bedingung	Zum Ausdruck der unerfüllbaren Bedingung der Gegenwart, vor allem nach if, if only, as if und as though.	• If we all **lived** in poverty. • He talks as though he **knew** everything about it.
would sooner, would rather	Nach would sooner, would rather steht der past subjunctive oder would prefer + Objekt + Infinitiv + to bei verschiedenen Subjekten. Bei gleichem Subjekt steht der Infinitiv ohne to.	• She wants to go by car but I would rather she **went** by train. • She wants to go by car but I would prefer her **to go** by train. • Peter and Mary would rather **spend** their holidays in Scotland.
it is time	Nach it is time kann der past subjunctive oder for + Objekt + Infinitiv + to stehen.	• It is time we **went**. • It is time **for us to go**.

Der Past Perfect Subjunctive

unerfüllbarer Wunsch	Zum Ausdruck unerfüllbarer Wünsche, des Wunschgedankens der Vergangenheit. Der past perfect subjunctive steht dabei vor allem nach to wish, das auch im past tense stehen kann.	• I wish it **had been** true. • I wish I **had known**. • I wish I **had been** you. • I wished it **had been** true. • I wished I **had known**. • I wished I **had been** you.
unerfüllte Bedingung	Zum Ausdruck der unerfüllten Bedingung, vor allem nach if, if only, as if und as though.	• If we all **had lived** in poverty. • He talked as though he **had known** everything about it.

Der Imperativ (The Imperative)

Der Imperativ, die so genannte Befehlsform, drückt einen Befehl, eine Aufforderung aus.

Es ist zu beachten, dass nach einem Imperativsatz nur dann ein Ausrufezeichen steht, wenn es sich wirklich um einen Ausruf handelt.

Der Imperativ kann nur in der 2. Person Singular und Plural gebildet werden. Er hat dieselbe Form wie der Infinitiv ohne to. Für die fehlende 3. Person Singular und Plural sowie für die 1. Person Plural treten Ersatzformen ein. Für die 1. Person Singular steht keine Form zur Verfügung.

Ausrufezeichen nur bei Ausrufen

Der Imperativ steht zum Ausdruck eines Befehls, einer Aufforderung, die an die 2. Person Singular oder Plural (you) gerichtet ist. Damit sind eine oder mehrere Personen gemeint, die man duzt (du, ihr) oder siezt (Sie). Einem Befehl wird durch to do oder das Hinzufügen des entsprechenden Subjekts mehr Nachdruck verliehen.	▪ **Be** quiet. (Sei, seid, seien Sie ruhig!) ▪ **Do be** quiet. ▪ Peter, you **do** your homework now.	Befehl, Aufforderung an die 2. Person
Zwei Imperative werden durch and verbunden. Der zweite Imperativ wird im Deutschen häufig mit dem Infinitiv + *zu* übersetzt.	▪ **Sit down** and **be** quiet. ▪ **Stop talking** and **begin** to work. ▪ **Try** and **read** clearly. (Versuche deutlich zu lesen.)	zwei Imperative
Der verneinte Imperativ wird stets mit to do umschrieben.	▪ **Don't forget** your books. ▪ **Don't go** into this room.	verneinter Imperativ
Als Ersatz für die 1. Person Plural und die 3. Person Singular und Plural steht to let. Die Verneinung wird nur mit not gebildet, das hinter das entsprechende Pronomen tritt.	▪ **Let us (let's)** go. ▪ **Let him do** his homework. ▪ **Let them do** their homework. ▪ **Let us not** go. ▪ **Let them not** go away.	Befehl, Aufforderung an die 1., 3. Person

Der Infinitiv

Der Infinitiv (The Infinitive)

Der Infinitiv gehört zu den infiniten Verbformen und ist die Grundform des Verbs.

Der Present Infinitive

Gleichzeitigkeit	Der present infinitive steht zum Ausdruck der Gleichzeitigkeit, d. h. die Handlung von Haupt- und Nebensatz findet gleichzeitig statt.	• I saw her come into the house. (Ich sah sie ins Haus kommen.) (Das Sehen und Kommen findet gleichzeitig statt.)
im Aktivsatz, im Passivsatz,	Der present infinitive active steht im Aktivsatz (der Handelnde wird genannt), aber auch im Passivsatz (der Handelnde wird nicht genannt), nach there is, there was und nach Adjektiven, besonders nach hard, easy, difficult, nice, pleasant.	• Mrs Brown allowed the boys to play in her garden. (Mrs Brown ist die Ausführende der Handlung.) • The boys were allowed to play in Mrs Brown's garden. (Wer die Erlaubnis gibt, wird nicht mitgeteilt.) • There was no time to lose. (Es war keine Zeit zu verlieren.)
im Passivsatz	Der present infinitive passive steht im Passivsatz (der Handelnde wird nicht genannt) und zwar besonders nach to be, to remain, there is there was. Die passive Form wird immer mit der Präposition to angeschlossen.	• He ordered the job to be done. (Er befahl die Arbeit zu erledigen.) (Wer die Arbeit erledigt wird nicht mitgeteilt.) • There was no time to be lost. (Es war keine Zeit zu verlieren.) • A lot of things remained to be done. (Eine Menge blieb zu tun.)

Der Perfect Infinitive

Vorzeitigkeit	Der perfect infinitive steht zum Ausdruck der Vorzeitigkeit, d. h. die Handlung des Nebensatzes findet vor der des Hauptsatzes statt.	• I was happy to have bought the car. (Ich war froh das Auto gekauft zu haben.) (Das Kaufen findet zuerst statt.)
im Aktivsatz, im Passivsatz,	Der perfect infinitive active steht im Aktivsatz (der Handelnde wird genannt), aber auch im Passivsatz (der Handelnde wird nicht genannt), nach there is, there was und nach Adjektiven, besonders nach hard, easy, difficult, nice, pleasant.	• I was happy to have bought the car. (I ist der Ausführende der Handlung.) • It is nice to have finally met Susan. (Es ist nett, Susan doch noch getroffen zu haben.) (Wer Susan trifft, wird nicht mitgeteilt.)
im Passivsatz	Der perfect infinitive passive steht im Passivsatz (der Handelnde wird nicht genannt) und zwar besonders nach to be. Die passive Form wird immer mit der Präposition to angeschlossen.	• It is nice to have been chosen for this honour. (Es war nett für diese Ehre ausgewählt worden zu sein.) (Wer auswählt, wird nicht mitgeteilt.) • Nobody was to have been told about the surprise.

Der Infinitiv

Der Present Continuous Infinitive

Der present continuous infinitive steht zum Ausdruck der Gleichzeitigkeit, d. h. die Handlung von Haupt- und Nebensatz findet gleichzeitig statt.
Er steht vor allem nach to seem, to appear, nach den Modalverben und nach dem Passiv der Verben to believe, to know, to report, to say, to suppose, to think und to understand.

- He seems to be telling the truth.
  (Er scheint die Wahrheit zu sagen.) (Der Anschein und das Sagen findet gleichzeitig statt.)
- He must be telling the truth.
- He is supposed to be doing this work already.
- He is thought to be hiding an awful secret.

Gleichzeitigkeit

Der Perfect Continuous Infinitive

Der perfect continuous infinitive steht zum Ausdruck der Vorzeitigkeit, d. h. die Handlung des Nebensatzes findet vor der des Hauptsatzes statt.
Er steht vor allem nach to seem, to appear, nach den Modalverben und nach dem Passiv der Verben to believe, to know, to report, to say, to suppose, to think und to understand.

- He seems to have been telling the truth.
  (Er scheint die Wahrheit gesagt zu haben.)
  (Das Sagen findet zuerst statt.)
- Why weren't you helping him? You should have been helping him.
- He was supposed to have been doing this work as soon as possible.

Vorzeitigkeit

Der Infinitiv

Die Infinitive können in der Funktion eines Subjekts, nach bestimmten Verben oder Adjektiven stehen, und sie sind ein wichtiges Stilmittel zur Verkürzung von Nebensätzen.
Sie werden als reiner Infinitiv (ohne Präposition) oder mit der Präposition to verwendet.

	Infinitiv + to	Infinitiv ohne to
als Subjekt	Als Subjekt steht der Infinitiv + to am Satzanfang, vor allem in bestimmten Redewendungen und nach it is of (no) use. • **To solve** this problem would be difficult. • It is of no use **to cry** over spilt milk.	
to do		Nach dem Hilfsverb to do steht der Infinitiv ohne to. • She **does play** the piano very well. (Sie **spielt** sehr gut Klavier.) • **Does** he always **tell** the truth?
Modalverben	Nach den folgenden Modalverben steht der Infinitiv mit to. Nach den Modalverben ought to, used to und nach den Ersatzformen to have to und to be able to wird der Infinitiv häufig weggelassen und durch die Präposition to repräsentiert. • ought to (sollen) • used to (pflegen) • dare (wagen)	Nach den folgenden Modalverben und Ausdrücken steht der Infinitiv ohne to. • can (kann) • I cannot but (ich kann nicht umhin) • could (konnte; könnte) • I could not but (ich konnte nicht umhin) • may (darf) • might (durfte, dürfte) • need (brauchen) • must (müssen) • shall (sollen) • should (sollte) • will (wollen) • would (würden) • I would rather (ich möchte lieber) • I would sooner (ich möchte lieber) • dare (wagen) • I had better (ich täte gut daran) • I had rather (ich möchte lieber) • I had sooner (ich möchte lieber)

Der Infinitiv

Infinitiv + to

Das Modalverb dare schließt den Infinitiv mit to an, wenn es mit to do, will oder would verbunden wird.

- You ought to say something.
- Do you go to school by bus? Yes, I used to (go to school by bus).
- He wouldn't dare to tell him everything about it.

Nach den unpersönlichen Verben und nach unpersönlichen Ausdrücken wie it is/was/would be, that is/was/would be + Substantiv oder Adjektiv steht der Infinitiv + to häufig mit einem vorangehenden Objekt + for oder of.

- It is advisable to tell the truth.
- It is kind of you to help me.
- It is time for me to go.
- That would be an awful thing to do.

Nach vielen transitiven Verben steht der Infinitiv + to.
Der Infinitiv steht hier in der Funktion eines direkten Objekts.

- to agree — zu-, übereinstimmen
- to attempt — versuchen
- can't bear — nicht ausstehen können
- to begin — anfangen, beginnen
- to cease — aufhören
- to continue — weitermachen
- to decide — entscheiden
- to forget — vergessen
- to hope — hoffen
- to intend — beabsichtigen
- to learn — lernen; erfahren
- to manage — führen, leiten
- to mean — meinen; bedeuten
- to neglect — vernachlässigen
- to offer — anbieten
- to pretend — vorgeben, -täuschen
- to promise — versprechen
- to propose — vorschlagen

Infinitiv ohne to

Das Modalverb dare kann den Infinitiv ohne to anschließen, auch wenn es mit to do, will oder would verbunden wird.

- You need not say anything.
- He dare not come.
- He wouldn't dare tell him everything about it.
- You had better tell him the truth.
- I would rather go to the coast tomorrow.

unpersönliche Verben und Ausdrücke

transitive Verben

Der Infinitiv

	Infinitiv + to	Infinitiv ohne to
	<ul><li>to refuse — verweigern</li><li>to remember — erinnern</li><li>to start — anfangen, beginnen</li><li>to try — versuchen</li><li>to wish — wünschen</li></ul>	
	• I promise **to come** as soon as I can. • I'll try **to do** this work as soon as possible.	
Verben des Veranlassens, Zulassens	Im Passiv steht der Infinitiv + to nach den folgenden Verben des Veranlassens.	Im Aktiv steht der Infinitiv ohne to mit vorangehendem Objekt nach den folgenden Verben des Veranlassens. Im Passiv steht der Infinitiv ohne to auch nach to let.
	<ul><li>to bid — bieten</li><li>to make — (veran)lassen</li></ul>	<ul><li>to bid — bieten</li><li>to have — lassen</li><li>to let — (zu)lassen</li><li>to make — (veran)lassen</li></ul>
	• He was made **to tell** the truth. (Er wurde veranlasst die Wahrheit **zu sagen**.) • She was made **to go** immediately. (Sie wurde veranlasst sofort **zu gehen**.)	• He made me **tell** the truth. (Er veranlasste mich, die Wahrheit **zu sagen**.) • They were let **go**. (Man ließ sie **gehen**.) • I had Peter **wash** my car for me. (Ich ließ Peter mein Auto **waschen**.)
	Nach den folgenden Verben des Veranlassens, Zulassens, Befehlens, Bittens steht der (aktive und passive) Infinitiv + to mit vorangestelltem Objekt. Ist das Subjekt des Infinitivs nicht auch Subjekt des gesamten Satzes, so muss dieses Subjekt dem Infinitiv vorangestellt werden.	
	<ul><li>to advise — raten</li><li>to allow — erlauben</li><li>to ask — bitten</li><li>to beg — bitten</li><li>to cause — veranlassen</li><li>to command — befehlen</li><li>to expect — erwarten</li><li>to force — zwingen</li><li>to get — jn. bringen zu</li><li>to induce — jn. bewegen zu</li><li>to lead — veranlassen</li></ul>	

Der Infinitiv

Infinitiv + to

- to order — befehlen
- to permit — erlauben
- to persuade — überreden
- to require — erfordern, verlangen
- to tell — auffordern
- to urge — zwingen
- to warn (not to) — warnen nicht zu tun

- The boys were allowed **to play** in the garden.
- He caused me **to tell** him the truth.
- He induced me **to tell** him everything about it.

Im Passiv steht der Infinitiv + to nach den folgenden Verben der Sinneswahrnehmung.

- to feel — fühlen
- to hear — hören
- to notice — wahrnehmen
- to observe — beobachten
- to see — sehen
- to watch — ansehen

- She was seen **to read** a book.
  (Man sah sie ein Buch lesen.)
- He was heard **to come**.
  (Man hörte ihn kommen.)

Nach den folgenden Verben des Seins oder Scheinens steht der Infinitiv + to.

- to appear — scheinen
- to be — sein
- to remain — bleiben

- The best thing would be **to do** it immediately.
- He seems **to tell** the truth.

Infinitiv + to

Nach den Verben des Sagens und Denkens steht der Infinitiv + to mit vorangehendem Objekt in der Regel nur, wenn der Infinitiv to be oder to have been ist, wobei to be fehlen kann.

Infinitiv ohne to

Im Aktiv steht der Infinitiv ohne to mit vorangehendem Objekt nach den folgenden Verben der Sinneswahrnehmung.

Verben der Sinneswahrnehmung

- to feel — fühlen
- to hear — hören
- to notice — wahrnehmen
- to observe — beobachten
- to see — sehen
- to watch — ansehen

- I saw her **read** a book.
  (Ich sah sie ein Buch lesen.)
- I heard him **come**.
  (Ich hörte ihn kommen.)

Verben des Seins, Scheinens

Nebensatz mit that

Nach den Verben des Sagens und Denkens steht ein Nebensatz mit that meist in der Umgangssprache oder wenn der Infinitiv nicht to be oder to have been ist.

Verben des Sagens, Denkens

Der Infinitiv

	Infinitiv + to	Nebensatz mit that
⚠ Reflexivpronomen, wenn Subjekt und Objekt die gleiche Person bezeichnen	Wenn Subjekt und Objekt dieselbe Person bezeichnen, steht nicht das Personal-, sondern das Reflexivpronomen. - to assume — annehmen - to believe — glauben - to consider — erwägen - to declare — erklären - to find — finden - to guess — annehmen - to imagine — sich vorstellen - to know — wissen, kennen - to prove — beweisen - to recommend — empfehlen - to suppose — vermuten - to think — denken - to understand — verstehen	- to assume — annehmen - to believe — glauben - to consider — erwägen - to declare — erklären - to deny — abstreiten - to find — finden - to guess — annehmen - to imagine — sich vorstellen - to know — wissen, kennen - to prove — beweisen - to recommend — empfehlen - to suppose — vermuten - to think — denken - to understand — verstehen
	- We believe him **to be** an expert. - We believe him **to have been** an expert. - He declared himself **to be** innocent.	- We believe **that he didn't tell the truth.** - He declared **that he has never seen a thing like that.** - I guess **that I will never meet a person like him.**
		Nach den folgenden Verben des Sagens und Denkens steht grundsätzlich ein Nebensatz mit oder ohne that. - to answer — antworten - to hope — hoffen - to reply — antworten - to say — sagen
		- I hope **(that) he will soon arrive.** - She said **(that) she had seen him last week.**
Verben des Wünschens	Nach den folgenden Verben des (Nicht-)Wünschens steht der Infinitiv + to + vorangehendes Objekt. Häufig wird der Infinitiv weggelassen und nur durch die Präposition to repräsentiert. Im Deutschen wird dies häufig durch einen Nebensatz mit *dass* übersetzt.	Nach den folgenden Verben des (Nicht-)Wünschens (außer nach to want) kann auch ein Nebensatz mit that stehen.

Der Infinitiv

Infinitiv + to

- to desire — wünschen
- to hate — nicht mögen, hassen
- to like — mögen
- to love — lieben
- to prefer — bevorzugen
- to want — wünschen, wollen
- to wish — wünschen
- I should hate — ich will nicht haben
- I should like — ich möchte, dass
- I should prefer — ich hätte lieber

Nach to want steht nie ein Nebensatz mit that, sondern immer ein Objekt.

- I want you to go home.
  (Ich möchte, dass du nach Hause gehst.)
- I should prefer you to do that immediately.
  (Ich hätte es lieber, wenn du das sofort machtest/machen würdest.)
- Did you go by bus? I wanted to (go by bus).

Nach den folgenden Verben des persönlichen Empfindens steht der Infinitiv + to zum Ausdruck eines besonderen Einzelfalles, besonders in Verbindung mit would, should und in Konditionalsätzen.

- to fear — fürchten
- to hate — hassen
- to like — mögen
- to love — lieben
- to prefer — bevorzugen
- to think wise — für weise halten
- to think right — für richtig halten

- I like to read books before I fall asleep.
- Would you like to come and see me in my new house?
- She likes to go to the dentist regularly (she thinks it is wise).

Der Infinitiv steht mit to zum Ausdruck der Absicht, des Zwecks. Dies kann durch in order to, so as to verstärkt werden.

Nebensatz mit that

- to desire — wünschen
- to hate — nicht mögen, hassen
- to like — mögen
- to love — lieben
- to prefer — bevorzugen
- to wish — wünschen
- I should hate — ich will nicht haben
- I should like — ich möchte, dass
- I should prefer — ich hätte lieber

- I hate that you are always late.
- I wish that you do your work precisely.
- I should prefer that you do this work immediately.
- Should we go by bus? I prefer that we take the train.

kein Nebensatz nach to want

Verben des persönlichen Empfindens

Absicht, Zweck

Der Infinitiv

Infinitiv + to

- We finished our work as soon as possible (in order) **to**/so as **to leave** early.

too, enough + Adjektiv, Adverb	Nach Konstruktionen wie too, enough + Adjektiv/Adverb steht der Infinitiv + to. Dem Infinitiv geht häufig eine Konstruktion aus for + Substantiv/Pronomen voraus.

- The problem is too difficult (for us) **to solve**.
  (Das Problem ist uns zu schwierig zu lösen.)
- He is honest enough **to tell** the truth.
  (Er ist ehrlich genug, die Wahrheit zu sagen.)

so + Adjektiv, such + Substantiv **so/such + as to**	Nach so + Adjektiv oder such + Substantiv wird der Infinitiv mit as to angeschlossen.

- Will you please be so kind **as to help** me?
  (Wären Sie so freundlich mir zu helfen?)
- This is of such a difficulty **as to make** one think it over again.
  (Dies ist so schwierig, dass man nochmals darüber nachdenken muss.)

anstelle von Relativsätzen	Anstelle von Relativsätzen steht der Infinitiv + to nach Substantiven oder Pronomen. Präpositionen stehen vor allem in der Umgangssprache nach dem Infinitiv, in der Schriftsprache können sie dem Relativpronomen vorangestellt werden.

- Do you have a car **to take** me to the airport?
  (Do you have a car with which you can take me to the airport?)
- Do you have a good book **to study with**?
  (Do you have a good book with which to study?)

Anstelle von Relativsätzen steht der Infinitiv + to nach Zahlwörtern wie the first, the last, the only thing etc.

- Peter was the last **to reach** the winning-post.
  (Peter was the last who reached the winning-post.)

Der Infinitiv

Infinitiv + to

Anstelle von Relativsätzen steht der Infinitiv + to nach Superlativen.

- He was **the best** reader **to represent our group**.
  (He was **the best** reader **who could represent our group**.)

Anstelle von indirekten Fragesätzen steht der Infinitiv + to unmittelbar nach dem Fragewort.
Im Deutschen wird dies durch einen Nebensatz mit *können, sollen* oder *müssen* ausgedrückt.
Solche Infinitivkonstruktionen stehen besonders nach den folgenden Verben.

- to fear — fürchten
- to ask — fragen
- to decide — entscheiden
- to explain — erklären
- to forget — vergessen
- to know — wissen, kennen
- to learn — lernen; erfahren
- to remember — erinnern
- to see — sehen
- to show — zeigen
- to tell — erzählen
- to wonder — sich fragen

- Peter asked me what **to do**.
  (Peter asked me **what he should do**.)
- Mary wondered how **to get** to school on Monday.
  (Mary wondered **how she should get to school on Monday**.)

anstelle von indirekten Fragesätzen

Der Infinitiv

Übungen zum Infinitiv

1. Setzen Sie to ein wo nötig.

1. Little children were made ... work in factories for twelve hours or more every day.

2. Dr Davies made Billy ... open his mouth wide.

3. Let ... come what may.

4. You had better ... begin by reading this article.

5. On the way back he heard the telephone ... ring.

6. He saw her ... throw the letter into the waste-paper basket.

7. Bob watched Simon ... help Carol into the boat.

8. He did not know what had made him ... pour out this stream of rubbish.

9. That wonderful opportunity was let ... slip.

10. We had better ... get started.

11. I was amazed to hear him ... tell her a lie.

12. They were told ... come.

13. What did you see him ... do after that.

14. For the first time since he had known Ben, Philip could feel him ... hesitate.

15. The more you try to make him ... do something, the more determined he is not ... do it.

richtig   falsch

2. Ersetzen Sie die folgenden Sätze durch eine Infinitivkonstruktion.

1. The suitcase is too heavy. I can't carry it.

2. The coffee is too hot. I can't drink it.

3. He was quick. He followed their advice.

4. I think you were right. You told us.

Der Infinitiv

5. You are very kind. You don't tell him.

6. She was naughty. She pulled the kitten's tail.

7. We can't miss the opportunity. It is too favourable.

8. He will succeed. It is sure.

9. He racked his brain. He wanted to say something sensible.

10. The text is too difficult. I can't understand it.

richtig   falsch

3. Ersetzen Sie die blau gedruckten Nebensätze durch eine Infinitivkonstruktion.

1. You should say something. I want ...

2. Would you prefer that I help you?

3. Peter says that you should go home now. Peter wants ...

4. You must leave in the morning. He wanted ...

5. The unemployment rate was over 12.5 % this spring. We hope that we will reduce it to 11 % in the autumn.

6. People think that Mr Templeton has been a very cautious man all his life.

7. I should hate that you have to ask him a favour.

8. It is said that the natives of these islands are cannibals. (passive voice)

9. We believed that she has lied. (passive voice)

10. She bought a small camera with which she wanted to take pictures.

11. He hasn't got a chair on which he can sit.

12. There's a table on which you can write.

13. This is a depressing message that I must send to you and I regret it.

14. Mrs Miller was the first who discovered the broken window.

15. Peter was the next who arrived at the bottom of the hill.

Der Infinitiv

16. Peter was the only one **who returned to the hotel.**

17. It was the best thing **that we could do.**

18. She didn't really mind having no friends **with whom she could play.**

19. He is not an easy man **with whom you can get along.**

20. I have nine TV channels **from which I can choose,** but I usually watch sport.

21. The millionth guestworker **who entered the country** was given an honorary welcome in front of the press.

22. To the American, whose country is so huge, a few hundred miles are no impediment **of which he would** speak.

23. Without TV people would not know **what they should do in their spare time.**

richtig   falsch

4. Setzen Sie die Verben in Klammern in den present infinitive passive.

1. This parcel is **(handle)** carefully.

2. The news had **(keep)** secret.

3. Even Julia seemed **(impress).**

4. The opinions seem **(divide).**

5. I want **(trust).**

6. There was no fire **(see),** only clouds of smoke.

7. It is too urgent **(put off).**

8. His age has **(to take account of).**

9. It is **(doubt)** if she will ever make it.

10. She was very much what has come **(call)** a personality.

richtig   falsch

5. Setzen Sie den present infinitive active oder present infinitive passive ein.

1. He was busy and didn't want **(disturb).**

Der Infinitiv

2. I propose (have) a conversation with you this evening.

3. He didn't seem (notice) the difference.

4. The chief carpenter called his apprentice and ordered him (make) a bed.

5. The paper is (find) in the first drawer to the right.

6. The plants have (water), or they won't grow.

7. We'd love your friends (come).

8. Do I have (blame) for that?

9. English drivers never seem (get) excited or lose their tempers.

10. He caused the engine (go) slower, so that he could stop at any time.

                                                                                        richtig   falsch

6. Setzen Sie die Verben in Klammern in den perfect infinitive active.

1. It seems (get) colder.

2. They ought (know).

3. He is thought (leave) the house at 7 p.m.

4. They are supposed (lose) their way.

5. (Make) the same mistake twice was unforgivable.

6. She appeared not (see) him.

7. The introduction of the health service seems (do) much to improve the condition of people's teeth in general.

8. I knew Mrs Miller had said hello to me, but I pretended not (hear).

9. What effect is that likely (have) on him?

10. I am pleased (survive) the crash.

                                                                                        richtig   falsch

7. Setzen Sie die Verben in Klammern in den perfect infinitive passive.

1. For a moment he seemed (deprive) of the power of speech.

Der Infinitiv

2. Nothing seems (disarrange).

3. (Educate) at one of the private universities of high prestige is a great advantage in the pursuit of a good job.

4. Oxford's first college claims (found) in 1249.

5. (Visit) by the queen was something special.

                                                                             richtig   falsch

8. Setzen Sie die Verben in Klammern in den present und perfect infinitive active und übersetzen Sie jeden Satz.

1. I regret (displease) you, sir.

2. The sun seemed (grow) hotter.

3. I am sorry (keep) you waiting.

4. We seem (lose) something.

5. She ought not (say) that.

6. I should like (see) it.

7. We ought (trust) him.

8. I pretended not (understand) her.

9. They seem (do) that job pretty well.

10. The parents are glad (have) their child back home safe.

                                                      richtig   falsch

Die entsprechenden Lösungen befinden sich auf Seite 432ff.

Das Gerund

Das gerund ist eine (infinite) Verbform, die durch Anhängen der Endung *-ing* an den Verbstamm gebildet wird. Eine entsprechende Verbform gibt es im Deutschen nicht, das gerund wird im Deutschen in der Regel mit dem Infinitiv mit und ohne *zu* ausgedrückt.
Das gerund ist nicht zu verwechseln mit der continuous form.

nicht zu verwechseln mit der continuous form

Das Present Gerund

Das present gerund steht zum Ausdruck der Gleichzeitigkeit bzw. Vorzeitigkeit, d. h. die Handlung des Nebensatzes findet gleichzeitig mit bzw. vor der Handlung des Hauptsatzes statt.	I don't allow smoking here. (Ich erlaube nicht, dass hier geraucht wird.) (Das Erlauben und Rauchen findet gleichzeitig statt.) He was accused of deserting the ship. (Er wurde beschuldigt, das Schiff im Stich gelassen zu haben.) (Das im Stich lassen findet zuerst statt.)	Gleichzeitigkeit, Vorzeitigkeit
Das present gerund active steht im Aktivsatz (der Handelnde wird genannt), aber auch im Passivsatz (der Handelnde wird nicht genannt), nach to need, to require, to want.	I like going for a walk in the early morning. (*I* ist der Ausführende der Handlung.) The motor needs oiling. (Wer den Motor ölt wird nicht mitgeteilt)	im Aktivsatz, im Passivsatz
Das present gerund passive steht im Passivsatz (der Handelnde wird nicht genannt) und zwar besonders nach to need, to require, to want.	Do you mind being taken to hospital? (Wer die Person ins Krankenhaus bringt wird nicht mitgeteilt.)	im Passivsatz

Das Perfect Gerund

Das perfect gerund steht zum Ausdruck der Vorzeitigkei, d. h. die Handlung des Nebensatzes findet vor der des Hauptsatzes statt. Statt des perfect gerund wird in der modernen Sprache immer mehr das present gerund verwendet.	He was accused of having deserted the ship. (Er wurde beschuldigt, das Schiff im Stich gelassen zu haben.) (Das im Stichlassen findet zuerst statt.)	Vorzeitigkeit
Das perfect gerund active steht im Aktivsatz (der Handelnde wird genannt) und besonders nach to deny.	He is afraid of having failed the exam. (*He* ist der Ausführende der Handlung.)	im Aktivsatz
Das perfect gerund passive steht im Passivsatz (der Handelnde wird nicht genannt).	He came in without having been seen. (Er kam herein ohne gesehen worden zu sein.) (Wer ihn hätte sehen können wird nicht mitgeteilt.)	im Passivsatz

Das Gerund

Das gerund kann Substantiv oder Subjekt sein, es steht nach bestimmten Verben, und es ist ein wichtiges Stilmittel zur Verkürzung von Nebensätzen.

Das Gerund als, beim Substantiv

als Substantiv

Das gerund wird zum Substantiv, wenn ihm der Artikel vorangestellt wird. Es kann als solches den Plural bilden, durch Adjektive näher bestimmt werden, eine Beifügung + of bei sich haben oder zusammengesetzte Substantive bilden. Viele gerunds sind längst echte Substantive geworden. In dieser Funktion heißt das gerund auch Verbalsubstantiv.

- The **beginning** is always difficult.
- My **feelings** on this case have remained unchanged.
- What do you think: is mobility a **blessing** or a curse?
- The Empire State Building is one of the highest **buildings** in the world.
- The **learning** of languages is great fun.
- Have you seen my **walking-stick**?

- being — Wesen
- beginning — Anfang
- blessing — Segen
- crossing — Kreuzung, Überweg
- dining-room — Esszimmer
- drinking-water — Trinkwasser
- driving-licence — Führerschein
- ending — Endung
- feeling — Gefühl
- gathering — Versammlung
- living-room — Wohnzimmer
- meaning — Bedeutung

- meeting — Zusammenkunft
- misunderstanding — Missverständnis
- painting — Gemälde
- sailing-boat — Segelschiff
- savings — Ersparnisse
- saying — Sprichwort
- sewing-machine — Nähmaschine
- sitting-room — Wohnzimmer
- suffering — Leiden
- waiting-room — Wartezimmer
- walking-stick — Spazierstock

als Subjekt

Das gerund kann als Subjekt stehen und zwar besonders nach den folgenden Ausdrücken:

- **Learning** languages is great fun.
- It is no good **complaining** about the same mistake again and again.

- it is no good — es nützt nichts
- it is not much good — es nützt nicht viel
- it is (no) use — es nützt (nichts)

- it is useless — es ist nutzlos
- it is (not) worthwhile — es lohnt sich (nicht)
- there is no ... — es gibt nicht ...

in Sprichwörtern

Das gerund steht in kurzen Sprichwörtern und Verboten, die sich nicht an eine bestimmte Person richten.

- No **smoking**.
  (**Rauchen** verboten)
- No **loitering**.
- **Seeing** is **believing**.

Subjekt des gerunds

Bezeichnet das gerund eine andere Person als das Subjekt des Hauptsatzes, so muss diese dem gerund als attributives Possessiv-, Personalpronomen oder Substantiv im possessive case voranstehen. In der Umgangssprache steht statt des possessive case meist der common case.

- He insisted on **doing** it himself.
- He insisted on your **doing** it yourself.
- Do you mind my **smoking**?
- Do you mind me **smoking**?
- Do you mind my brother's **smoking**?
- Do you mind my brother **smoking**?

Das Gerund

Das gerund steht nach Substantiven, die eng mit einer Präposition verbunden sind. Als Präpositionen gelten auch like, near, past, far from.

- There is no chance of escaping.
- He has a lot of experience in cooking.
- Mary takes great interest in learning languages.

Substantive + Präposition

chance of	Chance zu
danger of	Gefahr von
difficulty in	Schwierigkeit mit
experience in	Erfahrung mit
for fear of	aus Angst vor
to be in the habit of	die Gewohnheit haben zu
hope of	Hoffnung auf
intention of	Absicht zu
interest in	Interesse an
necessity of	Notwendigkeit zu
objection to	Einwand gegen
opportunity of	Gelegenheit zu
pleasure in/of	Vergnügen an
to be on the point of	dabei sein zu
prospect of	Aussicht auf
reason for	Grund für
way of	Art, Weise zu

Das Gerund beim Verb

Das gerund steht nach to be, besonders nach to be busy, to be like, to be near und to be worth als prädikative Ergänzung.

- My favourite occupation is sitting at the window and observing the birds.
- Peter and Mary are busy preparing their wedding next month.

to be

Das gerund steht nach den folgenden transitiven Verben. Das gerund ist dann direktes Objekt.
Die Verben mit * können auch mit Infinitiv stehen.

- How can I prevent you from making this mistake again?
- I couldn't help calling him a liar.

transitive Verben

to anticipate	vorausahnen
to attempt *	versuchen
to avoid	vermeiden
cannot avoid	nicht umhin können
to begin *	beginnen, anfangen
to cease *	aufhören
to continue *	weitermachen
to defer	aufschieben
to delay	verzögern
to endure	aushalten
to escape	flüchten, entkommen
to excuse	entschuldigen
to finish	beenden
to forgive	vergeben
cannot help	nicht umhin können
to involve	einbeziehen
to miss	vermissen
to pardon	verzeihen
to postpone	verschieben
to practise	ausüben
to prevent	verhindern
to put off	verschieben
to recollect	erinnern
to resist	widerstehen
to risk	riskieren
to save	retten
to start *	beginnen

Das gerund kann nach den folgenden Verben des Sagens und Denkens stehen.
Die mit * versehenen Verben können auch einen Nebensatz mit that anschließen.

- He would never admit having a secret bank account.
- Can you imagine his brother having stolen the car?
- Can you imagine that his brother stole the car?

Verben des Sagens und Denkens

to admit *	eingstehen, zugeben
to appreciate *	(hoch)schätzen
to consider *	erwägen
to contemplate	überdenken, erwägen
to deny *	abstreiten
to fancy	sich vorstellen

Das Gerund

- to imagine * sich vorstellen
- to mention * erwähnen
- to neglect vernachlässigen

- to propose * vorschlagen
- to suggest * vorschlagen
- to understand * verstehen

Verben des persönlichen Empfindens

Nach den Verben des persönlichen Empfindens drückt das gerund etwas allgemein Gültiges, Gewohnheitsmäßiges aus.
Es steht besonders, wenn to like, to love, to hate und to prefer im present oder past tense stehen.
Verben mit * können auch mit dem Infinitiv stehen.

- She fears not having passed the examination.
- I hated getting up early in the morning.

- to appreciate (hoch)schätzen
- cannot bear nicht aushalten können
- to detest verabscheuen
- to dislike nicht mögen
- to dread * (sich) fürchten
- to enjoy genießen
- to fear * fürchten
- to feel like Lust haben

- to hate * hassen
- to like * mögen
- to love * lieben
- to mind Acht geben; beachten
- to prefer * bevorzugen
- to regret * bereuen
- to resent verabscheuen
- cannot stand nicht aushalten können

to mind

To mind steht vor allem in fragenden und verneinten Sätzen und zum Ausdruck, dass ein Vorgang schon begonnen hat.

- Do you mind my smoking in your room?
- I don't mind living in the country.

Verben des Erlaubens, Empfehlens

Nach den Verben des Erlaubens, Empfehlens steht das gerund vor allem dann, wenn die betreffende Person nicht erwähnt wird.
Die Verben mit * können auch mit dem Infinitiv stehen.

- I don't allow smoking in my room.
- U.S. Customs does not permit bringing meat products into the country.

- to advise * raten
- to allow * erlauben

- to permit * gestatten, erlauben
- to recommend * empfehlen

Verben der Gewohnheit

Das gerund steht nach to be used to zum Ausdruck der Gewohnheit.

- I was always used to taking a walk in the evening.

Verben mit Präposition

Das gerund steht nach den Verben, die eng mit einer Präposition verbunden sind. Als Präpositionen gelten auch like, near, past und far from.

- He was accused of having murdered his mother.
- He was accustomed to getting up before 6 o'clock in the morning.

- to accuse of anklagen wegen
- to be accustomed to gewöhnt sein an
- to apologize for sich entschuldigen für
- to be against/for gegen/für etw. sein
- to believe in glauben an
- to burst out herausplatzen
- to care for sorgen für
- to complain of sich beklagen über

- to delight in Freude haben an
- to depend on abhängen von
- to despair of verzweifeln an
- to excuse for sich entschuldigen für
- to give up aufgeben
- to go on weitermachen
- to insist on bestehen auf
- to keep from abhalten von

Das Gerund

to keep on	weitermachen	to see about	sich kümmern um
to leave off	auslassen	to speak about/of	sprechen über/von
to look forward to	sich freuen auf	to succeed in	gelingen
to object to	einwenden gegen	to talk about/of	sprechen über/von
to prevent from	abhalten von	to thank for	danken für
to pride o.s. on	sich rühmen wegen	to worry about	sich sorgen wegen
to put off	verschieben	to think of/about	denken an
to quarrel about	streiten über	to be used to	gewöhnt sein an
to rely on	verlassen auf		

Das Gerund beim Adjektiv

Das gerund steht nach Adjektiven, die eng mit einer Präposition verbunden sind. Als Präpositionen gelten auch like, near, past und far from.

- He is afraid of not having passed the exam.
- He is angry at your being so late.

Adjektive mit Präposition

absorbed in	vertieft, -sunken in	glad of/about	froh über
accustomed to	gewöhnt an	happy about	glücklich über
afraid of	ängtlich wegen	incapable of	unfähig zu
angry at	ärgerlich auf	interested in	interessiert an
annoyed at/about	verärgert über	keen on	begierig auf
capable of	fähig zu	proud of	stolz auf
engaged in	beschäftigt mit	responsible for	verantwortlich für
far from	entfernt von	sad about	traurig über
fond of	gerne tun	tired of	satt haben
free from	frei von	used to	gewöhnt an

Das gerund steh nach how about, what about (wie wäre es, wie steht's mit).

- How about going for a walk?
- What about reading a book?

how about, what about

Das Gerund anstelle von Nebensätzen

Anstelle von temporalen Nebensätzen steht das gerund nach temporalen Konjunktionen, vor allem nach after, before, on und since. Nach after kann auch das perfect gerund stehen, jedoch wird das present gerund immer mehr bevorzugt. Temporale Nebensätze geben die Zeit an.

- After spending some days in London, we went to Scotland.
- After having spent some days in London, we went to Scotland.
- You must do your homework before leaving.

temporale Nebensätze

Anstelle von kausalen Nebensätzen steht das gerund nach kausalen Konjunktionen, vor allem nach for, from, at.
Kausale Nebensätze geben den Grund, die Ursache an.

- He got a headache from lying too long in bed.
  (He got a headache because he lay too long in bed.)
- He was sentenced to death for having killed his wife.

kausale Nebensätze

Das Gerund

konzessive Nebensätze	Anstelle von konzessiven Nebensätzen steht das gerund nach konzessiven Konjunktionen, vor allem nach apart from, despite, in spite of. Konzessive Nebensätze drücken die Einräumung aus.	• In spite of **working** day and night, he couldn't pay back his debts. (**Although he worked day and** ...) • In spite of Peter **having done** everything for her, she abandoned him. • Apart from **being convicted** to a fine of $ 10,000, he got off lightly.
konditionale Nebensätze	Anstelle von konditionalen Nebensätzen steht das gerund nach konditionalen Konjunktionen, vor allem nach in the event of. Konditionale Nebensätze drücken eine Bedingung aus.	• In the event of not **passing** the exam, you will have to repeat the whole term. (**If you don't pass the exam**, you ...) • In the event of **losing** your wallet, you should call the police.
modale Nebensätze	Anstelle von modalen Nebensätzen steht das gerund nach modalen Konjunktionen, vor allem nach without, with, in, instead of. Modale Nebensätze drücken die Art und Weise, das Mittel aus.	• He passed the exam without **having learnt** anything. (**Although he hadn't learnt anything**, he passed the exam.)

Das Gerund

Übungen zum Gerund

1. Setzen Sie die Verben in Klammern ins gerund.

1. She hasn't finished (do) her exercise yet.
2. I can't help (laugh).
3. My father doesn't mind (wash up) on Sundays.
4. My sister enjoys (travel) by train, but some people may prefer (fly).
5. He suggested (go).
6. It seemed impossible that he could avoid (be) discovered.
7. Don't keep (ask) me.
8. We are looking forward to (see) you.
9. I could have died (laugh).
10. Sorry I've kept you (wait).
11. Keep on (try).
12. She insisted on (get) my address.
13. It gave me an opportunity of (settle) the affair.
14. Rockets are the only known motors that are capable of (propel) a vehicle in empty space.
15. She succeeded in (convince) him.

richtig   falsch

2. Ersetzen Sie die blau gedruckten Sätze durch das gerund.

1. After they had defeated the Norwegians at Stamford Bridge, King Harold and his tired men marched south.
2. We asked a solicitor for advice before we went to court.
3. She taught the class although she was feeling bad.
4. She had a headache because she was sitting in the sun.
5. Although he had a cold, the swimmer succeeded in crossing the channel.

Das Gerund

6. Although I trust you, I must make some inquiries.

7. He was sent to prison because he stole.

8. The boy was reprimanded because he was disobedient.

9. If you were any good, you'd help me and you would not stand there criticising.

10. They quarrelled, left each other and didn't make friends again.

                                                                                                                  richtig   falsch

3. Ersetzen Sie die Verben in Klammern durch das gerund oder den infinitive.

1. She sat down and began (knit) a jacket for Mike.

2. Have you started (learn) to drive yet?

3. I hate (interfere) in other people's affairs.

4. The tramp said he didn't like (work).

5. I think I prefer (stay) outside.

6. Simon proposed (leave) before the show was over.

7. You must remember (post) the letter.

8. Bob remembered (go) to a cocktail party with Simon Atkinson.

9. I don't know what you want me (say).

10. I couldn't help (cry) when I heard the news.

11. He took his shoes off so he could put his feet up on the sofa, lay back on a pillow, and continued (read) Bob's letter.

12. A growing number of people prefer (watch) sporting events on TV to (attend) them.

13. All the petunias want (water), very badly.

14. When they saw that Mary did not like the questions, they at once stopped (ask).

15. It's no use (object) to his taking risks.

                                                                                                                  richtig   falsch

Das Gerund

4. Setzen Sie die Verben in Klammern ins gerund und die Personalpronomen in den object case oder verwenden Sie das entsprechende Possessivpronomen.

1. I strongly resent (you, come) late.
2. My sister Caroline hates (I, eat) with dirty fingers.
3. That shouldn't prevent (you, go).
4. Forgive (I, leave) you alone.
5. I rely on (you, return) the book soon.
6. She taught the class in spite of (her mother, be) ill.
7. How do you think I can do Latin with (you, interrupt) me every few seconds?
8. Mary can't remember (he, post) the letter.
9. I won't have (you, smoke) at your age.
10. Will the new job involve (you, be) away.

richtig   falsch

5. Setzen Sie die Verben in Klammern ins present gerund passive.

1. He said nothing for fear of (misunderstand).
2. I came as near to them as I could without (see).
3. She hates (stare at).
4. Adults rightly resent (treat) as children.
5. It seemed impossible that he could avoid (discover).
6. After (welcome) by Mr Smith, they were shown round the building.
7. After (capture), escaping and finally (recapture), Charles I was executed in London on 30 January, 1649.
8. If there was any sensation he hated, it was that of (follow).
9. He is faced with the danger of his secret (know).
10. Nobody likes (laugh at).

richtig   falsch

Das Gerund

6. Ersetzen Sie die Verben in Klammern durch das present gerund active oder das present gerund passive.

1. He avoided (answer) directly.

2. Mary and Bob burst out (laugh).

3. On a rainy day he couldn't go (swim). So he went to the museum.

4. He was not a man who would forgive (deceive).

5. He bit hungrily into his bread and swallowed a couple of mouthfuls, then continued (speak).

6. He may have an opportunity of (appoint) a Queen's Counsel.

7. He passed by with studied indifference, his face averted, eyes fixed straight ahead, as though to avoid (see) her.

8. Not (bind) to the direction of time - as so other media are - the printed book is still the most valuable medium for learning.

9. There is virtually no erosion on the moon and footprints can last for 500,000 years before (erase) by the invisible rain of micrometeorites.

10. There was a table under the window where Bob and Mary could talk without fear of (overhear).

richtig   falsch

7. Setzen Sie die Verben in Klammern ins perfect gerund active.

1. At least you have the satisfaction of (do) your duty.

2. She denied (eat) it.

3. We remember (leave) the book on the table.

4. He got an award for (save) the boy's life.

5. He remembered (see) the man the evening before.

6. Does he regret (study) so hard?

7. I told him not to mind about (fail).

8. Of course he could not pay at once, (give up) all his money.

9. (Appoint) a Prime Minister the Queen appoints other ministers and public servants on his advice.

Das Gerund

10. I am 40 years old, in perfect health, never **(know)** a day's illness.

richtig   falsch

8. Setzen Sie die Verben in Klammern ins **perfect gerund passive**.

1. Both President Ford and Vice-President Rockefeller held office without **(elect),** but appointed through consultation.

2. After **(recognize),** he could not go and sit at a table with an unattended girl.

3. His sister, conscious of **(rob)** of something, had set up a feeble wail.

4. After **(sentence)** to death for his crimes Cunningham was taken to a small single room with a fireplace and a barred window.

richtig   falsch

9. Setzen Sie die Verben in Klammern ins **present gerund active** oder ins **perfect gerund active**.

1. I regret **(trouble)** you, Sir.

2. Please return the enclosed letter after **(read)** it.

3. He remembered **(see)** the man.

4. After not **(find)** this book he left the shop without buying anything.

5. After **(reach)** the River Thames, Roger joined a gang of smugglers.

6. After **(try)** to get a job in a restaurant without success, he wanted to find a job in an office.

7. When questioned about the disappearance of a bicycle from the school cycle sheds, the boy flatly denied **(have)** anything to do with it.

8. Finding the evening extremely dull, Mr Burton cursed himself for **(accept)** the invitation.

9. I avoided **(speak to)** her, as she isn't a nice person.

10. He continued **(send)** me roses but I did not react to this.

richtig   falsch

Die entsprechenden Lösungen befinden sich auf Seite 434ff.

Die Partizipien

Die Partizipien (The Participles)

Die Partizipien sind (infinite) Verbformen. Sie können nach bestimmten Verben, in der Funktion eines Adjektivs und anstelle von Nebensätzen stehen.

Das Present Participle

continuous form — Das present participle dient zur Bildung der continuous form. Es kann nach bestimmten Verben, in der Funktion eines Adjektivs und anstelle von Nebensätzen stehen.

- I am writing.
- He sat there listening to the noises coming from the other room.
- London's surrounding country is beautiful.
- While doing his homework, he heard the telephone ring.

im Aktivsatz, im Passivsatz — Das present participle active steht im Aktivsatz, d. h. der Handelnde wird genannt.

- I saw them whispering to each other.
  (Ich sah sie miteinander flüstern.)
  (I ist der Ausführende der Handlung.)

im Passivsatz — Der present participle passive steht im Passivsatz. d. h. der Handelnde wird nicht genannt.

- Her friend being hurt, she began to cry.
  (Da ihr Freund verletzt war, begann sie zu weinen.)
  (Wer den Freund verletzt hat, wird nicht mitgeteilt.)

Das Past Participle

zusammengesetzte Zeiten, Passiv — Das past participle dient zur Bildung der zusammengesetzten Zeiten und des Passivs. Es kann nach bestimmten Verben, in der Funktion eines Adjektivs und anstelle von Nebensätzen stehen.

- I have read a book.
- We were invited to his party.
- He lay discouraged on his bed and cried.
- He is a highly respected citizen.
- If begun at once, the work will be finished by this evening.

Das Perfect Participle

anstelle von Nebensätzen — Das perfect participle steht anstelle von Nebensätzen.

- (After) having closed off the site of the accident, she called the police.
- (After) having started up the computer, he saw the $-sign appear.

im Aktivsatz, im Passivsatz — Der perfect participle active steht im Aktivsatz, d. h. der Handelnde wird genannt.

- Having prepared everything, he left the house.
  (Nachdem er alles vorbereitet hatte, verließ er das Haus.)
  (He ist der Ausführende der Handlung.)

Die Partizipien

Der perfect participle passive steht im Passivsatz. d. h. der Handelnde wird nicht genannt.

- **Having been bitten** twice, the postman refused to come into our house.
(*Da* der Briefträger zweimal *gebissen worden war*, weigerte er sich in unser Haus zu kommen.)
(*Wer den Briefträger gebissen hat, wird nicht mitgeteilt.*)

Das Subjekt des Partizips

Bezeichnet das Subjekt des Partizips eine andere Person als das Subjekt des Hauptsatzes, so muss dieses dem Partizip vorangestellt werden (unverbundenes Partizip).
Bezeichnet das Subjekt des Partizips und das Subjekt des Hauptsatzes dieselbe Person, steht das Partizip alleine (verbundenes Partizip).

- Her friend **being hurt**, she began to cry.
(*Da* ihr Freund *verletzt war*, begann *sie* zu weinen.)
- **Being hurt**, she began to cry.
(*Da* sie *verletzt war*, begann *sie* zu weinen.)
- **Arriving** at the station, she saw that the train was gone.
Nicht:
Arriving at the station, the train was gone.

unterschiedliche Subjekte in Haupt- und Nebensatz müssen genannt werden

Die Partizipien

	Present Participle	Past Participle
Verben der Ruhe	Als prädikative Ergänzung zum Subjekt nach den folgenden Verben der Ruhe. ▪ to lie — liegen ▪ to remain — bleiben ▪ to sit — sitzen ▪ to stand — stehen • He sat there listening to the noises coming from the other room.	Als prädikative Ergänzung zum Subjekt nach den folgenden Verben der Ruhe. ▪ to lie — liegen ▪ to remain — bleiben ▪ to sit — sitzen ▪ to stand — stehen • He lay discouraged on his bed and cried.
Verben der Bewegung	Als prädikative Ergänzung zum Subjekt, nach den Verben der Bewegung. • He came running down the street.	
Verben der Sinneswahrnehmung	Nach den Verben der Sinneswahrnehmung steht es in aktivem Sinn als prädikative Ergänzung zum Objekt. Das present participle steht des Weiteren nach den folgenden Verben, wenn sie im Passiv stehen. ▪ to find — finden ▪ to hear — hören ▪ to notice — wahrnehmen ▪ to observe — beobachten ▪ to see — sehen • I saw them whispering to each other. • I heard her crying in her room. • He was heard singing softly to himself.	Nach den Verben der Sinneswahrnehmung steht es in aktivem und passivem Sinn als prädikative Ergänzung zum Objekt. • I heard a song sung by Mary. • He found the vase smashed to pieces. • The vase was found smashed to pieces.
Verben des Scheinens, Seins	Als prädikative Ergänzung zum Subjekt, steht es nach den folgenden Verben des Seins und Scheinens.	Als prädikative Ergänzung zum Subjekt, steht es nach den folgenden Verben des Seins und Scheinens.

Die Partizipien

Present Participle	Past Participle	
• to appear scheinen • to be sein • to feel fühlen • to look aussehen • to seem scheinen • to sound klingen	• to appear scheinen • to be sein • to feel fühlen • to look aussehen • to seem scheinen • to sound klingen	
To be + present participle bilden die continuous form.	To be + past participle bilden das Passiv.	
• This looks very discouraging. • He was reading in his room. (continuous form)	• He looked surprised. • I was invited to his party. (Passiv)	
Nach den Verben des Veranlassens, ist es prädikative Ergänzung zum Objekt.	Nach den Verben des Veranlassens, besonders nach to have und to get. Es ist prädikative Ergänzung zum Objekt.	Verben des Veranlassens
• I sent them shopping for groceries. • He kept me waiting for more than an hour. • They left me standing in the cold. • We have a bottle of champagne chilling in the refrigerator.	• He leaves nothing undone. • I got my car repaired. (Ich habe mein Auto reparieren lassen.) • I had my hair cut. (Ich habe mir die Haare schneiden lassen.) Beachte: • I had cut my hair. (Ich hatte die Haare geschnitten.)	have + Objekt + past participle heißt *etwas machen lassen*
In der Funktion eines Adjektivs steht es zur näheren Bestimmung eines Substantivs. Es kann als solches substantiviert und gesteigert werden und Adverbien bilden.	In der Funktion eines Adjektivs steht es zur näheren Bestimmung eines Substantivs. Es kann als solches substantiviert und gesteigert werden und Adverbien bilden.	als Adjektiv
• London's surrounding country is beautiful. • His behaviour was even more surprising than his remarks. • His looks were surprisingly elegant.	• He is a highly respected citizen of our town. • The outcast live in a ghetto on the outskirts of town. • She seemed interested in the history of Europe.	

Die Partizipien

	Present Participle	Past Participle	Perfect Participle
temporale Nebensätze	Anstelle eines temporalen Nebensatzes, gegebenenfalls mit einer temporalen Konjunktion (while, when etc.). Temporale Nebensätze geben die Zeit an. Das present participle steht, wenn ausgedrückt werden soll, dass zwei Vorgänge gleichzeitig stattfinden.	Anstelle eines temporalen Nebensatzes, gegebenenfalls mit einer temporalen Konjunktion (while, when etc.). Temporale Nebensätze geben die Zeit an.	Anstelle eines temporalen Nebensatzes, gegebenenfalls mit einer temporalen Konjunktion (while, when etc.). Temporale Nebensätze geben die Zeit an. Das perfect participle drückt aus, dass ein Vorgang vor einem anderen stattfindet.
	■ While doing his homework, he heard the telephone ring. (While he was doing his homework, he heard the telephone ring.)	■ When finished, this article will appear in «The Times». (When this article is finished, ...)	■ (After) having started up the computer, he saw the $-sign appear on the screen. (After he had started up the ...)
kausale Nebensätze	Anstelle eines kausalen Nebensatzes, gegebenenfalls mit einer kausalen Konjunktion (as, for etc.). Kausale Nebensätze geben den Grund, die Ursache an.	Anstelle eines kausalen Nebensatzes, gegebenenfalls mit einer kausalen Konjunktion (as, for etc.). Kausale Nebensätze geben den Grund, die Ursache an.	Anstelle eines kausalen Nebensatzes, gegebenenfalls mit einer kausalen Konjunktion (as, for etc.). Kausale Nebensätze geben den Grund, die Ursache an.
	■ Having an old car, he took longer to get there. (As he had an old car ...)	■ Prepared for the worst, I was relieved when the plane landed safely. (Since I was prepared for the worst, ...)	■ Having had experience with cars, he was able to help us. (Since he had had experience with ...)
konzessive Nebensätze	Anstelle eines konzessiven Nebensatzes, gegebenenfalls mit einer konzessiven Konjunktion (although, even if etc.). Konzessive Nebensätze drücken die Einräumung, das Zugeständnis aus.	Anstelle eines konzessiven Nebensatzes, gegebenenfalls mit einer konzessiven Konjunktion (although, even if etc.). Konzessive Nebensätze drücken die Einräumung, das Zugeständnis aus.	Anstelle eines konzessiven Nebensatzes, gegebenenfalls mit einer konzessiven Konjunktion (although, even if etc.). Konzessive Nebensätze drücken die Einräumung, das Zugeständnis aus.
	■ Though hoping for a window seat, I was prepared to sit on the aisle. (Although I hoped for a window seat, ...)	■ Though seated near the window, he could not see the road. (Although he was seated near the window, ...)	■ Despite having driven all day, we weren't very tired. (Despite the fact that we had driven all day, ...)

Die Partizipien

	Present Participle	Past Participle	Perfect Participle	
	Anstelle eines konditionalen Nebensatzes, gegebenenfalls mit einer konditionalen Konjunktion (if (not) unless). Konditionale Nebensätze drücken die Bedingung aus.	Anstelle eines konditionalen Nebensatzes, gegebenenfalls mit einer konditionalen Konjunktion (if (not) unless). Konditionale Nebensätze drücken die Bedingung aus.	Anstelle eines konditionalen Nebensatzes, gegebenenfalls mit einer konditionalen Konjunktion (if (not) unless). Konditionale Nebensätze drücken die Bedingung aus.	konditionale Nebensätze
	• If **travelling** to the tropics, one should get a malaria shot. **(If one is travelling to the tropics, ...)**	• If **begun** at once, the work will be finished by this evening. **(If you begin at once ...)**	• If **having** your car **repaired,** be sure to get an estimate. **(If you are having your car repaired, ...)**	
	Anstelle eines modalen Nebensatzes, gegebenenfalls mit einer modalen Konjunktion (for, with, without). Nach with steht das Objekt vor dem Partizip. Modale Nebensätze geben die Art und Weise, das Mittel an.	Anstelle eines modalen Nebensatzes, gegebenenfalls mit einer modalen Konjunktion (for, with, without). Nach with steht das Objekt vor dem Partizip. Modale Nebensätze geben die Art und Weise, das Mittel an.	Anstelle eines modalen Nebensatzes, gegebenenfalls mit einer modalen Konjunktion (for, with, without). Nach with steht das Objekt vor dem Partizip. Modale Nebensätze geben die Art und Weise, das Mittel an.	modale Nebensätze
	• With their hands **clapping,** they stood at the gate and cheered the musicians.	• They stood there with their eyes and mouths widely **opened.**	• Without **having eaten** all day, we were looking forward to dinner.	
	Anstelle von Relativsätzen, vor allem nach Substantiven, Pronomen, Zahlwörtern (the first etc.), Superlativen. Beim present participle passive kann being entfallen.			Relativsätze
	• The person **coming up** the street is my father. (The person **who is coming up** the street is my father.) • He was the only musician **(being) invited** to this wedding.			

Die Partizipien

Übungen zu den Partizipien

1. Setzen Sie die Verben in Klammern ins present participle.

1. I heard her (whistle).

2. Remain (sit).

3. When I saw him (run down) the street I called to him from the kitchen window.

4. It doesn't sound (encourage).

5. She was found (lie) in the street.

6. Do you know what they heard me (say)?

7. He lay there (listen) to what they were arguing so loudly about.

8. Geraldine was very pale and sat (twist) her hands together.

9. We stopped outside a big film studio and stood (watch) the people going in and out, hoping to see a famous film-star.

10. Oh, you look (starve).

richtig   falsch

2. Verkürzen Sie die blau gedruckten Nebensätze durch das present participle.

1. I've fallen into the bad habit of eating dinner while I am watching TV.

2. Although he is rich, he is not happy.

3. I was passing the main gate, when I nearly ran into a man who was hurrying along.

4. A few days after the end of the war, Abraham Lincoln was shot by a fanatic Southerner while he was attending a theatre in Washington.

5. When I entered the house I knew at once that something terrible had happened.

6. The amount of the people who live in the fifty biggest metropolitan areas is growing steadily.

7. When he came home he found his wife in tears.

200 dnf

Die Partizipien

8. **While I was packing a suitcase,** I came across an envelope which for some unaccountable reason I had forgotten until now.

9. **When he looked up** he caught a glimpse of something red.

10. **While he was waiting in the rain,** he lost all count of time.

richtig   falsch

3. Setzen Sie die Verben in Klammern ins past participle.

1. He looked **(depress).**

2. He lay **(injure)** at my feet.

3. Carol's voice sounded **(lose)** already.

4. They felt **(relieve)** after the walk-out.

5. John, however, seemed **(occupy)** with his own thoughts.

6. Bob stood **(petrify)** with fear.

7. He remained **(seat)** for some minutes.

8. He felt **(discourage)** and only the prompt appearance of his father prevented him from bursting into tears.

9. Mr Red seemed **(please)** that Bob was taking his studies seriously.

10. Some students who fail to be elected to fraternities feel **(reject).**

richtig   falsch

4. Verkürzen Sie die blau gedruckten Nebensätze durch das past participle.

1. Does monarchy **as it is practised in England today** interfere with the principles of democracy?

2. **If the letter is posted at once,** the letter will arrive in time.

3. **When it is focused to a sharp point at very close range,** the laser can vaporize any substance on earth.

4. David stood **as if he was turned to stone.**

5. **As she was determined to earn her own living,** Martha had become a housemaid.

6. He never speaks of himself except **when he is compelled.**

Die Partizipien

7. Windsor Castle **which was founded by William the Conqueror,** stands on the Thames, 22 miles west of London.

8. Manhattan Island **which was bought for 25 dollars from the Indians in 1626,** is now the centre of New York.

9. The dangers of living in a hurricane zone seem acceptable **when we compare them with the other dangers** which have to be faced every day.

10. **Unless we were forced to return,** we should be there in time.

richtig   falsch

5. Setzen Sie die Verben in Klammern ins present participle oder past participle.

1. We can't sit here **(talk)**.

2. He sat **(hunch)** forward in an armchair, smoking and thinking.

3. It began to sound **(excite)** to him.

4. She sounded **(please)**.

5. She felt **(disappoint),** but wanting to appear polite, she smiled.

6. In the warm dim light the place looked **(invite)**.

7. I'll be very glad to help if I can, Bob said in a very **(excite)** voice.

8. For a while they sat in **(depress)** silence.

9. This is a **(depress)** message to send to you and I regret it.

10. In nature, excessive animal numbers are controlled by an **(increase)** death rate, a **(decrease)** birth rate, or migration.

richtig   falsch

6. Verkürzen Sie die blau gedruckten Nebensätze durch das perfect participle.

1. **As I had worked hard** I was very tired.

2. **As I have lost his telephone number** I couldn't ring him back.

3. **When I had finished my homework** I watched TV.

4. **If you have your car repaired,** be sure to get an estimate.

5. **As he had been betrayed once,** he never trusted anybody.

richtig   falsch

Die Partizipien

7. Setzen Sie die Verben in Klammern ins present participle passive.

1. Something was (do).
2. The orders were given so fast that I could scarcely understand what was (say).
3. He was (wait for) in the garden.
4. There was no way of knowing whether you were (watched) at.
5. I felt I had been a part of the Berlin Wall when it was (take down).

richtig   falsch

8. Setzen Sie die Verben in Klammern ins present participle active oder present participle passive.

1. As I lay (watch), I saw the boat draw near to the shore.
2. He could hear Laura (sing) to her doll.
3. It was awful to see her (run) straight into the lorry.
4. They were (look at).
5. We find him (have) an early breakfast.

richtig   falsch

9. Setzen Sie die Verben in Klammern ins perfect participle passive.

1. Bob glanced over the newspapers from Paris for an item about a boat (find) near Monaco.
2. Most primary schools are wholly owned by the local authorities, but about one-third belong to churches, (found) by religious bodies.
3. The disputes (settle), the men returned to work.
4. (Bite) twice the postman refused to come into our house.
5. (Bring up) in a big city, I know how to find my own way.

richtig   falsch

Die entsprechenden Lösungen befinden sich auf Seite 435ff.

Das deutsche *lassen*

Das deutsche Verb lassen wird im Englischen, je nachdem ob es in der Bedeutung *zulassen* oder *veranlassen* verwendet wird, folgendermaßen wiedergegeben.

Lassen im Sinne von *veranlassen*

To Have + Past Participle

> unterscheide
> have + Objekt
> + past participle *(etw. machen lassen)*
> und have +
> past participle *(etw. machen)*

Zum Ausdruck, dass jemand veranlasst wird etwas zu tun, steht to have + Objekt + past participle.

- I **had** my car **repaired**.
  (Ich ließ mein Auto reparieren.)
  Unterscheide:
- I **had repaired** my car.
  (Ich hatte mein Auto repariert.)

To Get + Past Participle

Zum Ausdruck, dass jemand veranlasst wird etwas zu tun, steht to get + Objekt + past participle als Alternative zu to have.

- I **got** my car **repaired**.
  (Ich ließ mein Auto reparieren.)
- I **got** my hair **cut**.
  (Ich ließ mir die Haare schneiden.)

To Make + Infinitiv

Zum Ausdruck, dass jemand veranlasst, gezwungen wird etwas zu tun, steht to make + Objekt + Infinitiv ohne to. Im Passiv muss der Infinitiv mit to angeschlossen werden.

- He **made** the pupils **learn** the text by heart.
  (Er ließ die Schüler den Text auswendig lernen.)
- The pupils **were made to learn** the text by heart.

To Cause + Infinitiv

Zum Ausdruck, dass jemand veranlasst wird etwas zu tun, steht to cause + Objekt + Infinitiv + to im Aktiv- und Passivsatz.

- The birth of his baby **caused** him **to think** about his life.
  (Die Geburt seines Kindes ließ ihn über sein Leben nachdenken.)

Lassen im Sinne von *zulassen*

To Let + Infinitiv

Zum Ausdruck, dass zugelassen, erlaubt wird, dass jemand etwas tut, steht to let + Objekt + Infinitiv ohne to. Der Infinitiv wird auch im Passivsatz ohne to angeschlossen.

- The teacher **let** the pupils **go** before the lesson was over.
  (Der Lehrer ließ die Schüler vor Unterrichtsende gehen.)
- The pupils **were let go** before the lesson was over.

Das deutsche *lassen*

To Allow, Permit + Infinitiv

Zum Ausdruck, dass zugelassen, erlaubt wird, dass jemand etwas tut, steht to allow, permit + Objekt + Infinitiv + to im Aktiv- und Passivsatz.

- The teacher **allowed** the pupils **to go** before the lesson was over.
  (Der Lehrer ließ die Schüler vor Unterrichtsende gehen.)
- The pupils **were allowed to go** before the lesson was over.

To Have + Infinitiv, Present bzw. Past Participle

Zum Ausdruck, dass etwas zugelassen wird, steht to have + Objekt + Infinitiv ohne to.

- I won't **have** you **say** such things.
  (Ich möchte nicht, dass du solche Dinge sagst.)
- I won't **have** you **do** that.

Zum Ausdruck, dass etwas zugelassen wird, steht im Aktivsatz to have + Objekt + present participle.

- I won't **have** you **saying** such things.
- I won't **have** you **doing** that.
- I won't **have** you **waiting** for me.

Zum Ausdruck, dass etwas zugelassen wird, steht im Passivsatz to have + Objekt + be + past participle.

- The teacher doesn't want **to have** the pupils **be left** alone in the classroom.
  (Der Lehrer möchte nicht, dass die Schüler im Klassenzimmer allein gelassen werden.)

To Keep, Leave + Present bzw. Past Participle

Zum Ausdruck, dass zugelassen wird, dass etwas geschieht, steht to keep, to leave + Objekt + present bzw. past participle.

- He **kept/left** me **waiting** for an hour.
  (Er ließ mich eine Stunde warten.)
- He **left** nothing **undone**.

Das deutsche lassen

Übungen zum deutschen *lassen*

1. Verwenden Sie to have zum Ausdruck des deutschen *lassen* und schreiben Sie die Sätze neu.

1. I (cut, my hair) (past tense simple) at the barber's.
2. Mrs Stevens (clean, the windows) every month. (present tense simple)
3. I (wash, my car) while I am doing my shopping. (present tense continuous)
4. I (wash, my car) before coming here. (past perfect simple)
5. I (wash, my car) before going to the check-up. (future perfect simple)
6. She (dye, her hair) (present perfect simple)
7. We (redecorate, our house) (present tense simple)
8. You (must take, another picture) (present tense simple)
9. In order to be able to vote in the U.S.A., you (to have to enter, your name) in a list called the electoral register. (present tense simple)
10. Any person (may test, his eyes) free of charge by an optician or eye specialist. (present tense simple)   richtig   falsch

2. Verwenden Sie to let zum Ausdruck des deutschen *lassen* und schreiben Sie die Sätze neu.

1. Please (hear, me) from you as soon as possible. (present tense simple)
2. She (go out, her cigarette) and was listening intently. (past perfect simple)
3. By the way, I suppose you haven't got any razor blades you can (have, me)? (present tense simple)
4. Oh please God, (not get away, him) (imperative)
5. They (do, you) what you'd like to do. (future tense simple)

Das deutsche *lassen*

6. Your father ever (drive, you) his car? (present perfect simple)

7. He (know, her) his address as soon as he had one. (conditional I)

8. We had both taken on quite a lot of martinis, but he looked capable of driving or of course I (not go home alone) (conditional II)

9. At first her parents refused to (go, her) but at last Mary managed to persuade them. (present tense simple)

10. One knew that it was all rubbish so why (worry, oneself) by it? (present infinitive)

                                                                                                                                                      richtig   falsch

3. Verwenden Sie to make zum Ausdruck des deutschen *lassen* und schreiben Sie die Sätze neu.

1. She swept the house and did the dishes and then she (get up, the children) and wash and dress. (past tense simple)

2. I want you to know that I do everything I can to (come back, Simon) (present tense simple)

3. Discussion (think, the students) (present tense simple)

4. What do you think (write, Consul Carrington) this letter? (past tense simple)

5. If I told you what strange things I made, it (laugh, you) at me? (conditional I)

                                                                                                              richtig   falsch

4. Verwenden Sie to keep und to leave zum Ausdruck des deutschen *lassen* und schreiben Sie die Sätze neu.

1. They can (lie about, everything). (present tense simple)

2. He (wonder, me) (past tense simple)

3. I (discuss, them) the matter and went to bed. (past tense simple)

4. (Play, them) (imperative)

5. Ben (wait, her) on a date? (past perfect simple)

                                                                                                              richtig   falsch

Das deutsche *lassen*

5. Verwenden Sie to allow zum Ausdruck des deutschen *lassen* und schreiben Sie die Sätze neu.

1. Peter thought his father might not (go, him) to the party. (present tense simple)

2. Her parents realized that they must (lead, her) her own life. (present tense simple)

3. Of course they (talk, him) to Mary. (conditional I)

4. Would they (call, him) his family? (present tense simple)

5. Some states (impose, local communities) their own speed limits. (present tense simple)   richtig falsch

6. Verwenden Sie to have, to let, to leave zum Ausdruck des deutschen *lassen*.

1. I (not wash, my car) ever since I have it. (present perfect simple)

2. I (wash, my car) while I watched the film. (past tense continuous)

3. (Show, me) you what I've bought. (imperative)

4. They had to (lie, the wounded soldiers) in the blazing sun. (infinitive)

5. We must not (grow, our hair) (present tense simple)

6. William (build, strong castles) all over his kingdom to keep the Saxons down. (past tense simple)

7. Why you (cut, your hair) (past tense simple)

8. I feel sure that she (know, me) (future tense simple)

9. (Run free, the dog) (negative imperative)

10. (See, the others) you. (negative imperative)   richtig falsch

Die entsprechenden Lösungen befinden sich auf Seite 436.

Der Artikel (The Article)

Der Artikel (Geschlechtswort) ist der Begleiter des Substantivs und hat im Englichen für alle drei Geschlechter (männlich, weiblich und sächlich) im Singular (Einzahl) und Plural (Mehrzahl) dieselbe Form.

Der bestimmte Artikel (The Definite Article)

Der bestimmte Artikel bezeichnet ein oder mehrere bestimmte Substantive im Singular oder Plural.

- The man I had seen yesterday was arrested.
- The books I had put on the table over there have been taken away.

Der unbestimmte Artikel (The Indefinite Article)

Der unbestimmte Artikel bezeichnet ein unbestimmtes, zählbares Substantiv im Singular. Unbestimmte Substantive im Plural stehen ohne Artikel.

- Yesterday, I saw a dog roaming around in the park.
- Priests are not allowed to get married.

Die Formen der Artikel (The Forms of the Articles)

	Numerus	Bestimmter Artikel	Unbestimmter Artikel
Vor Konsonant	Singular	the	a *2)
	Plural	the	-
Vor Vokal und stummem -h	Singular	the *1)	an
	Plural	the	-

*1) Vor Vokal und stummem -h wird the wie [θi] ausgesprochen.
*2) Vor Vokal, der wie ein Konsonant gesprochen wird (konsonantischer Anlaut) wird a nicht an verwendet (a university [juniversiti]).

Der Artikel

Der bestimmte und der unbestimmte Artikel (The Definite and the Indefinite Article)

	Unbestimmter Artikel	Kein Artikel
zählbare/ nicht zählbare Substantive	Zählbare Substantive im Singular, die keine bestimmte Person oder Sache bezeichnen (vor allem, wenn sie zum ersten Mal erwähnt werden).	Nicht zählbare Substantive generell. Zur Verdeutlichung, dass sie im Singular stehen, können sie mit folgenden Ausdrücken verbunden werden. - any - some - a piece of - a stroke of Im Deutschen steht meist der unbestimmte Artikel.
	- A tree is a plant. - A frog is an animal.	- That's good advice. (Das ist ein guter Rat.) - That's an interesting piece of advice. (Das ist ein interessanter Rat.)
	Zählbare Substantive im Singular, die in Ausrufen stehen.	Zählbare Substantive im Plural, die in Ausrufen stehen.
	- What a nice little girl! aber (nicht zählbar): - What a pity! - What a shame!	- What nice little girls! - What big dogs!
	Zählbare Substantive im Singular, die eine bestimmte Gruppe von Sachen vertreten.	
	- A plant needs water and light. (All plants need water and light.)	
	Zählbare Substantive, die nach as stehen.	
	- I will give it to him as a birthday present.	

Der Artikel

	Bestimmter Artikel		Kein Artikel	
Substantive im possessive case	Substantive im possessive case.			
	- The book's contents. - The contents of this book.			
Abstrakta	Abstrakta, die durch ein Substantiv + of, ein Adjektiv oder einen Relativsatz näher bestimmt sind.		In allgemeiner Bedeutung verwendete Abstrakta, auch wenn sie durch ein Adjektiv näher bestimmt sind. Abstraktum und Adjektiv bilden eine zusammengehörende Einheit. Conditions, matters und things, wenn sie in der Bedeutung *Situation, Lage* stehen.	
	- The writing of novels is a very interesting occupation. - We often discussed the meaning of life. - The important thing is that you are happy.		- I studied (modern) art. - Public opinion is sometimes very unjust. - Writing is a way of expression. - You can't imagine how difficult things are.	
Gattungsnamen	Gattungsnamen, die durch ein Substantiv + of, ein Adjektiv oder einen Relativsatz näher bestimmt sind.		Gattungsnamen, die in allgemeiner Bedeutung verwendet werden.	
	- The cats of Africa are very powerful creatures. - Can you introduce me to the nice lady over there? - The boys who are playing over there are very noisy.		- They live like cat and dog. - Dogs must be kept on the lead. - Cats are very independent animals. - Jim is very interested in reptiles.	
	Ein oder mehrere Vertreter (Einzelwesen) aus einer Gattung.		Gattungsnamen im Plural bzw. bei man oder woman, wenn sie die ganze Gattung bezeichnen.	
	- When the cat is away the mice will play.		- Dogs must be kept on the lead. - Man cannot live by bread alone.	

Der Artikel

	Bestimmter Artikel	Kein Artikel
Stoffnamen	Stoffnamen, die durch ein Substantiv + of, ein Adjektiv oder einen Relativsatz näher bestimmt sind.	In allgemeiner Bedeutung verwendete Stoffnamen, auch wenn sie durch ein Adjektiv näher bestimmt sind. Stoffname und Adjektiv bilden einen zusammengehörenden Begriff.
	• The gold of Fort Knox is guarded very well. • The gold that was found in this chest was false.	• Coffee is imported from South America. • Italian wines are famous all over the world.
Sammelnamen	Sammelnamen, die durch ein Substantiv + of, ein Adjektiv oder einen Relativsatz näher bestimmt sind.	Sammelnamen, die in allgemeiner Bedeutung verwendet werden.
	• The society of our time is often considered to be cruel. • The society they live in is often considered to be cruel.	• Mankind has profited by the discoveries of medical science. • Posterity will have to cope with a lot of difficulties.
Eigennamen	Eigennamen, die durch ein Substantiv + of, ein Adjektiv oder einen Relativsatz näher bestimmt sind.	Eigennamen im Singular.
	• The City of New York is a melting pot. • The successful Thomas Edison died in 1931. • The Thomas Edison, who was the most successful inventor, died in 1931.	• New York is a melting pot. • Thomas Edison was the most successful inventor. • Peter is a very nice little boy.
Personennamen		Personennamen generell, auch wenn sie mit den folgenden Adjektiven stehen oder die Mitglieder einer Familie bezeichnen.

Der Artikel

Bestimmter Artikel	Kein Artikel
	• dear — lieb • good — gut • little — klein • old — alt • poor — arm • saint (St.) — Sankt • tiny — winzig • young — jung
	• Peter and Mary are good friends. • Dear Mary ... • Father and Mother have already gone. • Little Rachel was named after dear old Aunt Rachel.
	Personennamen in Verbindung mit Verwandtschaftsbezeichnungen. • I met Aunt Mary at the station. • Yesterday, I saw Uncle Tom washing his car.

Bestimmter Artikel	Unbestimmter Artikel	Kein Artikel	
Familiennamen, die eine bestimmte Person bezeichnen und Familiennamen, die im Plural stehen.	Familiennamen, die eine Person bezeichnen, die dem Sprecher unbekannt ist, vor allem in Verbindung mit Mr, Mrs und Miss.	Familiennamen generell.	Familiennamen
• The Mrs Smith I met at the station. • The Walkers spent their holiday at the seaside.	• A Mrs Smith explained them the way. • I met a certain Mr Jones today.	• I met Mrs Smith at the station. • Do you already know Mr and Mrs Olson?	

Bestimmter Artikel	Kein Artikel	
Englische Titel, auf die ein Substantiv + of folgt.	Englische Titel + Eigenname, auf die kein Substantiv + of folgt.	Titel
• The Prince of Wales is the successor to the throne.	• Queen Elizabeth arrived for an official visit in Germany.	

dnf 213

Der Artikel

	Bestimmter Artikel	Kein Artikel
im Deutschen steht die Präposition *zu*, im Englischen kein *to*	Nicht-englische Titel generell.	Titel, die auf die nachstehenden Verben folgen, stehen grundsätzlich ohne Artikel. - to be — sein - to become — werden - to crown — krönen - to elect — wählen - to make — machen - to turn — werden
	• **The** Emperor Napoleon I was born in 1769.	• He was elected President of the United States. (Er wurde zum Präsidenten der Vereinigten Staaten gewählt.)
		Titel, die auf nachstehende Ausdrücke folgen. - the office of - the post of - the rank of - the title of
		• Charles, son of Queen Elizabeth II, holds the title of Prince of Wales.
		Titel, die nur einmal vorhanden sind.
		• Queen Elizabeth I was born in 1533.

	Unbestimmter Artikel	Kein Artikel
Berufs- und Standesbezeichnungen	Zum Ausdruck von Berufsbezeichnungen, besonders nach *to be* und *to become*. Die Verneinung lautet meist *not a* (kein, nicht). Im Deutschen steht hier kein Artikel.	Berufs- und Standesbezeichnungen, wenn sie in Verbindung mit einer Beifügung + *of* stehen.
kein Artikel im Deutschen	• Her father is a doctor. (Ihr Vater ist Arzt.) • He is a teacher, not a doctor.	• He earned the title of doctor. • He earned the rank of lieutenant.

Der Artikel

Unbestimmter Artikel	Kein Artikel	
Zum Ausdruck der Nationalität, Rasse, besonders nach to be und to become. Die Verneinung lautet meist not a (kein, nicht). Im Deutschen steht hier kein Artikel. - Peter is an Englishman and Susanne is a German. (Peter ist Engländer und Susanne ist Deutsche.) - Mr Smith is an American and his friend Pierre is a Frenchman.		Nationalität, Rasse kein Artikel im Deutschen
	Politische Begriffe, die einmalig sind. - Parliament represents the two chambers House of Commons and House of Lords. (Das (englische) Parlament umfasst die beiden Kammern Oberhaus und Unterhaus.)	politische Begriffe
Zum Ausdruck der Zugehörigkeit einer Person zu einer religiösen Vereinigung oder Gruppe, besonders nach to be und to become. Die Verneinung lautet meist not a (kein, nicht). Im Deutschen steht hier kein Artikel. - Martin Luther King was a Protestant. (Martin Luther King war Protestant.) - His wife is not a Protestant, but a Catholic.	Religiöse Begriffe, die einmalig sind. Zum Ausdruck der Zugehörigkeit einer Person zu einer religiösen Vereinigung oder Gruppe können religiöse Begriffe auch ohne Artikel stehen. - Help yourself and Heaven will help you. - Go to Hell. - His wife is Catholic, but he is Protestant.	religiöse Begriffe kein Artikel im Deutschen
Bestimmter Artikel	**Kein Artikel**	
	Erdteile, auch wenn sie durch ein Adjektiv nä-	Erdteile

dnf 215

Der Artikel

	Bestimmter Artikel	Kein Artikel
		her bestimmt sind. Erdteil und Adjektiv bilden einen zusammengehörenden Begriff. • They left (old) Europe to find a new home in America. • We sailed from southeast Asia to Africa.
Länder, Inseln	Länder- und Inselnamen, die durch eine Beifügung näher bestimmt sind oder die in Verbindung mit einem Substantiv + of stehen oder die im Plural stehen (Inselgruppen). • The Great Britain described in his new novel … • The America of Roosevelt's days … • The Bahamas are beautiful islands.	Länder- und Inselnamen generell, auch wenn sie durch ein Adjektiv näher bestimmt sind. Länder- oder Inselname und Adjektiv bilden einen zusammengehörenden Begriff. • Merry old Britain is such a beautiful country. • The last five years, I spent my holidays in beautiful Malta. • Jim is taking his vacation in sunny California.
Städte		Städtenamen stehen grundsätzlich ohne Artikel, auch wenn sie durch ein Adjektiv näher bestimmt sind. Städtename und Adjektiv bilden einen zusammengehörenden Begriff. • Berlin • beautiful London • downtown Manhattan
Berge	Die Namen der Berge nicht englischsprachiger Länder stehen in der Regel mit dem bestimmten Artikel. • the Alps • the Andes • the Matterhorn	Die Namen der Berge englischsprachiger Länder stehen in der Regel ohne Artikel. • Ben Nevis • Snowdon • Wicklow

Der Artikel

Bestimmter Artikel	Kein Artikel	
Die Namen der Berge, die durch eine Beifügung näher bestimmt sind oder in Verbindung mit einem Substantiv + of stehen oder mit of an den Ausdruck Mount angeschlossen werden oder im Plural stehen (Bergketten, Gebirge).	Die Namen der Berge, die ohne of an den Ausdruck Mount angeschlossen werden.	
- The beautiful Ben Nevis - The Mount of Olives	- Ben Nevis is in Scotland. - Mount Everest is the highest mountain in the world.	
Meeres- und Küstennamen, besonders wenn sie mit of an Ausdrücke wie Cape, Bay und Harbour, Gulf, Sea und Strait angeschlossen werden.	Meeres- und Küstennamen, die ohne of an Ausdrücke wie Cape, Bay und Harbour angeschlossen werden.	Meere
- The Atlantic - The Cape of Good Hope - The Bay of Biscay - The Harbour of New York - The Gulf of Mexico - The Sea of Japan - The Strait of Gibraltar	- Cape Horn - Hudson Bay - Boston Harbour - Puget Sound	
Die Namen von Seen, die mit of auf die Ausdrücke Lake, Loch, Harbour folgen.	Die Namen der Seen, die ohne of an die Ausdrücke Lake, Loch, Harbour angeschlossen werden.	Seen
- The Lake of Geneva - The Port of San Francisco	- Lake Erie - Loch Ness	
Flussnamen stehen in der Regel mit dem bestimmten Artikel.		Flüsse
- The Thames - The Rhine		

Der Artikel

	Bestimmter Artikel	Kein Artikel
Himmelsrichtungen	Die Himmelsrichtungen stehen in der Regel mit dem bestimmten Artikel.	Himmelsrichtungen in den Ausdrücken from north to south und from east to west, oder wenn sie als Adjektive, Adverbien verwendet werden.
	▪ Russia lies in the east, America lies in the west. ▪ The wind came from the north-east.	▪ They travelled through America from east to west. ▪ We drove north to Scotland. ▪ We had a strong west wind.
Straßen	Straßennamen generell. Hierzu gehört auch der Ausdruck High Street.	Straßennamen, die vor Street, Road und Avenue stehen.
	▪ The Champs-Elysées ▪ The High Street is the main street.	▪ 5th Avenue ▪ Fleet Street
Plätze		Die Namen von Plätzen, vor allem wenn Ausdrücke wie Square, Circus, Park, Gardens oder Station folgen.
		▪ Trafalgar Square ▪ Piccadilly Circus ▪ Hyde Park ▪ Victoria Station
Brücken	Die Namen von Brücken, vor allem wenn eine Beifügung + of folgt.	Die Namen von Brücken, wenn der Ausdruck Bridge folgt.
	▪ the Tower of London	▪ Tower Bridge
Gebäude	Gebäudenamen, vor allem wenn sie aus Adjektiv + Substantiv oder Substantiv + of-Genitiv bestehen. Gebäudenamen wie cathedral, office, cinema und theatre stehen immer mit dem bestimmten Artikel.	Viele Gebäudenamen, besonders wenn sie nicht aus Adjektiv + Substantiv oder Substantiv + of-Genitiv bestehen.
	▪ The Houses of Parliament	▪ St. Paul's Cathedral ▪ Westminster Abbey

Der Artikel

Bestimmter Artikel	Kein Artikel
• **The** House of Representatives • He goes to **the** office every day. • He goes to **the** cinema tonight.	• Windsor Castle • Capitol Hill • Trump Tower
Folgende Gebäudenamen, wenn sie nur das Gebäude, den Ort an sich bezeichnen. • bed — Bett • camp — Lagerplatz • chapel — Kapelle • church — Kirche • class — Klassenzimmer • college — College • court — Gerichtsgebäude • hospital — Krankenhaus • market — Marktplatz • prison — Gefängnis • school — Schule • university — Universität • work — Arbeitsplatz	Folgende Gebäudenamen, wenn sie den Zweck, die Funktion des Gebäudes, Ortes bezeichnen. • bed — Bett-, Nachtruhe • camp — Zeltlager • chapel — Gottesdienst • church — Gottesdienst • class — Unterricht • college — Studium • court — Gerichtsverhandlung • hospital — Krankenlager • market — Markt, Handel • prison — Gefangenschaft • school — Unterricht • university — Studium • work — Arbeit, Werk
• You will find the library in **the** university.	• Every Sunday he goes to church at 9 o'clock.
Körperteile generell. Im Deutschen steht hier kein Artikel.	Bei Körperteilen, die zum Subjekt gehören, steht das entsprechende Possessivpronomen.
• He took me by **the** arm. (Er nahm mich am Arm.)	• Raise **your** right hand. (Hebe deine rechte Hand.)
Kleidungsstücke generell. Im Deutschen steht kein Artikel.	Bei Kleidungsstücken, die zum Subjekt gehören, steht das entsprechende Possessivpronomen.
• He took me by **the** collar. (Er nahm mich am Kragen.)	• He took off **his** coat. (Er zog den Mantel aus.)
Musikinstrumente generell.	
• He learnt to play **the** piano.	

Körperteile

kein Artikel im Deutschen

Kleidungsstücke

kein Artikel im Deutschen

Musikinstrumente

Der Artikel

	Bestimmter Artikel	Kein Artikel
Jahreszeiten, Monatsnamen, Wochentage, Feiertage	Näher bestimmte Jahreszeiten, Wochentage, Feiertage. Bei den Jahreszeiten kann der bestimmte Artikel nach *in* stehen.	In allgemeiner Bedeutung verwendete Jahreszeiten, Monatsnamen, Wochen-, Feiertage. Bei den Jahreszeiten kann der Artikel nach *in* entfallen.
	▪ That year **the** summer was very hot. ▪ They always go on holiday **in the** winter. ▪ **The** Friday before the election was very cold.	▪ I don't like winter. ▪ They always go on holiday in winter. ▪ July is the hottest month. ▪ Friday is the beginning of the weekend.
Tageszeiten	Näher bestimmte Tageszeiten, und die Tageszeiten, die mit einer Präposition, die einen Zeitraum bezeichnet (*in, during, through*), verbunden sind.	Tageszeiten, die in allgemeiner Bedeutung verwendet werden, und Tageszeiten, die mit einer Präposition, die einen Zeitpunkt bezeichnet (*at, from - to* etc.), verbunden sind.
	▪ The baby was crying all **through the** night.	▪ I always work from morning to night.

	Bestimmter Artikel	Unbestimmter Artikel	Kein Artikel
Mahlzeiten	Näher bestimmte Mahlzeiten, oder Mahlzeiten, die die Speisen an sich bezeichnen.	Mahlzeiten, die durch ein Adjektiv näher bestimmt sind.	Mahlzeiten, die in allgemeiner Bedeutung verwendet werden.
	▪ Do you mean **the** dinner when Lord Farnsworth was our guest?	▪ We had **a** really good breakfast. ▪ Have **a** nice lunch.	▪ Dinner will be served at 8 o'clock. ▪ I don't eat much for breakfast.
Zeiteinheiten	Folgende Zeiteinheiten können mit dem bestimmten Artikel stehen, besonders wenn die Art des Unterrichts, der Arbeit etc. gemeint ist, oder wenn sie näher bestimmt sind.	Zeiteinheiten stehen in der Regel mit dem unbestimmten Artikel, vor allem wenn die Zeit an sich gemeint ist. Im Deutschen wird dies oft durch *je, pro* wiedergegeben.	Folgende Zeiteinheiten können auch ohne Artikel verwendet werden, vor allem wenn die Unterrichts-, Arbeitszeit etc. gemeint ist.
	▪ business hours — Geschäftszeiten		▪ business hours — Geschäftszeiten

Der Artikel

Bestimmter Artikel	Unbestimmter Artikel	Kein Artikel
▪ dinner time — Abendessenzeit ▪ last — zuletzt ▪ lesson — Unterricht ▪ lunchtime — Mittagessenzeit ▪ next — nächster ▪ question time — Fragestunde ▪ school hours — Unterrichtszeiten ▪ tea time — Teatime ▪ term — Semester ▪ working hours — Arbeitszeiten Last und next stehen mit dem bestimmten Artikel, wenn ab der Vergangenheit oder Zukunft gerechnet wird.		▪ dinner time — Abendessenzeit ▪ last — zuletzt ▪ lesson — Unterricht ▪ lunchtime — Mittagessenzeit ▪ next — nächster ▪ question time — Fragestunde ▪ school hours — Unterrichtszeiten ▪ tea time — Teatime ▪ term — Semester ▪ working hours — Arbeitszeiten Last und next stehen ohne Artikel, wenn von der Gegenwart aus gerechnet wird.
▪ **The lessons** of Professor Blackwell are very interesting. ▪ One night he came home very late and **the next day** he overslept.	▪ My car runs 120 miles **an** hour. (Mein Auto fährt 120 Meilen **pro** Stunde.) ▪ We all have to pay 500 pounds **a** term.	▪ You must attend every English lesson. ▪ Last night I was at home and read. ▪ Next month I will be on holiday.
Der bestimmte Artikel steht nach den folgenden Mengenangaben. Im Deutschen steht der Artikel vor der Mengenangabe. ▪ both — beide ▪ double — doppelt ▪ half — halb ▪ treble — dreimal ▪ twice — zweimal	Bei folgenden Maß-, Gewichts- und Mengeneinheiten. Im Deutschen steht oft *je, pro*. Der unbestimmte Artikel steht nach half. ▪ a couple — ein paar ▪ a great deal of — eine Menge ▪ a dozen — ein Dutzend ▪ half a dozen — ein halbes Dutzend ▪ a gross — 144 Pfund ▪ a hundred/thousand — hundert, tausend etc. ▪ a lot of — viele ▪ a great many of — eine Menge ▪ a score — 20 Stück	Folgende Mengeneinheiten stehen ohne Artikel. ▪ both — beide

Maß- und Gewichtseinheiten der Artikel steht *nach* der Mengenangabe

Der Artikel

	Bestimmter Artikel	Unbestimmter Artikel	Kein Artikel
	• Both the students passed the exam. • He spent half the money on this house. • A jet can fly at twice the speed of a prop plane.	• He spent 100 pounds a square meter for this real estate. (Er gab 100 Pfund pro Quadratmeter für dieses Grundstück aus.)	• Both students passed the exam.
all	All steht zur Bezeichnung von *allen* aus einer bestimmten Anzahl mit dem bestimmten Artikel.		All steht ohne Artikel zur Bezeichnung von *allen* generell.
	• All the sheets on the table have to be distributed among the pupils.		• All sheets have to be distributed among the pupils.
few, little	Mit dem bestimmten Artikel hat few meist negativen Sinn (die wenigen).	Few, little haben mit dem unbestimmten Artikel positiven Sinn (einige, ein paar, ein bisschen).	Few, little haben ohne Artikel meist negativen Sinn ((wenig, wenige).
	• The few who came to his party were in a very bad mood.	• He bought a few books. • He has only a few friends. • He spent a little time with her.	• Few students passed the exam. • We had little time for amusement.
most			Most im Sinne von *die meisten, fast alle*.
			• Most houses in this town are sold.
part of	Part of steht zur Bezeichnung eines Teils aus einer bestimmten Anzahl mit dem bestimmten Artikel.	Part of kann, wenn es mit einem Adjektiv verbunden ist, mit dem unbestimmten Artikel stehen.	Part of steht zur Bezeichnung einer unbestimmten Größe ohne Artikel.
	• Part of the 100 pounds goes to Gary.	• We spent a good part of our time reading.	• Fran was in Ireland for part of last year.
plenty of	Plenty of steht zur Bezeichnung eines Teils aus einer bestimmten Anzahl mit dem bestimmten Artikel.		Plenty of steht zur Bezeichnung einer unbestimmten Größe ohne Artikel.
	• Plenty of the people I work with are married.		• He has always plenty of time.

Der Artikel

Bestimmter Artikel

Substantivierte Adjektive, die eine bestimmte Gruppe von Personen oder Dingen bezeichnen.	Adjektive
- There is no peace for any but **the** dead. - **The** rich always get richer.	
Vor Superlativen und dem Adverb only.	
- Mr Smith is **the** richest man in our town. - He is **the** only person to solve this problem.	

Der Artikel

Übungen zum Artikel

1. Setzen Sie den bestimmten oder unbestimmten Artikel ein wo notwendig.

1. ... Archbishop Cranmer, ... author of some of our most magnificent collects, was burned alive at Oxford.

2. ... Chairman of ... House of Commons is ... Speaker.

3. ... little Bob couldn't remember the names very well.

4. ... Lord Chancellor of England presides over the debates from the Woolsack - a red cloth couch stuffed with wool.

5. ... man must eat to live.

6. ... Mrs Burton wrote a postcard to ... Harrison family.

7. ... Tom came home from school the other day, and his mother asked him: «Are you getting on well at school, ... Tom?»

8. He was raised to the rank of ... Colonel.

9. If ... House of Lords should reject a bill which has been passed by ... Commons, the bill can go no further for a few months.

10. If ... men were more reasonable, there would be no more war.

11. In some states of the U.S.A .... boys and ... girls are allowed to drive a car at the age of sixteen.

12. Peter lived in London, and he was visiting ... aunt in New York for a few months.

13. She was ... daughter of a leading New England Presbyterian minister and ... wife of a professor of theology.

14. She was taken away by ... ambulance.

15. Sheila Anderson's father was ... acrobat in a famous circus, which travelled all over England.

16. Soon after Christmas ... Robinsons went to Aspen, Colorado.

17. The committee appointed Mr Stevens ... chairman.

18. The Queen was crowned, like her predecessors, by ... Archbishop of Canterbury in Westminster Abbey.

19. The woman we visited was my ... aunt Martha.

20. This is ... book I have been speaking of all ... time.

richtig   falsch

2. Setzen Sie den bestimmten oder unbestimmten Artikel ein wo notwendig.

1. ... church is a place where people can meet other Christians.

2. ... Mall and ... Strand are two famous London streets.

3. ... Matterhorn was first scaled in 1865.

4. ... Regent Street runs from ... Piccadilly Circus to ... Oxford Street.

5. ... St. James's Park is near ... Buckingham Palace.

6. ... Tower of London used to be a state prison.

7. Because ... England is old, ... Englishman lays great store by tradition.

8. Every year thousands of visitors from ... Continent come to ... England by boat from ... Ostend or ... Calais.

9. Founded by William the Conqueror, Windsor Castle stands on ... Thames, 22 miles west of ... London.

10. From ... Boston to ... Los Angeles is as far as from ... France to ... Central Asia, and from ... east to ... west there are five time zones.

11. Harold marched north and defeated the Norsemen in a great battle near ... Stamford Bridge.

12. By six o'clock ... school is empty and the caretaker and the cleaners can finish their work in peace.

13. I am ... Englishman.

14. In 1984 the Olympic Games returned to ... City of LA.

15. In the morning a lot of people go to ... church.

16. Linda was standing at the corner of ... Broadway.

17. More than 2,000,000 migrants have arrived, the largest groups coming from ... United Kingdom and ... Ireland, from ... Italy,

Der Artikel

... Greece, ... Germany, and ... Netherlands.

18. People who wanted to get from ... East to ... West could go by three routes: round ... Cape Horn, across ... Isthmus of Panama, or overland by wagon.

19. Side streets to the right of ... Fifth Avenue are called 41st ... East Street, while streets to the left are called 41st ... West Street.

20. Sir Edmund Hillary was the first conqueror of ... Mount Everest.

richtig   falsch

3. Setzen Sie den bestimmten oder unbestimmten Artikel ein wo notwendig.

1. We are going to Italy next ... summer.

2. ... summer of 1987 was very hot.

3. Thousands of holiday-makers visit the Highlands in ... summer, hoping for good luck with the weather.

4. Scotland is not particularly cold, and in ... winter the west is one of the mildest parts of Britain.

5. He's not coming back all ... winter?

6. Mrs Taft lives in Florida during ... winter.

7. The tramp who came on ... April 1st was a friendly man.

8. No more school till ... Monday morning.

9. What's he going to do about ... Christmas?

10. He'll stay all ... night.

11. He remembered having seen the man ... evening before.

12. He has been writing all ... morning.

13. Tomorrow the wind will change during ... morning, and there will be rain in ... afternoon.

14. The last time Adam was seen by anybody was ... February fifteenth.

15. Susan was the only one he felt like telling about his European trip, and he went to see her on ... Thursday before he sailed.

richtig   falsch

Der Artikel

4. Setzen Sie den bestimmten Artikel oder das entsprechende Possessivpronomen ein.

1. Look me in ... eyes.

2. He crossed the road by the zebra-crossing and caught her by ... arm.

3. Take her by ... hand.

4. I rose to ... feet, bowed and left the room.

5. Don't pick stamps up with ... fingers.

6. He was struck on ... head from behind.

7. Little children can't put on ... shoes. So their parents must help them.

8. They have winter staring them in ... face.

9. Britain is a parliamentary democracy with the Queen at ... head.

10. He took ... shoes off so he could put ... feet up on the sofa, lay back on a pillow, and continued reading Steven's letter.   richtig   falsch

Die entsprechenden Lösungen befinden sich auf Seite 436ff.

Der Artikel

Die Stellung des Artikels (The Position of the Article)

Der Artikel steht meist unmittelbar vor dem Substantiv, das er begleitet. Tritt zum Substantiv eine der folgenden Mengenangaben, steht der Artikel nach der Mengenangabe. Im Deutschen steht der Artikel vor dem Substantiv mit Mengenangabe.

> Artikel steht im Englischen nach, im Deutschen vor der Mengenangabe

Die Stellung des bestimmten Artikels

all, both, double, twice, half, treble, triple	Der bestimmte Artikel steht nach all, both, double, twice, half, treble (BE) und triple (AE). Bei both kann der bestimmte Artikel weggelassen werden.	• He only told me half **the** truth. (Er sagte mir nur **die** halbe Wahrheit.) • All **the** children were crying. • Both **(the)** children were crying.

Die Stellung des unbestimmten Artikels

half, quite, rather	Der unbestimmte Artikel steht nach half, quite, rather.	• Can you give me half **a** pound? (Kannst du mir **ein** halbes Pfund geben?)
such, many	Der unbestimmte Artikel steht nach such und many.	• His failure is such **a** pity. • They talked for many **an** hour.
as, so, too, how, however	Der unbestimmte Artikel steht nach einem Adjektiv, das mit as, so, too, how und however eng verbunden und damit besonders betont ist.	• This is as good **a** book as I have ever read. (Nie zuvor habe ich **ein** so gutes Buch gelesen.) • This was too difficult **a** problem for us.
what	Der unbestimmte Artikel steht nach what im Ausruf.	• What **a** pity! • What **an** elegant suit you are wearing!

Übungen zur Stellung des Artikels

1. Setzen Sie den bestimmten oder unbestimmten Artikel an die richtige Position.

1. Mr Brenton asked Bob how **(close, friend)** Simon had been of Daniel Robins.

2. Henry had seldom tasted so **(good, dish)**.

3. I have lost my key and have been looking for it for **(half, hour)**.

4. This is too **(important, question)** to leave open.

5. The news was **(quite, relief)** to him.

6. How **(terrible, prospect)**!

7. A few years ago, Mrs Smith took lessons in cooking **(twice, week)**.

8. That sounds **(quite, possibility)**.

9. It was too **(small, reward)** for such a great deed.

10. We have more than **(twice, acreage)** of woodland than we inherited at the turn of the century.

richtig falsch

Die entsprechenden Lösungen befinden sich auf Seite 437.

Der Artikel

Die Wiederholung des Artikels (The Repetition of the Article)

In Aufzählungen zusammengehörender Personen oder Sachen braucht der Artikel nicht wiederholt zu werden. In den folgenden Fällen ist die Wiederholung des Artikels jedoch erforderlich.

Hervorhebung	Zur Hervorhebung oder Gegenüberstellung einzelner Personen oder Sachen wird der Artikel wiederholt.	• It was not only **the** woman but also **the** man who complained about it. • It was **the** brothers of Peter and **the** brothers of John who had a fight.
mehrere Adjektive	Der Artikel wird wiederholt vor mehreren Adjektiven unterschiedlicher bzw. gegensätzlicher Bedeutung, die vor einem Substantiv im Singular stehen.	• The economic differences between **the** industrial and **the** developing world are enormous.
	Der Artikel wird nicht wiederholt, wenn mehrere Adjektive unterschiedlicher bzw. gegensätzlicher Bedeutung vor einem Substantiv im Plural stehen.	• The economic differences between industrial and developing countries are enormous.

Das Substantiv (The Noun)

Substantive (Hauptwörter, Dingwörter, Nennwörter, Nomen) bezeichnen Lebewesen, Pflanzen, Gegenstände oder sonstige Begriffe.

Konkreta (Concrete Nouns)

Substantive, die Gegenstände bezeichnen (Gegenstandswort).

- book
- table

Abstrakta (Abstract Nouns)

Substantive, die das Nichtgegenständliche bezeichnen, d. h. Dinge, die man nicht berühren kann (Begriffswort).

- love
- beauty
- courage

Appellativa (Common Nouns)

Substantive, die eine Gattung von Lebewesen oder Dingen bezeichnen und zugleich jedes einzelne Lebewesen oder Ding dieser Gattung (Gattungsnamen).

- man
- woman
- child
- dog

Kollektiva (Collective Nouns)

Substantive, die eine Gruppe gleichartiger Lebewesen oder Dinge bezeichnen (Sammelnamen).

- team
- group

Stoffnamen (Substantial Nouns)

Stoffnamen sind Masse- und Materialbezeichnungen.

- water
- gold

Eigennamen (Proper Nouns)

Substantive, die Sachen und Personen bezeichnen, die einmalig sind.

- Great Britain
- London

Das Substantiv

Ursubstantive (Original Nouns)

Nicht durch ein Suffix (Nachsilbe), Präfix (Vorsilbe) veränderte Substantive.

- water
- book

Abgewandelte Substantive (Modified Nouns)

Substantive, die durch ein Suffix (Nachsilbe) oder Präfix (Vorsilbe) abgewandelt sind.

- reproduction
- subway
- underground

Abgeleitete Substantive (Derivative Nouns)

Von einer anderen Wortart (z. B. Verb, Adjektiv) abgeleitete Substantive.

- happy - happiness
- busy - business

Zusammengesetzte Substantive (Compound Nouns)

Aus verschiedenen Wortarten zusammengesetzte Substantive (z. B. Substantiv + Substantiv, Substantiv + Verb etc.).

- apple-tree
- father-in-law
- looker-on

Das Substantiv

Das Geschlecht des Substantivs (The Gender of the Noun)

Im Gegensatz zum Deutschen ist es im Englischen nicht am Artikel zu erkennen, ob ein Substantiv männliches (maskulines), weibliches (feminines) oder sächliches (neutrum) Geschlecht (Genus) hat. Welches Geschlecht ein Substantiv hat, ist nur noch zu erkennen, wenn es durch ein Personal- oder Possessivpronomen (he, she, it etc.) ersetzt wird.
Bei Personen und Tieren entspricht das grammatische Geschlecht meist dem natürlichen Geschlecht. Substantive, die keine Lebewesen bezeichnen, werden meist durch ein sächliches Pronomen (it etc.) ersetzt.
Im Übrigen sind bezüglich des Geschlechts folgende Besonderheiten zu beachten.

Männliches Geschlecht | Weibliches Geschlecht

Männliches Geschlecht	Weibliches Geschlecht	
Einige männliche Substantive haben für das weibliche Substantiv eine besondere Bezeichnung.	Einige weibliche Substantive haben für das männliche Substantiv eine besondere Bezeichnung. Einige weibliche Substantive hängen an das männliche Substantiv -ess oder -ine an.	unterschiedliche Bezeichnung für männliche und weibliche Substantive

- actor — Schauspieler
- boy — Junge
- brother — Bruder
- duke — Herzog
- emperor — Kaiser
- father — Vater
- heir — Erbe
- hero — Held
- host — Gastgeber
- husband — Ehemann
- king — König
- man — Mann
- master — Herr, Gebieter
- nephew — Neffe
- prince — Prinz
- son — Sohn
- steward — Steward
- uncle — Onkel

- actress — Schauspielerin
- girl — Mädchen
- sister — Schwester
- duchess — Herzogin
- empress — Kaiserin
- mother — Mutter
- heiress — Erbin
- heroine — Heldin
- hostess — Gastgeberin
- wife — Ehefrau
- queen — Königin
- woman — Frau
- mistress — Herrin, Gebieterin
- niece — Nichte
- princess — Prinzessin
- daughter — Tochter
- stewardess — Stewardess
- aunt — Tante

- **Peter** is a very nice **boy**. **He** always helps me with the dishes.
- **Mary** is a very nice **girl**. **She** always helps me with the dishes.

Einige Substantive sind sowohl weiblich als auch männlich.	Einige Substantive sind sowohl weiblich als auch männlich.	gleiche Bezeichnung für männliche und weibliche Substantive

Das Substantiv

Männliches Geschlecht	Weibliches Geschlecht
Welches Geschlecht das Substantiv hat, geht meist aus dem Zusammenhang hervor. Um Missverständnisse zu vermeiden, können boy, gentleman, man, male zur Kennzeichnung des männlichen Geschlechts hinzugefügt werden.	Welches Geschlecht das Substantiv hat, geht meist aus dem Zusammenhang hervor. Um Missverständnisse zu vermeiden, können girl, lady, woman, female zur Kennzeichnung des weiblichen Geschlechts hinzugefügt werden.
▪ artist — Künstler ▪ assistant — Assistent ▪ author — Autor ▪ clerk — Büroangestellter ▪ companion — Begleiter ▪ cook — Koch ▪ cousin — Vetter, Cousin ▪ customer — Kunde ▪ dancer — Tänzer ▪ doctor — Arzt ▪ driver — Fahrer ▪ friend — Freund ▪ journalist — Journalist ▪ officer — Beamter ▪ painter — Maler ▪ pupil — Schüler ▪ reporter — Reporter ▪ rider — Reiter ▪ servant — Diener ▪ singer — Sänger	▪ artist — Künstlerin ▪ assistant — Assistentin ▪ author — Autorin ▪ clerk — Büroangestellte ▪ companion — Begleiterin ▪ cook — Köchin ▪ cousin — Cousine ▪ customer — Kundin ▪ dancer — Tänzerin ▪ doctor — Ärztin ▪ driver — Fahrerin ▪ friend — Freundin ▪ journalist — Journalistin ▪ officer — Beamtin ▪ painter — Malerin ▪ pupil — Schülerin ▪ reporter — Reporterin ▪ rider — Reiterin ▪ servant — Dienerin ▪ singer — Sängerin
▪ Peter attended the same school as his **cousin** John. ▪ Mary has a nice **boy friend**.	▪ Mary attended the same school as her **cousin** Pamela. ▪ John has a nice **girl friend**.

child, baby

Männliches Geschlecht	Weibliches Geschlecht	Sächliches Geschlecht
Child und baby sind männlich, wenn ihr natürliches Geschlecht männlich ist.	Child und baby sind weiblich, wenn ihr natürliches Geschlecht weiblich ist.	Ist das natürliche Geschlecht von child und baby unbekannt, sind sie sächlich.
▪ Peter is a tall **child** for his age.	▪ What's the name of the **baby**. Her name is Ann.	▪ The **baby** doesn't want to eat its meal.

Tiernamen

Ist das natürliche Geschlecht eines Tieres	Ist das natürliche Geschlecht eines Tieres	Ist das natürliche Geschlecht eines Tieres

Das Substantiv

Männliches Geschlecht	Weibliches Geschlecht	Sächliches Geschlecht
männlich, so ist sein grammatisches Geschlecht auch männlich. Gelegentlich werden große Tiere auch als männliche Lebewesen angesehen und haben somit männliches Geschlecht. Viele Tiernamen stehen für männliches und weibliches Geschlecht. Um Missverständnisse zu vermeiden, kann dem männlichen Tiernamen **male, he** bzw. **cock** (bei Vögeln) vorangestellt werden.	weiblich, so ist sein grammatisches Geschlecht auch weiblich. Gelegentlich werden kleine Tiere auch als weibliche Lebewesen angesehen und haben somit weibliches Geschlecht. Viele Tiernamen stehen für männliches und weibliches Geschlecht. Um Missverständnisse zu vermeiden, kann dem weiblichen Tiernamen **female, she** bzw. **hen** (bei Vögeln) vorangestellt werden.	unbekannt, so ist es sächlich.
▪ Last night, a big **bear** went straight through our camp. **He** ate our provisions. ▪ What's the sex of your dog? Is it a **he-dog/ male dog**?	▪ My **cat** is a rather independent animal. **She** likes roaming around for days. ▪ What's the sex of your dog? Is it a **she-dog/ female dog**?	▪ I cannot ride this **horse**. **It** is ill. ▪ What a cute **penguin**! Look how **it** can swim under water.
Einige männliche Tiernamen haben andere weibliche Tiernamen. ▪ bull — Bulle, Stier ▪ cock — Hahn ▪ dog — Hund ▪ drake — Enterich ▪ gander — Gänserich ▪ horse — Pferd ▪ lion — Löwe ▪ ox — Ochse ▪ tiger — Tiger	Einige weibliche Tiernamen haben andere männliche Tiernamen. ▪ cow — Kuh ▪ hen — Henne ▪ bitch — Hündin ▪ duck — Ente ▪ goose — Gans ▪ mare — Stute ▪ lioness — Löwin ▪ cow — Kuh ▪ tigress — Tigerin	
▪ My aunt Mary has a **cock** and ten hens.	▪ My mother has a **goose** named Samantha.	
	Ländernamen können, wenn sie nicht in rein geografischer Bedeutung stehen, auch weibliches Geschlecht haben.	Ländernamen sind, besonders wenn sie in rein geografischer Bedeutung verwendet werden, sächlich.

Ländernamen

Das Substantiv

	Weibliches Geschlecht	Sächliches Geschlecht
	• Many countries took **Great Britain** and **her** parliamentary system as an example.	• **Scotland** is part of Great Britain. **It** lies north of England.
Städtenamen	Städtenamen können, wenn sie nicht in rein geografischer Bedeutung stehen, auch weibliches Geschlecht haben.	Städtenamen sind, besonders wenn sie in rein geografischer Bedeutung verwendet werden, sächlich.
	• **London** is a modern city. **She** has one of the most important banking centers in the world.	• **London** is the capital of Great Britain. **It** has more than 7 million inhabitants.
Verkehrsmittel, Maschinen	Die Namen von Autos, Flugzeugen, Lokomotiven, Maschinen und besonders von Schiffen können auch weibliches Geschlecht haben.	Die Namen von Autos, Flugzeugen, Schiffen, Lokomotiven und Maschinen sind in der Regel sächlich.
	• The ship **Britannia** is used by the royal family. **She** is, however, very controversial because **she** costs a lot of money.	• Can you see the **Airbus** over there? **It** is one of the most important planes in the world.

Das Substantiv

Übungen zum Geschlecht des Substantivs

1. **Setzen Sie das entsprechende Personal- oder Possessivpronomen ein.**

    1. Since the second world war Australia has enjoyed ... greatest period of economic growth.

    2. Under the rule of the Tudor monarchs, among them Henry VIII and Elizabeth I, England regained ... national unity.

    3. When did you feed the dog? I fed ... an hour ago.

    4. This is our dog, ... name is Jimmy.

    5. That's Brian's girl friend. What's ... name. Sheila.

    6. I want some of your special stamps: They're for my German pen-friend Klaus. ... collects stamps.

    7. If there was a snake we'd hunt ... and kill ....

    8. No teacher would profess that ... knows all the answers.

    9. Our teacher Miss Taylor said this morning ... can't teach me anything.

    10. America is convinced that all ... institutions and achievements are the biggest and best in the world.

    11. Canada won ... freedom without rebellion.

    12. The cat lay on ... side on the floor, panting.

    13. Don't tease the dog, lest ... should bite you.

    14. His mother drew her arm round the child and pressed ... face against her breast.

    15. The passenger cannot claim ... seat unless he takes possession of it by the time the train leaves the station.

                                                                                          richtig   falsch

    Die entsprechenden Lösungen befinden sich auf Seite 437.

Das Substantiv

Der Numerus des Substantivs (The Number of the Noun)

Die meisten Substantive erhalten im Plural (Mehrzahl) ein -s. Einige Substantive haben jedoch besondere Pluralformen.

Singular	Plural	Singular	Plural
-ch	-ches	Endung einiger Substantive im Singular.	Pluralform der im Singular auf -ch endenden Substantive. Das -e in der Endung -ches wird ausgesprochen [i].
		• witch • inch	• witches [wit∫iz] • inches
-f(e)	-ves	Endung einiger Substantive germanischer Herkunft im Singular.	Pluralform der im Singular auf -f(e) endenden Substantive germanischer Herkunft.
		• knife • wife	• knives • wives
-f(e)	-f(e)s	Endung einiger Substantive romanischer Herkunft im Singular.	Pluralform der im Singular auf -f(e) endenden Substantive romanischer Herkunft.
		• handkerchief • safe	• handkerchiefs • safes
-o	-oes	Endung einiger Substantive im Singular.	Pluralform der im Singular auf -o endenden Substantive, wenn dem -o ein Konsonant vorausgeht.
		• potato • tomato	• potatoes • tomatoes
-o	-os	Endung einiger Substantive im Singular.	Pluralform der im Singular auf -o endenden Substantve, die als Fremdwörter gelten.
		• folio • photo • piano	• folios • photos • pianos
-oof	-oofs	Endung einiger Substantive im Singular.	Pluralform der im Singular auf -oof endenden Substantive.

Das Substantiv

Singular	Plural	Singular	Plural
		▪ pr**oof** ▪ r**oof**	▪ pr**oofs** ▪ r**oofs**
-sh	**-shes**	Endung einiger Substantive im Singular.	Pluralform der im Singular auf -sh endenden Substantive. Das -e in der Endung -shes wird ausgesprochen [i].
		▪ dish ▪ wish	▪ dish**es** [diʃiz] ▪ wish**es**
-ss	**-sses**	Endung einiger Substantive im Singular.	Pluralform der im Singular auf -ss endenden Substantive. Das -e in der Endung -sses wird ausgesprochen [i].
		▪ cla**ss** ▪ gla**ss**	▪ cla**sses** [kla:siz] ▪ gla**sses**
-x	**-xes**	Endung einiger Substantive im Singular.	Pluralform der im Singular auf -x endenden Substantive. Das -e in der Endung -xes wird ausgesprochen [i].
		▪ a**x** ▪ bo**x**	▪ a**xes** [æksiz] ▪ bo**xes**
-y	**-ies**	Endung einiger Substantive im Singular.	Pluralform der im Singular auf -y endenden Substantive, wenn dem -y ein Konsonant vorausgeht.
		▪ bab**y** ▪ famil**y**	▪ bab**ies** ▪ famil**ies**
-y	**-ys**	Endung einiger Substantive im Singular.	Pluralform der im Singular auf -y endenden Substantive, wenn dem -y ein Vokal vorausgeht.
		▪ bo**y** ▪ da**y**	▪ bo**ys** ▪ da**ys**

Das Substantiv

Singular	Plural	Singular	Plural
-a-	-e-	Einige Substantive germanischer Herkunft haben besondere Pluralformen.	Substantive germanischer Herkunft wandeln das -a im Plural in -e um.
		• man • woman [wumən]	• men • women [wimin]
-oo-	-ee-	Einige Substantive germanischer Herkunft haben besondere Pluralformen.	Substantive germanischer Herkunft wandeln -oo im Plural in -ee um.
		• foot • tooth	• feet • teeth
-ous-	-ic-	Einige Substantive germanischer Herkunft haben besondere Pluralformen.	Substantive germanischer Herkunft wandeln -ous im Plural in -ic um.
		• louse • mouse	• lice • mice

Das Substantiv

Singular	Plural	
Stoffnamen bezeichnen in der Regel etwas Nichtzählbares und werden daher nur im Singular verwendet.	Einige Stoffnamen können zur Bezeichnung von Einzelstücken, verschiedenen Sorten etc. im Plural verwendet werden.	Substantive, die nur im Singular, Plural vorkommen

- Mary is a fan of dried **fruit**.
  (Mary ist ein Fan von Dörr**obst**.)
- Her **hair** is beautiful.
  (Ihr (Kopf)**Haar** ist schön.)
- Waiter, will you please remove **this hair** from my plate.
  (Herr Ober, nehmen Sie bitte **dieses Haar** aus meinem Teller!)

- In summer, you can see the farmers reaping their **fruits**.
  (Im Sommer kann man die Bauern beim Ernten ihrer **Früchte** sehen.)
- He has absolutely no **hairs** on his head.
  (Er hat absolut keine **Haare** auf dem Kopf.)

Folgende Substantive kommen nur im Singular vor.
Sie können nicht in Verbindung mit dem unbestimmten Artikel stehen. Um deutlich zu machen, dass es sich bei diesen Substantiven um einzelne Dinge handelt, können sie mit **a, (two, three ...) piece(s) of** verbunden werden.

- advice — Rat, Ratschläge
- ash — Zigarettenasche
- business — Geschäft(e)
- equipment — Ausrüstung(en)
- evidence — Beweis(e)
- food — Lebensmittel
- furniture — Möbel
- homework — Hausaufgabe(n)
- information — Information(en)
- knowledge — Kenntnis(se)
- machinery — Maschinen
- merchandise — Ware(n)
- news — Nachricht(en)
- produce — Erzeugnis(se)
- progress — Fortschritt(e)
- remorse — Reue
- strength — Kraft, Kräfte

Folgende Substantive kommen nur im Plural vor.

- arms — Waffen
- ashes — Asche (im Ofen)
- belongings — Habseligkeiten
- clothes — Kleidung
- contents — Inhalt
- doings — Taten
- earnings — Verdienst
- goods — Ware(n)
- the Middle Ages — Mittelalter
- oats — Hafer
- outskirts — Randgebiet
- premises — Grundstück
- riches — Reichtum
- stairs — Treppe
- surroundings — Umgebung
- thanks — Dank
- victuals — Lebensmittel

- He fainted when he heard this terrible **(piece of) news.**
  (Er fiel in Ohnmacht, als er diese schreckliche **Nachricht** hörte.)
- He gave me **three pieces of information**: the time of departure, the time of arrival and the meeting place.
  (Er gab mir **drei Informationen** ...)

- My **earnings** are $ 1,000 a week.
- We have a house on the **outskirts** of Chicago.
- He expressed his **thanks** for the wonderful hospitality.
- She has several maple trees on the **premises**.

Das Substantiv

Singular	Plural
	Einige Substantive, vor allem solche, die Werkzeuge und Kleidungsstücke bezeichnen, die aus zwei Teilen bestehen, kommen nur im Plural vor. Um deutlich zu machen, dass es sich bei diesen Substantiven um einzelne Stücke handelt, können sie mit some pairs of oder a (two, three ...) pair(s) of verbunden werden.

- binoculars — Fernglas
- braces — Hosenträger
- breeches — enge Kniehose
- compasses — Zirkel
- glasses — Brille
- goggles — Schutzbrille
- jeans — Jeanshose
- knickerbockers — Knickerbocker
- lungs — Lunge
- pants — Unterhose
- pincers — Kneifzange
- pliers — Kombizange
- pyjamas — Pyjama
- scales — Waage
- scissors — Schere
- shears — Heckenschere
- shorts — kurze Hose
- spectacles — Brille
- suspenders (AE) — Hosenträger
- tights — Strumpfhose
- tongs — Feuerzange
- trousers — lange Hose

- These **scissors** are not sharp enough.
  (Diese **Schere** ist nicht scharf genug.)
- This pair of **scissors** is not sharp enough.
  (Diese **Schere** ist nicht scharf genug.)
- These pairs of **scissors** are not sharp enough.
  (Diese **Scheren** sind nicht scharf genug.)

Substantive im Singular mit Plural-s; Substantive im Plural ohne -s

Singular	Plural
The United States und the Netherlands gelten als Substantive im Singular und stehen daher mit einem Verb im Singular.	Bezeichnungen der Nationalität (meist substantivierte Adjektive), die auf Zischlaut enden, erhalten kein Plural-s.
- The Netherlands is the country of cheese and wind mills.	- The Dutch are famous for their cheese and wind mills.

Das Substantiv

Singular	Plural	
Substantivierte Adjektive auf -ch, -sh zur Bezeichnung der Nationalität können nicht als Substantive im Singular verwendet werden. Sie haben für den Singular ein besonderes Wort. Die Substantive die auf -man enden, hängen für die weibliche Bezeichnung -woman an.	Die Substantive, die im Singular auf -man und -woman enden, können im Plural -men und -women anhängen.	Substantive auf -ch, -sh, -ss, -se, -man, -woman

- Dutch — a Dutchman
  holländisch — ein Holländer
- English — an Englishman
  englisch — ein Engländer
- French — a Frenchman
  französisch — ein Franzose
- Scotch — a Scotsman
  schottisch — ein Schotte
- Spanish — a Spaniard
  spanisch — ein Spanier
- Swedish — a Swede
  schwedisch — ein Schwede
- Polish — a Pole
  polnisch — ein Pole
- Turkish — a Turk
  türkisch — ein Türke

- Peter is **an Englishman,** but his father is **a Frenchman**.
- This morning, I met three **Englishmen** at the station.

Die Namen von Wissenschaften auf -ics sind Substantive im Singular.	Die Namen praktischer Tätigkeiten auf -ics (vor allem Sportarten) sind Substantive im Plural.	Substantive auf -ics

- **Mathematics is** an exact science.
  (**Die Mathematik** ist eine exakte Wissenschaft.)
- **Athletics are** a very popular sport.
  (**Leichtathletik** ist ein sehr beliebter Sport.)

Die Namen von Krankheiten sind Substantive im Singular.		Krankheiten

- **Measles is** not a serious illness.
  (**Masern** sind keine ernste Krankheit.)

Die Namen von Spielen sind Substantive im Singular.		Spiele

- **Darts is** a very popular game.
  (**Darts** ist ein sehr beliebtes Spiel.)

In der Bedeutung *Volk* kann people mit dem unbestimmten Artikel und einem Verb im Singular stehen und zur Bezeichnung des Plurals (Völker) ein -s erhalten.	Die Substantive cattle (Vieh) und people (Leute) sind Substantive im Plural, auch wenn sie nicht auf Plural-s enden.	people cattle

Das Substantiv

Substantive mit gleicher Form im Singular und Plural

Singular	Plural
▪ The Americans are said to be **a** rich **people**. (Man sagt, die Amerikaner seien *ein* reiches **Volk**.) ▪ America is a country of many different **peoples**. (Amerika ist ein Land vieler verschiedener **Völker**.)	▪ He has about *one hundred* **cattle** to sell. (Er hat ungefähr 100 Stück **Vieh** zu verkaufen). ▪ This morning, I met *two* strange **people** at the station. (Heute Morgen traf ich *zwei* seltsame **Leute** am Bahnhof.)
Die folgenden Sammelnamen gelten als Substantive im Singular und stehen folglich auch mit einem Verb im Singular, wenn sie eine Gruppe von Personen bezeichnen.	Die folgenden Sammelnamen gelten als Substantive im Plural und stehen folglich auch mit einem Verb im Plural, wenn sie jede einzelne Person, jedes einzelne Ding einer Gruppe bezeichnen.
▪ army — Armee ▪ audience — Publikum ▪ class — Klasse ▪ company — Firma ▪ couple — Paar ▪ crew — Mannschaft ▪ crowd — Menge ▪ enemy — Feind ▪ family — Familie ▪ government — Regierung ▪ group — Gruppe ▪ majority — Mehrheit ▪ parliament — Parlament ▪ party — Partei ▪ police — Polizei ▪ public — Öffentlichkeit ▪ staff — Personal ▪ team — Team	▪ army — Armee ▪ audience — Publikum ▪ class — Klasse ▪ company — Firma ▪ couple — Paar ▪ crew — Mannschaft ▪ crowd — Menge ▪ enemy — Feind ▪ family — Familie ▪ government — Regierung ▪ group — Gruppe ▪ majority — Mehrheit ▪ parliament — Parlament ▪ party — Partei ▪ police — Polizei ▪ public — Öffentlichkeit ▪ staff — Personal ▪ team — Team
▪ The **police has** caught the criminal in the very act.	▪ There *are many* **police** in the town due to the football game.
Einige Substantive, vor allem Tiernamen, haben im Singular und Plural dieselbe Form.	Einige Substantive, vor allem Tiernamen, haben im Singular und Plural dieselbe Form. Diese Substantive erhalten, auch wenn sie im Plural verwendet werden, in der Regel kein -s.
▪ antelope — Antilope ▪ beaver — Biber ▪ cod — Kabeljau ▪ craft — Fahrzeug ▪ deer — Hirsch, Reh ▪ fish — Fisch ▪ pike — Hecht ▪ salmon — Lachs	▪ antelope — Antilopen ▪ beaver — Biber ▪ cod — Kabeljaus ▪ craft — Fahrzeuge ▪ deer — Hirsche, Rehe ▪ fish — Fische ▪ pike — Hechte ▪ salmon — Lachse

Das Substantiv

Singular	Plural
• sheep — Schaf • trout — Forelle	• sheep — Schafe • trout — Forellen
• Farmer O'Brian has **a** black **sheep** in his flock.	• Farmer O'Brian has two dogs to drive his **sheep** together.
Die folgenden Substantive haben im Singular und Plural dieselbe Form. Diese Substantive haben ein -s, auch wenn sie im Singular verwendet werden.	Die folgenden Substantive haben im Singular und Plural dieselbe Form.
• barracks — Kaserne • gallows — der Galgen • headquarters — Hauptquartier • means — das Mittel • series — Serie • species — Art • works — Fabrik, Werk	• barracks — Kasernen • gallows — die Galgen • headquarters — Hauptquartiere • means — die Mittel • series — Serien • species — Arten • works — Fabriken, Werke
• Is there **a means** of solving the problem? (Gibt es **ein Mittel** das Problem zu lösen?)	• There are **a lot of means** of solving the problem. (Es gibt **viele Mittel** das Problem zu lösen.)
	Einige Substantive haben zwei Pluralformen mit unterschiedlicher Bedeutung. — *Substantive mit zwei Pluralformen*
• **brother** — Bruder • **cloth** — Tuch • **die** — Würfel; Prägestempel • **penny** — Penny	• brothers — Brüder (leibliche) • brethren — Mitbrüder • clothes — Kleider • cloths — Tücher • dice — Würfel • dies — Prägestempel • pennies — Pennymünzen • pence — Pence (Wertangabe)
• This glass can be cleaned with **a** cotton **cloth**.	• These glasses can be cleaned with cotton **cloths**. • John has **a lot of** very expensive **clothes**.
	Einige Substantive haben eine Pluralform mit zwei verschiedenen Bedeutungen. — *Pluralformen mit unterschiedlichen Bedeutungen*
• colour — Farbe • compass — Kompass • custom — Sitte • force — Kraft • glass — Glas • manner — Art • mountain — Berg	• colours — Farben / Fahne • compasses — Kompasse / Zirkel • customs — Sitten / Zoll • forces — Kräfte / Streitkräfte • glasses — Gläser / Brille • manners — Arten / Benehmen • mountains — Berge / Gebirge

Das Substantiv

	Singular		Plural	
	• quarter	ein Viertel	• quarters	Viertel Quartier
	• scale	Schale, Schuppe	• scales	Schalen Waage
	• spectacle	Schauspiel	• spectacles	Schauspiele Brille
	• spirit	Geist	• spirits	Geister Laune; Schnaps
	• step	Schritt, Stufe	• steps	Schritte Leiter
	• trouble	Mühe	• troubles	Mühen Sorgen
	• wit	Geist, Esprit, Witz	• wits	Witze Verstand
	• work	Arbeit	• works	Werke Fabriken
	• Mount Everest is the highest **mountain** in the world.		• Switzerland has **a lot of mountains.** • John lives in the **mountains.**	

Substantive mit unregelmäßigen Pluralformen

	Plural	
	Einige Substantive haben unregelmäßige Pluralformen. Dies sind meist Fremdwörter, die die Pluralform ihrer Herkunftssprache behalten.	

Singular		Plural	
• analysis	Analyse	• analyses	Analysen
• appendix	Appendix	• appendices, -xes	Appendices
• axis	Achse	• axes	Achsen
• bacillus	Bazillus	• bacilli	Bazillen
• bacterium	Bakterie	• bacteria	Bakterien
• basis	Basis	• bases	Basen
• cactus	Kaktus	• cacti, cactuses	Kakteen
• child	Kind	• children	Kinder
• chorus	Chor	• choruses	Chöre
• crisis	Krise	• crises	Krisen
• datum	Datum	• data	Daten
• erratum	Druckfehler	• errata	Druckfehlerverzeichnis
• formula	Formel	• formulae	Formeln
• index	Inhaltsverzeichnis	• indices, indexes	Inhaltsverzeichnisse
• medium	Mittel	• media	Mittel
• memorandum	Merkzeichen	• memoranda	Merkzeichen
• oasis	Oase	• oases	Oasen
• ox	Ochse	• oxen	Ochsen
• parenthesis	Klammer	• parentheses	Klammern
• phenomenon	Phänomen	• phenomena	Phänomene
• prospectus	Prospekt	• prospectuses	Prospekte
• radius	Radius	• radii	Radien
• synthesis	Synthese	• syntheses	Synthesen
• terminus	Fachwort	• termini	Fachwörter
• thesis	These	• theses	Thesen

• Our country is recovering very slowly from **this** economic **crisis**.

• Last year was a year of **many** political **crises**.

Maßangaben

Maßangaben stehen, wenn sie mit dem Zahlwort 1 verbunden sind, im Singular. Wird der Maßangabe ein Zahlwort mit Bindestrich vorangestellt, steht die Maßangabe im Sin-

Maßangaben stehen, wenn sie mit einem Zahlwort über 1 verbunden sind, im Plural.
Folgt der Maßangabe ein geringerer Wert als der Wert vor der Maß-

Das Substantiv

Singular

gular. Folgt der Maßangabe ein geringerer Wert als der Wert vor der Maßangabe, kann die Maßangabe im Singular stehen. Die Maßangabe foot steht meist vor einem weiteren Zahlwort ohne zusätzliche Maßangabe. Die Maßangabe stone steht grundsätzlich im Singular.

- He earns one **dollar** an hour.
- He gave me a **five-pound** note.
- He earns five **pound** four a week.
- The height is five **foot** three.
- Its weight is twelve **stone**.

Folgende Mengenangaben stehen mit einem Verb im Singular, wenn sie sich auf ein Substantiv im Singular beziehen.

- a certain amount of — ein gewisser Betrag
- a bit of — ein bisschen
- a good/great deal of — eine Menge
- a lot of — eine Menge
- lots of — viele
- the number of — eine Anzahl
- part of — ein Teil
- plenty of — ziemlich viele

- A good deal of **time** is necessary.
- A lot of **money** was raised for cancer research.

Die Mengenangaben dozen, hundred, thousand und million stehen im Singular, wenn sie mit einem Zahlwort oder a few, several verbunden sind.

- Five **thousand** people lost their lives in the earthquake.
- He lives a few **thousand** miles away.

Körperteile und Kleidungsstücke, wenn sie sich auf eine Person beziehen.

- The boy had his **hand** in his **pocket**.

Plural

angabe, kann die Maßangabe im Plural stehen. Die Maßangabe feet steht meist, wenn kein Zahlwort folgt.

- He earns two **dollars** an hour.
- He earns five **pounds** a week.
- He earns five **pounds** four a week.
- She is five **feet** tall.
- We climbed 2,000 **feet**.

Folgende Mengenangaben können mit Substantiven im Plural verbunden werden. Sie verlangen dann auch ein Verb im Plural.

- a few (of) — ein paar
- a good many (of) — ziemlich viele
- a number of — eine Anzahl
- a lot of — eine Menge
- lots of — viele
- part of — ein Teil
- plenty of — ziemlich viele

- A number of **students** have passed the exam.
- A lot of **research grants** were awarded.

Die Mengenangaben dozen, hundred, thousand und million stehen im Plural, wenn sie nicht mit einem Zahlwort oder wenn sie mit many verbunden sind.

- **Thousands** of people lost their lives in the earthquake.
- Many **hundreds** of protesters assembled in the street.

Körperteile und Kleidungsstücke, wenn sie sich auf mehrere Personen beziehen. Diese stehen im Deutschen oft im Singular.

- The boys had their **hands** in their **pockets**.
  (Die Jungen hatten die Hand in der Tasche.)

Mengenangaben

Körperteile, Kleidungsstücke im Deutschen oft Singular

Das Substantiv

death,
life,
mind,
temper

Singular	Plural
Die Substantive death, life, mind und temper stehen im Singular, wenn sie sich auf ein Wort im Singular beziehen.	Die Substantive death, life, mind und temper stehen, wenn sie sich auf Wörter im Plural beziehen, im Plural. Im Deutschen stehen sie meist im Singular.
▪ The man lost his **life** in the accident.	▪ Thousands of people lost their **lives** in the earthquake. (Tausende von Menschen verloren bei dem Erdbeben ihr **Leben**.)

Pluralbildung zusammengesetzter Substantive

Für die Pluralbildung zusammengesetzter Substantive lassen sich keine allgemein gültigen Regeln aufstellen. Als Faustregel gilt jedoch, dass in Zusammensetzungen, die aus einem Substantiv und anderen Wortarten (Adjektive, Präpositionen etc.) bestehen, generell das Substantiv das Plural-s erhält.

In Zusammensetzungen aus mehreren Substantiven erhält generell das Grundwort das Plural-s. In Zusammensetzungen aus Substantiv und anderen Wortarten ist das Substantiv das Grundwort und erhält das Plural-s.	• My uncle has a lot of **apple-trees** in his garden. • May I introduce you to John and Peter? They are my **brothers-in-law**. • Our school has three **reading-rooms**.	Zusammensetzungen mit Grundwort
Ist kein Grundwort vorhanden, so wird das Plural-s am letzten Teil der Zusammensetzung angehängt. Dies gilt besonders für Zusammensetzungen, die kein Substantiv enthalten.	• She is very ill. Last month, she had three nervous **break-downs**. • **Grown-ups** have to pay two pounds, students and children have to pay one pound.	Zusammensetzungen ohne Grundwort
Bei Mengenangaben auf -ful wird das Plural-s an den letzten Teil der Zusammensetzung angehängt.	• He had only eaten three **spoonfuls** when his boss wanted to see him.	Mengenangaben auf -ful
In Zusammensetzungen mit man und woman werden, zur Bezeichnung des Geschlechts, beide Teile in den Plural gesetzt.	• She prefers to go to **women-doctors**. • He prefers to go to **men-doctors**.	Zusammensetzungen aus man und woman

Das Substantiv

Übungen zum Numerus des Substantivs

1. Setzen Sie die folgenden Substantive in den Plural.

1. box
2. buffalo
3. church
4. crisis
5. difficulty
6. journey
7. life
8. roof
9. studio
10. success
11. wish
12. tie
13. tax
14. ghetto
15. ax

richtig   falsch

2. Setzen Sie die entsprechende Form von to be im present tense simple ein.

1. Athletics ... my favourite subject.
2. I think a pair of binoculars ... just as expensive as a camera.
3. Part of the class ... late.
4. The majority ... poor and uneducated.
5. His mathematics ... not so good as it was.
6. The Netherlands ... an agricultural country.

Das Substantiv

7. He thinks that the news ... of great importance.

8. Curious people ... standing round the car.

9. The stairs ... steep and slippery.

10. Although the United States ... a rich society, poverty exists there.

11. The police ... going to wonder where the hell he went to.

12. Southern politics ... different.

13. His progress ... continuous.

14. Automation and technological progress ... essential to the general welfare.

15. The public ... taught that staying up to date is one of the first duties of man.

richtig falsch

Die entsprechenden Lösungen befinden sich auf Seite 437.

Das Substantiv

Common und Possessive Case

Das moderne Englisch kennt nur zwei Kasusformen beim Substantiv, den common case (Subjekt-, Objektfall) und den possessive case (Besitzfall). Der possessive case gibt den Besitzer, den Urheber einer Handlung an und wird durch Anhängen von `s gebildet. Substantive im Singular erhalten die Endung `s, Substantive im Plural oder solche, die bereits auf -s enden erhalten die Endung `.
In bestimmten Fällen kann der possessive case neben dem Apostroph-s auch durch eine Beifügung + of ausgedrückt werden.

Objektfall;
Besitzfall
kein Apostroph-s
im Deutschen

Common Case	Possessive Case
Ein Substantiv steht im common case, wenn es Subjekt oder direktes oder indirektes Objekt ist. Seine Form ändert sich dabei nicht.	Ein Substantiv steht im possessive case, wenn es den Besitz ausdrückt. Es ist zu beachten, dass das -s im Deutschen ohne Apostroph an das Substantiv angehängt wird.
• The boy is playing in the garden. • Peter gives his sister the book. • Peter gives the book to his sister. • Peter buys a book.	• Yesterday, I met my brother's friend at school. (Gestern traf ich den Freund meines Bruders in der Schule.) • Yesterday, I met my brothers' friend at school. (Gestern traf ich den Freund meiner Brüder in der Schule.) • The children play in St. James' [dʒeimziz] Park. • The children play in St. James's [dʒeimziz] Park.
	In der Regel steht der possessive case vor dem näher zu bestimmenden Substantiv. Ist dieses mit dem unbestimmten Artikel, einem Zahlwort, einem Demonstrativ- oder Indefinitpronomen verbunden, so steht der possessive case + of (doppelter Genitiv)

Das Substantiv

Common Case	Possessive Case	
	hinter dem näher zu bestimmenden Substantiv. - Yesterday, I saw **Peter's** mother at the station. - Yesterday, I saw a friend of **Peter's** at the station. - At the moment, I read three books of **Shakespeare's**. - This morning, I met this friend of **Peter's**. - I invited some friends of **Peter's** to my party.	

Possessive Case	Beifügung + of	
Zur Bezeichnung des Besitzers oder des Urhebers einer Handlung steht der possessive case bei Lebewesen sowie bei personifizierten Substantiven. - Yesterday, I met **Peter's** friend. - The **birds'** singing can be heard everywhere. - **Great Britain's** history is taught to all children. - **God's** love is boundless. (Die Liebe **Gottes** ist grenzenlos.)	Besitzer oder Urheber einer Handlung werden mit of angeschlossen, wenn es sich nicht um ein Lebewesen, sondern um Sachen handelt. Einzelwesen, die näher bestimmt sind oder Personen, die Gegenstand einer Handlung sind, werden mit of angeschlossen. - The author of this **book** is very successful. - This is the car of my sister **Mary**. - The love of **God** means to act with responsibility. (Die Liebe zu Gott bedeutet verantwortungsbewusst zu handeln.)	Lebewesen; Sachen

Possessive Case	Beifügung + of	
Eigennamen werden an die folgenden Substantive nie mit of angeschlossen. - **number** Zahl - **river** Fluss	Eigennamen werden an die folgenden Substantive (vor allem geografische Begriffe) stehts mit of angeschlossen. - **city** Stadt - **continent** Kontinent	Eigennamen

Das Substantiv

	Common Case	Beifügung + of
	▪ year — Jahr ▪ word — Wort	▪ country — Land ▪ dignity — Hoheit ▪ hour — Stunde ▪ kind — Art, Weise ▪ kingdom — Königreich ▪ month — Monat ▪ name — Name ▪ office — Amt ▪ post — Posten ▪ province — Provinz ▪ rank — Rang ▪ sort — Sorte ▪ state — Staat ▪ title — Titel ▪ town — Stadt ▪ village — Dorf
	▪ Queen Elizabeth II was crowned in the **year 1952**.	▪ **The City of New York** is a melting pot. ▪ **The month of January** is one of the coldest months of the year.
	Eigennamen zur Bezeichnung historischer Ereignisse stehen weder im *possessive case*, noch mit einer Beifügung + *of*. ▪ **the Geneva Convention** ▪ **the Gulf War** ▪ **the Helsinki Accords** ▪ **the Watergate hearings** ▪ **the Berlin airlift**	
Sammelnamen		Sammelnamen werden grundsätzlich mit *of* angeschlossen. ▪ The needs **of this minority** are being discussed in the meeting.
	Possessiv Case	Beifügung + *of*
Titel	Ordnungszahlen werden an den Herrschernamen im *possessive case* angeschlossen.	Titel werden immer mit *of* angeschlossen.

Das Substantiv

Possessive Case	Beifügung + of	
Elizabeth the First's reign lasted from 1588 to 1603.	**The Duke of Edinburgh** is Queen Elizabeth's husband.	
	Substantivierte Adjektive werden grundsätzlich mit of angeschlossen.	substantivierte Adjektive
	She sacrificed herself for the needs **of the poor** and the ill.	
Zur Bezeichnung des Zeitraums. Die Dauer von Kriegen wird immer nur mit dem possessive case bezeichnet.	Bezeichnungen des Zeitraums werden mit of angeschlossen oder durch ein zusammengesetztes Adjektiv ausgedrückt.	Zeitangaben
We waited for two **hours'** time. During the **Thirty Years' War,** many people lost their lives.	We waited for a time **of two hours.** A **five-hour** walk lay still in front of us.	
Bei Ortsbestimmungen (mit at und to), wenn ein öffentliches Gebäude, ein Geschäft, ein Haus oder eine Wohnung zu bezeichnen ist.	Ortsangaben zu geschichtlichen Ereignissen.	Ortsangaben
During our holiday in Great Britain, we also visited **St. Paul's** (Cathedral). We will meet at **Peter's** (pub) tonight. On your way to town, you have to go to your **sister's** (house).	Napoleon was defeated in the **Battle of Waterloo** in 1815. **The Treaty of Versailles** was signed on June the 28th, 1919. **The Norman Invasion of England** took place in 1066.	

Common Case	Possessive Case	Beifügung + of	
Die Zahlwörter hundred, thousand, million und dozen werden ohne of angeschlossen, wenn eine Grundzahl vorausgeht.	Die Begriffe dollar, pound und money können, wenn ihnen ein Possessivpronomen oder Zahlwort vorausgeht, im possessive	Nach Mengen- und unbestimmten Zahlenangaben (partitiver Genitiv). ▪ a bundle of ein Bündel	Maß-, und Mengenangaben

Das Substantiv

Common Case	Possessive Case	Beifügung + of
	case stehen, wenn ihnen der Begriff worth nachfolgt.	▪ a cup of — eine Tasse ▪ a glass of — ein Glas ▪ a great deal of — eine Menge ▪ a group of — eine Gruppe ▪ hundreds of — Hunderte von ▪ thousands of — Tausende von ▪ a lot of — viele ▪ a number of — eine Anzahl von ▪ a packet of — ein Pack von ▪ a large part of — ein großer Teil von ▪ a piece of — ein Stück von ▪ a pound of — ein Pfund von ▪ a slice of — eine Scheibe von
▪ Two **million** people attended the museum this year. ▪ I would like three **dozen** eggs, please.	▪ She sold 100,000 **pounds'** worth of gold. ▪ Nowadays it is not easy to get your **money's** worth.	▪ Every evening, I drink **a glass of** milk. ▪ **All of us** were surprised about this news.
Bezeichnungen der Entfernung können mit zusammengesetzten Adjektiven ausgedrückt werden.	Zur Bezeichnung der Entfernung steht der possessive case nur in Verbindung mit dem Wort distance.	Bezeichnungen der Entfernung können mit of angeschlossen werden.
▪ A **ten-mile** walk still lay in front of us.	▪ He observed them from a 20 **yards'** distance. ▪ We were still a ten **miles'** distance from home.	▪ He observed them from a **distance of** 20 yards.

Das Substantiv

Übungen zum Common und Possessive Case

1. Setzen Sie die blau gedruckten Substantive in den possessive case.

1. Parents sometimes invite their children ... friends to a party.
2. Oliver doesn't know Jenny ... address.
3. How many times have you washed your father ... car?
4. St. James ... Park is the largest of the London parks.
5. Tom's mother went to a parents ... evening at school.
6. I can hardly wait to see the boys ... faces at school tomorrow.
7. Joan took a post as superintendent of a women ... hospital.
8. The envelope containing Mrs Stevens ... letter had disappeared.
9. He was a welcome guest at gentlemen ... parties.
10. Smith ... companions were killed in an accident.

richtig   falsch

2. Verwenden Sie den possessive oder common case oder eine Beifügung mit of.

1. He is a drinker and he would sell his soul for a (bottle, wine).
2. Mr Robinson drew a (hundred, pounds) from the bank yesterday.
3. (Mrs Stevens, husband) had been a heavy drinker.
4. The (chairman, the House of Commons) is the Speaker.
5. Oxford University is the oldest of (Britain, universities) and was founded in the 12th century.
6. In the spring of 1775 the (City, Boston) on the east coast of America was full of English soldiers.
7. The church whose dome looks like half a football is called (St. Paul)
8. The (River, Thine) is longer than the (River, Thames)
9. He wanted to fly to Paris to stay there for three weeks with the Dubois, some friends of his (father).

Das Substantiv

10. There isn't much bread left. Someone must go to the **(baker)**.

11. Bob's father had a good job as a train driver on the London Underground and his mother worked part-time in **(Woolworth)**.

12. For more than **(a hundred, years)** Britain was **(Australia, chief customer)** for wool and meat.

13. She never rests till she knows every detail of **(everybody, family secrets)**.

14. Queen Victoria was proclaimed **(Empress, India)** in 1876.

15. The Greyhound Bus company provides tickets for unlimited travel all over the United States for a **(three months, period)**.   richtig   falsch

Die entsprechenden Lösungen befinden sich auf Seite 437ff.

Das Adjektiv (The Adjective)

Das Adjektiv (Eigenschaftswort, Wiewort) drückt eine Eigenschaft aus und bezieht sich im Satz auf ein oder mehrere Substantive. Es ist stets unveränderlich.

Attributives Adjektiv (Attributive Adjective)

Das attributive Adjektiv steht eng beim Substantiv.

- an **intelligent** child
- a **nice** boy

Prädikatives Adjektiv (Predicative Adjective)

Das prädikative Adjektiv wird durch ein Verb (meist to be) mit dem Substantiv verbunden.

- This flower is **beautiful.**
- This book is **interesting.**
- This child is **intelligent.**

Das Adjektiv wird durch Voranstellen des bestimmten Artikels zum Substantiv. Es bezeichnet dann alle Personen einer bestimmten Gruppe oder bei Sachen ein Abstraktum.
Adjektive, die als Substantive gelten, können auch den Plural bilden. Völkernamen auf -ch, -sh, -se und -ss haben im Singular und Plural dieselbe Form.

- The **rich** always grow richer, and the **poor** always grow poorer.
- We had no other choice but hope for the **best.**
- Who do you think will win the election, the **Republicans** or the **Democrats**?
- The **English** and the **Germans** have a lot of interests in common.

Das Adjektiv

Die Steigerung des Adjektivs (The Comparison of the Adjective)

Das Englische kennt neben der Grundstufe die folgenden Steigerungsformen beim Adjektiv. Dabei unterscheidet man die germanische und romanische Steigerungsart.

Positiv (Positive)

Der Positiv ist die Grundstufe des Adjektivs. Er drückt aus, dass zwei oder mehr Wesen oder Dinge in Bezug auf eine Eigenschaft gleich sind; gleicher Grad.
Zur Verstärkung des Positivs dienen very (sehr) und most (überaus).

- Mary and Peggy are young.
- These books are interesting.
- My mother and Father are busy.
- Peter is as nice as John.
- Mary is very nice and most honest.
  (Mary ist sehr nett und überaus aufrichtig.)

Komparativ (Comparative)

Der Komparativ drückt aus, dass zwei Wesen oder Dinge in Bezug auf eine Eigenschaft ungleich sind; ungleicher Grad.
Germanisch: Adjektiv + -er
Romanisch: more + Adjektiv

- Mary is younger than Peggy.
- Peter is nicer than John.
- These houses are smaller.
- This boy is more intelligent.
- These books are more interesting.

Zur Verstärkung des Komparativs dienen much (viel), even (sogar noch), still (noch) und far (weit) und by far (bei weitem), das dem Komparativ stets nachgestellt wird.

- Mary is much younger than Peggy and still younger/even younger than Susan.
- Mary is younger than Peggy by far.

Der Komparativ wird durch no oder not any verneint.

- This problem is no easier/not any easier to solve than that one.

Die allmählich zunehmende Steigerung (immer) wird bei den germanisch gesteigerten Adjektiven durch Wiederholung des Komparativs und bei den romanisch gesteigerten Adjektiven durch more and more + Adjektiv ausgedrückt.

- Peter always gets younger and younger.
  (Peter wird immer jünger.)
- The problem grew more and more difficult.
  (Das Problem wurde immer schwieriger.)

Superlativ (Superlative)

Der Superlativ drückt aus, dass von mindestens drei Wesen oder Dingen einem der höchste Grad einer Eigenschaft zukommt; höchster Grad.
Germanisch: (the) Adjektiv + -est
Romanisch: (the) most + Adjektiv

- Mary is the youngest girl in our class.
- Peter is the nicest boy I know.
- These books are the most interesting books I have ever read.

Das Adjektiv

Zur Verstärkung des Superlativs dienen by far (bei weitem), das dem Superlativ vorangestellt wird und of all, das nach dem Superlativ steht.

- Mary was by far the youngest girl in our group.
- Mary was the youngest girl of all (girls in our group).

	Positiv	Komparativ	Superlativ	Allmähliche Steigerung
Germanisch	Adjektiv	Adjektiv + -er	Adjektiv + -est	Komparativ and Komparativ
Romanisch	Adjektiv	more + Adjektiv	(the) most + Adjektiv	more and more + Adjektiv
Verstärkung	very most	much, even, still, (by) far	by far of all	

Für die Wahl der Steigerungsart lassen sich bei den zweisilbigen Adjektiven keine verbindlichen Regeln aufstellen. Vielmehr hängt es oft auch von der Absicht und vom Klangempfinden des Sprechers ab, ob die germanische oder die romanische Steigerungsart gewählt wird.

Das Adjektiv

	Germanisch gesteigerte Adjektive	Romanisch gesteigerte Adjektive
einsilbige; mehrsilbige Adjektive	Alle einsilbigen Adjektive.	Alle drei- und mehrsilbigen Adjektive und alle Partizipien. Dabei steht most mit dem bestimmten Artikel, wenn ein Substantiv aus einer bestimmten Gruppe besonders hervorgehoben werden soll. Dies ist besonders beim Vergleich der Fall.
	- **deep - deeper - deepest** - **great - greater - greatest** - **young - younger - youngest**	- **difficult - more difficult - most difficult** - My brother Tom is **the most intelligent** boy in his class.
zweisilbige Adjektive	Zweisilbige Adjektive auf -y, -le, -er, -ow und die zweisilbigen Adjektive, die auf der zweiten Silbe betont werden.	Die meisten zweisilbigen Adjektive, die auf der ersten Silbe betont werden.
	- **easy - easier - easiest** - **happy - happier - happiest** - **polite - politer - politest**	- **polished - more polished - most polished** - **rapid - more rapid - most rapid**
	Folgende Adjektive werden auf germanische Art gesteigert, wenn sie vor Substantiven stehen.	Folgende Adjektive werden auf romanische Art gesteigert, wenn sie nicht vor Substantiven stehen.
	- clever — klug - common — gemeinsam - cruel — grausam - handsome — schön, stattlich - pleasant — angenehm - quiet — ruhig, still - solid — fest - stupid — dumm	- clever — klug - common — gemeinsam - cruel — grausam - handsome — schön, stattlich - pleasant — angenehm - quiet — ruhig, still - solid — fest - stupid — dumm
	- His **stupidest** mistake was to leave without saying anything.	- Peter's behaviour was **more stupid** than John's.

Das Adjektiv

Unregelmäßig gesteigerte Adjektive

Positiv		Komparativ	Superlativ
good	gut	**better**	**best**
bad	schlecht	**worse**	**worst**
evil	böse	**worse**	**worst**
ill	krank	**worse**	**worst**
many	viele	**more**	**most**
much	viel	**more**	**most**

Einige Adjektive haben im Komparativ und Superlativ verschiedene Formen. Es liegt dann auch ein Unterschied in der Bedeutung vor.

Bedeutungsunterschied

Positiv		Komparativ	Superlativ
far	weit (Entfernung)	**farther**	**farthest**
far	weit (übertragen)	**further**	**furthest**
late	spät	**later**	**latest**
late	letzter, letzt	**(the) latter**	**(the) last**
little	klein	**smaller**	**smallest**
little	gering	**less**	**least**
near	nahe (Entfernung)	**nearer**	**nearest**
near	nahe (Reihenfolge)	**nearer**	**next**
old	alt (wirkliches Alter)	**older**	**oldest**
old	alt (Vergleich von Familienmitgliedern)	**elder**	**eldest**

Das Adjektiv

Übungen zur Steigerung des Adjektivs

1. **Setzen Sie die Adjektive in Klammern in den Komparativ oder Superlativ.**

   1. Digital technology will make teleconferences (cheap) as well as (easy) to arrange.

   2. He was (pale) than before and breathless.

   3. It proved to be a (difficult) operation than they had thought.

   4. Nearly everything in New York is (big), (large), (noisy), (mad), and (fascinating) than in most other cities in the world.

   5. Comprehensive schools allow children to mix out of class with other children (poor) or (rich) than themselves.

   6. The (massive) a body is the (big) is its pull.

   7. You are (early) than today.

   8. Rapid economic growth made it less attractive to leave Europe with its (varied) scenery and culture.

   9. The curse of noise around airports was being dealt with by the development of (quiet) jet engines.

   10. The (simple) and (little) disturbing way of moving heavy loads, provided that there is no great hurry, is by water.   richtig   falsch

   Die entsprechenden Lösungen befinden sich auf Seite 438.

Das Adjektiv

Das Adjektiv mit einem Stützwort (The Adjective with a Prop-Word)

Das Adjektiv steht mit einem Stützwort, wenn einzelne Personen oder Dinge bezeichnet werden. Stützwörter sind Substantive und besonders das Pronomen one, ones, um zu vermeiden, dass ein zuvor genanntes Substantiv ständig wiederholt wird. One steht bezüglich eines Substantivs im Singular, ones steht bezüglich eines Substantivs im Plural.

Substantive als Stützwort	Kein Stützwort	
Als Stützwörter für einzelne Personen, Sachen dienen Substantive wie man, woman, person, thing etc.	Zur Bezeichnung mehrerer Personen oder Sachen, kann das Adjektiv durch Voranstellen des bestimmten Artikels substantiviert werden.	einzelne; mehrere Personen oder Sachen
• You need not help the rich man because he has enough money and knows a lot of people with great influence.	• You need not help the rich because they have enough money and know a lot of people with great influence.	

one, ones	Kein Stützwort	
Nach Komparativen oder Superlativen, die nicht mit dem bestimmten Artikel verbunden sind.	Nach Komparativen und Superlativen, die mit dem bestimmten Artikel stehen.	Komparativ, Superlativ
• These notepads are too thick. Haven't you got any thinner ones? (... Haven't you got thinner notepads?)	• The African peoples are the poorest of all peoples in the world.	
	Nach den Adjektiven few und many.	few, many
	• I cannot give you more. I have got only a few.	
	Nach den Grundzahlen bezüglich eines zuvor erwähnten Substantivs.	Grundzahlen
	• He has got five cars. We have got only two.	
Nach Ordnungszahlen, besonders zur Bezeichnung einer bestimmten Person oder Sache aus einer Anzahl.	Nach den Ordnungszahlen und zwar besonders nach the first, the second und the third.	Ordnungszahlen
• Which song from the CD do you like best? I like the fourth one.	• Our first teacher was much more polite than the second.	
	Nach dem Possessivpronomen + own.	Possessivpronomen + own
	• Is this car your own? • He hasn't paid his own?	

Das Adjektiv

Übungen zum Stützwort des Adjektivs

1. Setzen Sie das Stützwort one, ones ein wo nötig.

1. There was not a single bad ... among them.

2. What do you think of these two cars? I like the blue ... better than the red ....

3. I had a secretary who was with me for 9 years and then she decided to get married and I had to get a new ....

4. The bridges in London are the highest ... I ever saw.

5. The Millers have three children. The eldest ..., Kevin, is at a boarding school, so he only comes home during the holidays.

6. Alexander Graham Bell was one among many ..., who were experimenting with the possibility of transmitting speech by wire.

7. The United Kingdom is a unitary state, not a federal ...

8. The two armies were about equal in number, but Duke William's was the stronger ...

9. Of a population of about 50,000 aborigines, today only few ... still live a primitive life as nomadic hunters.

10. Not wanting to wait a year for our house, we built a prefabricated ....

richtig   falsch

Die entsprechenden Lösungen befinden sich auf Seite 438.

Das Adjektiv

Die Stellung des Adjektivs (The Position of the Adjective)

Normalerweise steht das Adjektiv unmittelbar vor dem Substantiv, das es näher bestimmt. In einigen Fällen kann das Adjektiv dem Substantiv auch nachgestellt werden.

Vor dem Substantiv	Nach dem Substantiv	
Attributive Adjektive, auch wenn sie durch ein Adverb näher bestimmt sind.	Attributive Adjektive, die durch ein anderes Wort, eine andere Wortgruppe als durch ein Adverb näher bestimmt sind.	attributive Adjektive
▪ He was an unusually intelligent boy.	▪ There were many horses decorated with wonderful plumes and flowers.	
	Attributive Adjektive, die besonders hervorgehoben werden sollen, können dem Substantiv nachgestellt werden.	
	▪ They needed all the information available to solve this problem.	
	Adjektive, die unmittelbar von einem Verb abgeleitet sind.	Adjektive verbalen Ursprungs
	▪ Opportunities seized are better than opportunities lost.	
	In einigen besonderen Redewendungen tritt das Adjektiv hinter das Substantiv.	Redewendungen
	▪ court martial — Kriegsgericht ▪ Lords Spiritual — geistliche Lords ▪ Lords Temporal — weltliche Lords ▪ the member present — anwesende Mitglieder ▪ Poet Laureate — Hofdichter ▪ Prince Consort — Prinzgemahl ▪ Princess Royal — älteste Tochter des Königs ▪ Solicitor General — Oberstaatsanwalt	
	▪ All the Lords Temporal and the Lords Spiritual assembled in the chamber.	

Das Adjektiv

Der Vergleich (The Comparison)

(No) ... than

bei Komparativen — Nach dem Komparativ wird der Vergleich durch than (als, wie) ausgedrückt.
Die Verneinung wird ausgedrückt durch no ... than (nicht ... als, wie).

- He is taller than I.
  (Er ist größer als ich.)
- He is no taller than I.
  (Er ist nicht größer als ich.)

Like

vor Substantiven, Pronomen — Vor Substantiven und Pronomen wird der Vergleich durch like (wie) ausgedrückt.
Like ist eine Präposition und kann nur in der Umgangssprache wie eine Konjunktion zur Verbindung zweier Satzteile verwendet werden.

- He cried like a baby.
  (Er weinte wie ein Baby.)
- He made the same mistake like his brother (had made).
  (Er machte den gleichen Fehler wie sein Bruder.)

As

vor Substantiven, Pronomen — Vor Substantiven und Pronomen wird der Vergleich durch as (wie) ausgedrückt, vor allem wenn ein ganzer Satz folgt.

- He made the same mistake as his brother (had made).
  (Er machte den gleichen Fehler wie sein Bruder.)

(Not) as ... as

bei Adjektiven, Adverbien — Bezüglich eines Adjektivs oder Adverbs wird der Vergleich ausgedrückt durch as ... as ((eben)so ... wie).
Die Verneinung lautet not as ... as (nicht so ... wie).

- His sister is as old as my brother.
  (Seine Schwester ist so alt wie mein Bruder.)
- His sister is not as old as my brother.
  (Seine Schwester ist nicht so alt wie mein Bruder.)

The ... the

vor Komparativen — The ... the (je ... desto) steht jeweils vor dem Komparativ.

- The harder he works the more tired he gets.

The + Komparativ

vor Komparativen — In der Bedeutung *je mehr* steht the vor dem Komparativ.

- I am becoming more efficient the longer I practise.

Das Adjektiv

All the

All the (umso, noch mehr) steht vor dem Komparativ.

- You have to be **all the** more careful when the streets are wet. — vor Komparativen

	Vor dem Komparativ	Vor Substantiven und Pronomen	Vor Adjektiven und Adverbien
than (als, wie)	(no ...) than		
like (wie)		like	
as (wie)		as (+ ganzer Satz)	
as ... as (so ... wie)			(not) as ... as
so ... as (so ... wie)			(not) so ... as
the ... the (je ... desto)	the ... the		
the (je mehr)	the		
all the (umso)	all the		

dnf 269

Das Adjektiv

Übungen zum Vergleich

1. Setzen Sie than, like oder as ein.

1. I found Venice much bigger ... I had supposed.
2. I see you do not trust me ... Miss Sheila trusts me.
3. I'm afraid I'm not as clever ... Charles is.
4. She behaved ... an angel.
5. They act ... amateurs.
6. Today there are no less ... 10 million scouts in 70 countries.
7. From our space lab, the sun, the moon, and the stars look brighter ... they do from the earth.
8. In some western states there are already more than half ... many cars ... people.
9. It was impossible to move ... much ... a centimetre in any direction.
10. Some jungle tribes still live ... their fathers lived for centuries before them.
11. The steam-engine did not put the horse out of action ... motors have done.
12. America buys only about half ... many dailies per person ... the United Kingdom.
13. He ran his fingers through his hair, ... his father sometimes did when he was irritated.
14. His smooth face was pale ... bone.
15. Tom wanted his Swedish to be ... good ... Bob's.

richtig falsch

Die entsprechenden Lösungen befinden sich auf Seite 438.

Das Adverb (The Adverb)

Das Adverb (Umstandswort) kann als adverbiale Bestimmung mit einem Verb stehen oder als Attribut zum Substantiv, Adjektiv oder zu einem anderen Adverb treten. Das Adjektiv steht zur näheren Bestimmung von Substantiven und Pronomen. Das Adverb dient zur Definition der Art und Weise (adverbs of manner), des Ortes (adverbs of place), der Zeit (adverbs of time), der Menge (adverbs of frequency) und des Grades, der Intensitiät (adverbs of degree).

Ursprüngliche Adverbien (Original Adverbs)

Die ursprünglichen Adverbien haben keine besondere Form.

- I slept quite well.
- He has come here.

Abgeleitete Adverbien (Derivative Adverbs)

Abgeleitete Adverbien hängen generell an das Adjektiv die Endung -ly an. Die genauen Ableitungsregeln gehen aus der folgenden Tabelle hervor.

- He spoke patiently.
- He works precisely.
- This rule can easily be understood.
- He is highly excited by the news.

	Adjektiv	Adverb
Adjektiv ohne besondere Endung	patient-	patient-ly
-y am Adjektivende wird zu -i	happy	happi-ly
-e nach Konsonant bleibt erhalten	extreme	extreme-ly
-e nach Vokal entfällt	true	tru-ly
-le nach Vokal bleibt erhalten	pale	pale-ly
-le nach Konsonant entfällt	simple	simp-ly
-le entfällt in -able und -ible	capable sensible	capab-ly sensib-ly
-l am Adjektivende bleibt erhalten	usual	usual-ly
-ll wird zu -l	full	ful-ly
-ic hängt -ally an	poetic	poetic-ally
-ly am Adjektivende bedingt Umschreibung	friendly	in a friendly way

Einige Adverbien haben eine endungslose und eine auf -ly endende Form. Es liegt dann meist ein Bedeutungsunterschied vor. Die Form auf -ly hat meist übertragene Bedeutung.

- He works hard from morning to night.
  (Er arbeitet hart von morgens bis abends.)
- I could hardly control myself.
  (Ich konnte mich kaum beherrschen.)

Bedeutungsunterschied

Das Adverb

• cheap	billig		• cheaply	billig; leicht
• clear	klar		• clearly	deutlich
• close	dicht		• closely	genau
• dear	lieb, teuer		• dearly	zärtlich; teuer
• deep	tief		• deeply	zutiefst, sehr
• direct	direkt		• directly	sofort
• fair	schön, ehrlich		• fairly	recht, ziemlich
• hard	schwer, hart		• hardly	kaum
• high	hoch		• highly	äußerst, höchst
• just	gerade		• justly	gerecht, mit Recht
• late	spät		• lately	kürzlich, neulich
• loud	laut		• loudly	prahlerisch, auffallend
• low	niedrig		• lowly	niedrig; gering
• near	nahe		• nearly	fast, beinahe
• right	richtig		• rightly	zu Recht
• short	kurz		• shortly	in kurzem
• tight	eng		• tightly	fest
• wrong	falsch		• wrongly	zu Unrecht

Häufig wirken die Adverbien auf -ly schwerfällig und werden deshalb häufig durch folgende Stilmittel ersetzt.

Umschreibung durch
in a ... manner/way,
it is + Adjektiv,
with + Substantiv

Einige Adjektive enden schon auf -ly oder das Adverb klingt schwerfällig. In diesen Fällen bedient man sich der Umschreibung mit in a ... manner, in a ... way, it is + Adjektiv oder with + Substantiv.

- They treated me **in a friendly way**.
- **It is difficult** for me to solve this problem all alone.
  (Dieses Problem kann ich nur **schwer** alleine lösen.)
- She could only solve this problem **with difficulties**.

verbaler Ausdruck

Häufig wird im Englischen ein verbaler Ausdruck verwendet, wo im Deutschen ein Adverb steht.

- He **was about** to leave the house, when the telephone rang.
  (Er war **gerade dabei** das Haus zu verlassen, als das Telefon klingelte.)

• to be about to	gerade dabei sein zu		• to like better	lieber
• to be afraid that	leider		• to be likely to	wahrscheinlich
• to chance to	zufällig		• to be on the point of	gerade dabei sein zu
• to continue	weiter		• to prefer	lieber
• to expect that	voraussichtlich		• to be said to	angeblich
• to finish by	zuletzt, schließlich		• that is to say	nämlich
• to be fond of	gern		• to seem to	anscheinend
• to be glad of	froh		• to be sorry	leider
• to go on	weiter		• to suppose	vermutlich
• to happen to	zufällig		• to be supposed to	vermutlich
• to hope	hoffentlich		• to be sure	sicherlich
• to keep on	weiter		• to be true	zwar
• to like to	gern			

Das Adverb

Übungen zur Bildung des Adverbs

1. Ändern Sie die folgenden Adjektive in Adverbien.

1. angry
2. attentive
3. careful
4. cool
5. cruel
6. dry
7. due
8. dull
9. extreme
10. full
11. gay
12. sure
13. terrible
14. true
15. lucky
16. pale
17. practical
18. radical
19. shy
20. usual

richtig   falsch

Die entsprechenden Lösungen befinden sich auf Seite 438.

Das Adverb

Die Steigerung des Adverbs (The Comparison of the Adverb)

Das Englische kennt neben der Grundstufe die folgenden Steigerungsformen beim Adverb. Dabei unterscheidet man die germanische und romanische Steigerungsart.

Positiv (Positive)

Der Positiv ist die Grundstufe des Adverbs. Er drückt aus, dass zwei oder mehr Wesen oder Dinge in Bezug auf ein Merkmal gleich sind; gleicher Grad.
Zur Verstärkung des Positivs dienen very (sehr) und most (überaus).

- Mary and Pamela will soon arrive.
- You must do your homework carefully.
- Peter answered my question correctly.
- Mary works as precisely as Peggy.
- Mrs Smith listens very patiently.
- Mary works most precisely.

Komparativ (Comparative)

Der Komparativ drückt aus, dass zwei Wesen oder Dinge in Bezug auf ein Merkmal ungleich sind; ungleicher Grad.

Germanisch: Adverb + -er

Romanisch: more + Adverb

- Mary arrived sooner than Pamela did.
- You must do your homework more carefully.
- Mary works more precisely than Peter.

Zur Verstärkung des Komparativs dienen much (viel), even (sogar noch), still (noch) und far (weit) und by far (bei weitem), das dem Komparativ stets nachgestellt wird.

- Mary works much more precisely than Peggy.
- Peter answered my question more correctly by far.

Der Komparativ wird durch no oder not any verneint.

- Mary did not arrive any sooner than Pamela did.

Die allmählich zunehmende Steigerung (immer) wird bei den germanisch gesteigerten Adverbien durch die Wiederholung des Komparativs und bei den romanisch gesteigerten Adverbien durch more and more + Adverb ausgedrückt.

- He spoke faster and faster.
  (Er sprach immer schneller.)
- His situation gets worse and worse.
  (Seine Lage verschlechtert sich immer mehr.)
- Mary works more and more carefully.
  (Mary arbeitet immer sorgfältiger.)

Superlativ (Superlative)

Der Superlativ drückt aus, dass von mindestens drei Wesen oder Dingen einem der höchste Grad eines Merkmals zukommt; höchster Grad.

Germanisch: (the) Adverb + -est

Romanisch: (the) most + Adverb

- Four o'clock is the soonest I can be there.
- Of all our employees, Mary works the most precisely.

Das Adverb

Zur Verstärkung des Superlativs dienen by far (bei weitem), das dem Superlativ vorangestellt wird und of all, das nach dem Superlativ steht.

- Four o'clock is by far the soonest I can be there.
- Of all our employees, Mary works the most precisely of all.

	Positiv	Komparativ	Superlativ	Allmähliche Steigerung
Germanisch	Adverb	Adverb + -er	Adverb + -est	Komparativ and Komparativ
Romanisch	Adverb	more + Adverb	(the) most + Adverb	more and more + Adverb
Verstärkung	very, most	much, even, still, (by) far	by far, of all	

Für die Wahl der Steigerungsart ist zu beachten, um welches Adverb es sich handelt. Der folgenden Tabelle ist zu entnehmen, welche Adverbien germanisch und welche romanisch gesteigert werden.

Das Adverb

	Germanisch gesteigerte Adverbien	Romanisch gesteigerte Adverbien
ursprüngliche; abgeleitete Adverbien	Ursprüngliche Adverbien werden auf germanische Art gesteigert.	Abgeleitete Adverbien (mit der Endung -ly) werden auf romanische Art gesteigert.
	▪ The **harder** you work the more successful you will be.	▪ The problem is **more simply** solved than I had expected.
einsilbige; zwei- und mehrsilbige Adverbien	Einsilbige Adverbien und das Adverb **early** werden auf germanische Art gesteigert.	Zwei- und mehrsilbige Adverbien werden auf romanische Art gesteigert.
	▪ Mary arrived **sooner** than I had expected.	▪ Peter did his homework **more carefully** than John.
gleiche Form von Adjektiv und Adverb	Adverbien, die die gleiche Form haben wie das entsprechende Adjektiv werden in der Regel auf germanische Art gesteigert.	
	▪ The **earlier** you start the **sooner** you will arrive.	
Partizipien		Partizipien, die in der Funktion eines Adverbs stehen.
		▪ Bob behaved even **more surprisingly** than John.

Unregelmäßig gesteigerte Adverbien

Die Steigerungsformen der unregelmäßig gesteigerten Adverbien gleichen meist denen der entsprechenden Adjektive.

Positiv		Komparativ	Superlativ
badly	schlimm; schlecht	worse	worst
far	weit (räumlich)	farther	farthest
far	weit (übertragen)	further	furthest
ill	schlimm, schlecht	worse	worst
little	wenig, gering	less	least
much	viel	more	most
well	gut	better	better

Das Adverb

Übungen zur Steigerung des Adverbs

1. Setzen Sie die Adverbien in Klammern in den Komparativ oder Superlativ.

1. I will put it (precisely).

2. If I should return (late), you might put the key in the place known to both of us.

3. She began walking (close) and (close) to me.

4. Tell them to work (fast).

5. Officials said that these delicate activities were (good) conducted in secrecy.

6. The pilot flew (low) and tried the landing.

7. They were pleased that he was writing (often).

8. As much as they hate to admit it, the computer can operate the machinery much (efficiently) and (accurately).

9. During the Hungry Forties many workers who could no (long) make a living in Britain arrived in New Zealand.

10. The Chancellor said that if the nation were to work (hard) and increase output, wage increases would be fully justified.

11. He did not look the (little) surprised.

12. Actions speak (loud) than words.

13. George's eyebrows lifted a trifle (high).

14. He had no (soon) seated himself at his desk when Charles entered.

15. Carol quizzed him (acutely) than any police officer.

richtig   falsch

Die entsprechenden Lösungen befinden sich auf Seite 438.

Das Adverb

Die Stellung des Adverbs (The Position of the Adverb)

Zur Stellung des Adverbs lassen sich keine allgemein gültigen Regeln aufstellen. Es ist vielmehr von der Satzmelodie und nicht zuletzt vom Empfinden des Sprechers abhängig, an welcher Stelle er das Adverb platziert. Im Gegensatz zum Deutschen steht das Adverb im Englischen jedoch nie zwischen Verb und direktem Objekt.

	Vor dem Vollverb	Nach dem Vollverb	Nach dem 1. Hilfsverb, nach to be
Adverbien der Art und Weise	Adverbien der Art und Weise stehen in den einfachen Zeiten vor dem Vollverb. • He **quickly** left the house. • He **obviously** worked hard.	Adverbien der Art und Weise stehen in der Regel nach dem Vollverb, wenn kein Objekt folgt. • He worked **precisely**. • He went **slowly** out of the room.	Adverbien der Art und Weise stehen in den zusammengesetzten Zeiten und im Passiv nach dem ersten Hilfsverb. • He has **quickly** left the house. • The house has **obviously** been abandoned.
			Adverbien der Art und Weise stehen in den einfachen Zeiten in der Regel nach den Formen von to be. • This essay is **simply** brilliant. • She is **extremely** friendly.
Adverbien der Menge, Häufigkeit	Adverbien der Menge, Häufigkeit, besonders **always** und **usually**, stehen in den einfachen Zeiten vor dem Vollverb. • He **often** left the house before 6 o'clock. • I **usually** walk to work. • I **normally** get up at 6 o'clock.	Adverbien der Menge, Häufigkeit, außer **always** und **usually**, können nach dem Vollverb stehen, wenn kein Objekt folgt. • We met **regularly** for lunch. • We swim **daily**.	Adverbien der Menge, Häufigkeit stehen in den zusammengesetzten Zeiten und im Passiv nach dem ersten Hilfsverb. • He has **often** left the house before 6 o'clock. • This rule has **often** been repeated in class.
			Adverbien der Menge, Häufigkeit stehen in den einfachen Zeiten in der Regel nach den Formen von to be.

Das Adverb

Vor dem Vollverb	Nach dem Vollverb	Nach dem 1. Hilfsverb, nach to be	
Adverbien des Grades stehen in den einfachen Zeiten vor dem Vollverb. - He **nearly** finished his work yesterday. - I **almost** hope we miss our train.		- He is **always** behind time. - They were **always** nervous. Adverbien des Grades stehen in den zusammengesetzten Zeiten und im Passiv nach dem ersten Hilfsverb. - He had **nearly** finished his work when he was called to see the boss. - This problem has **nearly** been solved. Adverbien des Grades stehen in den einfachen Zeiten in der Regel nach den Formen von to be. - He is **quite** nervous. - They were **rather** upset.	Adverbien des Grades
Adverbien der unbestimmten Zeit stehen in den einfachen Zeiten vor dem Vollverb. - He **sometimes** left the house before 6 o'clock. - She **sometimes** plays the piano for us.	Adverbien der unbestimmten Zeit stehen in der Regel nach dem Vollverb, wenn kein Objekt folgt. - The children played **sometimes** in the garden.	- He has **sometimes** left the house before 6 a.m. - This rule has **often** been repeated in class. Adverbien der unbestimmten Zeit stehen in den einfachen Zeiten in der Regel nach den Formen von to be. - He is **sometimes** there before 8 o'clock.	Adverbien der unbestimmten Zeit
Vor dem Infinitiv Adverbien, die zur näheren Bestimmung eines Infinitivs einge-			Adverbien beim Infinitiv

Das Adverb

	Vor dem Infinitiv	
kein Adverb zwischen Infinitiv und to	setzt sind, stehen in der Regel unmittelbar vor diesem. Not steht immer vor dem Infinitiv. Es sollte vermieden werden, ein Adverb zwischen to und den Infinitiv zu setzen.	
	• He left her **never to come back** again. • He told her **not to come back** before 8 o'clock in the evening. • I planned an entire vacation, **only to find out** that I had scheduled the wrong week.	

	Vor dem Bezugswort	Nach dem Bezugswort
Adverbien des Grades	Adverbien des Grades stehen meist direkt vor dem Wort, das sie näher bestimmen.	
	• The crowd was **quite nervous** when the police arrived. • I **quite** understand.	
only	Only steht in der Regel unmittelbar vor dem Wort, das es näher bestimmt. Steht dieses Wort am Satzende, kann only auch hinter dieses treten.	Zur näheren Bestimmung eines Wortes kann only nach diesem stehen. Statt only kann auch alone stehen.
	• **Only you** can do this work successfully. • The dog obeys **only Father**. • The dog obeys **Father only**.	• You **only** can do this work successfully. • He **alone** is able to solve this problem.
too		Too steht in der Regel nach dem Substantiv, zu dem es gehört.
		• My mother and father **too** have left the house.

Das Adverb

Vor Adjektiven	Nach Adjektiven	
	Enough steht generell nach dem prädikativen Adjektiv. • Is the drink cold enough for your guest?	enough
Too steht vor Adjektiven, zu denen es gehört. • This problem was too difficult.		too

Vor Adverbien	Nach Adverbien	
Ortsadverbien stehen meist vor einem Adverb der Art und Weise. • I will see you there shortly. Ortsadverbien stehen am Satzende meist vor Adverbien der Zeit und sonstigen Zeitbestimmungen (Ort vor Zeit). • I have lived here for more than ten years.		Ortsadverbien
	Enough steht grundsätzlich nach einem anderen Adverb. • Does he run fast enough?	enough
Too steht in der Regel vor den Adverbien, zu denen es gehört. • I was driving too quickly.		too

Satzanfang	Satzende	
Adverbien der Art und Weise können, wenn sie besonders betont sind, an den Satzanfang treten.	Adverbien der Art und Weise können, wenn sie besonders betont sind, an das Satzende treten.	Adverbien der Art und Weise

Das Adverb

	Satzanfang	Satzende
	- **Of course,** everybody wanted to see the Queen.	- He left the house **quickly.**
Adverbien der Menge, Häufigkeit	Adverbien der Menge, Häufigkeit können, wenn sie besonders betont sind, an den Satzanfang treten.	Adverbien der Menge, Häufigkeit können, wenn sie besonders betont sind, an das Satzende treten.
	- **Several times** we talked this text over.	- We talked this text over **several times.**
Adverbien der bestimmten Zeit	Adverbien, die eine bestimmte Zeit bezeichnen, können an den Satzanfang treten.	Adverbien, die eine bestimmte Zeit bezeichnen, können an den Satzanfang treten.
	- **Yesterday,** I met your sister. - **Last night,** I read all the books.	- I met your sister **yesterday.** - I read all the books **last night.**
Adverbien der unbestimmten Zeit	Adverbien der unbestimmten Zeit können, wenn sie besonders betont sind, an den Satzanfang treten.	Adverbien der unbestimmten Zeit können, wenn sie besonders betont sind, an das Satzende treten.
	- **Sometimes** we spent our holidays in Scotland.	- They talked to each other on the telephone **sometimes.**
Ortsadverbien	Ortsadverbien können, wenn sie besonders betont werden sollen, am Satzanfang stehen.	Ortsadverbien stehen meist am Satzende.
	- **There,** I found my peace.	- I found my peace **there.**

Das Adverb

Übungen zur Stellung des Adverbs

1. Setzen Sie die Adverbien in Klammern vor oder hinter das blau gedruckte Verb.

1. Philip spoke. (absently)
2. He wants to spend the winter in Miami. (apparently)
3. I shall call Rome, the officer answered and picked up the telephone on his desk. (calmly)
4. The hunter followed the trace. (cautiously)
5. It can be very lonely out there. (certainly)
6. We are not concerned with it. (directly)
7. The dawn was breaking over London. (just)
8. He drew himself up and took off his tie. (calmly)
9. This parcel is to be handled. (carefully)
10. The plan was worked out, but within a year it was judged to have been a failure. (thoroughly and carefully)

richtig   falsch

2. Setzen Sie die Adverbien in Klammern vor oder hinter das blau gedruckte Adjektiv oder Adverb.

1. A patient must normally go to the doctor with whom he is actually registered. (only)
2. Claire had her hat on and had just come from the village (clearly).
3. I could see it clearly and I felt uneasy (enough).
4. The house was certainly big. (enough)
5. The package had arrived on January sixth. (only)
6. George was smoking a cigarette which he held horizontal. (carefully)
7. You shouldn't go by bus, it's a bad service. (awfully)
8. His wife felt extremely annoyed but George seemed unreasonable. (absolutely)

Das Adverb

9. I like this hotel with its hallways barely wide to walk through. **(enough)**

10. We were nearly broke when we arrived - 50 cents left. **(only)**

richtig falsch

3. Setzen Sie die Adverbien in Klammern an den Satzanfang oder ans Satzende.

1. No one had found anything. **(apparently)**

2. He folded the letter and put it back into his pocket. **(carefully)**

3. They reached the Grand Union canal, which runs from London to Birmingham. **(eventually)**

4. A little girl did come along and she was carrying a basket of food. **(finally)**

5. Visiting the neighbours is the best way to maintain good relationships with them. **(regularly)**

6. A warm wave of relief flowed through him. **(instantly)**

7. People have shown themselves quite ready to build houses in areas which are subject to danger from hurricanes. **(curiously)**

8. I met your sister. **(yesterday)**

9. Most people have understood the importance of this matter. **(finally)**

10. We wanted to see the Queen. **(of course)**

richtig falsch

4. Setzen Sie die Adverbien in Klammern an die richtige Stelle.

1. He was sitting on the sofa, listening. **(attentively)**

2. Some experts believe that the price will drop. **(eventually)**

3. Corporations merge into big trusts. **(frequently)**

4. It is nice to hear those kind words. **(certainly)**

5. The doctor on the rescue boat treated the injured people. **(badly)**

6. He turned his head away. **(abruptly)**

Das Adverb

7. The wide-spread motorization of the population has created new occupations and reduced others. (drastically)

8. Henry went upstairs, washed, brushed his teeth and changed his shirt. (briefly, hurriedly, quickly)

9. It was by chance that they had met. (actually)

10. We do not hope, but, we hope. (greatly, still)

richtig falsch

Die entsprechenden Lösungen befinden sich auf Seite 439.

Das Adverb

Adverb oder Adjektiv (Adverb or Adjective)

Adverb und Adjektiv haben unterschiedliche Funktionen im Satz, d. h. Adjektive stehen zur näheren Bestimmung von Substantiven und Pronomen, und Adverbien können als adverbiale Bestimmung in Verbindung mit einem Verb stehen oder als Attribut zum Substantiv, Adjektiv oder zu einem anderen Adverb treten.

	Adverb	Adjektiv

beim Substantiv	Einige Adverbien werden als attributive Adjektive verwendet, d. h. sie stehen zur näheren Bestimmung des Substantivs.
	
	▪ the above remark
	  die obige Bemerkung
	▪ in years to come
	  in späteren Jahren
	▪ in an off street
	  in einer Seitenstraße
	▪ the then minister
	  der damalige Minister
		Adjektive stehen zur näheren Bestimmung von Substantiven und Pronomen. Sie beschreiben deren Eigenschaften.

	▪ The **then** **minister** arrived on an official visit in London.	▪ Peter is **intelligent.** ▪ John is always **happy.**
beim Verb	Bezüglich eines Verbs steht das Adverb. Das Adverb beschreibt die Art und Weise einer Tätigkeit.	Nach den folgenden Verben des Seins, Scheins oder Werdens. Das Adjektiv ist dann prädikative Ergänzung zum Subjekt. ▪ to be sein ▪ to become werden ▪ to get bekommen ▪ to grow werden ▪ to look schauen ▪ to seem scheinen
	▪ He works **precisely.** ▪ He listens **patiently.** ▪ He reads **concentratedly.**	▪ It is **terrible.** ▪ It was getting **dark.** ▪ He looks **awful.**
		Nach den folgenden Verben der Ruhe bzw. der Bewegung. Das Adjektiv ist dann prädikative Ergänzung zum Subjekt. ▪ to arrive ankommen ▪ to leave verlassen ▪ to lie liegen ▪ to remain bleiben

Das Adverb

Adverb	Adjektiv	
	■ to return — zurückkehren ■ to sit — sitzen ■ to stand — stehen	
	■ He lay **silent** on his bed and read. ■ He stood **nervous** in the corner.	
	Nach den Verben des Handelns, Dafürhaltens und Erklärens. Das Adjektiv ist dann prädikative Ergänzung zum Objekt.	
	■ We find his attitude **wrong**. ■ We think his behaviour **irresponsible**.	
Einige Adverbien haben dieselbe Form und dieselbe Bedeutung wie die entsprechenden Adjektive.	Einige Adjektive haben dieselbe Form und dieselbe Bedeutung wie die entsprechenden Adverbien.	Form- und Bedeutungsgleichheit von Adverb und Adjektiv
■ best — am besten ■ better — besser ■ daily — täglich ■ early — früh ■ enough — genug ■ far — weit ■ fast — schnell ■ hourly — stündlich ■ last — zuletzt ■ least — mindestens ■ less — weniger ■ little — wenig ■ long — lang(e) ■ monthly — monatlich ■ much — viel ■ straight — gerade; direkt ■ weekly — wöchentlich ■ worse — schlechter ■ worst — am schlimmsten ■ yearly — jährlich	■ best — am besten ■ better — besser ■ daily — täglich, Tages- ■ early — früh ■ enough — genug ■ far — weit ■ fast — schnell ■ hourly — stündlich ■ last — zuletzt ■ least — mindestens ■ less — weniger ■ little — wenig ■ long — lang ■ monthly — monatlich ■ much — viel ■ straight — gerade; direkt ■ weekly — wöchentlich ■ worse — schlechter ■ worst — am schlimmsten ■ yearly — jährlich	
■ I go **daily** to the sports centre for one hour. (Ich gehe **täglich** eine Stunde ins Sportzentrum.)	■ «The Times» is a **daily** paper. («Die Times» ist eine **Tages**zeitung.)	
Einige Adverbien haben dieselbe Form wie die entsprechenden Adjektive, jedoch eine andere Bedeutung.	Einige Adjektive haben dieselbe Form wie die entsprechenden Adverbien, jedoch eine andere Bedeutung.	gleiche Form, unterschiedliche Bedeutung
■ only — nur ■ pretty — ziemlich ■ still — noch ■ well — gut	■ only — einzig ■ pretty — hübsch ■ still — still ■ well — wohl	

Das Adverb

	Adverb	Adjektiv
	▪ This problem is **pretty** difficult. (Dieses Problem ist **ziemlich** schwierig.) ▪ You can **only** wait. (Du kannst **nur** warten.)	▪ Peter is a **pretty** boy. (Peter ist ein **hübscher** Junge.) ▪ The **only** thing you can do is wait. (Das **Einzige** was du tun kannst, ist warten.)
unterschiedliche Form, unterschiedliche Bedeutung	Einige Adverbien haben zwei Formen, eine endungslose Form (wie das Adjektiv) und eine Form auf -ly. Die auf -ly endende Form wird meist in übertragener Bedeutung verwendet.	Einige Adjektive haben dieselbe Form wie die endungslose Form der entsprechenden Adverbien. Die Bedeutung wird meist aus dem Zusammenhang deutlich.

Adverb			
▪ cheap billig	▪ cheaply billig; leicht
▪ clear klar	▪ clearly deutlich
▪ close dicht	▪ closely genau
▪ dear lieb, teuer	▪ dearly teuer; zärtlich
▪ deep tief	▪ deeply zutiefst, sehr
▪ direct direkt	▪ directly sofort
▪ fair schön, ehrlich	▪ fairly ziemlich
▪ hard schwer	▪ hardly kaum
▪ high hoch	▪ highly äußerst
▪ just gerade	▪ justly gerecht
▪ late spät	▪ lately kürzlich
▪ loud laut	▪ loudly prahlerisch
▪ low niedrig	▪ lowly gering
▪ near nahe	▪ nearly beinahe
▪ right richtig	▪ rightly zu Recht
▪ short kurz	▪ shortly in kurzem
▪ tight eng	▪ tightly fest
▪ wrong falsch	▪ wrongly zu Unrecht

Adjektiv	
▪ cheap	billig
▪ clear	klar, deutlich
▪ close	dicht; genau
▪ dear	lieb, teuer
▪ deep	tief
▪ direct	direkt
▪ fair	schön; ehrlich
▪ hard	hart, schwer
▪ high	hoch
▪ just	gerecht
▪ late	spät; verstorben
▪ loud	laut
▪ low	niedrig
▪ near	nahe; beinahe
▪ right	richtig
▪ short	kurz
▪ tight	eng
▪ wrong	falsch

- An eagle can fly very **high**.
- He was **highly** excited when he heard the news.

- Mount Everest is the **highest** mountain in the world.

Das Adverb

Übungen zum Adverb und Adjektiv

1. Ändern Sie die Wörter in Klammern in Adjektive oder Adverbien.

1. All he cared for was to lie (quiet) on his bed.
2. Behind him was Harry, fighting to get (close).
3. He came to my house in the (early) hours of the morning.
4. He remained (attentive) to all his wishes.
5. He shouted (angry) at his wife and demanded an explanation.
6. He stood (close) to the wall.
7. Her face seems (bad) hurt.
8. I haven't the (little) (superlative) idea where Philip is.
9. It makes (little) difference.
10. Elizabeth seldom had an evening (complete) free.
11. I've been doing quite a lot of night work (late).
12. They were all below, eating their (late) dinner, he supposed.
13. In the teaching profession there is no (clear) distinction between elementary and advanced-level school-teachers.
14. Speak (clear).
15. Enjoy a voyage that will take you through the beautiful countryside, (pretty) villages, and old towns of England.
16. This is (pretty) difficult.
17. The slaves tried to forget their (hard) life by singing religious songs.
18. The patient will (hard) live to see another day.
19. This news, if it can be relied upon, is (high) significant.
20. Although immigration has been (fair) low for fifty years, the population has recently grown much faster than ever before.

richtig   falsch

Die entsprechenden Lösungen befinden sich auf Seite 439.

Das Zahlwort

Die Grundzahlen (The Cardinal Numbers)

Einer		Zehner		Hunderter, Tausender	
0	zero	10	ten	100	a/one hundred
1	one	11	eleven	101	a hundred and one
2	two	12	twelve	102	a hundred and two
3	three	13	thirteen	120	a hundred and twenty
4	four	14	fourteen	121	a hundred and twenty-one ..
5	five	15	fifteen	200	two hundred
6	six	16	sixteen	300	three hundred
7	seven	17	seventeen	400	four hundred
8	eight	18	eighteen	500	five hundred
9	nine	19	nineteen	600	six hundred
		20	twenty	700	seven hundred
		21	twenty-one	800	eight hundred
		22	twenty-two ...	900	nine hundred
		30	thirty	1,000	a/one thousand
		40	forty	2,000	two thousand
		50	fifty	10,000	ten thousand
		60	sixty	100,000	a hundred thousand
		70	seventy	200,000	two hundred thousand
		80	eighty	1,000,000	a/one million
		90	ninety	2,000,000	two million
				10^{12}	a/one billion, a thousand millions (BE)*

kein Punkt bei Dezimalstellen

* veraltet

Das Zahlwort

Cipher, nil, nought, o, zero

cipher	bezeichnet das Schriftzeichen, die Ziffer Null,
nil	die Punktzahl bei Sportergebnissen und in Statistiken,
nought	den Zahlenwert Null,
o [ou]	die Null in Fernsprechnummern,
zero	den Nullpunkt einer Skala.

- If you add a **cipher** to ten you will have one hundred.
- Manchester United beat Port Vale two to **nil** (2 : 0).
- Twenty minus twenty leaves **nought**.
- My telephone number is two, two, five, o.
- The temperature has fallen below **zero**.

(One, a) hundred, thousand, million, billion, trillion

Hundred, thousand, million, billion und trillion können nicht wie im Deutschen alleine stehen, sie müssen stets mit a oder one stehen. A wird verwendet, wenn die Zahlwörter alleine stehen, one steht zur Hervorhebung und immer bei Jahreszahlen.

- He gave me one **hundred** dollars.
  (Er gab mir **hundert** Dollar.)
- He gave me a **hundred** dollars.
- A **hundred**, a **thousand**, a **million**, a **billion**, a **trillion**.
- In the year one **hundred** and twenty-five.

hundred, thousand etc. stehen mit a, one

Hundred, thousand, million, billion und trillion können als Substantive verwendet werden und erhalten dann im Plural ein -s, es sei denn, es folgt ein Substantiv oder es geht eine kleinere Zahl voraus. Sie stehen mit einer Beifügung + of.

- There were **hundreds** of people.
- He asked me **thousands** of questions.
- He spent **millions** of dollars on this business.
- He spent five **million** dollars on this business.

Einer- und Zehnerzahlen

Einer- und Zehnerzahlen können ebenfalls als Substantive verwendet werden. Auch sie erhalten dann ein Plural-s.

- She is a girl in her **thirties**.
- The **twenties** of the last century are called the golden **twenties**.

Zahlen von vier und mehr Stellen

Zahlen von vier und mehr Stellen werden je drei Stellen von rechts durch Komma (nicht durch Punkt) abgetrennt.

- 10,000
- 100,000
- 100,000,000

kein Punkt bei Dezimalstellen

dnf 291

Das Zahlwort

Die Ordnungszahlen (The Ordinal Numbers)

Einer		Zehner		Hunderter, Tausender	
1st	first	10th	tenth	100th	a/one hundredth
2nd	second	11th	eleventh	101st	a hundred and first
3rd	third	12th	twelfth	102nd	a hundred and second
4th	fourth	13th	thirteenth	120th	a hundred and twentieth
5th	fifth	14th	fourteenth	121st	a hundred and twenty-first
6th	sixth	15th	fifteenth	200th	two hundredth
7th	seventh	16th	sixteenth	300th	three hundredth
8th	eighth	17th	seventeenth	400th	four hundredth
9th	ninth	18th	eighteenth	500th	five hundredth
		19th	nineteenth	600th	six hundredth
		20th	twentieth	700th	seven hundredth
		21st	twenty-first	800th	eight hundredth
		22nd	twenty-second	900th	nine hundredth
		30th	thirtieth	1,000th	a/one thousandth
		40th	fortieth	2,000th	two thousandth
		50th	fiftieth	10,000th	ten thousandth
		60th	sixtieth	100,000th	one hundred thousandth
		70th	seventieth	200,000th	two hundred thousandth
		80th	eightieth	1,000,000th	a/one millionth
		90th	ninetieth	2,000,000th	two millionth
				10^{12}	a billionth, a thousand millionth (BE)*

* veraltet

Das Zahlwort

st, nd, rd, th

Als Ziffern geschrieben müssen die letzten beiden Buchstaben der Ordnungszahl an die Ziffer angeschlossen werden.

- first   - 1st
- second   - 2nd
- third   - 3rd
- fourth   - 4th

Herrschernamen

Die Ordnungszahlen werden zur Bezeichnung von Herrschernamen verwendet. Bei der Verwendung von Ziffern stehen römische Ziffern ohne Punkt.

- Elizabeth I   - Elizabeth the First
- Henry XIII   - Henry the Eighth
- Charles V   - Charles the Fifth
- Elizabeth II - Elizabeth the Second

kein Punkt bei römischen Ziffern

First ... last, at first ... at last

Zur Bezeichnung der Reihenfolge steht first (als erstes) ... last (als letztes). Zum Ausdruck des Gegensatzes steht at first (anfangs) ... at last (schließlich).

- First I tried to call him and last of all I went to see him personally.
- At first he was very ambitious to win the match but at last he gave up.

Firstly, secondly, thirdly, fourthly, in the fifth place

In Aufzählungen wird an die vier ersten Ordnungszahlen -ly angehängt, die fünfte und alle weiteren Ordnungszahlen müssen mit in the fifth etc. place umschrieben werden.

- Firstly we unpacked our suitcases, secondly we took a rest for half an hour, thirdly we went to the beach, fourthly we ate something at a restaurant and in the fifth place we went to bed.

Das Zahlwort

Die Bruchzahlen (Fractional Numbers)

Gemeine Brüche (Vulgar Fractions)

Für die gemeinen Brüche gilt folgende Formel:

$$\frac{\text{Zähler}}{\text{Nenner}} = \frac{\text{Grundzahl}}{\text{Ordnungszahl}}$$

Ist die Grundzahl > 1, so erhält die Ordnungszahl ein Plural-s.
Ist die Grundzahl = 1, kann one oder a verwendet werden.

- $\frac{2}{5}$ - two fifths
- $\frac{1}{5}$ - a, one fifth

Bei Brüchen, die eine ganze Zahl enthalten, wird zwischen der ganzen Zahl und dem Bruch and eingefügt.

- 2 2/5 - **two** and **two fifths**
- 1 ½ - **one** and **a half**
- 3 ½ - **three** and **a half**

Die Brüche one half (1/2) und a fourth, a quarter (1/4) weichen von der obigen Formel ab.
A fourth und a quarter stehen, wenn kein Substantiv folgt. Folgt ein Substantiv kann nur a quarter stehen. Die Benennung wird mit of angeschlossen.

- ½ - **a/one half**
- ¼ - **a/one quarter, a/one fourth**
- How much do you want? Give me **a fourth/quarter.**
- How many miles is it to London. It is only **a quarter** of a mile.

Dezimalbrüche (Decimal Fractions)

Für die Dezimalbrüche gilt folgende Formel:

Grundzahl Punkt Grundzahl

| kein Komma bei Dezimalbrüchen

Dezimalbrüche werden im Englischen durch Punkt und nicht wie im Deutschen durch Komma abgetrennt.
Im britischen Englisch steht der Punkt vorzugsweise in der Mitte, im amerikanischen Englisch auf der Zeile.

- **3·23 three point twenty-three** (BE)
- **3.23 three point two three** (AE)

Das Zahlwort

Die Vervielfältigungszahlwörter (Multiplying Numbers)

Grundzahlen + -fold

Bis auf die ersten vier unregelmäßigen Formen wird an die Grundzahl -fold angehängt. Im Deutschen wird dies mit der Grundzahl + -fach übersetzt.

- I would like a **double** scotch.
- She had a **triple** scoop ice cream cone.
- He painted the room with a **single** coat of blue.
- We received a **fivefold** return on our investment.

- simple, single — einfach
- double — doppelt
- triple, treble (threefold) — dreifach

- quadruple (fourfold) — vierfach
- fivefold etc. — fünffach

Grundzahlen + times

Bis auf die ersten beiden unregelmäßigen Formen wird an die Grundzahl times angehängt. Im Deutschen wird dies mit der Grundzahl + -mal übersetzt.

- Her car has **three times** the horsepower of mine.
- David earns **twice** what I do.
- She has won Wimbledon **four times**.
- I explained this rule **five times** to you.

- twice — einmal
- double — zweimal
- three times — dreimal

- four times — viermal
- five times etc. — fünfmal

Ausdrücke wie doppelt, dreimal ... so + Adjektiv (wie) werden mit der Grundzahl und dem Adjektiv + as gebildet, also three times as + Adjektiv + as.

- This car is **four times** as expensive as that one.
- This text is **five times** as long as that one.

Das Zahlwort

Die Uhrzeit und weitere Zeitangaben

Die Uhrzeit (The Time)

Bei Zeitangaben kann o'clock und minutes hinzugefügt werden. Minutes kann weggelassen werden, wenn es sich um mehr als vier Minuten handelt, bei weniger als vier Minuten muss es stehen. Im Gespräch wird bei weniger als zehn Minuten statt minutes oft o [ou] eingesetzt.

- It is **four o'clock**.
- It is **four**.
- It is four (o'clock) and **twenty (minutes)**.
- It is four (o'clock) and **three minutes**.
- It is now **four o seven**.
- The train leaves at **eight o four** p.m.

Bei offiziellen Zeitangaben werden im britischen Englisch 24 Stunden gezählt. Dabei wird o'clock grundsätzlich weggelassen.

- The train arrives at **twenty twelve** (20:12).
- The plane takes off at **twenty-three** (23:00).

Die Zeit von 24 Uhr bis 12 Uhr wird mit a.m (lat.: ante meridiem) und die Zeit von 12 Uhr bis 24 Uhr wird mit p.m. (lat.: post meridiem) bezeichnet.

- When will the train arrive? I think the train arrives at **7 a.m.**
- When will the plane take off? I think the plane takes off at **5 p.m.**

Das Datum (The Date)

Beim Datum stehen - wie im Deutschen - die Ordnungszahlen und zwar vor oder hinter dem Monat, der durch Komma von der Jahreszahl abgetrennt wird, wenn die Ordnungszahl nach dem Monat steht.

- **27th July (,) 1994**
  (the twenty-seventh of July, 1994)
- **July 27(th), 1994**
  (July the twenty-seventh, 1994)

Das Datum im Brief wird im britischen Englisch durch Punkt, im amerikanischen Englisch durch Schrägstrich getrennt. Außerdem steht im amerikanischen Englisch der Monat vor der Tageszahl.

- **27.7.1994** (BE)
  7/27/1994 (AE)
  (July 27, 1994) (AE)

Das Zahlwort

Die Uhrzeit (The Time)

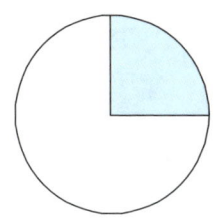

a quarter of an hour,
a quarter hour

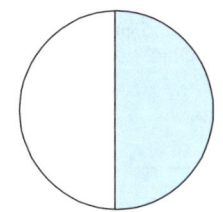

half an hour

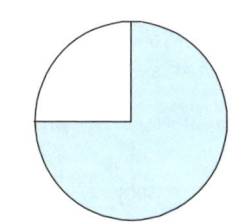

three quarters of an hour

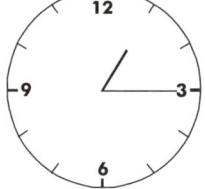

What time is it?

it is a quarter past one,
it is one fifteen

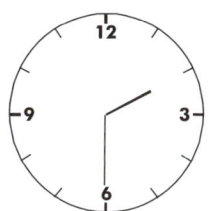

it is half past two,
it is two thirty

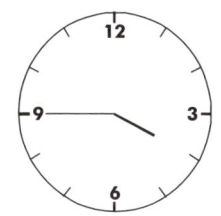

it is a quarter to four,
it is three forty-five

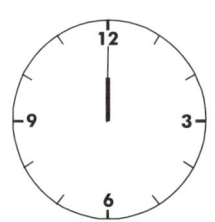

it is twelve o'clock,
it is midday/noon,
it is midnight

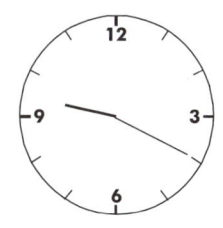

it is twenty past nine,
it is nine twenty

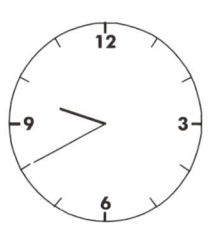

it is twenty to ten,
it is nine forty

Das Pronomen (The Pronoun)

Die Pronomen vertreten Personen und Sachen, die Subjekt sind, im possessive case stehen oder die indirektes Objekt oder direktes Objekt sind.

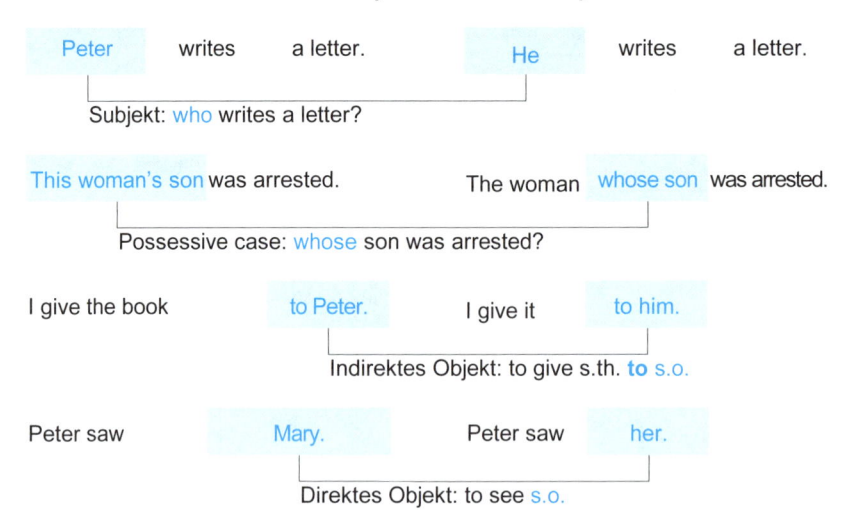

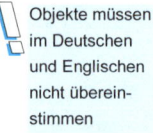

Peter writes a letter. **He** writes a letter.
Subjekt: *who* writes a letter?

This woman's son was arrested. The woman **whose son** was arrested.
Possessive case: *whose* son was arrested?

I give the book **to Peter.** I give it **to him.**
Indirektes Objekt: to give s.th. **to** s.o.

Peter saw **Mary.** Peter saw **her.**
Direktes Objekt: to see *s.o.*

> Objekte müssen im Deutschen und Englischen nicht übereinstimmen

Es ist zu beachten, dass ein Wort, das im Deutschen indirektes Objekt ist, im Englischen direktes Objekt sein kann und umgekehrt. Um welches Objekt es sich im einzelnen handelt, hängt davon ab, mit welcher Ergänzung das jeweilige Verb stehen kann. Indirekte Objekte können mit und ohne die Präposition *to* an das Verb angeschlossen werden und werden folglich auch durch ein indirektes Objektpronomen ersetzt. Direkte Objekte werden ohne Präposition an das Verb angeschlossen und folglich auch durch ein direktes Objektpronomen ersetzt.

Substantivische Pronomen (Substantival Pronouns)

Die substantivischen Pronomen können ohne ein Substantiv verwendet werden.

- I have lost my paper. Can you show me **yours**?

Attributive Pronomen (Attributive Pronouns)

Die attributiven Pronomen stehen in Verbindung mit einem Substantiv.

- Where is **your** book?
- I have seen **your** mother.

Das Personalpronomen (The Personal Pronoun)

Das Personalpronomen (persönliches Fürwort) vertritt Personen und Sachen, die Subjekt, indirektes Objekt oder direktes Objekt sind.

Nu.	Pers.	Gen.	Subjekt	Indirektes Obj.	Direktes Obj.
Sing.	1	mask.	I	me	me
		fem.			
	2	mask.	you (thou)	you (thee)	you (thee)
		fem.			
	3	mask.	he	him	him
		fem.	she	her	her
		neutr.	it	it	it
Plur.	1	mask.	we	us	us
		fem.			
	2	mask.	you (ye)	you (you)	you (you)
		fem.			
	3	mask.	they	them	them
		fem.			

Die Subjektpronomen

Die Subjektpronomen stehen anstelle eines Subjekts.

- Peter is doing his homework. **He** is doing his homework.

anstelle des Subjekt

Sie stehen als Ergänzung zu dem Verb to be. In der Umgangssprache stehen hier häufig die Objektpronomen, die Subjektpronomen sollten stehen, wenn ein Nebensatz folgt.

- It was **I** who called you last night. (It was **me** who called you last night.)
- It is only **he** who can solve this difficult problem.

Bezüglich einer zuvor genannten männlichen bzw. weiblichen Person im Singular oder Plural steht he bzw. she oder they. Bezüglich einer zuvor genannten Sache im Singular oder Plural steht it oder they. Im Deutschen steht hier oft *es, das*.

- May I introduce you to this gentleman? **He** is my father. (Darf ich Sie diesem Herrn vorstellen? **Es/das** ist mein Vater.)
- Can you see these girls over there? **They** are my sisters.

he, she, it, they

Bezüglich Personen oder Sachen, deren Geschlecht oder Zahl nicht bekannt ist oder deren Name erst nachher genannt wird.

- Who knocked at the door? **It** was your sister. (Wer klopfte an die Tür? **Es** war deine Schwester.)

it

Das Pronomen

bezüglich eines Satzinhalts	Es bezeichnet einen zuvor bereits erwähnten Vorgang oder einen ganzen Satzinhalt.	▪ My son passed the exam and I am very glad of it. (Mein Sohn bestand die Prüfung und ich bin sehr froh darüber.)
Hervorhebung is, was (Singular) auch bei einem Bezugswort im Plural	Zur Hervorhebung einzelner Satzglieder steht it is, it was. Selbst wenn das Bezugswort im Plural steht, steht immer nur is bzw. was.	▪ It was her brother who told me the truth. ▪ It was her brothers who told me the truth.
	Auf die Fragen who/what is it steht immer it is/was, selbst wenn das Bezugswort im Plural steht.	▪ Do you see the boys over there? Who is it? It is my brothers.
unpersönliche Ausdrücke	In einigen unpersönlichen Ausdrücken steht it als so genanntes Vorsubjekt (preparatory subject), wenn das folgende logische Subjekt ein Infinitiv + to, ein gerund oder Nebensatz ist.	▪ It is difficult to solve this problem in such a short time. ▪ It is no good crying over spilt milk. ▪ It is clear that he cannot solve this problem all by himself.

Die Objektpronomen

anstelle eines Objekts	Die Objektpronomen stehen anstelle eines Objekt.	▪ The teacher allowed the children to go earlier. The teacher allowed them to go earlier.
nach that is/was, it is/was	Statt der Subjektpronomen stehen in der Umgangssprache häufig die direkten Objektpronomen, besonders nach it is, it was und that is, that was.	▪ My husband and me spent our holidays in Scotland. (My husband and I ...) ▪ It was me who called you last night. (It was I who called you last night.)
bei Zahlwörtern, Indefinitpronomen	Sie stehen in Verbindung mit Zahlwörtern oder Indefinitpronomen, an die sie meist mit of angeschlossen werden.	▪ All of us went to school by bus. (Wir alle fuhren mit dem Bus zur Schule.) ▪ There were five of us who spent their holiday in Scotland.

Das Anredepronomen you

Personen, die man duzt, siezt	Das Anredepronomen you steht bei Personen, die man duzt oder siezt. Es hat im Singular und Plural und in im Subjekt- und Objektfall dieselbe Form.	▪ May I introduce this gentleman to you? (Darf ich Ihnen/dir/euch diesen Herrn vorstellen?) ▪ May I introduce you to this gentleman? (Darf ich Sie/dich/euch diesem Herrn vorstellen?)

Thou, thee, ye, you

Bibelsprache, veraltete Sprache	Diese Formen sind veraltet und kommen nur noch in der Bibel und in alten literarischen Werken und Dialekten vor.	▪ Oh Lord Jesus I ask Thee to help me in this difficult situation. (Oh Lord Jesus I ask you ...)

Das deutsche *es*

Die Personalpronomen he, she, they

Bezüglich einer zuvor genannten männlichen bzw. weiblichen Person im Singular oder Plural steht he bzw. she oder they.

- May I introduce you to this gentleman? He is my father.
(Darf ich Sie diesem Herrn vorstellen? Es/das ist mein Vater.)

bezüglich Personen

Das Personalpronomen it

Bezüglich Personen oder Sachen, deren Geschlecht oder Zahl nicht bekannt ist oder deren Name erst nachher genannt wird.

- Who knocked at the door? It was your sister Ann.
(Wer klopfte an die Tür? Es war deine Schwester Ann.)

bezüglich Personen, Sachen

Es bezeichnet einen zuvor bereits erwähnten Vorgang oder einen ganzen Satzinhalt.

- My son passed the exam and I am very glad of it.
(Mein Sohn bestand die Prüfung und ich bin sehr froh darüber.)

ganzer Satzinhalt

Zur Hervorhebung einzelner Satzglieder steht it is/was, selbst wenn das Bezugswort im Plural steht. Auf die Frage who/what is it steht immer it is/was, selbst wenn das Bezugswort im Plural steht.

- It was her brother who told me the truth.
- It was her brothers who told me the truth.
- Do you see the boys over there? Who is it? It is my brothers.

it is/was zur Hervorhebung is, was (Singular) auch bei einem Bezugswort im Plural

Nach betontem to do steht it, that oder so. It und that sind nachdrücklicher als so.

- Do you think he will tell her the truth? I don't know, but I will do it/that/so.
(... Ich weiß es nicht, aber ich werde es tun.)

betontes to do

In Angaben zum Wetter oder in Zeitangaben ist it ein unpersönliches, grammatisches Subjekt.

- Put your coat on, it is cold outside.
(Zieh deinen Mantel an, es ist kalt draußen.)
- It is six o'clock in the morning.

Zeitangaben, Angaben zum Wetter

Die unpersönliche Ausdrucksweise ist im Englischen viel weniger häufig als im Deutschen. Das Englische bevorzugt, wo immer möglich, die persönliche Ausdrucksweise.

- Shut the window please, I am cold.
(Schließ das Fenster bitte, es ist mir kalt.)
- Don't worry about me, I am very well.
(Mach dir keine Sorgen um mich, mir geht es sehr gut.)

persönliche Ausdrucksweise

- I am glad — es freut mich
- I am cold/warm — es ist mir kalt/warm
- I am (un)well — es geht mir (nicht) gut
- I am sorry — es tut mir Leid

- I succeed in — es gelingt mir
- I fail — es gelingt mir nicht
- I like — es gefällt mir
- I want — es fehlt mir an

In einigen unpersönlichen Ausdrücken steht it als so genanntes Vorsubjekt (preparatory subject), wenn das folgende logische Subjekt ein Infinitiv + to, ein gerund oder Nebensatz ist.

- It is difficult to solve this problem in such a short time.
- It is no good crying over spilt milk.
- It is clear that he cannot solve this problem all by himself.

unpersönliche Ausdrücke

Das Pronomen

Das Vorsubjekt there

als Vorsubjekt Es steht als so genanntes Vorsubjekt (preparatory subject), wenn das Verb des Satzes to be oder wenn noch ein Subjekt folgt, das ein Substantiv ist.

- There was nobody to be seen in the street.
- There were many people who wanted to see the Queen.

there is/was There is/was und there are/were (es gibt) muss stehen, wenn am Satzanfang ein Adverb oder eine adverbiale Bestimmung der Zeit steht. Nach adverbialen Bestimmungen des Ortes kann there weggelassen werden.

- Unfortunately, there were a lot of children who died in the catastrophe.
- This morning, there were two foreign persons standing in front of our house looking for something I don't know.

zur Hervorhebung Tritt there an den Satzanfang zur Hervorhebung des Subjekts, tritt das Subjekt hinter das Prädikat (Inversion.)

- There came a lot of people to see the Queen.

So

Verben des Sagens, Denkens Nach den Verben des Sagens und Denkens steht so bezüglich eines vorausgehenden ganzen Satzinhalts.

- Do you think she is happy? I hope so.
  (Denkst du, dass sie glücklich ist? Ich hoffe es.)
- Will he come to your party? I think so.

betontes to do Nach betontem to do steht so oder auch it oder that. It und that sind nachdrücklicher als so.
In der Bedeutung auch steht so nach den folgenden Verben:

- Do you think he will tell her the truth? I don't know, but I will do so/it/that.
  (... Ich weiß es nicht, aber ich werde es tun.)
- At the moment he is not alone like I am, but I think he will become so.
  (Im Moment ist er noch nicht allein wie ich, aber ich denke, er wird es noch werden.)

- to be   sein
- to become   werden
- to grow   werden

- to look   schauen
- to remain   bleiben
- to seem   scheinen

auch Zur nachdrücklichen Bestätigung der vorangegangenen Aussage steht so am Satzende in der Bedeutung auch. Enthält der Vordersatz ein Vollverb, wird dieses nach so durch to do wieder aufgenommen, enthält der Vordersatz ein Hilfs- oder Modalverb, wird dieses nach so wieder aufgenommen.

- I told him to do his homework right after lunch, and so he did.
  (Ich sagte ihm, er soll seine Hausaufgaben gleich nach dem Essen machen, und das tat er dann auch.)
- Mary can solve this problem all by herself and so can Peter.

Vergleich Zum Ausdruck des Vergleichs steht so am Satzende in der Bedeutung auch. Nach so steht to do oder ein Hilfs-, Modalverb, wenn der Vordersatz ein Vollverb oder Hilfs- bzw. Modalverb enthält. Das Subjekt tritt hinter das Prädikat (Inversion).

- His sister Elizabeth is very nice and so is he.
  (Seine Schwester Elizabeth ist sehr nett und er ist es auch.)
- Elizabeth likes reading and so does her brother Peter.

Das Pronomen

Das deutsche *es* bleibt unübersetzt

Nach den Modalverben, bleibt das deutsche *es* grundsätzlich unübersetzt.

> Do you think he can come? Yes, he **can**.
> (Denkst du er kann kommen? Ja(, er kann (es).)

Modalverben

Die Verben des Sagens und Denkens, vor allem to forget, to guess, to know, to promise, to remember, to tell und to try stehen, wenn sie betont werden, allein.

> Peter was one of the best students to pass the exam. Yes, I **know**.
> (... Ja, ich weiß es.)
>
> Do you think you will pass the exam? I don't know, but I will **try**.

Verben des Sagens, Denkens

In kurzen Antworten nach to be, to have und to do steht auch im Deutschen meist kein *es*.

> Are you happy? Yes, I **am**.
> (Bist du glücklich? Ja(, ich bin es).)
>
> Has he got a new car? No, he **hasn't**.

kurze Antworten

Im Deutschen weist *es* oder *daran*, *davon* auf einen folgenden Objektsatz oder Infinitiv, im Englischen bleibt dies unübersetzt.

> **I do not doubt** that Peter will pass the exam.
> (Ich zweifle nicht daran, dass Peter die Prüfung bestehen wird.)

unübersetzt

Das Pronomen

Übungen zum Personalpronomen

1. **Setzen Sie it, there, oder so + die entsprechende Form der Verben in Klammern im past tense simple ein.**

   1. When I had finished I was surprised to find someone waiting for me ... ... (be) Miss Davies.
   2. During October ... (come) heavy rains, so that I could not go out of my house.
   3. Are you two all right? I think ... .
   4. ... (be) your neighbours that spread the rumour.
   5. A hundred years ago, ... (be) no radio, ... (be) no aeroplanes, no cars and buses.
   6. He arrived in London late that afternoon, and ... (be) no bus to Milchester until the next morning at eleven.
   7. ... (be) my sister Caroline who was the cause of my few minutes delay.
   8. If he has an alibi, why doesn't he come forward and say ...?
   9. ... (be) deep lines of fatigue and grief in his face.
   10. ... (be) the areas nearest to the coasts which suffered most severely.

   richtig   falsch

   Die entsprechenden Lösungen befinden sich auf Seite 439.

Das Reflexivpronomen (The Reflexive Pronoun)

Das Reflexivpronomen (rückbezügliches Fürwort) bezieht sich «zurück» auf das Subjekt. Es kommt nur als indirektes und direktes Objekt vor und hat in beiden Fällen dieselbe Form.

Nu.	Pers.	Gen.	Indirektes Objekt	Direktes Objekt
Sing.	1	mask.	myself	myself
		fem.		
	2	mask.	yourself	yourself
		fem.		
	3	mask.	himself	himself
		fem.	herself	herself
		neutr.	itself	itself
			oneself	oneself
Plur.	1	mask.	ourselves	ourselves
		fem.		
	2	mask.	yourselves	yourselves
		fem.		
	3	mask.	themselves	themselves
		fem.		

Neben den reflexiven Verben, die immer mit einem Reflexivpronomen stehen, kann das Reflexivpronomen noch in den folgeden Fällen verwendet werden.

Das Reflexivpronomen kann zur Hervorhebung von Personen oder Dingen stehen. Ist die hervorzuhebende Person bzw. Sache ein Personalpronomen, entfällt dieses. Das Reflexivpronomen steht unmittelbar nach dem hervorzuhebenden Wort. Ist dieses Wort Subjekt, so kann das Reflexivpronomen auch am Satzende stehen.	Peter and (I) myself were washing the car. (Peter und ich wuschen das Auto.) My little sister has done this work herself. (Meine kleine Schwester hat diese Arbeit ganz allein gemacht.) The house itself is nice, but the colour is ugly. (Das Haus an sich ist schön, aber die Farbe ist hässlich.)	Hervorhebung
In Vergleichen steht das Reflexivpronomen statt des Personalpronomens besonders nach as, than und like.	Peter likes doing those things more than myself. (Peter macht solche Sachen lieber als ich.)	Vergleich
In Aufzählungen steht das Reflexivpronomen statt des Personalpronomens besonders nach and und or.	Peter, Mary and myself were washing the car. (Peter, Mary und ich wuschen das Auto.)	Aufzählungen

Das Pronomen

Präpositionen	Das Reflexivpronomen steht auch nach Präpositionen. Nach den Präpositionen des Ortes steht in der Regel das Personalpronomen, das Reflexivpronomen steht nur zur Hervorhebung.	▪ I saw Peter talking to **himself**. (Ich sah Peter mit sich selbst sprechen.) ▪ He placed the chair behind **him**. (Er stellte den Stuhl hinter sich.) ▪ I don't want to be left all by **myself**. (Ich möchte nicht ganz allein gelassen werden.)
except, but	Das Reflexivpronomen steht oft statt des Personalpronomens nach except und but.	▪ There is nobody else who can solve this difficult problem but **yourself**. (Niemand außer dir kann dieses schwierige Problem lösen.)
bezüglich eines unbestimmten Subjekt (one)	Das Reflexivpronomen oneself bezieht sich auf ein unbestimmtes Subjekt (one).	▪ There are some things one cannot do by **oneself**.

Das Pronomen

Übungen zum Reflexivpronomen

1. Setzen Sie das korrekte Reflexiv- oder Personalpronomen ein.

1. A sound behind him made ... turn.

2. Half an hour later Mr Cunningham, my mother and ... were in the train on the way to London.

3. He looked around ...

4. He saw the accident and Mrs Taylor's bleeding face before ... all the time.

5. He swore to ... he would stick to a job once he got it.

6. He thought that he could do the housekeeping for his daughter and ...

7. It was one of the few times in his life that he felt pleased with ...

8. McDonald was thinking the same thing as ... (1. Pers. Sing.)

9. She made porridge for him, George and ...

10. She preferred to be by ...

11. When he was twenty-one, Arthur Robinson married a beautiful woman some years older than ...

12. Charles wondered whether his friend Arthur was engaged on the same job as ...

13. He felt surer of ... now in every way.

14. He was beside ... with rage.

15. May I express the hope, sir, that you will honour Mrs Rose and ... by a visit to our apartment in the King's Road?

richtig   falsch

Die ensprechenden Lösungen befinden sich auf Seite 439ff.

Die Reziprokpronomen (The Reciprocal Pronouns)

Die Reziprokpronomen (Pronomen der Gegen-, Wechselseitigkeit) each other oder one another drücken die Gegenseitigkeit, Wechselseitigkeit aus (einander, gegenseitig). Sie beziehen sich nur auf Personen der 3. Person Plural.

Each other

bezüglich zweier Personen	Es bezieht sich auf zwei Personen(gruppen) und steht nach dem Verb. Präpositionen treten immer vor, nicht zwischen das Pronomen.	• Mary and Peter love **each other**. • The two presidents shook hands with **each other**. (Die zwei Präsidenten schüttelten einander die Hand.)

One another

bezüglich mehrerer Personen	Es bezieht sich auf mehrere Personen(gruppen) und steht nach dem Verb. Präpositionen treten immer vor, nicht zwischen das Pronomen.	• They helped **one another**. (Sie halfen einander.) • We all talked to **one another** on the phone.

Das Pronomen

Übungen zum Reziprokpronomen

1. Setzen Sie each other oder one another ein.

1. It was more than a week since they had seen ...

2. Sean and Jack are twins. They are like ... in every way.

3. Nearly all English people now live in towns or suburbs and most towns are very like ...

4. The boys and girls looked at ... with startled faces.

5. The pupils were doing their best to shout ... down.

6. They had been talking to ... for a couple of minutes.

7. We could hear them call to ...

8. What caused the police and the mob to start firing at ...?

9. They could do nothing except stand gazing into ... eyes.

10. You could see the two teams bashing ... from there.

11. There have been times in which the members of the Court have greatly disagreed with ...

12. Candidates for the Democratic nomination rival ... in their attempts to win the Democratic voters.

13. In the past, nations could pledge themselves to ... aid in case of attack.

14. Arthur and Susan smiled at ... with shy liking.

15. All political discussions balance the opposing views against ...

richtig   falsch

Die entsprechenden Lösungen befinden sich auf Seite 440.

Das Pronomen

Das Possessivpronomen (The Possessive Pronoun)

Das Possessivpronomen (besitzanzeigendes Fürwort) drückt ein Besitzverhältnis aus und steht stellvertretend für Personen und Sachen.

Das substantivische Possessivpronomen (The Possessive Pronoun)

Das substantivische Possessivpronomen steht nicht mit einem Substantiv. Es ist stets unveränderlich, unabhängig davon, ob es eine Person oder Sache im Singular oder Plural vertritt.

Genus	1. Pers. Sing.	2. Pers. Sing.	3. Pers. Sing.	1. Pers. Plur.	2. Pers. Plur.	3. Pers. Plur.
mask.			his			
fem.	mine	yours (thine)	hers	ours	yours (thine)	theirs
neutr.			its own			

Substantiv + of	Es steht mit of nach Substantiven mit unbestimmtem Artikel, Indefinit- oder Demonstrativpronomen.	▪ He is a friend of mine. ▪ That is no business of mine. ▪ This friend of mine is very reliable.
gehören	Es steht in Verbindung mit to be in der Bedeutung gehören. Diese Art der Formulierung ist weniger nachdrücklich als to be + attributives Possessivpronomen + own.	▪ The book on the table is mine. (Das Buch auf dem Tisch gehört mir.) (This is my book.) ▪ I found a bag under the table. Is it yours?
bei attributivem Possessivpronomen + Substantiv + and	Es steht mit and nach einem attributiven Possessivpronomen + Substantiv, um die Wiederholung zweier attributiver Possessivpronomen zu vermeiden.	▪ Your brother and mine are classmates. (Your brother and my brother are classmates.)
Anrede	Yours ist Anredepronomen für eine oder mehrere Personen, die man duzt oder siezt.	▪ This friend of yours is very reliable. (Ihr/dein/euer Freund ist sehr zuverlässig.) ▪ Yours (very) sincerely.
Bibelsprache, veraltete Sprache	Thine findet sich nur noch in alter literarischer Sprache oder der Bibelsprache.	▪ For Thine is the kingdom, and the power, and the glory forever.

Das attributive Possessivpronomen (The Possessive Adjective)

Das attributive Possessivpronomen steht stellvertretend für Personen und Sachen. Es steht immer mit einem Substantiv.
Es ist stets unveränderlich, unabhängig davon, ob es sich auf eine Person oder Sache im Singular oder Plural bezieht.

Genus	1. Pers. Sing.	2. Pers. Sing.	3. Pers. Sing.	1. Pers. Plur.	2. Pers. Plur.	3. Pers. Plur.
mask.			his			
fem.	my (mine)	your (thy, thine)	her	our	your (thy, thine)	their
neutr.			its			

Zur Bezeichnung von Körperteilen und Kleidungsstücken sowie bei house, bicycle, car, work, life, mind und temper, die zum Subjekt gehören.
Gehören Körperteil, Kleidungsstück zum Objekt oder Subjekt eines Passivsatzes, steht der bestimmte Artikel.

- He put his hands in his pockets.
  (Er steckte die Hände in die Hosentaschen.)
- He took her recklessly by the arm.
- I was hit on the head with a very sharp object.

Körperteile, Kleidungsstücke

Es steht zur Hervorhebung in Verbindung mit own in der Bedeutung *eigen* oder *selbst (ohne fremde Hilfe)*.

- I live in my own house.
  (Ich wohne in meinem eigenen Haus.)
- I repair my own car.
  (Ich repariere meinen Wagen selbst.)

mit own in der Bedeutung selbst, eigen

In der Regel steht own vor dem Substantiv. Es tritt allerdings hinter das Substantiv, wenn vor diesem der unbestimmte Artikel, kein Artikel, ein Zahlwort oder Indefinitpronomen steht.

- I live in my own house.
- I have a car of my own.
- I have two bikes of my own.
- I have no car of my own.

In Verbindung mit to be und own steht es in der Bedeutung *gehören*. Diese Art der Formulierung ist nachdrücklicher als to be + substantivisches Possessivpronomen.

- This is my own car.
  (This car is mine.)
  (Dieses Auto gehört mir.)
- Is this your own house?

to be + own in der Bedeutung gehören

Mine, thy, thine finden sich nur noch in der Bibelsprache und in alten literarischen Werken. Vor Substantiven, die mit Vokal beginnen, steht statt my und thy oft mine und thine.

- Drink to me only with thine eyes.
  (Ben Johnson)

Bibelsprache, veraltete Sprache

Das Pronomen

Übungen zum Possessivpronomen

1. Setzen Sie das attributive oder substantivische Possessivpronomen ein.

1. Does a scientist have to think about the possible consequences of ... work?

2. He is no friend of ... ... (1. Pers. Sing.)

3. Many people do not like Helen, but she can be very charming to ... friends.

4. Mr O'Neil saw his hat. He told the stewardess it was ...

5. Out of the corner of ... eye, I saw him running.

6. Philip begged Mary to keep ... marriage secret.

7. She had no money of ... own and was dependent on her brother-in-law's generosity.

8. That is no concern of ... (2. Pers. Sing.).

9. The children I invited were ... classmates.

10. These flowers are ... ... (3. Pers. Sing.).

11. Make good use of ... time.

12. Her eyes met ... ... (3. Pers. Sing.).

13. ... time was made good use of. (2. Pers. Sing.).

14. The investiture of ... Royal Highness the Prince of Wales at Caernarvon Castle means little to us.

15. He has come to Tahiti without ... girl friend.

richtig   falsch

2. Ändern Sie die blau gedruckten attributiven Possessivpronomen in substantivische Possessivpronomen.

1. Look at **his** car.

2. Bob left Liverpool after a cup of tea at Arthur's, where he said good-bye to some of **his** village acquaintances.

3. I had hoped that **my** visit would remain unnoticed.

Das Pronomen

4. Were they **your** friends?

5. I was talking recently to **your** friend.

6. The book on the table is **my** book.

7. Which glass is **your** glass?

8. He is my countryman and I am **his** countryman.

9. What about **your** interest in my patients?

10. **Your** friend is very reliable.

richtig   falsch

Die entsprechenden Lösungen befinden sich auf Seite 440.

Das Pronomen

Das Demonstrativpronomen (The Demonstrative Pronoun)

Das Demonstrativpronomen (hinweisendes Fürwort) weist auf eine oder mehrere bestimmte Personen oder Sachen und steht nur in der 3. Person.
Das Demonstrativpronomen kann substantivisch (demonstrative pronoun) und attributiv (demonstrative adjective) verwendet werden.

Nu.	Pers.	this	that	such
Sing.	3	this	that	such
Plur.	3	these	those	such

	this, these	that, those	
bezüglich des näher Liegenden; ferner Liegenden	Sie weisen in Gegenüberstellungen auf näher liegende Personen oder Sachen hin. This bezieht sich auf Personen oder Sachen im Singular, these bezieht sich auf Personen oder Sachen im Plural.	Sie weisen in Gegenüberstellungen auf ferner liegende Personen oder Sachen hin. That bezieht sich auf Personen oder Sachen im Singular, those bezieht sich auf Personen oder Sachen im Plural.	
	▪ Can you see **these** books over here? Can you give me **this** book? (Siehst du **diese** Bücher da? Kannst du mir **dieses** Buch geben?)	▪ Can you see **those** books over there? Can you give me **that** book? (Siehst du **jene** Bücher dort? Kannst du mir **jenes** Buch geben?)	

	this, these	that, those	such
bezüglich des Folgenden/ zuvor Genannten	Sie weisen auf etwas Folgendes hin.	Sie weisen auf etwas zuvor Genanntes hin oder auf etwas, das als bekannt vorausgesetzt wird.	Es weist auf etwas bereits Genanntes, Bekanntes. Bezüglich des Folgenden steht **such as** (wie zum Beispiel) häufig zur Einleitung von Aufzählungen.
	▪ Please remember **this**: We have to pick up Frances at 7 p.m.	▪ You lent Peter $ 1,000 half a year ago. I didn't know **that**.	▪ If I should have offended you, **such** was not my intention. ▪ He has already been to a lot of countries **such as** the USA, Great Britain, Japan.

Das Pronomen

this, these	that, those	
In Bezug auf eine vorher erwähnte Person (in der Nähe) muss es das Stützwort one erhalten. In Bezug auf eine vorher erwähnte (zählbare) Sache (in der Nähe) kann one entfallen. This is/was steht immer ohne one, auch in Bezug auf Personen. These steht in Bezug auf mehrere Personen oder Sachen und immer ohne one.	In Bezug auf eine vorher erwähnte Person (in der Ferne) muss es das Stützwort one erhalten. In Bezug auf eine vorher erwähnte (zählbare) Sache (in der Ferne) kann one entfallen. That is/was steht immer ohne one, auch in Bezug auf Personen. Those steht in Bezug auf mehrere Personen oder Sachen und immer ohne one.	mit dem Stützwort one
▪ That girl is younger than **this one.** ▪ I like that book much more than **this (one).** ▪ Those books are much better than **these.**	▪ This girl is younger than **that one.** ▪ I like this book much more than **that (one).** ▪ These books are much better than **those.**	
Sie weisen auf die Gegenwart oder (beim present perfect) auf einen Vorgang, der in der Vergangenheit begonnen hat und bis in die Gegenwart andauert.	Sie weisen auf die Vergangenheit hin.	bezüglich des Gegenwärtigen; Vergangenen
▪ Have you seen Mr Smith **this** morning? ▪ **These** last three years were very hard. (**Diese** letzten drei Jahre waren sehr hart.)	▪ The criminal was arrested on **that** day. ▪ **Those** three years were very hard. (**Jene** drei Jahre waren sehr hart.)	

this, these	that, those
In gefühlsbetonter Bedeutung ist es oft mit einem substantivischen Possessivpronomen verbunden, das hinter das Substantiv tritt. This, these und that, those sind in dieser Bedeutung austauschbar.	In gefühlsbetonter Bedeutung ist es oft mit einem substantivischen Possessivpronomen verbunden, das hinter das Substantiv tritt. This, these und that, those sind in dieser Bedeutung austauschbar.

Das Pronomen

	this, these	that, those
	• I love **this** uncomplicated way of his. (Ich liebe **diese** unkomplizierte Art an ihm.) • **These** cats of yours are always disturbing my kitchen-garden.	• I love **that** uncomplicated way of his. (Ich liebe **diese** unkomplizierte Art an ihm.) • **Those** cats of yours are always disturbing my kitchen-garden.

such

Hervorhebung	Zum Ausdruck der Hervorhebung kann **such** mit dem unbestimmten Artikel stehen, **such a** (solch ein). Für **such a** kann auch **so a** eintreten, wobei ein Adjektiv, im Gegensatz zum Deutschen, zwischen **so** und **a** tritt.
Adjektiv tritt zwischen so und a	• He got **such a** fright. (Er bekam **einen solchen** Schrecken.) • We spent **such a** nice weekend in the country. • With **so** charming **a** waiter, it's no wonder that the restaurant is full.
in der Bedeutung von much	**Such** kann auch in der Bedeutung von **much** verwendet werden. • We had **such** fun. (Wir hatten einen **Riesen**spaß, **so viel** Freude.)

316 dnf

Übungen zum Demonstrativpronomen

1. Setzen Sie this, these oder that, those ein.

1. I recommend ... book on London. This little one? Yes.
2. Give me ... telephone books over there.
3. I must get some sleep, even if it means taking four of ... tablets which you gave me.
4. Look Mary, there are our umbrellas. Hello, stewardess, ... umbrellas there are ours.
5. Look, how ... man over there is running. He wants to catch a plane I guess.
6. Some centuries ago, there were only very few roads, and even ... roads were narrow and bad.
7. We are flying across the Pacific. Land is in sight, ... city over there on the coast is Vancouver.
8. What has become of ... articles of value which you kept in the little box upon your dressing table?
9. He asked me if I would go out ... night and I said I wouldn't.
10. I am flying to Paris ... evening.

richtig   falsch

Die entsprechenden Lösungen befinden sich auf Seite 440.

Das Pronomen

Das Determinativpronomen (The Determinative Pronoun)

Das Determinativpronomen (bestimmendes Fürwort) weist auf ein oder mehrere folgende Personen oder Sachen oder auf einen folgenden Satz hin.

Das substantivische Determinativpronomen (The Determinative Pronoun)

Das substantivische Determinativpronomen weist auf einen unmittelbar folgenden Relativsatz, einen of-Genitiv oder es vertritt ein kurz zuvor genanntes Substantiv.
Das attributive Determinativpronomen steht unmittelbar bei einem näher zu bestimmenden Substantiv.

Nu.	Pers.	Gen.	that of	the one	(he) who	the one who
Sing.	3	mask.			(he) who	the one who
		fem.	that of	the one	(she) who	the one who
		neutr.			(that) which, what	the one (which)
Plur.	3	mask.			(they) who, (those) who	the ones who
		fem.	those of	the ones, those		
		neutr.			(those) which	the ones (which)

	that of	the one
stellvertretend für Personen und Sachen	Stellvertretend für eine oder mehrere Personen oder Sachen, wobei that of eine Person oder Sache vertritt und those of mehrere. In Vertretung für Personen kann statt of auch der **possessive case** stehen.	Stellvertretend für eine oder mehrere Personen oder Sachen aus einer Gruppe, wobei the one eine Person oder Sache vertritt und the ones, those mehrere.
	▪ Your father is much nicer than that of Mary. (Your father is much nicer than Mary's.) ▪ Your classrooms are much bigger than those of our school.	▪ Which boy is your son? The one with the black jacket on. ▪ Which books do you prefer? I prefer the ones/those (which) I read first.
	he who	the one who
vor Relativsätzen	Diese Determinativpronomen leiten einen folgenden Relativsatz ein. Sie stehen stellvertretend für eine oder mehrere Personen oder Sa-	Diese Determinativpronomen leiten einen folgenden Relativsatz ein. Sie stehen stellvertretend für eine oder mehrere zuvor genannte Per-

Das Pronomen

he who	the one who
chen, wobei he who, she who eine männliche, weibliche Person vertritt, that which vertritt eine Sache, they who und those who vertreten mehrere Personen, those which vertritt mehrere Sachen. Statt he who, she who steht, vor allem in der modernen Sprache, nur who. Für that which steht in der literarischen Sprache häufig und in der Umgangssprache immer what.	sonen oder Sachen, wobei the one who eine bestimmte Person, the one which eine bestimmte Sache vertritt, the ones who vertritt mehrere bestimmte Personen, the ones which vertritt mehrere Sachen. Which kann auch weggelassen werden.

- **He who** laughs last laughs best. **(Who** laughs last laughs best.)
- Heaven help **them/those who** help themselves.
- **They who** laugh last laugh best.
- Never trust to another **what (that which)** you can do yourself.

- Peter was **the one who** solved the problem.
- This action film is **the one (which)** I like best.
- Mary's brothers are **the ones who** repaired our roof.
- Action films are **the ones (which)** I like best.

Das Pronomen

Das attributive Determinativpronomen (The Determinative Adjective)

Das attributive Determinativpronomen steht unmittelbar bei dem näher zu bestimmenden Substantiv.
Das substantivische Determinativpronomen vertritt ein kurz zuvor genanntes Substantiv.

Nu.	Pers.	Gen.	that (who)	the (who)
Sing.	3	mask.	that (who)	the (who)
		fem.	that (who)	the (who)
		neutr.	that (which)	the (which)
Plur.	3	mask.	those (who)	the (who)
		fem.	those (who)	the (who)
		neutr.	those (which)	the (which)

	that (who)	the (who)
bezüglich Personen und Sachen	Bezüglich einer oder mehrerer Personen oder Sachen. That who bezieht sich auf eine Person, those who auf mehrere. That which bezieht sich auf eine Sache, those which auf mehrere. That, those (who/which) klingt bestimmter als the (who/which). Who und which können, sofern das Verb to be folgt, weggelassen werden.	Bezüglich einer oder mehrerer Personen oder Sachen. The who bezieht sich auf eine oder mehrere Personen, the which bezieht sich auf eine oder mehrere Sachen. The (who/which) klingt allgemeiner als that/those (who/which). Who und which können, sofern das Verb to be folgt, weggelassen werden.
	- Who is **that** boy **(who** is) playing in the garden? - **That** boy **(who** is) wearing the blue jacket is my son. - **That** money **(which** is) lying on the table is mine. - **Those** wine glasses **(which** are) on the top shelf are made of crystal.	- Who is **the** boy **(who** is) playing in the garden? - **The** boy **(who** is) wearing the blue jacket is my son. - **The** money **(which** is) lying on the table is mine. - **The** wine glasses **(which** are) on the top shelf are made of crystal.

Das Pronomen

Übungen zum Determinativpronomen

1. Setzen Sie that of, those of oder the one, the ones ein.

1. The area of Greater London is 620 square miles, almost twice ... New York City.

2. Across the road there was another hotel, an identical twin to ... where he was staying.

3. He handed Simon his letter and stuffed ... from Mr Atkinson into his pocket.

4. Robert liked the shops in London better than ... in his hometown.

5. Would you like a cappuccino or an espresso? Which is ... with milk? Cappuccino.

6. Australia is more than twice as big as India, yet it has a population of only 10 million - not much larger than ... London.

7. Each American is subject to two governments, ... his state and ... the Union.

8. Ghandi's most distinctive doctrine was ... non-violence.

9. The Queen makes appointments to all important State offices including ... judges, governors and diplomats.

10. Britain's economic comeback in many ways parallels ... the U.S.

richtig   falsch

2. Setzen Sie he who, those who oder that which, those which oder the one who, the ones who ein.

1. He is ... showed me how to do it.

2. ... is not for us is against us.

3. It was ... asked the questions.

4. It was ... won the game.

5. Many settlers died and ... survived lived in miserable conditions.

6. The Pilgrim Fathers, and many of ... followed them, left Europe to be free.

Das Pronomen

7. Although judges are well paid their current earnings are less than ... successful barristers receive.

8. The education committee of the local elected council is responsible for all the schools, except for ... are independent.

9. ... doesn't take advice can't be helped.

10. The working week for most Americans is forty hours, though this does not apply to ... have senior positions in management.

                                                                             richtig   falsch

3. Setzen Sie those who, the who oder the which ein.

1. She was one of ... people ... can go to sleep at any hour and in any position.

2. ... countries ... belong to the Commonwealth today were once colonies of the British Empire.

3. ... man ... was hurt died soon after.

4. ... noise ... was coming from the saloon could be heard down the street.

5. ... pupils ... live near the school walk or cycle home for lunch.

                                                                             richtig   falsch

Die entsprechenden Lösungen befinden sich auf Seite 440.

Das Relativpronomen (The Relative Pronoun)

Das Relativpronomen (bezügliches Fürwort) bezieht sich auf ein oder mehrere unmittelbar vorausgehende Substantive, die Subjekt, direktes oder indirektes Objekt sind oder im possessive case stehen. Es steht immer in der 3. Person. Es leitet einen Nebensatz, den so genannten Relativsatz ein.

Pron.	Nu.	Pers.	Gen.	Subjekt	Pos. Case	Indir.Obj.	Dir.Obj.
who	Sing.	3	mask.	who	whose	whom (who)	whom (who)
			fem.				
	Plur.	3	mask.	who	whose	whom (who)	whom (who)
			fem.				
which	Sing.	3	mask.	-	whose	-	-
			fem.				
			neutr.	which	of which, whose	which	which
	Plur.	3	mask.	-	whose	-	-
			fem.				
			neutr.	which	of which, whose	which	which
that	Sing.	3	mask.	(that)	-	(that)	(that)
			fem.				
			neutr.	that	-	that	that
	Plur.	3	mask.	(that)	-	(that)	(that)
			fem.				
			neutr.	that	-	that	that

Whoever, whichever, what, whatever, when, whenever, where, wherever, however können auch als Relativpronomen verwendet werden und sind unveränderlich.

Das Pronomen

	who	whom
bezüglich des Subjekts; Objekts	Es bezieht sich auf eine oder mehrere beliebige Personen, die Subjekt sind. Gelegentlich bezieht es sich auch auf Tiere, personifizierte Länder- und Städtenamen. In der Umgangssprache steht who häufig statt whom auch für Objekte. Präpositionen, die zum Verb gehören, bleiben beim Verb.	Es bezieht sich auf eine oder mehrere beliebige Personen, die Objekt sind. Präpositionen, die zum Verb gehören, treten vor whom. In der Umgangssprache können die Präpositionen auch beim Verb stehen.
	- The boy **who** was always playing with Peter has been taken to the hospital. (Der Junge, der immer mit Peter spielte, ...) - We have a dog **who** is always roaming around. - The man **who** (whom) we saw this morning had been arrested. (Der Mann, den wir heute Morgen sahen ...) - The man **who** you were talking **to** this morning had been arrested.	- The man **whom** we saw this morning had been arrested. (Der Mann, den wir heute Morgen sahen ...) - The man to **whom** you were talking this morning had been arrested. - The man **whom** you were talking to this morning had been arrested.

	who	which	that
bezüglich einzelner Personen und Sachen (aus einer Gruppe)	Es bezieht sich auf eine oder mehrere Personen aus einer Gruppe. Es ist jede einzelne Person gemeint.	Es bezieht sich auf eine oder mehrere bestimmte Sachen aus einer Gruppe. Which klingt förmlicher als that. Bezüglich einer Gruppe von Personen, wenn an die Gruppe als solche gedacht ist.	Es bezieht sich auf eine oder mehrere bestimmte Personen oder Sachen aus einer Gruppe, wobei bei Personen who bzw. whom in der modernen Sprache bevorzugt wird. That steht vor allem nach all, anything, everything, nothing, something, anybody, somebody, someone, nobody, no one, much,

Das Pronomen

who	which	that
		little und nach Superlativen wie the first, the last, the only. Vor that darf nie eine Präposition stehen, diese steht immer beim Verb.
• The boys who were always playing with Peter have been taken to the hospital. • The football team who won the World Cup were given a warm welcome.	• Give me the book which I bought yesterday. • I will buy the first book which you showed me. • They welcomed the football team which won the World Cup.	• The boy that was always playing with Peter has been taken to the hospital. • Give me the books that I bought yesterday. • I will buy the first book that you showed me. • This is the book that I have been talking about.

Präpositionen nie vor that

whose	of which
Es bezeichnet ein Besitzverhältnis, wobei der Besitzer eine oder mehrere Personen ist.	Es bezeichnet ein Besitzverhältnis, wobei der Besitzer eine oder mehrere Sachen oder Tiere ist. Of which klingt oft schwerfällig und wird daher häufig auch bei Sachen durch whose ersetzt.
• The man whose name nobody knows. (Der Mann, dessen Namen niemand kennt.) • The women whose children died very young.	• The cars, the motors of which had been exchanged, run very well now. (Die Autos, deren Motoren ausgetauscht wurden, fahren nun sehr gut.) • The cars whose motors had been exchanged run very well now.

Besitzverhältnis

which	what
Es bezieht sich auf einen vorangehenden Satz(inhalt) (was) und wird stets durch Komma abgetrennt.	Es bezieht sich auf einen folgenden Satz(inhalt) ((das) was).

bezüglich eines Satzinhalts

Das Pronomen

	which	what	
	■ He behaves like a fool, **which** really annoys me. (Er benimmt sich wie ein Verrückter, **was** mich wirklich ärgert.)	■ She works carefully and **what** is more, she often takes work home. ■ **What** she says is the truth. (**Das was** sie sagt, ist die Wahrheit.)	

	whoever	whichever	whatever
unbestimmte Personen und Sachen	Es bezeichnet eine oder mehrere unbestimmte Personen (wer auch immer).	Es bezeichnet eine oder mehrere unbestimmte Sachen aus einer Gruppe (welche/r/s auch immer).	Es bezeichnet eine unbestimmte Sache oder einen allgemeinen, folgenden Sachverhalt (was auch immer).
	■ **Whoever** did that will not be punished.	■ All of these cars are beautiful **whichever** you buy.	■ Don't believe her **whatever** she might say.

	when	where	that
nach Zeitangaben, Ortsangaben	Es leitet Relativsätze ein, die auf Zeitangaben folgen.	Es leitet Relativsätze ein, die auf Ortsangaben folgen.	Es leitet Relativsätze ein, die auf Zeitangaben folgen. Es steht nur bei notwendigen Relativsätzen und entfällt dann oft.
	■ This is the year **when** my mother was born.	■ This is the house **where** my mother was born.	■ Every time **(that)** he is in London he stays at the Ritz.

	whenever	wherever	however
Zeit; Ort; Art und Weise	Es bezeichnet einen unbestimmten Zeitpunkt, Zeitraum (wann auch immer).	Es bezeichnet einen unbestimmten Ort (wo auch immer).	Es bezeichnet die unbestimmte Art und Weise (wie auch immer).
	■ Come and see me **whenever** you like.	■ Have a rest **wherever** you like.	■ You can write the story **however** you wish.

Übungen zum Relativpronomen

1. Setzen Sie who oder whom ein.

1. Mary worked day and night among the wounded, ... she found crowded together in indescribably dirty barracks.
2. I don't know ... you mean.
3. It was she ... I had seen on Sunday.
4. It was the Millers ... called us.
5. Peggy was thinking only of Linda ... a doctor was examining.
6. The chairman's wife ... you met recently, was also bored.
7. There were few passengers ... escaped without serious injuries.
8. There were two letters, one to him from Simon's father, one to Simon from someone in New York ... Bob didn't know.
9. Queen Elizabeth I was the daughter of the Queen ... Henry had married in 1533 and beheaded three years later.
10. David is a delicate boy ... one shouldn't provoke all the time.

richtig   falsch

2. Setzen Sie which oder that, who oder whom ein.

1. Simon closed a book of poems ... had been lying face down on his studio couch.
2. Had he any enemies ... you know of?
3. He is the only man ... can speak English here.
4. One of the girls over there was a girl ... he often passed in the corridors.
5. Bob felt more comfortable at this party than at any other party ... he could remember.
6. You're the gentleman ... bought the young lady's keepsake album.
7. He had the appearance of being a person ... you could talk to.
8. I've got a wife ... I can't get rid of.

Das Pronomen

9. Navigation was one of the practical sciences ... benefitted from the new inventions.

10. The officer asked another question ... Bob pretended not to grasp. richtig falsch

3. Setzen Sie whose oder of which ein.

1. After passing the second reading stage a bill must then go to a committee for detailed examination, in the course ... there may be many proposals for amendment.

2. All members recognize the Queen as Head of the Commonwealth whether or not such states are republics or countries ... she is Queen.

3. Each chamber has galleries, parts ... are kept for the use of the public.

4. Is it the member of a fire department ... business it is to extinguish fires?

5. It was Arthur ... appearance had most impressed Charles.

6. The church ... dome looks like half a football is called St Paul's Cathedral.

7. The Conservative Party is a party ... basic aim is the protection of the individual.

8. The man ... car broke down in the forest had a pistol with him.

9. California has one place ... fame goes back to the early days of the great rush to prosperity and growth: Hollywood.

10. Supplementary benefits are provided for people ... incomes are too low for them to be able to live at a minimum standard. richtig falsch

Die entsprechenden Lösungen befinden sich auf Seite 440ff.

Das Interrogativpronomen (The Interrogative Pronoun)

Das Interrogativpronomen (Fragefürwort) leitet Fragesätze ein und fragt nach einer oder mehreren Personen oder Sachen die Subjekt, indirektes oder direktes Objekt sind oder im possessive case stehen. Es steht nur in der 3. Person.
Das Interrogativpronomen kann substantivisch (interrogative pronoun) und attributiv (interrogative adjective) verwendet werden.

Pron.	Nu.	Pers.	Gen.	Subjekt	Pos. Case	Indir. Obj.	Dir. Obj.
who	Sing.	3	mask. fem.	who	whose	whom (who)	whom (who)
who	Plur.	3	mask. fem.	who	whose	whom (who)	whom (who)
which	Sing.	3	mask. fem. neutr.	which	-	which	which
which	Plur.	3	mask. fem. neutr.	which	-	which	which
what	Sing.	3	mask. fem. neutr.	what	-	what	what
what	Plur.	3	mask. fem. neutr.	what	-	what	what

When, where, why, how sind Fragewörter. Sie sind unveränderlich.

Das Pronomen

	who	whose	whom
Fragen nach dem Subjekt; Objekt ⚠ Präpositionen müssen erhalten bleiben	Es leitet direkte und indirekte Fragesätze ein und fragt nach einer oder mehreren beliebigen Personen, die Subjekt sind. In der Umgangssprache fragt who häufig statt whom auch nach Objekten. Präpositionen, die zum Verb gehören, müssen erhalten bleiben, sie treten hinter das Verb oder an das Satzende.	Es leitet direkte und indirekte Fragesätze ein und fragt nach einer oder mehreren beliebigen Personen und Sachen im possessive case. Es fragt also nach dem Besitzer. Whose steht in Verbindung mit to be in der Bedeutung *gehören*.	Es leitet direkte und indirekte Fragesätze ein und fragt nach einer oder mehreren beliebigen Personen, die direktes oder indirektes Objekt sind. Präpositionen, die zum Verb gehören, treten vor whom. In der Umgangssprache können die Präpositionen auch hinter das Verb treten.
	• **Who** wrote this letter? (**Wer** schrieb diesen Brief?) • **Who** (whom) did you see in this room? (**Wen** hast du in diesem Zimmer gesehen?) • **Who** did you talk to? • **Who** did you give this letter to?	• **Whose** wife have you seen this morning? (**Wessen** Frau hast du heute Morgen gesehen?) • **Whose** book is this? (**Wem** gehört dieses Buch?)	• **Whom** did you see in this room? (**Wen** hast du in diesem Zimmer gesehen?) • **Whom** did you give the money? (**Wem** hast du das Geld gegeben?) • To **whom** did you talk. • **Whom** did you talk to?

	which	what
Fragen nach bestimmten Personen und Sachen ⚠ Präpositionen müssen erhalten bleiben	Es leitet direkte und indirekte Fragesätze ein und fragt nach einer oder mehreren bestimmten Personen oder Sachen aus einer Gruppe.	Es leitet direkte und indirekte Fragesätze ein und fragt nach einer oder mehreren Personen oder Sachen ganz allgemein. Präpositionen, die zum Verb gehören, müssen erhalten bleiben, sie treten entweder hinter das Verb oder an das Satzende.
	• **Which** boy (among these three) is your son? (**Welcher** Junge (unter diesen drei) ist Ihr Sohn?) • **Which** book (among these three) did you read?	• **What** people do things like this? (**Was für** Leute machen solche Sachen?) • **What** book did you read? (**Was für ein Buch** hast du gelesen?) • **What** are you looking for? (**Wonach** suchst du?)

Das Pronomen

what

In Fragen nach der Eigenschaft, dem Aussehen, der Größe etc.
What steht dabei mit to be oder in what kind/sort of, what does ... look, smell, taste etc. like.
Im Deutschen steht hier häufig ein Adjektiv + *wie*.

- **What** colour is the book?
  (**Welche** Farbe hat dieses Buch?)
- **What** is your age?
  (**Wie** alt bist du?)
- **What** kinds of books do you like best?
- **What** does this cake taste like?
- **What** is she like?
  (**Wie** ist sie?)

how

In Fragen nach der Art und Weise.
Es kann statt what in Verbindung mit Adjektiven stehen und es muss bei Adverbien und bei much und many stehen.

- **How** do I get to Buckingham Palace?
  (**Wie** komme ich zum Buckingham Palast?)
- **How** old are you?
  (**Wie** alt bist du?)
- **How** many books did you buy?
- **How** is she?
  (**Wie** geht es ihr?)

Fragen nach der Eigenschaft; Art und Weise

when

In Fragen nach der Zeit (wann?).

- **When** will you meet him?
- **When** will you arrive?

where

In Fragen nach dem Ort (wo?).
Präpositionen können nicht vor where stehen, sie stehen nach dem Verb. To entfällt.

- **Where** do you go?
- **Where** do you come from?

why

In Fragen nach dem Grund (warum?).

- **Why** don't you go home?
- **Why** are you late?

Fragen nach der Zeit; dem Ort; dem Grund

Präpositionen nicht vor where ❗

Das Pronomen

Übungen zum Interrogativpronomen

1. Ersetzen Sie die blau gedruckten Wörter durch who, whom oder whose.

1. He told me that.
2. I am calling my mother.
3. I believe Bob.
4. I blame Sheila.
5. I want your hat.
6. I'm going to share my room with Peter.
7. It is an architect's job to make plans for houses.
8. My neighbour is going to look after my children.
9. My sister helps me with my homework.
10. She married a friend of mine.
11. She was talking to the headmaster.
12. The black bag belongs to my brother.
13. The inspector might have asked the following question.
14. The inspector suspects the prisoner.
15. These are my socks.
16. They began to help the poor boy.
17. This was my fault.
18. We were making fun of Larry.
19. He was shielding a criminal.
20. I would call Stephenson the father of railroading.

richtig   falsch

2. Setzen Sie which oder what ein.

1. ... are you two going to do?

Das Pronomen

2. ... did they argue about?

3. ... do you think is wrong with him?

4. ... key is this one? The one for the garage.

5. ... must he adjust himself to?

6. ... people can possibly live in this desert?

7. ... of the brothers drove the car? The one who lived at this hotel.

8. ... of the following statements is true?

9. ... qualifications do you think a worker needs to get a well-paid job in a modern factory?

10. ... qualities do you think programmes must have to get high ratings?

11. ... of the two men leads the conversation?

12. ... wicked nonsense is this?

13. ... of these two bicycles would you buy? I think I'd buy the red one.

14. ... one of you two wants it?

15. ... did the judge find Harold Evans guilty of?

16. ... general rules would you consider important for successful team-work?

17. ... is being done about the situation?

18. ... is the best means of transport for oil from Alaska to the USA?

19. ... people are likely to read «The Times»?

20. ... of the two countries pioneered railroading - Britain or the United States?

richtig falsch

3. **Setzen Sie how oder what ein.**

1. ... is your Uncle Edward?

2. ... long would it take him to reach the house? Not more than five minutes.

Das Pronomen

3. ... was the weather like?
4. ... is your answer?
5. ... much did Mr Tillot pay you to keep your mouth shut?
6. ... sort of people might have made these remarks?
7. ... about a drink?
8. ... does it work?
9. ... many men were there?
10. ... was he like?
11. ... is your judgment?
12. ... old is he?
13. ... kind of interesting things happened on your trip?
14. ... well do you know the story?
15. ... is the ship called? The White Shark.
16. ... colour is your car?
17. ... size are you?
18. ... could the advance of urbanization be slowed down or stopped?
19. ... is it you are accusing me of?
20. ... far have advances in science in the last few decades given hope for the solution of many of our problems?

richtig   falsch

Die entsprechenden Lösungen befinden sich auf Seite 441.

Das Pronomen

Die Indefinitpronomen (The Indefinite Pronouns)

Die Indefinitpronomen (unbestimmte Fürwörter) stehen stellvertretend für eine oder mehrere unbestimmte Personen oder Sachen.

Some und any

Mit some wird etwas tatsächlich Vorhandenes oder etwas, das als vorhanden angesehen wird bezeichnet, während mit any das Vorhandensein verneint oder bezweifelt wird. Daher steht some überwiegend in bejahten Sätzen und any in verneinten Sätzen, in Frage- und Bedingungssätzen.
Wie some und any werden auch ihre Zusammensetzungen some-, anybody, some-, anyone, some-, anything, some-, anywhere etc. verwendet.

some	any
Es ist substantivisches und attributives Indefinitpronomen und steht in bejahten Sätzen zur Bezeichnung einer unbestimmten (zählbaren) Person oder Sache (irgendeiner) oder einer unbestimmten Menge (nicht zählbarer Substantive (irgendetwas)). In dieser Bedeutung steht some häufig mit of, vor Stoff- oder Gattungsnamen, Abstrakta oder den Namen der Mahlzeiten.	Es ist substantivisches und attributives Indefinitpronomen und steht in verneinten, fragenden Sätzen und in Bedingungssätzen zur Bezeichnung einer unbestimmten (zählbaren) Person oder Sache (keiner) oder einer unbestimmten Menge (nicht zählbarer Substantive) (etwas; nichts). In dieser Bedeutung steht any häufig mit of, vor Stoff- oder Gattungsnamen, Abstrakta oder den Mahlzeiten.

- **Some** boy came running up the street and asked for Peter.
  (**(Irgend)ein** Junge kam die Straße hochgerannt und fragte nach Peter.)
- I have **some** money to pay the bill.
  (Ich habe **etwas** Geld, um die Rechnung zu bezahlen.)
- **Some** of the money was spent to help the handicapped.
  (**Etwas** von dem Geld wurde ausgegeben, um den Behinderten zu helfen.)

- Peter and Mary haven't got **any** friends.
  (Peter und Mary haben **keine** Freunde.)
- Do you have **any** money to pay the bill?
  (Hast du **etwas** Geld um die Rechnung zu bezahlen?)
- If I had **any** time, I would help you.
  (Wenn ich **etwas** Zeit hätte, würde ich dir helfen.)
- I haven't had **any** food all day.
  (Ich hatte den ganzen Tag noch **nichts** zu essen.)

unbestimmte Personen, Sachen, Menge

Das Pronomen

	some	any
beliebige Person, Sache, Menge		In bejahten Sätzen zur Bezeichnung einer beliebigen Person, Sache oder einer beliebigen Menge (jeder beliebige, gleichgültig welcher). • **Any** person can do this work. (**Jeder** kann diese Arbeit tun.) • **Any** of the cars will do for me. • You may come at **any** time.
	• Now I have **some** time to help you. (Nun habe ich etwas Zeit, um dir zu helfen.) • Let's have **some** lunch. (Lass uns etwas essen.)	
unbestimmte Anzahl	In bejahten Sätzen zur Bezeichnung einer unbestimmten Anzahl (zählbarer) Personen oder Sachen (einige, manche).	In verneinten und fragenden Sätzen und in Bedingungssätzen zur Bezeichnung einer unbestimmten Anzahl (zählbarer) Personen oder Sachen (ein paar, irgendwelche; keine).
	• **Some children** came running up the street and asked for Peter. (**Einige Kinder** kamen die Straße hochgerannt und fragten nach Peter.) • **Some** books by this author are really difficult to understand. (**Manche** Bücher dieses Autors sind wirklich schwer zu verstehen.) • I haven't any more biscuits in the kitchen, but I put **some** on the table in the living-room. (Ich habe keine Kekse mehr in der Küche, aber ich habe welche auf den Tisch im Wohnzimmer gestellt.)	• Have you seen **any children** standing in front of the cinema? (Haben Sie vor dem Kino irgendwelche/ein paar Kinder stehen sehen?) • Are there **any** biscuits on the table in the living-room? I can't see **any**. (Stehen auf dem Tisch im Wohnzimmer irgendwelche Kekse? I kann keine sehen.) • I put some biscuits on the table in the living-room, but I didn't put **any** on the table in the dining-room. (Ich habe ein paar Kekse auf den Tisch im Wohnzimmer gestellt, aber ich habe keine auf den Tisch im Esszimmer gestellt.)

Das Pronomen

some	any	
	Ist die Bedeutung der Aussage insgesamt negativ, steht (auch im bejahten Satz) any und besonders nach hardly, scarcely und without. - They visited her without any presents to give to her.	im verneinten Satz
Im Fragesatz zum Ausdruck einer höflichen Frage, Einladung, besonders wenn eine bejahte Antwort erwartet wird. - May I have some more tea? Yes, you may. - Would you like some more tea?	Im Fragesatz steht überwiegend any und besonders, wenn eine verneinte Antwort erwartet wird oder wenn nicht sicher ist, welche Antwort gegeben wird. - May I have any more biscuits? (No, you may not.) - Do you have any more biscuits?	im Fragesatz
Im Bedingungssatz zum Ausdruck eines Wunsches oder einer erfüllbaren Bedingung. - If only we had some money to pay the rent with. - If we bought some presents for her, we might be invited.	Im Bedingungssatz steht meist any, besonders wenn die Bedingung nicht erfüllbar ist oder scheint. - If you had any self-respect, you wouldn't have done that. - If I had any money, I would pay the rent.	im Bedingungssatz
Vor Zahlwörtern steht some in der Bedeutung von *etwa, ungefähr*. - I waited some ten minutes before the bus came.	Vor Komparativen steht in der Regel any. Im Deutschen bleibt es häufig unübersetzt. - Can't you drive any faster? (Kannst du nicht (etwas, ein bisschen) schneller fahren?) - Can you come any earlier?	vor Zahlwörtern; Komparativen

Das Pronomen

Every und each

Wie each und every werden auch ihre Zusammensetzungen everyone, each one, everybody, everything, everywhere etc. behandelt.

	every	each
«jede» Person, Sache	Es ist attributives Indefinitpronomen und steht zur Bezeichnung «jeder» Person oder Sache ohne Ausnahme (jeder). Every wird im Deutschen oft durch *alle* wiedergegeben. Im Gegensatz zu all, das die Gesamtheit bezeichnet, bezeichnet every mehr den einzelnen.	Es ist substantivisches und attributives Indefinitpronomen zur Bezeichnung «jeder» einzelnen Person oder Sache aus einer Gruppe (jeder). Each wird oft mit of + Pronomen verwendet.
	▪ Every man has his duties. ▪ Every child has to go to school. ▪ He has collected every CD of this group. (Er hat jede CD, alle CDs dieser Gruppe gesammelt.)	▪ He brought some books with him and he gave us one each. ▪ He spoke to each of us. ▪ We each had £ 50 to spend on groceries.
größere; kleine Anzahl	Es steht normalerweise nicht bezüglich einer sehr kleinen Anzahl von Personen oder Dingen.	Es kann bezüglich zwei oder mehr Personen oder Sachen verwendet werden.
	▪ Every man has his duties. ▪ He had collected every disc of this group and they had produced about 200.	▪ Two teachers entered our classroom. Each (teacher) was carrying 20 sheets of our classwork.
in der Bedeutung *je, pro*		Nachgestelltes each steht in der Bedeutung *je, pro*. ▪ The price of these books is 20 pounds each.

Das Pronomen

All und whole

all

Es ist substantivisches und attributives Indefinitpronomen und bezeichnet «alle» Personen oder Sachen (alle) und bezieht sich auf zählbare Substantive im Plural.

- **All** inhabitants of the village were killed in the earthquake.
- **All** cars of this class cost more than $ 50,000.

«alle» Personen, Sachen

all

Es bezeichnet die Gesamtheit, das ungeteilte Ganze und bezieht sich auf Substantive im Singular (ganz, alles).

- He worked **all** day long from nine to five.
- **All** I know is that he saw her last week.

whole

Es ist substantivisches und attributives Indefinitpronomen und bezeichnet die Gesamtheit, das ungeteilte Ganze und bezieht sich auf Substantive im Singular (ganz).
Whole betont die Gesamtheit stärker als all. Bei Eigennamen steht the whole + of.

- He worked the **whole** day from nine to five.
- The **whole** of Great Britain was shocked by this news.

Gesamtheit

Much und many

much

Es ist substantivisches und attributives Indefinitpronomen und bezeichnet eine große Menge nicht zählbarer Substantive im Singular (viel).

many

Es ist substantivisches und attributives Indefinitpronomen und bezeichnet eine große Anzahl zählbarer Substantive im Plural (viele).

Menge, Anzahl nicht zählbarer; zählbarer Substantive

Das Pronomen

	much	many
	Es steht auch bei money, (obwohl Geld zählbar ist), da hier an die Gesamtheit gedacht wird und nicht an jede Münze oder an jeden Geldschein.	
	• There is not **much** time to catch the train. • He hasn't got **much** money. • I didn't have **much** trouble.	• She hasn't got **many** friends. • How **many** cars do you have? • How **many** CDs has she collected?
im bejahten Satz	Im bejahten Satz steht es nur, wenn es selbst Subjekt oder Teil dessen ist, oder wenn es mit den folgenden Ausdrücken verbunden ist. • as, so • too • how • if, whether • bestimmter Artikel • Komparativ	Im bejahten Satz steht es nur, wenn es selbst Subjekt oder Teil dessen ist, oder wenn es mit den folgenden Ausdrücken verbunden ist. • as, so • too • how • if, whether • bestimmter Artikel • Komparativ
	In allen anderen Fällen wird much im bejahten Satz, vor allem in der Umgangssprache, durch folgende Ausdrücke ersetzt: • a great/large amount of • a great/good deal of • a lot of, lots of • plenty of	In allen anderen Fällen wird many im bejahten Satz, vor allem in der Umgangssprache, durch folgende Ausdrücke ersetzt: • a large number of • several • a lot of, lots of • plenty of
	• In this rain, it is **much better** to wait until the taxi comes. • They spent **a lot of** money on this future project.	• **Many** of their neighbours own their houses. • Peter is very popular. He has **a lot of** friends.

Das Pronomen

Little und few

little	few
Es ist substantivisches und attributives Indefinitpronomen und bezeichnet eine geringe Menge nicht zählbarer Substantive im Singular (wenig). In Verbindung mit dem unbestimmten Artikel (a little) steht es in der Bedeutung *ein wenig, etwas*. Es wird meist nur in der Schriftsprache verwendet. In der Umgangssprache steht es meist nur nach very, too, extremely, comparatively etc. Statt little wird, vor allem in der Umgangssprache, eher hardly any, not much oder much mit einem verneinten Verb eingesetzt.	Es ist substantivisches und attributives Indefinitpronomen und bezeichnet eine geringe Anzahl zählbarer Substantive im Plural (wenige). In Verbindung mit dem unbestimmten Artikel (a few) steht es in der Bedeutung *einige, ein paar*. Es wird meist nur in der Schriftsprache verwendet. In der Umgangssprache steht es meist nur nach very, too, extremely, comparatively etc. Statt few wird, vor allem in der Umgangssprache, eher hardly any, not many oder many mit einem verneinten Verb eingesetzt.

geringe Menge; Anzahl

- She gave me **little** help.
- I have very **little** time. (I don't have **much** time.)

- Only **a few** biscuits were left.
- We have too **few** holidays.

Other und another

other	another
Es ist substantivisches und attributives Indefinitpronomen und bezeichnet eine oder mehrere «andere» Personen oder Sachen oder, in Verbindung mit dem bestimmten Artikel, «die andere(n)» Person(en) oder Sache(n) (anderer, der andere).	Es ist substantivisches und attributives Indefinitpronomen und bezeichnet «eine andere, weitere» Person oder Sache im Singular (ein anderer, noch einer, ein weiterer) oder «weitere» Personen oder Sachen im Plural (weitere, noch). Stellvertretend für ein

«andere» Personen, Sachen

Das Pronomen

other	another
Stellvertretend für ein vorangehendes, bestimmtes Substantiv im Singular steht the other one, bei einem Substantiv im Plural steht the other ones.	vorangehendes, unbestimmtes Substantiv im Singular steht another one (noch ein, ein weiteres).
• There are also **other ways** to solve the problem. • He waved to me from the **other** side of the street. • I only know these books. Can you show me **the other ones**?	• Can you show me **another** book? • He kept me waiting for **another** three hours. • I don't like this cake. Please give me **another one**.

No, none und nobody, no one

	no	none	nobody, no one
«keine» Person oder Sache	Es ist attributives Indefinitpronomen und bezeichnet «keine» Person oder Sache im Singular und Plural (keiner).	Es ist substantivisches Indefinitpronomen und bezeichnet «keine» Person oder Sache aus einer bestimmten Gruppe von mehr als zweien (keiner). Bei zweien wird neither verwendet. None steht nur bezüglich eines vorhergehenden oder folgenden Substantivs.	Es ist substantivisches Indefinitpronomen und bezeichnet «keine» Person im Singular (niemand, keiner). Sie können nicht - wie none - bezüglich eines vorhergehenden oder folgenden Substantivs stehen.
	• **No** person entered the room. • There is **no** cake for the children. • I am sorry, I have **no change** with me.	• **None** of these persons entered the room. • (**Neither** of these persons entered the room.) • I can afford **none** of these cars.	• **Nobody** entered the room. • **No one** entered the room. • We saw **no one** in the room.
	no	**none**	
	Es wird normalerweise nur als Subjekt und in Antworten, die aus nur einem Wort bestehen	Es wird normalerweise nur als Subjekt und in Antworten, die aus nur einem Wort bestehen,	

Das Pronomen

no	none
(nein), verwendet. Als Objekt klingt es sehr formell. Daher werden, vor allem in der Umgangssprache, Konstruktionen aus verneintem Verb + a, one, any vorgezogen.	verwendet. Als Objekt klingt es sehr formell. Daher werden, vor allem in der Umgangssprache, Konstruktionen aus verneintem Verb + a, one, any vorgezogen.
• **No** cakes were left. • Are there any cakes left? **No.** • He gave me **no** advice. (He did**n't** give me **any** advice.) • Well, you were **no** great help.	• **None** of the cars cost more than $ 15,000. • How many of these books have you read? **None.** • He read **none** of these books. (He did**n't** read **any** of these books.)

Either und neither

either	neither	
Es ist substantivisches und attributives Indefinitpronomen und bezeichnet «entweder die eine oder die andere» Person oder Sache, gleichgültig welche (jeder (von zweien, beide), entweder der eine oder der andere). Either steht in Verbindung mit einem verneinten Verb (keines von beiden).	Es ist substantivisches und attributives Indefinitpronomen und bezeichnet «keine, weder die eine noch die andere» von zwei Personen oder Sachen (keiner (von beiden). None bezeichnet «keine» Person oder Sache aus einer bestimmten Gruppe von mehr als zweien (keiner). Neither steht meist am Satzanfang oder in verneinten kurzen Antworten. Neither steht mit einem bejahten Verb.	«die eine oder andere» Person, Sache; «keine von zwei» Personen, Sachen
• His building site is situated on **either** side of this street. • Have you read one of these books? I have**n't** read **either**. • Would you like chicken	• **Neither** of these (two) persons entered the room. **(None** of these persons entered the room.) • Have you read one of these books? I have	either + verneintes Verb neither + bejahtes Verb

Das Pronomen

	either	neither
	or fish tonight? I'll take **either one**.	read **neither**. • Which of these books have you read? **Neither.**

Both und the two

	both	the two
zwei Personen oder Sachen	Es ist substantivisches und attributives Indefinitpronomen und bezeichnet zwei Personen oder Sachen, die zusammengehören ((alle) beide). Dabei steht es entweder vor dem Substantiv oder in der Mitte des Satzes. Zwischen both und Substantiv tritt entweder der bestimmte Artikel (+ of) oder ein Possessivpronomen (+ of).	Es ist substantivisches und attributives Indefinitpronomen und bezeichnet zwei Personen oder Sachen, die nicht zusammengehören oder sogar im Gegensatz zueinander stehen (beide, die zwei).
Artikel steht nach both	• **Both** (of) (the) students passed the exam. • **Both** (of) (her) sons lost their lives in an accident. • I have met both (of her) brothers.	• **The two** students passed the exam. • **The two** business men are bitter opponents. • Do you know Jim or Rachel? No, I've never met **the two**.

One

	one
unbestimmte Person	Es ist substantivisches Indefinitpronomen und bezeichnet eine unbestimmte Person (man). Statt one werden, vor allem in der Umgangssprache, Personalpronomen wie we, you,

Das Pronomen

one

they, eine Passivkonstruktion, there is (was) + gerund oder Ausdrücke wie people, man etc. bevorzugt.

- **One** should love one's neighbour as oneself.
- **You** never can tell how he will react.
- **This house is to be sold** immediately.
- **There was singing** and **drinking.**
- **People** gave the queen a warm welcome.

Übungen zum Indefinitpronomen

1. Setzen Sie some oder any ein.

1. Are there ... last instructions?
2. Did you ask ... of the people?
3. He said if ...thing ever happened to him, he wanted me to have his house.
4. I wonder if ... strangers have been seen round here.
5. Is there ... hope of help coming?
6. His attitude was not friendly and in ... ways even hostile.
7. He was excited, hoping to get ... important information.
8. He has not found ... of our ideas good enough.
9. This little town has 4,000 inhabitants and hardly ... hotels.
10. Suppose you are really a slave to the drug habit. Is there ... cure?
11. The English legal system is built up out of precedents, not on ... general principles.
12. Can ...one conceive of something more confusing than that?
13. He never showed ... liking for that place, did he?
14. Human ingenuity has not yet found ... means of mitigating the damage which hurricanes may cause to buildings.
15. All men are created equal. Not ... men. All men.
16. Do you want me to give the wounded man ... water?
17. Don't you think, under the circumstances, you should take ... steps?
18. I would buy the car if ...one gave me the money.
19. If only I could do ...thing useful!
20. If we had ... chewing-gum, we could stop the hole.

richtig   falsch

Das Pronomen

2. Setzen Sie every oder each ein.

1. Do you have to get up early ... day?

2. Glasgow and Newcastle upon Tyne, ... on a convenient river, became great centres of engineering and shipbuilding.

3. He is sure about ... single thing.

4. I have my car washed ... Saturday.

5. They have holidays of about four weeks over Christmas, two weeks ... at Easter and Whitsun, and about eleven weeks - from early August to mid-October - in the summer.

6. At the end of ... debate the Speaker puts the question whether or not to accept the motion that has been debated.

7. ... means was tried.

8. ... trifle must be paid for.

9. In streets where the houses are standing well back from the road, the postman does not come to the door of ... house, because ... house has a mailbox by the roadway.

10. Resignation often ends a politician's career as a leading politician, but not in ... case.

richtig   falsch

3. Setzen Sie all oder the whole oder a whole ein.

1. As soon as the crime was discovered ... forest was combed by search parties.

2. He said he would be away for ... day.

3. In these schools boys can learn ... about life-saving and rescues.

4. Richard Barton's father was an acrobat in a famous circus, which travelled ... over France.

5. What's ... this noise in the middle of the day?

6. Of course, we did not want to look at buildings and statues ... day long.

7. One evening Roger was walking along the shore ... by himself, when he saws a ship.

Das Pronomen

8. Sheila is having her birthday party today. She has been very busy ... week preparing the great event.

9. We have lost ... day.

10. When Jack and Jenny were back home, their friends Walter and Linda wanted to know ... about their trip to London.

11. Where do you get ... the money from?

12. He was giving me a hard time ... the while.

13. Social problems are problems which concern not only society as ... but also each of us individually.

14. ... place needs doing up.

15. If a single disaster were to occur in a nuclear power plant thousands of people might die and ... region be rendered uninhabitable.

richtig   falsch

4. Setzen Sie much oder many ein.

1. Did you get ... birthday presents? Yes I did.

2. He hasn't got ... money.

3. How ... chocolate have you got? Six bars.

4. It's surprising how ... space there is on a boat.

5. I've never seen so ... buses in my life.

6. The next day he regretted having drunk so ... beer.

7. Many people go by Underground because there is too ... traffic on the roads.

8. ... of what you say is not true.

9. Sheila wants to know how ... records Laura has got.

10. There isn't ... bread left. Someone must go to the baker's.

11. Bob hasn't ... hair, has he?

12. We could take as ... sweets as we liked.

13. We have as ... right to be here as the Johnsons.

Das Pronomen

14. A show at a prime evening hour can attract as ... as 7 million viewers.

15. I was here at four o'clock. And that wasn't ... use. You were asleep.

16. It may be said of both that they had too ... irons in the fire.

17. ... remains to be done before I can finish my studies.

18. When I'm working there is not ... chance to get a breather.

19. He has too ... good sense to be affronted at insults.

20. The English have never had ... reputation for their appreciation of good food or good cooking.

richtig   falsch

5. Setzen Sie little oder few ein.

1. A ... days ago, Richard and John were out for a bicycle ride.

2. Did you catch many fish? No, only a ...

3. He had ... money and no job.

4. His English is far better than my German, and he only makes a ... mistakes.

5. His speedometer gives him very ... information at all.

6. It'll take a ... time to get the sandwiches made.

7. Millions of American whites admired Martin Luther King. ... of them had ever seen him face to face.

8. Of a population of about 50,000 aborigines, today only ... still live a primitive life as nomadic hunters.

9. The Millers had very ... sunshine during their holiday in Scotland.

10. The night was clear, the road was dry, and there was ... traffic.

11. After a ... more unsuccessful attempts at getting information, I left, and drove back to London.

12. Behind us the cliff rolled away into the bush-covered hillside with a ... sheep grazing contentedly.

Das Pronomen

13. He proposed a treaty of friendship to the Indians, but they remained mistrustful, and his efforts to win their confidence made ... progress.

14. Mr Jackson had ... hope of doing business here.

15. The advances in science particularly in the last ... decades have sometimes been spectacular.

richtig   falsch

6. Setzen Sie no, none oder nobody ein.

1. He liked the fact that Venice had ... cars.

2. He looked in the drawer for some pens, but there were ...

3. I can't leave a tramp in the house with ... else about.

4. Knowing that there is ... water and ... air on the moon, we shan't find men or animals, trees or flowers.

5. ... had ever seen Mr Miller looking so angry before.

6. ... knew where he had gone.

7. Of all the games that Americans play and watch, ... is thought more typical of the country than baseball.

8. The phone rang and rang, but there was ... answer.

9. ... knows what I've been through in the last twenty-four hours.

10. ... would take you for an expert.

richtig   falsch

7. Setzen Sie either oder neither ein.

1. «I never drink anything for lunch,» she said. « ... do I,» I answered promptly.

2. ... Bob or Sean was responsible.

3. ... the son or the daughter is married.

4. If I can't live here, ... will you.

5. ... of them bothered to explain it to her.

6. ... of us, I think, was really afraid.

Das Pronomen

7. Perhaps he doesn't want to meet us. I'm not surprised. I don't want to meet him ...

8. Some 3,500,000 negro slaves had to do all the hard work that white people ... could not do or just refused to do.

9. You aren't allowed to walk on the grass ...

10. I can't remember exactly when I last saw him. It was ... the day before Christmas or a week later.   richtig   falsch

Die entsprechenden Lösungen befinden sich auf Seite 441ff.

Die Konjunktion (The Conjunction)

Konjunktionen sind Bindewörter und verbinden ganze Sätze oder Satzteile.

Nebenordnende, beiordnende Konjunktionen (Coordinating Conjunctions)

Nebenordnende oder beiordnende Konjunktionen verbinden gleichartige Satzglieder oder Sätze.

Unterordnende Konjunktionen (Subordinating Conjunctions)

Unterordnende Konjunktionen leiten Nebensätze ein.
Es steht eine Vielzahl von Konjunktionen zur Verfügung, die ihrer Bedeutung nach in folgende Gruppen eingeteilt werden.

Temporale Konjunktionen (Temporal Conjunctions)

Zeitpunkt, -raum

Die temporalen Konjunktionen geben einen Zeitraum, Zeitpunkt an.

- after — nachdem
- as — als, während
- as long as — so lange wie/als
- as often as — so oft wie/als
- as soon as — so bald als
- before — bevor
- hardly ... when — kaum als
- now — nun, jetzt

> **While** I was writing a letter, my mother entered the room.

- no sooner ... than — kaum als
- scarcely ... when — kaum als
- since — seit
- till — bis
- until — bis
- when — wenn, als
- while — während
- whilst (veraltet für while) — während

Bei gleichem Subjekt im Haupt- und Nebensatz steht *after* + gerund.
Diese Konstruktion ist eleganter als das Subjekt nochmals zu nennen.

> **After having done** his homework, he watched TV.
> (**After he had done** his homework, he watched TV.)

Finale Konjunktionen (Final Conjunctions)

Absicht, Zweck

Die finalen Konjunktionen drücken eine Absicht, einen Zweck aus.

- lest — damit nicht
- in case — falls
- in order that — so dass

> He studied hard **so that** he would pass the exam.

- so that — so dass
- that — dass, so dass

Kausale Konjunktionen (Causative Conjunctions)

Grund, Ursache

Kausale Konjunktionen geben den Grund, die Ursache an.

> **As** he has finished all his work, he can go home now.

Die Konjunktion

- as — da, weil
- because — da, weil
- for — da, weil
- in that — darum, weil, insofern als
- seeing that — in Anbetracht dessen, dass
- since — da, weil

Because leitet einen nachgestellten Nebensatz ein und sollte nicht am Anfang eines Satzgefüges stehen. As und since können dagegen voran- und nachgestellte Nebensätze einleiten.

- He can go home now because he has finished all his work.
- As he has finished all his work, he can go home now.
- Since he has finished all his work, he can go home now.

For sollte nicht am Anfang des Satzgefüges stehen und kann nicht auf not oder but folgen.
Es kann nicht in Aussagen, die bereits gemacht wurden oder in Antworten auf Fragen verwendet werden.

- He can go home now for he has finished all his work.
- He stole not because he wanted the money but because he liked stealing.
- Why did you read the book? I read it because I liked it.

Konsekutive Konjunktionen (Consecutive Conjunctions)

Konsekutive Konjunktionen drücken die Folge, die Wirkung aus.

- It rained all the morning so that he could not go for a walk. — Folge, Wirkung

- so — somit
- so/such that — so dass
- that — so dass
- therefore — deshalb, folglich

Konzessive Konjunktionen (Concessive Conjunctions)

Konzessive Konjunktionen dienen zum Ausdruck der Einräumung, des Zugeständnisses.

- Although it rained all the morning, he went for a walk. — Einräumung

- although — obwohl, obgleich
- as — obwohl, wenn auch
- even if — selbst wenn
- however — dennoch, jedoch
- notwithstanding that — obgleich, wenn auch
- though — obwohl, obgleich

Konditionale Konjunktionen (Conditional Conjunctions)

Konditionale Konjunktionen dienen zum Ausdruck der Bedingung. Dabei ist die Zeitenfolge im Bedingungssatz zu beachten.

- If it rains, I will come.
- If it rained, I would come.
- If it had rained, I would have come.

Bedingung

im if-Satz kein will oder would

- if — wenn
- on condition that — unter der Bedingung, dass
- in case — im Falle, dass
- provided that — vorausgesetzt, dass
- supposing that — angenommen, dass
- unless, if not — wenn nicht

Modale Konjunktionen (Modal Conjunctions)

Modale Konjunktionen bezeichnen die (Begleit)Umstände, die Mittel, die Art und Weise.

- With their hands clapping, they stood at the gate and cheered the musicians. — Art und Weise, Mittel

Die Konjunktion

- for — dafür, dass
- with — mit
- without — ohne dass, wenn nicht

Adversative Konjunktionen (Adversative Conjunctions)

Gegensatz

Adversative Konjunktionen stehen zum Ausdruck der Gegenüberstellung von Aussagen, zum Ausdruck des Gegensatzes.

- but — aber, sondern
- however — aber, hingegen, dennoch
- whereas — während

> He is not a gentleman **while** his wife is a real lady.
> I wished to tell him all about it **but** I could not.

- while — während
- whilst (veraltet für while) — während
- yet — dennoch, trotzdem

However steht in der Regel nicht am Satzanfang. Es kann, durch Komma abgetrennt, hinter das Subjekt treten.

> He is a nice boy, **however,** he is not very well brought-up.
> He is an independent man, **however,** he is lonely.

Vergleichende Konjunktionen (Comparative Conjunctions)

Vergleich

Vergleichende Konjunktionen bringen einen Vergleich zum Ausdruck.

- as — wie, so wie
- as ... as — ebenso ... wie
- as if — als ob, als wenn
- as though — als ob, als wenn

> Do **as** you are told.
> He is **as** tall **as** his brother.

- like — (ebenso, so ...) wie
- not as ... as — nicht so ... wie
- than — als

Nach Komparativen wird der Vergleich durch than ausgedrückt.

> Peter's behaviour was more stupid **than** John's.

Zum Ausdruck des Vergleichs steht as nach Adjektiven und Adverbien oder wenn ein ganzer Satz folgt.

> Tired **as** he was, he couldn't help her.
> He made the same mistake **as** his brother had made.

Zum Ausdruck des Vergleichs steht like vor Substantiven oder Pronomen.

> He cried **like** a baby.
> Peter and Mary want a house **like** ours.

Anreihende Konjunktionen (Copulative Conjunctions)

Verbindung von Sätzen

Anreihende Konjunktionen dienen zur Verbindung zweier Sätze oder Satzteile.

- also — auch
- and — und
- as well as — so ... wie
- both ... and — sowohl ... als auch
- either ... or — entweder ... oder
- not either — auch nicht

> **Both** her son **and** her daughter were killed in an accident.

- likewise — ebenso, gleichfalls
- neither ... nor — weder ... noch
- nor — auch nicht, noch
- not only ... but also — nicht nur ... sondern auch
- or — oder

Die Konjunktion

Statt *also* wird *as well* oder *too* bevorzugt. Außerdem sollte *also* nicht am Satzanfang stehen.

- You have done your homework. I **also** finished mine.
- You have done your homework. I finished mine, **too/as well.**

As well as steht meist ungetrennt hinter dem ersten Satzglied.

- My brother **as well as** my sister are older than I.

Both ... and wird getrennt und umschließt das erste Satzglied.

- **Both** my sister **and** my brother are older than I.

Die Präposition (The Preposition)

Mit der Präposition (Verhältniswort) werden bestimmte Verhältnisse und Beziehungen gekennzeichnet.
Für den Gebrauch der Präpositionen lassen sich keine allgemein gültigen Regeln aufstellen. Nicht jede Präposition kann in Verbindung mit jedem beliebigen Wort verwendet werden. Häufig ändert die Präposition die Bedeutung eines Wortes. Es empfiehlt sich daher jedes Wort von Anfang an mit den wichtigsten Präpositionen zu lernen.

Präposition	In räumlicher Bedeutung	In zeitlicher Bedeutung	In übertragener Bedeutung
aboard	an Bord		
about	um ... herum, umher	um, etwa, gegen	an, auf, bei, darüber, um, wegen, etwa, ungefähr
above	oberhalb, über		(erhaben) über
according to			gemäß, laut
across	jenseits, quer ... durch, über		
after	hinter ... (her)	nach	gemäß, nach
against	an, gegen(über), zu		gegen, wider
along	längs(seits), neben, entlang		nach, gemäß
amid(st)	(in)mitten (unter)		unter
among(st)	(in)mitten (unter), zwischen		zwischen, unter
around	nahe bei, um ... herum	um, ungefähr, etwa, gegen	ungefähr, etwa
at	am, an, bei, in, vor, zu	um	an, bei, in, über, um, zu
because of			wegen, infolge
before	in Gegenwart von, vor	vor, früher als	vor (Rang, Würde)
behind	hinter	hinter, nach	hinter
below	unter(halb)		unter (Rang, Würde)
beneath	unter(halb)		unter (Rang, Würde)
beside	neben		außer, neben
besides			außer, neben
between	zwischen (2)	zwischen	zwischen, unter

Die Präposition

Präposition	In räumlicher Bedeutung	In zeitlicher Bedeutung	In übertragener Bedeutung
beyond	jenseits, über	über ... hinaus	(erhaben) über
but			außer
by	am, an, durch, über	an, bei, bis, gegen, um	durch, mit, mittels, nach, von, über
despite			trotz, ungeachtet
down	herunter, hinunter	durch	bis
during		während	
except			außer, ausgenommen
for	zu, nach	... lang, seit (Zeitraum)	aus, für, nach, um, vor, wegen
from	von (weg), aus	von ... an	vor, aus
in front of	vor		
in	auf, in	am, in, im	auf, im, in, mit
inside	innerhalb		
into	in ... hinein	bis in	in, in ... hinein
near	nahe (bei)	nahe	
of	aus, bei, von	an, in, von, vor	an, auf, aus, für, mit, von
off	von ... herunter, von ... weg		
on	auf, an	an, am	von
out	(her)aus		aus
outside	außerhalb		
over	über	über (hinaus)	mehr als, über
past	an ... vorbei	nach	über ... hinaus
per		für, je, pro	durch, gemäß, laut, per, pro
round	um ... herum	gegen, ungefähr um	um
since		seit (Zeitpunkt)	
through	durch	durch	durch

Die Präposition

Präposition	In räumlicher Bedeutung	In zeitlicher Bedeutung	In übertragener Bedeutung
throughout	durch ... hindurch	hindurch, während	
till		bis, erst	
to	zu, nach	bis	mit, zu, bei
toward(s)	auf ... zu	gegen	zu
under	unter	unter, weniger als	unter
until		bis, erst	
up	hinauf		
upon	auf, an		von
via	über, via		durch, mit, mittels
with			mit
within	innerhalb	innerhalb	
without			ohne

Übungen zur Präposition

1. Setzen Sie die korrekte Präposition ein.

1. They arrived ... Paddington Station.
2. Your flight will be announced ... 10:15.
3. They arrived ... lunch.
4. Where shall we be ... 10 years' time?
5. The door opened, and two men came ...
6. Mr Atkinson came ... the room.
7. Charles covered his face ... his hands.
8. We always have chicken ... Sunday.
9. Throwing paper ... the ground is forbidden.
10. Your father bought this car ... you.

richtig falsch

2. Setzen Sie die korrekte Präposition ein.

1. I don't agree ... you.
2. Bob and Mary can never agree ... anything.
3. The driver stopped to ask ... the way.
4. His son believed ... him.
5. Impossible to call ... help.
6. They were congratulated ... their success.
7. You should look ... your little brother.
8. What are you looking ...?
9. That will be easy, put ... Harry.
10. Put ... your hands!
11. I shall just have to put ... with that.

Die Präposition

12. I put ... my ankle socks.
13. We had to put ... going on holiday.
14. Send ... the doctor.
15. Speak .....!
16. I succeeded ... passing my examination.
17. He did not wait ... a reply.
18. You will have to account ... that error.
19. His age has to be taken account ...
20. The children all burst ... laughter.
21. Mac and Henry burst ... laughing.
22. What did he die ...?
23. Smiling she gave ...
24. We gave ... teasing him.
25. What did the bishops and barons live ...?

richtig   falsch

3. Setzen Sie die korrekte Präpostion ein.

1. Note the difference ... meaning.
2. We had great difficulty ... translating the text.
3. There is no doubt ... that.
4. It did not make much impression ... her.
5. He does not take any interest ... reading.
6. What is your opinion ... these questions?
7. He had no opportunity ... speaking to him.
8. They did not discuss the possibility ... getting married.
9. The chance ... meeting him was poor.
10. My chances ... promotion aren't so hot.

Die Präposition

11. Madam, my congratulations ... your rehabilitation.

12. She kept quiet for fear .....being fired.

13. The early Americans had great faith ... constitutions.

14. The improvement ... her appearance was startling.

15. I was at a loss ... an answer.

richtig   falsch

4. Setzen Sie die korrekte Präposition ein.

1. Bob's mother is angry ... him.

2. He'll get angry ... nothing.

3. We are not directly concerned ... it.

4. He was crazy ... thirst.

5. I was crazy ... a hot bath and a good meal.

6. When I had finished this work I was delighted ... it.

7. Scottish towns look very different ... English towns.

8. Are you good ... drawing horses?

9. You are expected to be interested ... the job you have been offered.

10. The worst thing I can imagine is to be late ... school.

11. We are prepared ... the worst.

12. I'm proud ... you.

13. I feel sorry ... her.

14. I was surprised ... the news.

15. Feeling slightly ashamed ... himself, he sat up against the bedhead.

richtig   falsch

Die entsprechenden Lösungen befinden sich auf Seite 442.

Der Satz

Der Satz (The Clause)

Ein Satz besteht aus mindestens einem Hauptsatz (main, principal clause) oder einem Hauptsatz und einem Nebensatz (subordinate clause). Sätze, die aus Haupt- und Nebensatz bestehen, nennt man Satzgefüge (compound sentence). Der Hauptsatz ist der übergeordnete Teil eines Satzgefüges und kann, im Gegensatz zum Nebensatz, jederzeit alleine stehen.
Folgende Satzglieder können in einem Satz enthalten sein.

Subjekt (Subject)

wer tut etwas?

Das Subjekt oder der Satzgegenstand drückt aus, wer oder was eine Handlung ausführt. Das Subjekt steht im Nominativ (wer-Fall) und wird daher erfragt durch: wer oder was tut etwas?

- I read a book.
  (Wer liest das Buch? Ich.)
- The book is very interessant. (Wer oder was ist sehr interessant? Das Buch.)

Prädikat (Predicate)

was wird getan?

Das Prädikat oder die Satzaussage ist das Verb und besteht aus Vollverb oder Vollverb und Hilfsverb. Es drückt aus, was getan, welche Handlung ausgeführt wird und wird daher erfragt durch: was wird getan?

- I read a book.
  (Was tue ich? Lesen.)
- I have written a letter.
  (Was habe ich getan? Geschrieben.)

Objekt (Object)

Das Objekt ist ein Satzglied, das im possessive case steht, das indirektes oder direktes Objekt ist. Im Deutschen unterscheidet man Genitiv (wessen-Fall), Dativ (wem-Fall) und Akkusativ (wen-Fall).

Possessive Case

Der possessive case wird bei Substantiven im Singular durch 's und bei Substantiven im Plural durch ' gebildet wird. Bei Substantiven auf -s steht 's oder '. Sachen werden durch of angeschlossen.

- Whose car is this? Peter's car.
- Which boy is Mrs Stone's son? The boy with the blue jacket on.
- The children play in St. James' Park.
- Yesterday, I met my brothers' friend.
- The author of this book is very successful.

Indirektes Objekt

Das indirekte Objekt ist meist eine Person und wird im Englischen mit oder ohne to angeschlossen.

- Mary taught John English.
- Mary explained the case to John.

Der Satz

Direktes Objekt

Das direktes Objekt wird im Englischen ohne Präposition angeschlossen.

- This morning, I met Peter at the bus station.

Präpositionales Objekt

Das präpositionale Objekt ist ein Objekt mit einer Präposition. Welche Präposition das ist, hängt davon ab, welche Präposition das Verb verlangt.

- This morning, I spoke to Peter.
  (to speak with s.o.)

Es ist zu beachten, dass ein Wort, das im Deutschen direktes Objekt ist im Englischen indirektes Objekt sein kann und umgekehrt. Es kommt darauf an, mit welchem Objekt, welcher Ergänzung ein Verb stehen kann.

! Objektergänzungen können im Deutschen und Englischen verschieden sein

Prädikative Ergänzung (Predicative Complement)

Die prädikative Ergänzung kann ein Adjektiv oder Substantiv sein und bezieht sich entweder auf das Subjekt oder Objekt.

- Mary is very nice.
  (Prädikative Ergänzung zum Subjekt)
- I have a very interesting book.
  (Prädikative Ergänzung zum Objekt)

Adverbiale Bestimmungen (Adverbial Elements)

Adverbiale Bestimmungen (Umstandsbestimmungen) sind Zeit- oder Ortsangaben, Angaben zur Art und Weise, des Grundes.

- This morning, I wrote a letter.
- The children read this book at school.
- He did his homework in a very careful way.

Der Satz

Der Aussagesatz (The Clause of Statement)

Im Aussagesatz wird ein Sachverhalt mitgeteilt bzw. behauptet.

Der bejahte Aussagesatz (The Affirmative Clause of Statement)

Subjekt(pronomen)	Prädikat	Objekt
Mary	writes	a letter.
She	has written	a letter.

Präpositionen werden nicht vom Prädikat getrennt

Eng mit dem Prädikat verbundene Präpositionen oder Adverbien werden nicht vom Prädikat abgetrennt, es sei denn, sie sollen besonders betont werden oder das Objekt ist ein Pronomen, dann treten sie an das Satzende.

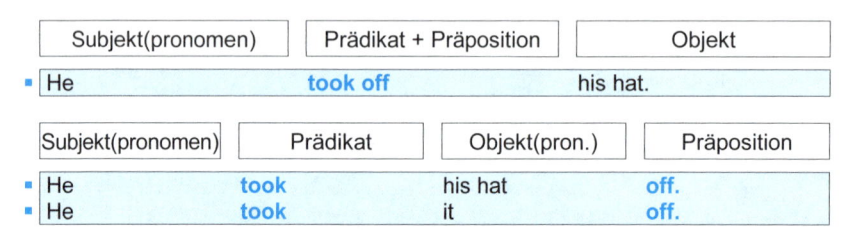

Subjekt(pronomen)	Prädikat + Präposition	Objekt	
He	took off	his hat.	

Subjekt(pronomen)	Prädikat	Objekt(pron.)	Präposition
He	took	his hat	off.
He	took	it	off.

Aussagesatz mit 2 Objekten

In Aussagesätzen mit zwei Objekten steht das indirektes Objekt (meist eine Person) im Allgemeinen vor dem direkten Objekt (meist eine Sache).

Subjekt(pron.)	Prädikat	indirektes Objekt	direktes Objekt
Mary	taught	John	English.

Das direkte Objekt tritt vor das indirekte Objekt, das dann mit *to* angeschlossen wird, wenn das indirekte Objekt besonders hervorgehoben werden soll, wenn es länger ist als das direkte Objekt oder wenn das direkte Objekt *it* oder *them* ist. Es ist zu beachten, dass manche Verben das indirekte Objekt mit der Präposition *to* anschließen.

Subjekt(pron.)	Prädikat	direktes Objekt	indirektes Objekt
Mary	explains	the case	to John.
Mary	writes	a letter	to her cousin Jill.
Mary	explained	it	to him.

Aussagesatz mit prädikativer Ergänzung

Prädikative Ergänzungen stehen generell nach dem Prädikat, gleichgültig, ob sie sich auf das Subjekt oder auf das Objekt beziehen.

Der Satz

Subjekt(pronomen)	Prädikat	präd. Ergänzung
Mary	is	very nice.

Subjekt(pronomen)	Prädikat	präd. Ergänzung	direktes Objekt
I	read	a very interesting	book.

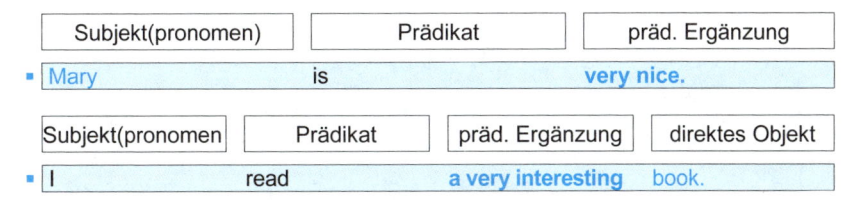

Aussagesatz mit adverbialen Bestimmungen

Adverbiale Bestimmungen können sowohl am Satzanfang als auch am Satzende stehen. Am Satzanfang stehen besonders adverbiale Bestimmungen und Adverbien wie here, so, thus, then und there, die dann durch Komma abgetrennt werden.

Adv. Bestimmung	Subjekt(pronomen)	Prädikat	Objekt
This morning,	Peter	wrote	a letter.

Subjekt(pronomen)	Prädikat	Objekt	adv. Bestimmung
The children	read	this book	at school.

Hervorhebung des Subjekts

Zur Hervorhebung des Subjekts dienen Ausdrücke wie it is (was) ... who/which/that, die das Subjekt umschließen. Es ist zu beachten, dass is und was immer im Singular stehen, auch wenn das Bezugswort im Plural steht.

> is, was stehen immer im Singular

It is/was	Subjekt(pron.)	who, which, that	Prädikat	Objekt
It was	Mary	who	wrote	that letter.
It was	her brothers	who	repaired	our roof.

Hervorhebung von Objekten

Das hervorzuhebende direkte oder präpositionale Objekt wird an den Anfang des Satzgefüges gestellt. Auf das Objekt folgt das Subjekt. Beim Objekt stehen häufig (attributive) Demonstrativpronomen wie this, that und such.

Objekt	Subj.(pron.)	Prädikat	Objekt	adv. Best.
This letter I had waited for,	I	received	it	today.
About this actress,	they	wrote		a lot.

Wie das Subjekt, kann auch das Objekt durch Ausdrücke wie it is (was) ... whom/which/that, die das Objekt umschließen, hervorgehoben werden. Präpositionale Objekte werden durch it is (was) ... that hervorgehoben.
Es ist zu beachten, dass is und was immer im Singular stehen, auch wenn das Bezugswort m Plural steht.

> is, was stehen immer im Singular

Der Satz

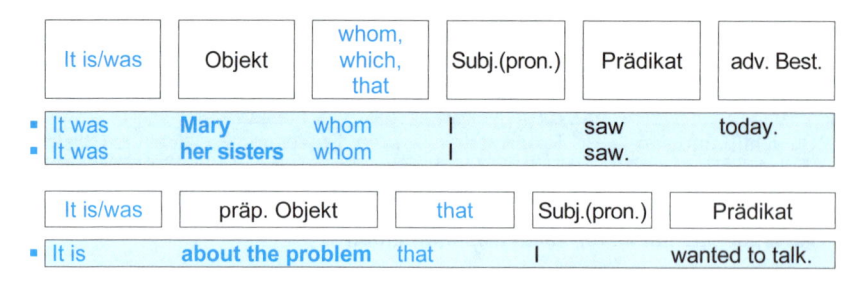

It is/was	Objekt	whom, which, that	Subj.(pron.)	Prädikat	adv. Best.
It was	**Mary**	whom	I	saw	today.
It was	**her sisters**	whom	I	saw.	

It is/was	präp. Objekt	that	Subj.(pron.)	Prädikat
It is	**about the problem**	that	I	wanted to talk.

Inversion des Subjekts

Inversion des Subjekts heißt, das Subjekt tritt hinter das Prädikat.

In Sätzen, die einen Wunschgedanken ausdrücken, steht das Hilfs- bzw. Modalverb am Satzanfang. Das Subjekt steht unmittelbar danach.

Hilfs-, Modalverb	Subjekt(pron.)	Prädikat	Objekt
May	**God**	save	the Queen.

In Bedingungssätzen, die ohne einleitende Konjunktion (if, whether etc.) stehen, tritt das Prädikat an den Satzanfang. Das Subjekt wird vom Prädikat umschlossen.

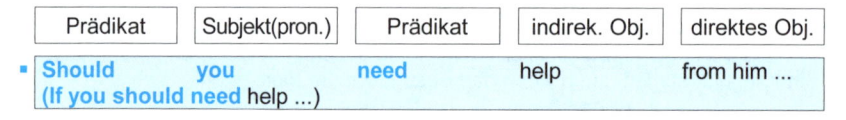

Prädikat	Subjekt(pron.)	Prädikat	indirek. Obj.	direktes Obj.
Should	**you**	**need**	help	from him ...
(If you should need help ...)				

Zur Hervorhebung kann das Subjekt an das Satzende treten. Dies ist besonders in kurzen Sätzen mit Verben wie to be, to come, to follow, to lie und to stand der Fall, wenn der Satz durch Adverbien wie first, here, there, then, next eingeleitet wird.

Adverb	Prädikat	Subjekt
Here	**comes**	**the guest of honour.**

Bei gefühlsbetont verwendeten prädikativen Adjektiven tritt das Subjekt hinter das Prädikat. Die Adjektive stehen am Satzanfang. Auch das Prädikat wird segmentiert, d. h. der erste Teil des Prädikats tritt vor das Subjekt.

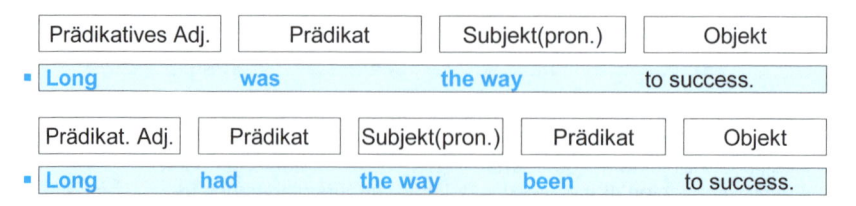

Prädikatives Adj.	Prädikat	Subjekt(pron.)	Objekt
Long	**was**	**the way**	to success.

Prädikat. Adj.	Prädikat	Subjekt(pron.)	Prädikat	Objekt
Long	**had**	**the way**	**been**	to success.

In Kurzsätzen, die durch so (auch) eingeleitet werden, tritt das Subjekt hinter das Prädikat. Ist das Prädikat ein Vollverb, so wird dieses durch to do wieder aufgenommen. Ist es ein Hilfs- oder Modalverb, so wird das Hilfs- bzw. Modalverb im Kurzsatz wieder aufgenommen.

Der Satz

Vordersatz	so	Prädikat	Subjekt(pron.)
He **took** French leave.	So	did	I.
He **has taken** French leave.	So	have	I.

Das Subjekt tritt ans Satzende, wenn vor dem Verb eine betonte prädikative Ergänzung steht, besonders wenn die prädikative Ergänzung in Verbindung mit so oder such oder einem Adverb wie in, out, off, up, das eng zum Prädikat gehört, steht. Ist das Subjekt ein Pronomen, so steht die regelmäßige Wortstellung (Subjekt - Prädikat - Objekt).

Prädikative Ergänzung	Prädikat	Subjekt
So exhausting	was	the climb.
Off	went	the handle of my cup.

In Einleitungssätzen einer direkten Rede, wie zum Beispiel he said, he replied etc., kann das Subjekt hinter das Prädikat treten, wenn der Einleitungssatz nicht vor, sondern nach der direkten Rede steht.

Direkte Rede	Prädikat	Subjekt
«Can you call back later?»	asked	Peter.

Ist das Subjekt ein Pronomen, so gilt die regelmäßige Wortstellung (Subjekt - Prädikat - Objekt) auch im nachgestellten Einleitungssatz der direkten Rede.

Direkte Rede	Subjektpronomen	Prädikat
«Can you call back later?»	he	asked.

Der Satz

Der verneinte Aussagesatz (The Negative Clause of Statement)

Im verneinten Aussagesatz wird ein Sachverhalt verneint. Die Verneinung wird durch Adverbien, Pronomen oder Konjunktionen der Verneinung ausgedrückt.

Not (nicht)

Dieses Adverb der Verneinung gehört zu denjenigen, die am häufigsten verwendet werden.
Ist das Prädikat des Satzes ein Vollverb, so muss dieses bei der Bidung des verneinten Satzes mit to do umschrieben werden. Zu beachten ist, dass to do und das Hilfsverb to have auch Vollverben sein können. Sie werden dann auch mit to do umschrieben.

> die Vollverben to have bzw. to do werden mit to do umschrieben

Subjekt(pron.)	Prädikat	direktes Objekt
Peter	did **not** pass	the exam.
I	do **not** do	it.
I	did **not** have	lunch.

Ist im Prädikat ein Hilfsverb oder ein Modalverb enthalten, so wird dieses bei der Bildung des verneinten Satzes verneint. Das Verneinungsadverb not folgt unmittelbar auf das Hilfsverb oder das Modalverb.

Subjekt(pron.)	Prädikat	direktes Objekt
He	has **not** made	this mistake.
I	can**not** solve	this problem.

No (kein, keiner; nein)

Das Indefinitpronomen no bezeichnet «keine» Person oder Sache und steht unmittelbar vor dem zu verneinenden bzw. einzuschränkenden Wort. Es steht in Verbindung mit einem bejahten Verb, es erfolgt demnach auch keine Umschreibung mit to do.

No	Subjekt	Prädikat	Objekt
No	person	entered	the room.
No	person	has entered	the room.

Es steht normalerweise nur als Subjekt. Als Objekt klingt es sehr formell. Daher werden, vor allem in der Umgangssprache, Konstruktionen aus verneintem Verb + a, one, any vorgezogen.

No + Subjekt	Prädikat	adverbiale Bestimmung
No cakes	were left	yesterday.

Der Satz

Subjekt	Prädikat	indirektes Objekt	no + dir. Objekt
He	gave	me	**no** advice.
He	did**n't** give	me	**any** advice.

Es steht in kurzen, verneinten Antworten in der Bedeutung *nein*. Es kann in dieser Funktion alleine stehen, was jedoch häufig als schroff empfunden wird. Um dies zu vermeiden, wird das Verb des Fragesatzes in der Antwort wieder aufgenommen und verneint, sofern dieses ein Hilfsverb oder Modalverb ist. Ist das Verb des Fragesatzes ein Vollverb, wird es durch to do + not wieder aufgenommen.

Fragesatz	(Antwort mit) no
Are there any cakes left?	**No**(, there aren't).
You met him at the station?	**No**(, I didn't).

None (keiner)

Das Indefinitpronomen none bezeichnet «keine» Person oder Sache aus einer bestimmten Gruppe von mehr als zweien und steht unmittelbar vor dem einzuschränkenden oder zu verneinenden Wort, an das es mit of angeschlossen wird. Es steht in Verbindung mit einem bejahten Verb, es erfolgt demnach auch keine Umschreibung mit to do.

None of	Subjekt	Prädikat	Objekt
None of	these persons	entered	the room.

Es steht normalerweise nur als Subjekt. Als Objekt klingt es sehr formell. Daher werden, vor allem in der Umgangssprache, Konstruktionen aus verneintem Verb + a, one, any vorgezogen.

None of + Subjekt	Prädikat	prädikative Ergänzung
None of these cars	cost	more than $ 15,000.

Subjekt	Prädikat	none + direktes Objekt
He	read	**none of** these books.
He	didn't read	**any of** these books.

Es kann in kurzen, verneinten Antworten alleine stehen.

Fragesatz	none
How many of these children do you know?	**None.**

Any (kein)

Da no und none als Objekt sehr förmlich klingen, wird diesen, vor allem in der Umgangssprache, any vorgezogen. Auch any steht unmittelbar vor dem zu verneinenden oder einzuschränkenden Wort.

Der Satz

Da any in Verbindung mit einem verneinten Verb steht, muss dieses, sofern es ein Vollverb ist, mit to do umschrieben werden. Ist im Prädikat ein Hilfs- oder Modalverb enthalten, entfällt die Umschreibung mit to do.

Subjekt(pron.)	Prädikat	Objekt	any	Objekt
He	didn't give	me	any	advice.
He	cannot give	me	any	of these books.

Nobody, no one (keiner, niemand)

Sie sind Indefinitpronomen und bezeichnen «keine» Person und stehen ohne ein vorangehendes oder folgendes Bezugswort. Sie stehen in Verbindung mit einem bejahten Verb, es erfolgt demnach auch keine Umschreibung mit to do.

Nobody, no one	Prädikat
Nobody	entered.
No one	has entered.

Neither (weder der eine noch der andere, keiner von beiden)

Das Indefinitpronomen neither bezeichnet «weder die eine, noch die andere» Person oder Sache, «keine von beiden».
None steht bezüglich mehrerer Personen oder Sachen aus einer Gruppe.
Neither steht unmittelbar vor dem einzuschränkenden oder zu verneinenden Wort, an das es mit of angeschlossen wird. Es steht in Verbindung mit einem bejahten Verb, es erfolgt demnach auch keine Umschreibung mit to do.

Neither of	Subjekt	Prädikat	Objekt
Neither of	these (two) persons	entered	the room.

In verneinten Antworten steht es unmittelbar nach dem (bejahten) Prädikat oder es kann auch alleine stehen.

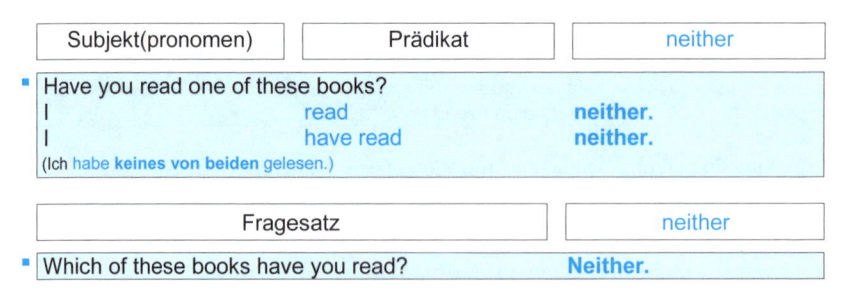

Subjekt(pronomen)	Prädikat	neither
Have you read one of these books?		
I	read	neither.
I	have read	neither.
(Ich habe **keines von beiden** gelesen.)		

Fragesatz	neither
Which of these books have you read?	**Neither.**

Neither (auch nicht)

Es steht in kurzen Antworten am Satzanfang. Das Verb des Fragesatzes wird in der Antwort durch to do wieder aufgenommen. Ist im Prädikat des Fragesatzes ein Hilfsverb oder Modalverb enthalten, so wird dieses in der Antwort wieder aufgenommen. In der Umgangssprache steht statt neither häufig not either.

Fragesatz	neither	Prädikat	Subjekt
Do you like reading?	**Neither**	do	I.
Has he already gone?	**Neither**	has	she.

Either (entweder der eine oder der andere, keiner von beiden)

Das Indefinitpronomen either bezeichnet «entweder die eine oder die andere» Person oder Sache oder «keine von beiden». Es steht in Verbindung mit einem verneinten Prädikat, das, sofern es ein Vollverb ist, mit to do umschrieben werden muss. Enthält es ein Hilfs- oder Modalverb, wird das Hilfsverb bzw. das Modalverb verneint.

Subjekt(pronomen)	Prädikat	either
Have you read one of these books?		
I	didn't read	**either.**
I	haven't read	**either.**
(Ich habe keines von beiden gelesen.)		

Not ... either (auch nicht)

Es steht in kurzen Antworten nach dem Subjekt in Verbindung mit einem verneinten Prädikat, das, sofern es ein Vollverb ist, mit to do umschrieben werden muss. Enthält es ein Hilfs- oder Modalverb, wird das Hilfsverb bzw. das Modalverb verneint. In der Umgangssprache wird not ... either häufig statt nor und neither verwendet.

Fragesatz	Subjekt	Prädikat	either
Do you like reading?	Mary	doesn't	**either.**
Has he already gone?	Mary	hasn't	**either.**

Nor (auch nicht)

Es steht in kurzen Antworten am Satzanfang. Das Verb des Fragesatzes wird in der Antwort durch to do wieder aufgenommen. Ist im Prädikat des Fragesatzes ein Hilfsverb oder Modalverb enthalten, so wird dieses in der Antwort wieder aufgenommen. In der Umgangssprache steht statt nor häufig not either.

Fragesatz	nor	Prädikat	Subjekt
Do you like reading?	**Nor**	do	I.
Has he already gone?	**Nor**	has	she.

Einschränkende oder verneinende Bestimmungen

Verneinende oder einschränkende Bestimmungen wie hardly ... when, in vain, no sooner ... than, never, not only ... but, rarely, scarcely, seldom stehen in der Regel mit einem bejahten Verb, da diese Bestimmungen bereits die Verneinung

Der Satz

ausdrücken. Einschränkende oder verneinende Bestimmungen können am Satzanfang stehen, das Prädikat des Satzes wird mit to do umschrieben (jedoch ohne not), wenn es ein Vollverb ist. Das Subjekt des Satzes tritt zwischen to do und Vollverb. Diese Art der Formulierung findet sich nur noch in der literarischen und veralteten Sprache.

Verneinende Best.	Prädikat	Subjekt	Prädikat
In vain	did	he	come.
Never	did	he	come.

Steht die verneinende oder einschränkende Bestimmung nicht am Satzanfang, so wird das (bejahte) Prädikat nicht mit to do umschrieben. Die Bestimmung tritt entweder vor das Prädikat oder an das Satzende.

Subjekt(pron.)	Prädikat	verneinende Bestimmung
He	came	**in vain.**

Subjekt(pron.)	verneinende Bestimmung	Prädikat
He	**never**	came.

Zur besonderen Hervorhebung kann die Umschreibung mit to do im present und past tense eingesetzt werden.

Subjekt(pron.)	verneinende Best.	Prädikat	Objekt
He	**never**	does drink	hard liquor.

Übungen zur Formulierung von verneinten Sätzen mit und ohne to do finden Sie auf Seite 58ff.

Der Satz

Der Fragesatz (The Interrogative Clause)

Im Fragesatz wird eine Frage formuliert.

Die direkte Frage (The Direct Interrogative Clause)

Direkte Fragen bilden selbst den Hauptsatz, sie werden nicht wie die indirekten Fragen in einen Nebensatz eingebettet und durch ein Verb des Sagens und Denkens eingeleitet.

Die Entscheidungsfrage (The Yes-/No-Question)

Entscheidungsfragen enthalten kein Fragewort. Sie bedingen eine Ja- oder Nein-Antwort. Zu den Entscheidungsfragen gehören die im Folgenden aufgeführten.

Die Intonationsfrage (The Intonated Question)

Die Frage wird durch die Intonation kenntlich gemacht, d. h. die Satzmelodie geht am Satzende nach oben. Die Wortstellung entspricht der des einfachen, bejahten Aussagesatzes. Diese Art der Fragestellung wird, vor allem in der gesprochenen Sprache, sehr häufig verwendet.

Subjekt(pronomen)	Prädikat	Objekt
Mary	knows	Peter?

Die Inversionsfrage (The Inversion Question)

Bei dieser Art der Fragestellung tritt das Subjekt(pronomen) hinter das Verb (Inversion des Subjekts).
Ist das Prädikat ein Vollverb, so muss dieses bei der Bildung des Fragesatzes mit to do umschrieben werden. Zu beachten ist, dass to do und to have selbst Vollverb sein können. Sie werden dann auch mit to do umschrieben.

To do	Subjekt(pron.)	Prädikat	Objekt
Does	Mary	know	Peter?
Did	he	do	his homework?
Does	he	have	a car?

die Vollverben to have bzw. to do werden mit to do umschrieben

Ist das Prädikat ein Hilfs- oder Modalverb, so wird dieses zur Bildung des Fragesatzes verwendet.

Hilfsverb	Subjekt(pron.)	Vollverb	Objekt
Have	you	done	your homework?
Could	Mary	solve	this problem?

Der Satz

Die Frage mit Fragewort (The Question With a Question Word)

Diese Fragen enthalten ein Fragewort (who, what, how, when etc.), das am Satzanfang steht.

Ist das Fragewort selbst Subjekt oder ein Teil dessen, d. h. der Satz enthält kein anderes Subjekt (he, Peter etc.), so wird nicht mit to do umschrieben.

Fragewort	Prädikat	direktes Objekt
Who	solved	the problem?
Who	has solved	the problem?

Ist das Fragewort nicht selbst Subjekt oder ein Teil dessen, d. h. der Satz enthält schon ein anderes Subjekt (he, Peter etc.), so muss das Vollverb mit to do umschrieben werden. Das Subjekt des Satzes tritt zwischen to do und das Vollverb.

Fragewort	Prädikat	Subjekt	Prädikat	adv. Best.
Whom	did	you	meet	at the station?
Where	is	he	going?	

Fragesätze mit Fragewort, die ein Hilfsverb oder Modalverb enthalten, werden nicht mit to do umschrieben, gleichgültig ob das Fragewort selbst Subjekt des Satzes ist oder nicht. Das Subjekt des Satzes tritt hinter das Hilfsverb bzw. Modalverb oder, sofern das Fragewort nicht selbst Subjekt des Satzes ist, unmittelbar hinter das Fragewort.

Fragewort	Prädikat	Subjekt(pron.)	Prädikat	dir. Objekt
Where	has	Peter	been?	
Where	can	you	meet	him?

Fragewort als Teil des Subjekts	Prädikat	Subj.(pron.)	Prädikat
Whose books	have	you	taken away?

Die indirekte Frage (The Indirect Interrogative Clause)

Indirekte Fragen (Fragen in der indirekten Rede) sind in einem Nebensatz, der von einem Verb des Sagens und Denkens (say, think, believe, answer etc.) eingeleitet wird, eingebettet. Sie werden vom Einleitungssatz nicht durch Komma abgetrennt und nicht durch Fragezeichen, sondern durch Punkt abgeschlossen.

Indirekte Fragen ohne Fragewort

Indirekte Fragen ohne Fragewort (indirekte Entscheidungsfragen) werden mit whether oder if eingeleitet, wobei whether zutreffender ist als if, if jedoch, vor allem in der Umgangssprache, häufiger ist. Die Wortstellung entspricht der des einfachen Aussagesatzes.

Der Satz

Einleitung	whether, if	Subjekt(pron.)	Prädikat	Objekt
Mary asked	**whether/if**	he	had done	his homework.

Indirekte Fragen mit Fragewort

In indirekten Fragen mit Fragewort wird das Fragewort wiederholt. Die Wortstellung entspricht der des einfachen Aussagesatzes.

Einleitung	Fragewort	Subjekt(pron.)	Prädikat	adv. Best.
He wondered	**what**	she	had done	in his room.

Übungen zur Formulierung von Fragesätzen mit und ohne to do finden Sie auf Seite 58ff.

Der Satz

Die Question Tags

Die question tags oder Kurzfragen sind eine Besonderheit im Englischen, die immer dann eingesetzt werden, wenn der Sprecher vom Gesprächspartner eine Bestätigung seiner Aussage erwartet (*nicht wahr?, so?, wirklich?, oder?*). Das Vollverb der vorangehenden Aussage wird im question tag durch to do wieder aufgenommen. Enthält die vorangehende Aussage ein Hilfs- oder Modalverb, so wird dieses im question tag wieder aufgenommen. Wird das Verb im question tag verneint, steht immer die Kurzform (n't) und nicht not. Das Subjekt des question tags ist immer ein Pronomen und nie ein Substantiv.

kein Substantiv im question tag

Question Tag bejaht	Question Tag verneint
Eine verneinte vorangehende Aussage wird bejaht wiederholt. Hardly und scarcely geben dem Satz einen negativen Sinn, daher wird die vorangehende Aussage bejaht wiederholt.	Eine bejahte vorangehende Aussage wird verneint wiederholt. Ist das Verb des Vordersatzes ein Vollverb, wird im question tag to do eingesetzt, ist das Verb im Vordersatz ein Hilfs- oder Modalverb, wird dieses im question tag wieder aufgenommen.
▪ He doesn't go home, **does he?** ▪ He isn't at home, **is he?** ▪ We can't take your car, **can we?** ▪ There was hardly anybody to be seen, **was there?**	▪ He goes home, **doesn't he?** ▪ He is at home, **isn't he?** ▪ We can take your car, **can't we?**

verneinte; bejahte Aussage

question tag ist gleich der vorangehenden Aussage

Eine bejahte vorangehende Aussage wird bejaht wiederholt, wenn die Aussage einen Imperativ enthält. Der Imperativ wird im question tag durch will - oder für die 1. Person Plural - shall wiederholt.	
▪ Stop talking, **will you?** ▪ Come punctually, **will you?** ▪ Let's have a party, **shall we?**	
Eine bejahte vorangehende Aussage wird bejaht wiederholt, wenn im question tag persönliche Gefühle (Überraschung, Freude etc.) zum Ausdruck gebracht werden sollen.	
▪ The teacher told the pupils to burn their books, **did he?**	

Der Satz

Übungen zu den Question Tags

1. Setzen Sie den entsprechenden question tag ein.

1. He doesn't like me, ...?
2. He never showed any liking for that place, ...?
3. He wasn't waiting there for us, ...?
4. He won't do it, ...?
5. He's getting desperate, ...?
6. I can't really take all the prize myself, ...? We both won it, ...?
7. I don't know, ...?
8. I tried to do my best, ... ?
9. I won't see you again, ...?
10. I'm being selfish, brother, ...?
11. Sam, I'm going to be all right, ...?
12. They could hide it, ...?
13. They both look very funny, ...?
14. They didn't help, ...?
15. They don't actually believe Harry killed him, ...?
16. Your uncle wanted to give us something, ...?
17. Jack looks weaker than John, ...?
18. You know where we go now, ...?
19. They have always been making trouble, ...?
20. Jack has big ears, ...?
21. Bob doesn't look strong, ...?
22. Bob hasn't much hair, ...?
23. Bob is very fat, ...?

Der Satz

24. Bob isn't very good-looking, ...?
25. We had better push the barrow together, ...?
26. We haven't failed yet, ...?
27. We'll be happier now, ...?
28. We'll just please ourselves, ...?
29. We're not far from London, ...?
30. Whatever we do we're laughed at, ...?
31. You can watch that on television, ...?
32. You don't like Bill, ...?
33. You knew, ...?
34. You know the trouble, ...?
35. You were asleep, ...?
36. You weren't very careful, ...?
37. You weren't whispering, ...?
38. You'll go when we get there, ...?
39. You're going to ask her, ...?
40. Sit down, ...?

richtig   falsch

Die entsprechenden Lösungen befinden sich auf Seite 443.

Der Satz

Der Aufforderungssatz (The Imperative Clause)

Im Aufforderungssatz wird ein Befehl, eine Aufforderung mit den Formen des Imperativs ausgedrückt.
Der Aufforderungssatz wird im Gegensatz zum Deutschen nicht mit Ausrufezeichen, sondern mit Punkt abgeschlossen.

kein Ausrufezeichen im Aufforderungssatz

Eine Aufforderung wird durch die Formen des Imperativs ausgedrückt, die an den Anfang des Satzes treten.

- Be quiet.
  (Sei, seid, Seien Sie ruhig!)
- Let's go now.

Eine Aufforderung kann durch Hinzufügen von to do oder des entsprechenden Subjekts besonders betont werden.

- Do be quiet.
- Peter, you do your homework now.
- Mary, you go home now.

Der verneinte Aufforderungssatz wird in der 2. Person Singular und Plural mit to do not gebildet. In der 1. Person Plural und in der 3. Person Singular und Plural kann auch nur not verwendet werden.

- Don't forget your books.
- Don't go into this room.
- Don't let him go/Let him not go.
- Don't let us go/Let us not go.
- Don't let them go/Let them not go.

Der Satz

Der Ausrufesatz (The Exclamatory Clause)

Im Ausrufesatz wird eine persönliche Empfindung (Erstaunen, Verwunderung, Überraschung etc.) in einem Ausruf formuliert.
Der Ausrufesatz wird nur dann mit einem Ausrufezeichen (exclamation mark) versehen, wenn es sich tatsächlich um einen Ausruf handelt.

Ausrufezeichen nur beim Ausruf

Ausrufesätze ohne Ausrufewort (Exclamatory Clauses Without an Interjection Word)

Bei Ausrufesätzen, die nicht durch ein Ausrufewort eingeleitet werden, gilt dieselbe Wortstellung wie im bejahten und verneinten Aussagesatz.

- **Impossible not to see her(!)**
  (Unmöglich, sie nicht zu sehen!)
- **If only I could make her acquaintance(!)**
  (Wenn ich sie nur kennen lernen könnte!)

Ausrufesätze mit Ausrufewort (Exclamatory Clauses With an Interjection Word)

Ausrufesätze können mit Ausrufewörtern (Interjektionen) wie *what a* und *how* eingeleitet werden.
What a steht, wenn ein Substantiv folgt. Vor das Subjekt tritt das Objekt bzw. die prädikative Ergänzung zum Subjekt. *How* steht, wenn ein Adjektiv folgt und das Subjekt tritt hinter das Prädikat (Inversion des Subjekts).

- **What an elegant lady(!)**
  (Was für eine elegante Frau!)
- **What an elegant lady Mary-Ellen is(!)**
  (Was für eine elegante Dame Mary-Ellen doch ist!)
- **How beautiful(!)**
  (Wie schön!)
- **How beautiful this countryside is(!)**
  (Wie schön diese Landschaft ist!)

Der Nebensatz (The Subordinate Clause)

Der Nebensatz ist der untergeordnete Teil eines Satzgefüges und kann im Gegensatz zum Hauptsatz nicht alleine stehen.
Einige Satzarten sind immer Nebensätze, sie können nie Hauptsätze sein. Diese Satzarten sind im Folgenden aufgeführt.

Der Subjektsatz (The Nominative Clause)

Ein Subjektsatz ist ein Nebensatz anstelle des Subjekts.

- **Whether he is coming** is uncertain.
  (**Ob er kommt**, ist ungewiss.)
  (**Das** ist ungewiss.)

Der Objektsatz (The Objective Clause)

Ein Objektsatz ist ein Nebensatz anstelle eines Objekts.

- I don't know **if he is coming**.
  (Ich weiß nicht, **ob er kommt**.)
  (Ich weiß **es** nicht.)

Der Adverbialsatz (The Adverbial Clause)

Ein Adverbialsatz ist ein Nebensatz anstelle einer adverbialen Bestimmung und wird mit einer Konjunktion eingeleitet.

Der Temporalsatz (The Temporal Clause)

Der Temporalsatz gibt einen Zeitpunkt, Zeitraum an und wird durch eine temporale Konjunktion eingeleitet.

- **When my father arrived,** we had prepared everything.

Zeitpunkt, -raum

Der Finalsatz (The Final Clause)

Der Finalsatz bringt eine Absicht, einen Zweck zum Ausdruck und wird durch eine finale Konjunktion eingeleitet.

- He studied hard **so that he would pass the exam.**

Absicht, Zweck

Der Kausalsatz (The Causative Clause)

Der Kausalsatz bringt eine Begründung zum Ausdruck und wird durch eine kausale Konjunktion eingeleitet.

- **Since he has finished all his work,** he can go home now.

Grund

Der Konsekutivsatz (The Consecutive Clause)

Der Konsekutivsatz bringt eine Folge, Wirkung zum Ausdruck und wird

- It rained all morning **so he could not go for a walk.**

Folge, Wirkung

Der Satz

durch eine konsekutive Konjunktion eingeleitet.

Der Konzessivsatz (The Concessive Clause)

Einräumung

Im Konzessivsatz wird eine Einräumung formuliert. Er wird durch eine konzessive Konjunktion eingeleitet.

- **Although it rained all morning,** he went for a walk.

Der Konditionalsatz (The Conditional Clause)

Bedingung

Im Konditionalsatz wird eine Bedingung ausgedrückt. Er wird durch eine konditionale Konjunktion eingeleitet. Zu beachten ist die Zeitenfolge in Konditionalsätzen.

im if-Satz kein will oder would

- **If it rains,** I will come.
- **If it rained,** I would come.
- **If it had rained,** I would have come.

Der Attributsatz (The Attributive Clause)

Beifügung

Ein Attributsatz ist ein Nebensatz anstelle eines Attributs. Das Attribut ist eine Beifügung, die zum Verständnis des Satzes nicht notwendig ist, jedoch diesen näher erklärt.

- The task **of translating the whole book** was very difficult.
- His expectation **of winning the prize** was not fulfilled.

Der Relativsatz (The Relative Clause)

Nebensatz mit Relativpronomen

Ein Relativsatz wird durch ein Relativpronomen eingeleitet, das unmittelbar nach dem Wort bzw. der Wortgruppe steht, auf das bzw. auf die es sich bezieht.

Der notwendige Relativsatz (The Defining Relative Clause)

Notwendige Relativsätze sind für das Verständnis des Hauptsatzes unbedingt erforderlich und können demnach nicht weggelassen werden. Sie werden auch nicht durch Komma vom Hauptsatz getrennt.
Das Relativpronomen, das sich auf das Objekt bezieht, wird in der Umgangssprache meist, in der Schriftsprache gelegentlich weggelassen. Bezieht es sich auf das Subjekt, darf es nicht weggelassen werden. Präpositionen, die zum Verb gehören, müssen erhalten bleiben, sie treten meist hinter das Verb.

kein Komma vor notwendigen Relativsätzen

- My friend **who took his exam last week** went to England.
  (Mein Freund, **der letzte Woche sein Examen ablegte,** ging nach England.)
- The children **who played in the garden this morning** were taken to the hospital.
- The man **(whom/that) I saw this morning** was arrested.
  (Der Mann, **den ich heute Morgen sah,** wurde verhaftet.)
- The man **(who) you were talking to this morning** was arrested.
  (Der Mann, **mit dem du heute Morgen gesprochen hast,** wurde verhaftet.)

Der ausmalende, nicht notwendige Relativsatz (The Non-Defining Relative Clause)

Ausmalende Relativsätze sind für das Verständnis des Hauptsatzes nicht unbedingt erforderlich und können demnach auch weggelassen werden. Sie werden vom Hauptsatz durch Komma abgetrennt und kommen meist nur in der Schriftsprache vor.

- A young man, **whom I don't know,** left the house a few minutes ago.
- Peter left some books, **which he bought yesterday,** on the table over there.
- Mary, **who is a very nice girl,** visits her grandmother every day.

Die Rechtschreibung

Groß- und Kleinschreibung (The Use of Capital and Small Letters)

Grundsätzlich wird im Englischen alles kleingeschrieben.

Satzanfang	Der Anfangsbuchstabe des ersten Wortes eines Satzes wird großgeschrieben.	• He is very happy to see you. • This book is very interesting.
Personalpronomen I	Das Personalpronomen I wird immer großgeschrieben. Alle anderen Pronomen werden, außer am Satzanfang, kleingeschrieben.	• My brothers and sisters and I grew up in the country. • My sister and your sister are classmates.
Eigennamen	Die Eigennamen werden grundsätzlich großgeschrieben. Hierzu zählen auch die von den Eigennamen abgeleiteten Adjektive.	• Peter and Mary are classmates. • Every year, I go to Great Britain in my holidays to improve my English. • June, July and August are the hottest months.
von Eigennamen abgeleitete Adjektive	Adjektive, die von Eigennamen abgeleitet sind, werden großgeschrieben. Vorsilben, die mit dem Adjektiv durch Bindestrich verbunden sind, werden kleingeschrieben.	• English • Elizabethan • un-English • anti-American • pro-French
Titel	Titel, die mit dem zugehörigen Namen in Verbindung stehen. Titel ohne Namen werden ebenfalls großgeschrieben, wenn dabei an eine bestimmte Person gedacht ist.	• Queen Elizabeth • the Queen (of Great Britain) • the President (of the United States) aber: • Once there lived a queen.
Ordnungszahlen in Herrschernamen	Ordnungszahlen in Verbindung mit Titeln werden großgeschrieben.	• Elizabeth the Second • Henry the Eighth
Himmelsrichtungen	Himmelsrichtungen werden zur Bezeichnung von Gebieten großgeschrieben.	• the West and the East aber: • France is west of Germany.
Direkte Rede	Das erste Wort der direkten Rede wird, auch wenn ein Komma vorausgeht, großgeschrieben.	• Mr Smith asked the passer-by, «Can you tell me how I get to St. Paul's Cathedral?»
Überschriften, Buchtitel	Die wichtigsten Wörter (Substantive, Adjektive etc.) in Überschriften und Buchtiteln mit Ausnahme von a, an, the, and, or, Präpositionen oder anderen Wörtern mit weniger als vier Buchstaben, werden großgeschrieben.	• For Whom the Bell Tolls • The Catcher in the Rye • The Old Man and the Sea • The Plague • Modern Life in Great Britain

Das erste Wort der Schluss- und Anredeformeln in Briefen wird großgeschrieben.

- **Yours** sincerely
- **With** best wishes
- **Dear** Peter, ...

Schlussformel, Anredeformel in Briefen

Die Rechtschreibung

Besonderheiten bei der Schreibung

Beim Anfügen von Endungen, Nachsilben und in Wortzusammensetzungen ändert sich häufig die Schreibweise, da die Aussprache des Grundwortes gehalten werden soll. Es sind daher die folgenden Besonderheiten zu beachten.

	Ursprüngliche Endung bleibt erhalten	Ursprüngliche Endung entfällt, ändert sich
Konsonant am Wortende	Konsonanten am Wortende werden nicht verdoppelt, wenn diesen ein unbetonter Vokal oder zwei Vokale vorausgehen.	Konsonanten am Wortende werden verdoppelt, wenn Endungen, die mit Vokal beginnen angehängt werden und wenn dem Konsonant ein einfacher (nicht zwei) betonter Vokal vorausgeht.

	▪ look - looked
	       - looker-on
	       - looking
	▪ conquer - conquered
	       - conqueror
		▪ begin - beginning
		       - beginner
		▪ stop - stopped
		       - stopper
		       - stopping
		Wichtige Ausnahmen:
		▪ bus - buses (BE)
		       - busses (AE)
		▪ gas - gases

Endkonsonant -l	-l am Wortende wird nicht verdoppelt, wenn ihm kein einfacher, sondern zwei Vokale vorausgehen.	-l am Wortende wird verdoppelt, wenn Endungen, die mit Vokal beginnen, angehängt werden. Im Amerikanischen wird es nicht immer verdoppelt.

	▪ boil - boiled
	▪ cool - cooler, coolest
	▪ fail - failed
	▪ sail - sailing
	Wichtige Ausnahmen:
	▪ wool - woolen
		▪ control - controlled
		▪ quarrel - quarrelled (BE)
		       - quarreled (AE)
		▪ travel - traveller (BE)
		       - traveler (AE)
		Wichtige Ausnahmen:
		▪ parallel - paralleled
		▪ peril - perilous

	-l am Wortende wird nicht verdoppelt, wenn Endungen wie -ic, -ish, -ism, -ist, -ity und -ize angehängt werden.	
	▪ angel - Angelic ▪ devil - devilish ▪ liberal - liberalism ▪ royal - royalist ▪ total - totality ▪ equal - equalize Wichtige Ausnahmen: ▪ duel - duellist ▪ metal - metallic	

Die Rechtschreibung

Ursprüngliche Endung bleibt erhalten	Ursprüngliche Endung entfällt, ändert sich	
	Die Endkonsonanten -ll in einsilbigen Wörtern werden in Zusammensetzungen zu -l.	Endkonsonanten -ll
	- all - almost - fill - fulfil - full - fulfil - till - until	
-r am Wortende wird nicht verdoppelt, wenn ihm kein einfacher, sondern zwei Vokale vorausgehen.	-r wird nach einfachem, betontem Vokal grundsätzlich verdoppelt, wenn Endungen, die mit Vokal beginnen, angehängt werden.	Endkonsonant -r
- pour - poured - repair - repairing	- bar - barred - occur - occurrence - prefer - preferring	
Stummes -e am Wortende bleibt erhalten, wenn Endungen, die mit Konsonant beginnen, angehängt werden.	Stummes -e am Wortende entfällt, wenn Endungen, die mit Vokal beginnen, angehängt werden.	stummes -e
- care - careful - excite - excitement Wichtige Ausnahmen: - argue - argument - awe - awful - due - duly - true - truly - nine - ninth - whole - wholly	- love - loved - live - living - nice - nicer, nicest Wichtige Ausnahmen: - dye - dyeing - queue - queueing	
-ce und -ge bleiben erhalten, wenn Endungen angehängt werden, die mit -a, -o und -u beginnen.	-ce wird in einigen Fällen zu -ci, wenn die Endung -ous angehängt wird.	-ce und -ge
- change - changeable - courage - courageous - notice - noticeable	- grace - gracious - space - spacious - vice - vicious	
-ee am Wortende bleibt erhalten, wenn die Endungen -ing und -able angehängt werden.	-ee am Wortende wird zu -e, wenn Endungen, die mit -e beginnen, angehängt werden.	-ee
- agree - agreeable - see - seeing	- see - seer - free - freer, freest	
-f(e) am Ende von Wörtern romanischer Herkunft bleibt erhalten, wenn	-f(e) am Ende von Wörtern germanischer Herkunft wird zu -ve, wenn	-f(e)

Die Rechtschreibung

	Ursprüngliche Endung bleibt erhalten	Ursprüngliche Endung entfällt, ändert sich
	ein Plural-s angehängt wird.	ein Plural-s angehängt wird.
	• gulf - gulfs • proof - proofs • safe - safes	• calf - calves • half - halves • knife - knives
-ie		-ie am Ende von Verben wird zu -y, wenn die Endung -ing angehängt wird. • to die - dying • to lie - lying • to tie - tying
-o	Bei Wörtern, die als Fremdwörter gelten, bleibt das -o am Wortende erhalten, wenn ein Plural-s angehängt wird. • folio - folios • photo - photos • piano - pianos • radio - radios • studio - studios	Geht dem -o am Wortende ein Konsonant voraus, wird es zu -oe, wenn ein Plural-s oder das -s der 3. Person Singular present tense angehängt wird. • do - does • go - goes • negro - negroes • tomato - tomatoes
-oe	-oe am Wortende bleibt erhalten. • canoe - canoeing • shoe - shoeing	
-y	-y bleibt erhalten, wenn dem -y ein Vokal vorausgeht. • enjoy - enjoyed • gay - gayer • play - playing • pay - paying	-y wird zu -i, wenn dem -y ein Konsonant vorausgeht. • beauty - beautiful • cry - cried • mercy - merciless • victory - victorious
	y bleibt erhalten, wenn -ing folgt. • cry - crying • pay - paying • try - trying	
	-y bleibt erhalten, wenn ein Plural-s oder das Endungs-s der 3. Person Singular des present tense angehängt wird und wenn dem -y ein Vokal vorausgeht.	-y wird zu -ie, wenn ein Plural-s oder das Endungs-s der 3. Person Singular des present tense angehängt wird und wenn dem -y ein Konsonant vorausgeht.

Die Rechtschreibung

Ursprüngliche Endung bleibt erhalten		
enjoy	-	he enjoys
pay	-	he pays
boy	-	boys
way	-	ways

Eigennamen, die auf -y enden, behalten das -y im Plural.

| Mr Henry | - | the Henrys |
| Mr Kennedy | - | the Kennedys |

Einsilbige Wörter auf -y erhalten das -y, vor allem vor den Endungen -ness und -ly.

| dry | - | dryness |
| shy | - | shyly |

Wichtige Ausnahmen:

| day | - | daily |
| gay | - | gaily |

Ursprüngliche Endung entfällt, ändert sich		
cry	-	he cries
marry	-	he marries
lady	-	ladies
story	-	stories

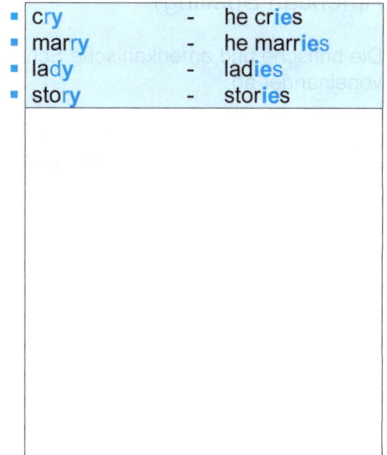

Die Rechtschreibung

Britische und amerikanische Schreibweise (British and American Spelling)

Die britische und amerikanische Schreibweise weicht in den folgenden Punkten voneinander ab.

BE	AE	Britische Schreibweise	Amerikanische Schreibweise	Deutsche Bedeutung
-ce	-se	defence	defense	Verteidigung
		licence	license	Lizenz, Erlaubnis
		offence	offense	Beleidigung
		pretence	pretense	Vorwand
-gement	-gment	abridg(e)ment	abridgment	Verkürzung
		acknowledg(e)ment	acknowledgment	Anerkennung
		judg(e)ment	judgment	Urteil, Beurteilung
-iae-	-ie-	mediaeval (medieval)	medieval	mittelalterlich
-l-	-ll-	enrol	enroll	einrollen
		fulfil	fulfill	erfüllen
		fulfilment	fulfillment	Erfüllung
		wilful	willful	eigenwillig
		wilfulness	willfulness	Eigenwille
-ll-	-l-	marvellous	marvelous	wundervoll
		modelled	modeled	modelliert
		modelling	modeling	modellierend
		travelled	traveled	gereist
		traveller	traveler	Reisender
		travelling	traveling	reisend
		woollen	woolen	wollen, aus Wolle
-mme	-m	gramme	gram	Gramm
		programme	program	Programm
-œ-	-e-	manoeuvre	maneuver	Manöver
-ogue	-og	analogue	analog	analog
		catalogue	catalog	Katalog
		dialogue	dialog	Dialog

Die Rechtschreibung

BE	AE	Britische Schreibweise	Amerikanische Schreibweise	Deutsche Bedeutung
-oul	-ol	mould	mold	Gussform
		smoulder	smolder	schwelen
-ou-	-u-	moustache	mustache	Schnurrbart
-ough	-ow	plough	plow	Pflug
-our	-or	armour	armor	Rüstung, Panzer
		colour	color	Farbe
		favour	favor	begünstigen
		favourite	favorite	Lieblings-
		honour	honor	Ehre
		honourable	honorable	ehrenhaft
		parlour	parlor	Besuchszimmer
-que	-ck	cheque	check	Scheck
-re	-er	centre	center	Zentrum
		fibre	fiber	Faser, Glas
		litre	liter	Liter
		meagre	meager	mager
		sombre	somber	düster, trübe
		spectre	specter	Gespenst
		theatre	theater	Theater
-xe	-x	axe	ax	Axt, Beil

Die Zeichensetzung (The Punctuation)

Bis auf die Verwendung des Kommas, des Bindestrichs und des Ausrufezeichens weicht die Zeichensetzung (Interpunktion) im Englischen im Allgemeinen nicht wesentlich von der deutschen ab.

Der Punkt (The Full Stop (BE), Period (AE))

Der Punkt steht am Ende eines Satzes.

- Peter is a very nice boy.
- They have just arrived.

Das Komma (The Comma)

Die Kommasetzung weicht im Englischen stark vom Deutschen ab. Während im Deutschen das Komma hauptsächlich zur Trennung von Satzteilen gesetzt wird, werden im Englischen mit Kommas Sprechpausen angezeigt. Im Allgemeinen werden im Englischen viel weniger Kommas gesetzt als im Deutschen, daher empfiehlt es sich das Komma in Zweifelsfällen besser wegzulassen.

	Komma	Kein Komma
Subjekt-, Objektsätze		Vor und nach Subjekt- und Objektsätzen steht kein Komma. - Whether he is coming is uncertain. (Subjektsatz) - I don't know whether he is coming. (Objektsatz)
Nebensätze	Nebensätze, die vor einem Hauptsatz stehen, werden, auch wenn sie verkürzt sind, durch Komma vom Hauptsatz abgetrennt. - During the English lesson, Peter fell asleep.	Vor kurzen adverbialen Nebensätzen, die unmittelbar nach dem Hauptsatz stehen und mit diesem eng verbunden sind. - Wait until I am ready.
kein Komma vor that		Nebensätze, die mit that (dass) eingeleitet werden, dürfen, im Gegensatz zum Deutschen, nicht durch Komma abgetrennt werden. - I told him that I never want to see him again. (Ich sagte ihm, dass ich ihn nie wieder sehen will.)
kein Komma vor notwendigen Relativsätzen	Nach ausmalenden Relativsätzen, die zum Verständnis des Satzes nicht notwendig sind.	Notwendige Relativsätze, die zum Verständnis des Satzes notwendig sind, dürfen nicht durch Komma abgetrennt werden.

Die Zeichensetzung

Komma	Kein Komma	
▪ A young man, whom I don't know, left the house a few minutes ago.	▪ My friend who took his exam last week went to England.	
Vor der direkten Rede kann statt des Doppelpunkts das Komma stehen.	Vor der indirekten Rede und in indirekten Fragen steht im Gegensatz zum Deutschen kein Komma.	direkte Rede; indirekte Rede kein Komma vor indirekter Rede, indirekten Fragen
▪ Peter asked me, «Can you give me 100 pounds?»	▪ Peter asked me if I could give him 100 pounds.	
	Vor dem reinen Infinitiv und dem Infinitiv + to.	Infinitiv
	▪ I heard him go into the house. ▪ They asked me to come.	
	Vor Konstruktionen mit gerund (Gerundialkonstruktionen).	gerund
	▪ He came back without telling us where he was.	
Die folgenden Adverbien und adverbialen Bestimmungen werden zwischen Kommas gesetzt, vor allem wenn eine Sprechpause gemacht wird.		adverbiale Bestimmungen
▪ anyhow — irgendwie ▪ besides — außerdem ▪ for example — zum Beispiel ▪ for instance — zum Beispiel ▪ however — jedoch ▪ indeed — in der Tat ▪ in fact — in der Tat ▪ moreover — überdies, außerdem ▪ of course — natürlich ▪ on the contrary — im Gegenteil ▪ on the other hand — andrerseits ▪ still — noch ▪ then — dann ▪ therefore — daher, deshalb ▪ though — obwohl ▪ too — auch		
▪ Peter, however, did his homework carefully.		
Nach adverbialen Bestimmungen am Satzanfang.		
▪ This morning, I met Peter at the station.		

Die Zeichensetzung

	Komma	Kein Komma
Auszählungen Komma auch vor and, or	In Aufzählungen, auch wenn die einzelnen Teile durch and oder or verbunden sind.	
	• He bought bread, cheese, milk, and butter.	
and	Vor and steht auch das Komma, wenn ein zweites Prädikat hinzukommt, das sich auf dasselbe Subjekt bezieht wie das erste.	
	• Our father leaves the house at 8 o'clock, and comes back at 5 o'clock.	
Datum	In Datumsangaben steht ein Komma vor der Jahreszahl, vor allem, wenn der Monatsname vor der Tageszahl steht.	In Datumsangaben kann das Komma fehlen, vor allem wenn die Tageszahl vor dem Monatsnamen steht.
	• April 15th, 1994 • April 15, 1994 • 15th April, 1994	• 15th April 1994
mehrstellige Zahlen kein Punkt in Dezimalstellen	In vier- und mehrstelligen Zahlen steht das Komma zur Abtrennung von je 3 Stellen, ausgenommen bei Jahreszahlen.	
	• 2,368 • 22,897 • 987,654,654	
Anrede kein Ausrufezeichen in der Anrede	Nach der Anrede am Satzanfang sowie bei der Anrede und in der Schlussformel von Briefen. Es steht im Gegensatz zum Deutschen hier kein Ausrufezeichen.	
	• My dear boy, will you please do your homework now. • Dear Peter, ... • Yours sincerely, ...	
Ausrufewörter	Nach Ausrufewörtern steht ein Komma oder ein Ausrufezeichen.	
	• Oh, I am sorry! • Oh! I am sorry!	

Die Zeichensetzung

Das Fragezeichen (The Question Mark; Mark/Note of Interrogation)

Das Fragezeichen steht zur Kennzeichnung einer Frage.

- Can you please pass me the salt?
- Where do you come from?

Das Ausrufezeichen (The Exclamation Mark/Note of Exclamation)

Das Ausrufezeichen steht zur Kennzeichnung eines Ausrufesatzes und nach Ausrufewörtern (Interjektionen). Beim Imperativ, der eine bloße Aufforderung ausdrückt, steht kein Ausrufezeichen.

- What a nice little boy! she cried out.
- Oh! I'm sorry!
- Oh, I'm sorry!
- Please pass me the salt.

kein Azusrufezeichen bei Aufforderungen

Der Doppelpunkt (The Colon)

Der Doppelpunkt kann zur Einleitung nachfolgender Aufzählungen oder eines folgenden Satzes oder zur Einleitung der direkten Rede stehen.

- Please find enclosed: our offer and three copies.
- Peter asked me: «Can you lend me your bicycle?»

Die Anführungszeichen (The Quotation Marks)

Die Anführungszeichen stehen am Anfang und Ende einer direkten Rede.
Im britischen Englisch werden diese «» Anführungszeichen bevorzugt, im amerikanischen Englisch jene " ".

- He said: «Read the text by tomorrow.»
- He said: "Read the text by tomorrow."

Der Bindestrich (The Hyphen)

Es lassen sich keine allgemein gültigen Regeln dafür aufstellen, wann ein Bindestrich gesetzt wird. Auch gibt es erhebliche Unterschiede zwischen britischem und amerikanischem Englisch. Im Zweifelsfall sollte der Bindestrich besser weggelassen werden und statt dessen ein Wort oder zwei Wörter geschrieben werden.

1 Wort (ohne Bindestrich)	Mehrere Wörter (ohne Bindestrich)
	Eigennamen, die aus zwei Wörtern bestehen.
	- Buckingham Palace - Windsor Castle - Central Park

Eigennamen

dnf 395

Die Zeichensetzung

	1 Wort (ohne Bindestrich)	Mehrere Wörter (ohne Bindestrich)
gebräuchliche Zusammensetzungen	Gebräuchliche Zusammensetzungen werden, sofern sie Gegenstände des täglichen Lebens bezeichnen und häufig verwendet werden und nur eine betonte Silbe (meist die erste) haben, zusammengeschrieben. - bedroom - handbag - suitcase	Zusammensetzungen werden, sofern sie weniger gebräuchlich sind, längere Bestandteile haben oder mehr als eine betonte Silbe haben, getrennt geschrieben. - insurance policy - school television - woman teacher
	Mit Bindestrich	Mehrere Wörter (ohne Bindestrich)
Substantiv + Substantiv	Zusammensetzungen aus mehreren Substantiven. - commander-in-chief - brother-in-law - merry-go-round	Zusammensetzungen aus mehreren durch of verbundene Substantive. - chief of staff - date of birth - Secretary of State
Substantiv + gerund	Zusammensetzungen aus Substantiv und gerund werden im britischen Englisch durch Bindestrich verbunden. - walking-stick - swimming-suit - dining-room	Zusammensetzungen aus Substantiv und gerund werden im amerikanischen Englisch getrennt geschrieben. Auch im britischen Englisch geht die Tendenz zur Getrenntschreibung. - walking stick - swimming suit - dining room
Substantiv + Adjektiv	Zusammensetzungen aus Substantiv und Adjektiv. - light-blue - sky-blue	Zusammensetzungen aus Substantiv und nachgestelltem Adjektiv. - director general - accounts receivable
Verb + Präposition	Zusammensetzungen aus Verb und Präposition. - knock-out - make-up - passer-by	
Adjektiv + Adjektiv	Zusammensetzungen aus Adjektiv und Adjektiv. - red-hot - brand-new	

Die Zeichensetzung

Mit Bindestrich	Kein Bindestrich (ein Wort)	
Zusammensetzungen aus Adjektiv und Partizip.	Zusammensetzungen aus Adjektiv und Partizip werden im Amerikanischen häufig zusammengeschrieben.	Adjektiv + Partizip
• old-fashioned • new-born	• oldfashioned • newborn	
Zusammensetzungen mit Vorsilben.	Zusammensetzungen mit Vorsilben werden im amerikanischen Englisch meist zusammengeschrieben.	Zusammensetzungen + Vorsilbe
• to co-operate • non-stop • to re-elect	• to cooperate • nonstop • to reelect	
Zahlen zwischen 21 und 99 werden durch Bindestrich verbunden.		die Zahlen 21 - 99
• twenty-one • fifty-three • ninety-nine		

Der Gedankenstrich (The Dash)

Der Gedankenstrich kennzeichnet den Wechsel des Themas, des Sprechers oder eine längere Pause, und er betont einen Gegensatz.

- In our last meeting we talked about this problem. – Has anybody seen Mr Smith?
- Be quiet!» – he cried out.
- He tried again and again – but it was useless.

Die Silbentrennung (Syllable Division, Syllabification)

Die Silbentrennung kann nur bei mehrsilbigen Wörtern vorgenommen werden und erfolgt im Englischen nach Sprechsilben und nach Wortbestandteilen. Da die Silbentrennung im Englischen recht kompliziert ist, empfiehlt es sich so wenig wie möglich zu trennen.

Silbentrennung nach Sprechsilben

Die Silbentrennung nach Sprechsilben erfolgt im Wesentlichen nach denselben Regeln wie im Deutschen.

1 Vokal am Wortanfang	Ein einzelner Vokal am Wortanfang darf nicht abgetrennt werden.	• about • ashamed
2 Vokale	Zwei aufeinander folgende Vokale werden getrennt, wenn jeder zu einer Sprechsilbe gehört.	• Janu-ary • re-ality • tri-umph
Vokal + Konsonant + Vokal	Ein Konsonant, der zwischen zwei Vokalen steht, wird an den zweiten Vokal angeschlossen.	• cha-rade • bro-cade • mo-ney
beonter Vokal + Konsonant	Ein kurzer, betonter Vokal bildet mit einem folgenden Konsonanten eine untrennbare Einheit.	• gov-ernment • lim-it • moth-er
Doppelkonsonant	Zwei gleiche Konsonanten werden getrennt.	• gram-mar • stop-ping
st	Die Konsonantenverbindung st wird getrennt, außer wenn das Wort mit einer Vorsilbe beginnt.	• chemis-try • hos-tage • con-struction
-ch, -ck, -dg, -ng, -ph, -sh, -th, -tch	Konsonantenverbindungen aus -ch, -dg, -ng, -ph, -sh, -th und -tch werden nicht getrennt und nach langem Vokal an die zweite Silbe angehängt. Nach kurzem, betontem Vokal werden sie an die erste Silbe angehängt. Die Verbindung ck und der Konsonant x werden stets an die erste Silbe angehängt.	• mer-chant • soph-is-ti-cat-ed • fa-ther • amor-phous • no-thing • pock-et • rack-et • ex-ample
Konsonant + -l, Konsonant + -r	Konsonant und nachfolgendes -l oder -r bilden eine untrennbare Einheit. Geht ihnen ein kurzer betonter Vokal voraus, dürfen sie getrennt werden.	• trou-ble • pan-try • prob-lem • pub-lish

Silbentrennung nach Wortbestandteilen

Flexionsendungen, die durch die Bildung von Partizipien, Steigerung von Adjektiven, Pluralbildung etc. entstehen und andere Ableitungsendungen werden abgetrennt.

- froz-**en**
- writ-**er**
- writ-**ing**
- nic-**er**
- child-**ren**

Flexionsendungen, Ableitungsendungen

Vorsilben werden vom Restwort abgerennt.

- **post**-pone
- **re**-turn

Vorsilben

Nachsilben werden vom vorangehenden Wort abgetrennt.

- incomprehens-**ible**
- remark-**able**

Nachsilben

Zusammegesetzte Wörter werden nach ihren ursprünglichen Bestandteilen getrennt.

- bed-room
- hair-dresser
- peace-time

Zusammensetzungen

Präfixe und Suffixe

Präfixe (Prefixes)

Das Englische kennt eine Reihe von Präfixen (Vorsilben), die an Substantive, Verben oder Adjektive angehängt werden können. Die Bedeutung eines Wortes verändert sich durch das Anhängen verschiedener Präfixe völlig oder teilweise. Es ist zu beachten, dass nicht jedes beliebige Präfix an jedes beliebige Substantiv, Verb oder Adjektiv angehängt werden darf. Auch kann durch das Anhängen eines Präfixes an eine bestimmte Wortart, z. B. ein Substantiv, eine andere Wortart, z. B. ein Verb entstehen.

Gegenteil	a-	a-, un-	**a**moral	amoralisch
	anti-	anti-, gegen-, wider-	**anti**christ	Antichrist
	contra-	kontra-, gegen-, wider-	**contra**distinction	Gegensatz
	counter-	gegen-, wider-	**counter**attack	Gegenangriff
	de-	ab-, aus-, de-, ent-, un-, zer-	**de**populate	entvölkern
	dis-	ab-, aus-, de-, ent-, un-, zer-	**dis**honest	unehrlich
	in-	in, un-	**in**attention	Unaufmerksamkeit
	il-	il-, un-	**il**legal	illegal
	im-	im-, un-, ver-	**im**mature	unreif
	ir-	ir-, un-	**ir**relevant	irrelevant
	mal-	un-	**mal**adjusted	unangepasst
	mis-	miss-	**mis**understand	missverstehen
	non-	un-	**non**sense	Unsinn
	un-	un-	**un**employment	Arbeitslosigkeit
	with-	wider-, ab-, ent-, zurück-	**with**draw	zurückziehen
Gleichheit	equi-	gleich-, equi-	**equi**distant	gleich weit entfernt
	uni-	uni-, ein-	**uni**colour	einfarbig
Steigerung, Verstärkung	ambi	beid-, zwei-	**ambi**dextrous	beidhändig
	arch-	erz-	**arch**bishop	Erzbischof
	bi-	bi-, zwei-, doppel-	**bi**polar	bipolar
	di-	di-, zwei-	**di**acid	zweisäurig
	extra-	extra-, sonder-, neben-	**extra**-thin	extra dünn
	hyper-	hyper-, über-	**hyper**critical	überkritisch
	mega-	mega-	**mega**-ton	Megatonne
	out-	aus-, über	**out**range	übertreffen
	over-	über-	**over**wind	überdrehen (Uhr)
	poly	poly-, mehr-, viel-	**poly**syllabic	mehrsilbig
	super-	super-, über-	**super**sensitive	überempfindlich

Präfixe und Suffixe

Steigerung, Verstärkung	**tri-**	tri-, drei-	**tri**colour	dreifarbig
	ultra-	ultra-	**ultra**violet	ultraviolett
	up-	auf-, an-, empor-, hoch-	**up**hold	hochhalten
Verminderung	**demi-**	halb-	**demi**god	Halbgott
	micro-	micro-	**micro**wave	Mikrowelle
	milli-	milli-	**milli**gramme	Milligramm
	mono-	mono-, ein-	**mono**syllable	einsilbig
	semi-	semi-, halb-	**semi**tone	Halbton
	sub-	unter-, sub-	**sub**divide	unterteilen
	under-	unter-	**under**ground	Untergrund
Wiederholung	**re-**	re-, wieder-, zurück-	**re**construction	Wiederaufbau
Ergebnis, Wirkung	**be-**	be-	**be**sieged	belagert
	co-	ko-, zusammen-	**co**operation	Kooperation
	com-	kom-, mit-, zusammen-	**com**position	Zusammensetzung
	em-	be-, er-, ein-, in-, ver-	**em**body	verkörpern
	en-	be-, er-, ein-, in-, ver-	**en**courage	ermutigen
	for-	ver-	**for**bid	verbieten
Vor-	**ante-**	vor-, voraus-, vorher-	**ante**room	Vorraum
	ex-	ex-	**ex**-president	Expräsident
	fore-	vorder-, vorher-	**fore**ground	Vordergrund
	pre-	prä-, vor-	**pre**war	Vorkriegs-
Nach-	**by-**	neben-, nach-, seiten-	**by**-election	Nachwahl
	post-	post-, nach-	**post**war	Nachkriegs-
Sonstige	**astr(o)-**	astro-	**astro**physics	Astrophysik
	audio-	audio-, hör-	**audio**-visual	audiovisuell
	auto-	auto-	**auto**biography	Autobiografie
	centi-	zenti-	**centi**metre	Zentimeter
	chrono-	chrono-	**chrono**meter	Chronometer
	con-	kon-, mit-	**con**form	anpassen, entsprechen
	dia-	dia-, durch-	**dia**meter	Diameter, Durchmesser
	hetero-	hetero-	**hetero**sexual	heterosexuell
	homo-	homo-	**homo**sexual	homosexuell
	hydro-	hydro-	**hydro**dynamic	hydrodynamisch

Präfixe und Suffixe

Sonstige	inter-	inter-, zwischen-	international	international
	intra-	intra-, inner-	intramural	innerhalb der Mauern
	intro-	intro-, inner-	introversion	Einwärtskehren
	neo-	neo-	neoclassical	neoklassisch
	physio-	physio-	physiotherapy	Physiotherapie
	pro-	pro-, für-	pro-revolutionary	pro-revolutionär
	proto-	proto-	prototype	Prototyp
	pseudo-	pseudo-	pseudo-intellectual	pseudointellektuell
	psycho-	psycho-	psychoanalysis	Psychoanalyse
	self-	selbst-	self-service	Selbstbedienung
	socio-	sozio-, gesellschafts-	socio-economic	sozioökonomisch
	trans-	trans-, über-	transplant	übertragen, transplantieren
	vice-	vize-	vice-president	Vizepräsident

Suffixe (Suffixes)

Das Englische kennt einige Suffixe (Nachsilben), die an Substantive, Verben oder Adjektive angehängt werden können. Die Bedeutung eines Wortes verändert sich durch das Anhängen verschiedener Suffixe völlig oder teilweise. Daher kann nicht jedes beliebige Suffix an jedes beliebige Substantiv, Verb oder Adjektiv angehängt werden. Auch kann durch das Anhängen eines Suffixes an eine bestimmte Wortart, z. B. an ein Substantiv, eine andere Wortart, z.B. ein Verb entstehen.

Suffixe beim Substantiv

Gesamtheit, Kollektivum	-age	-ung	breakage	Bruchstelle
	-an	-isch	Lutheran	lutherisch
	-ance	-anz, -enz	assistance	Hilfe, Beistand
	-ate	-schaft, -tum	electorate	Wählerschaft
	-cy	-lichkeit, -igkeit	accuracy	Genauigkeit
	-dom	-heit, -tum	freedom	Freiheit
	-ence	-anz, -enz	immanence	Immanenz
	-gamy	-gamie	monogamy	Monogamie
	-graphy	-grafie	photography	Fotografie
	-hood	-heit, -keit	childhood	Kindheit
	-(s, t)ion	-tion, -nis, -ung	relation	Beziehung
	-ism	-ismus	communism	Kommunismus

Präfixe und Suffixe

Gesamtheit, Kollektivum	-ment	-ung	development	Entwicklung
	-ness	-heit, -keit, -schaft	dryness	Trockenheit
	-ship	-schaft	friendship	Freundschaft
	-tude	-keit	exactitude	Genauigkeit
	-ty	-keit	honesty	Ehrlichkeit
	-ure	-ung, -ur	legislature	Gesetzgebung
Beruf, Amt, Tätigkeit	-ant	-ent	assistant	Helfer, Assistent
	-ary	-är	functionary	Funktionär
	-ator	-ator	stimulator	Stimulator
	-crat	-krat	democrat	Demokrat
	-ee	-er	employee	Angestellter
	-eer	-ator, -är	auctioneer	Auktionator
	-er	-er	runner	Läufer
	-ery	-erei	fishery	Fischerei
	-ian	-er	optician	Optiker
	-ist	-ist	publicist	Publizist
	-maniac	-mane	kleptomaniac	Kleptomane
	-or	-ter, -eur	governor	Gouverneur
	-ster	-er	songster	Sänger
Verkleinerung	-ee	-chen, -lein	bootee	Damenhalbstiefel
	-ie	-chen, -lein	auntie	Tantchen
	-let	-chen, -lein	booklet	Büchlein
	-ling	-chen, -lein	duckling	Entchen
Sonstige	-ade	-ade	lemonade	Limonade
	-cide	-zid	insecticide	Insektizid
	-cracy	-kratie	democracy	Demokratie
	-ess	-in	lioness	Löwin
	-gramme	-gramm	monogramme	Monogramm
	-ics	-ik	physics	Physik
	-ide	-id	chloride	Chlorid
	-ite	-it	dynamite	Dynamit
	-ity	-keit	oddity	Seltsamkeit
	-logue	-log	dialogue	Dialog
	-logy	-logie	biology	Biologie
	-mania	-manie	kleptomania	Kleptomanie

Präfixe und Suffixe

Sonstige	-oid	-oid	aster**oid**	Asteroid
	-ory	-orium	labora**tory**	Laboratorium
	-osis	-ose	hypn**osis**	Hypnose
	-philia	-philie	Anglo**philia**	Anglophilie
	-phobia	-phobie	claustro**phobia**	Klaustrophobie
	-phone	-fon	tele**phone**	Telefon
	-ry	-tät	rival**ry**	Rivalität
	-scape	-schaft	land**scape**	Landschaft
	-scope	-skop	micro**scope**	Mikroskop
	-sphere	-sphäre	hemi**sphere**	Hemisphäre

Suffixe beim Verb

Neben den nachstehend aufgeführten Suffixen bei Verben, werden die Verben häufig von einem Substantiv abgeleitet, indem man das Suffix des Substantivs weglässt (z. B. assistance - to assist).

Suffixe bei Verben	**-ate**	-ieren	stimul**ate**	stimulieren
	-fy	-ern	beauti**fy**	verschönern
	-ize, -ise	-sieren	tyrann**ize**, tyrann**ise**	tyrannisieren

Das Suffix -ise findet sich im britischen Englisch an veralteten Stammwörtern (wenn man die Endung -ise wegstreicht, bleibt kein sinnvolles Wort mehr übrig), -ize findet sich an modernen Stammwörtern (streicht man die Endung weg, bleibt ein erkennbares englisches Wort übrig. Im amerikanischen Englisch werden beide Endungen eingesetzt.

Suffixe beim Adjektiv

Diese Suffixe können an ein Substantiv, den Stamm eines Verbs oder an ein Adjektiv angehängt werden, um so ein neues Adjektiv zu bilden.

Ergebnis, Wirkung	**-able**	-isch, -lich, -bar	fashion**able**	modisch
	-al	-isch, -haft	magic**al**	magisch, zauberhaft
	-ant	-ant, -end	signific**ant**	bedeutend
	-ate	-lich	passion**ate**	leidenschaftlich
	-ative	-ativ	quantit**ative**	quantitativ
	-ed	-t	talent**ed**	talentiert
	-en	-en, -ern	earth**en**	irden, tönern
	-ent	-lich	differ**ent**	unterschiedlich

Präfixe und Suffixe

Ergebnis, Wirkung	**-esque**	-isch	pictur**esque**	malerisch
	-fic	-lich, -isch	horri**fic**	schrecklich
	-ful	-voll, -lich	peace**ful**	friedlich
	-ial	-lich	essent**ial**	wesentlich
	-ible	-isch, -lich, -bar	respons**ible**	verantwortlich
	-ic(al)	-isch	systemat**ical**	systematisch
	-ive	-iv	act**ive**	aktiv
	-less	-los	end**less**	endlos
	-ly	-lich	coward**ly**	feige
	-oid	-förmig, -oid	rhomb**oid**	rautenförmig
	-ory	-isch	illus**ory**	illusorisch
	-ous	-ig, -lich	danger**ous**	gefährlich
	-some	-ig, -lich	quarrel**some**	streitsüchtig
	-wise	-weise, -mäßig	cross**wise**	kreuzweise
	-worthy	-wert, -würdig, -lich	praise**worthy**	lobenswert, löblich
	-y	-ig, -lich	dust**y**	staubig
Nationalität, Ort	**-an**	-isch	Americ**an**	amerikanisch
	-ese	-isch	Japan**ese**	japanisch
	-ian	-(n)isch	Brazil**ian**	brasilianisch
	-ward(s)	-wärts	home**ward**	heimwärts
Gesamtkeit, Kollektivum	**-ary**	-isch	planet**ary**	planetarisch
	-cratic	-kratisch	demo**cratic**	demokratisch
	-ish	-isch	child**ish**	kindisch
	-like	-gleich, -ähnlich, -haft	lady**like**	damenhaft
Steigerung	**-er**	-er (Komparativ)	strong**er**	stärker
	-fold	-fach	ten**fold**	zehnfach

Fachausdrücke

Fachausdrücke

A

Abstraktum (abstract noun)
Substantiv, mit dem etwas Nichtgegenständliches bezeichnet wird; *Begriffswort*

Adjektiv (adjective)
bezeichnet eine Eigenschaft, ein Merkmal; *Eigenschafts-, Wiewort*

Adjektiv, attributives (attributive adjective)
Adjektiv, das beim Substantiv steht

Adjektiv, prädikatives (predicative adjective)
Adjektiv, das mit dem Substantiv durch ein Verb verbunden ist

Adverb (adverb)
bezeichnet die Art und Weise, den Ort oder die Zeit, die Menge, den Grad, die Intensität; *Umstandswort*

Adverb, abgeleitetes (derivative adverb)
von einem Adjektiv abgeleitetes Adverb, das im Englischen auf -ly endet

Adverb, ursprüngliches (original adverb)
hat keine besondere Form

Adverbialsatz (adverbial clause)
Nebensatz anstelle einer adverbialen Bestimmung

Akkusativ (accusative)
der vierte der vier Kasus; *wen-Fall*

Aktiv (active voice)
Handlung, die vom Subjekt durchgeführt wird; *Tatform, Tätigkeitsform* (vgl. Passiv)

Antonym (antonym)
Wort, welches das Gegenteil ausdrückt; *Gegen(satz)wort*

Appelativum
vgl. Gattungsname

Apposition (apposition)
substantivisches Attribut, das meist im gleichen Kasus steht wie das Wort, auf das es sich bezieht; *Beisatz*

Artikel (article)
Begleiter des Substantivs; *Geschlechtswort*

Artikel, bestimmter (definite article)
der, die, das; the

Artikel, unbestimmter (indefinite article)
ein, eine; a, an

Attribut (attribute)
hinzugefügtes Satzglied, das für das Verständnis des Satzes nicht notwendig ist; *Beifügung*

Attributsatz (attributive clause)
Nebensatz anstelle eines Attributs

Aufforderungssatz (imperative clause)
Satz, der eine Aufforderung, einen Befehl ausdrückt

Ausrufesatz (exclamatory clause)
Satz, in dem ein Ausruf ausgedrückt wird

Ausrufewort
vgl. Interjektion

Aussagesatz (clause of statement)
Satz, in dem ein Sachverhalt behauptet oder mitgeteilt wird

B

Bedingungssatz
vgl. Konditionalsatz

Befehlsform
vgl. Imperativ

Begriffswort
vgl. Abstraktum

Beifügung
vgl. Attribut

Beisatz
vgl. Apposition

Bestimmung, adverbiale (adverbial element)
Zeit-, Ortsangaben, Angaben der Art und Weise, des Grundes und der Ursache; *Umstandsbestimmung*

Beugung
vgl. Flexion

Bindewort
vgl. Konjunktion

C

Common case
Substantiv, das im Nominativ steht, also Subjekt ist; *Objektfall* (vgl. possessive case)

Continuous form
Verbform, die den Verlauf, die Kontinuität

Fachausdrücke

bezeichnet (progressive form); vgl. simple form

D

Dativ (dative)
der dritte der vier Kasus, *wem-Fall*

Deklination (declination)
Abwandlung der Form von Substantiven, Artikeln, Pronomen und Adjektiven

Direktes Objekt (direct object)
Satzglied, das im Englischen ohne Präposition an das Verb angeschlossen wird und im Deutschen im Akkusativ steht

Demonstrativpronomen (demonstrative pronoun)
weist auf eine bestimmte Person oder Sache hin; *hinweisendes Fürwort*

Determinativpronomen (determinative pronoun)
weist auf eine folgende Person oder Sache hin; *bestimmendes Fürwort*

Diphthong (diphthong)
Doppellaut, Gleitlaut aus zwei Vokalen

Dingwort
vgl. Substantiv

E

Eigenschaftswort
vgl. Adjektiv

Eigenname (proper noun)
Substantive, die Sachen und Personen bezeichnen, die einmalig sind

Einzahl
vgl. Singular

Entscheidungsfrage (yes-/no-question)
Frage, bei der als Antwort eine Ja-/Nein-Antwort erwartet; *Satzfrage*

Ergänzung, prädikative (predicative complement)
Adjektiv oder Substantiv, das sich auf das Subjekt oder Objekt bezieht

Erlebte Rede (substitutionary narration, interior monologue)
Aussagen einer Person A werden durch eine Person B an eine dritte Person C weitergegeben. Sie ist ein Stilmittel der literarischen Sprache

F

Fall
vgl. Kasus

Femininum (feminine)
das weibliche der drei Genera (Geschlechter)

Finalsatz (final clause)
Nebensatz, der einen Zweck, eine Absicht ausdrückt und durch eine finale Konjunktion eingeleitet wird

Finitum (finite verb)
Verbform, die nach Person, Numerus, Modus und Tempus bestimmt ist; *finite Verbform, Personalform*

Flexion (inflection)
zusammenfassende Bezeichnung für Deklination und Konjugation; *Beugung*

Frage, direkte (direct question)
Frage, die selbst den Hauptsatz bildet

Frage, indirekte (indirect question)
Frage, die in einem Nebensatz, der von einem Verb des Sagens und Denkens eingeleitet wird, eingebettet ist

Fragefürwort
vgl. Interrogativpronomen

Fragesatz (interrogative clause)
Satz, in dem eine Frage formuliert wird

Fragewort (interrogative pronoun)
Wort, mit dem eine Frage eingeleitet wird (z. B. Interrogativpronomen, Adverb)

Fürwort
vgl. Pronomen

Fürwort, besitzanzeigendes
vgl. Possessivpronomen

Fürwort, bestimmendes
vgl. Determinativpronomen

Fürwort, bezügliches
vgl. Relativpronomen

Fürwort, fragendes
vgl. Interrogativpronomen

Fürwort der Gegenseitigkeit

Fachausdrücke

vgl. Reziprokpronomen

Fürwort, hinweisendes
vgl. Demonstrativpronomen

Fürwort, persönliches
vgl. Personalpronomen

Fürwort, rückbezügliches
vgl. Reflexivpronomen

Fürwort, unbestimmtes
vgl. Indefinitpronomen

Futur I
Zeit, die die Zukunft ausdrückt; *unvollendete Zukunft*

Futur II
Zeit, die ausdrückt, dass zu einem bestimmten Zeitpunkt in der Zukunft eine Handlung abgeschlossen sein wird; *vollendete Zukunft*

Future tense
Zeitform zur Bezeichnung von Vorgängen, die von der Gegenwart aus gesehen in der Zukunft liegen

Future perfect
Zeitform zur Bezeichnung von Vorgängen, die an einem Zeitpunkt der Zukunft abgeschlossen sein werden

Future in the past
Zeitform zur Bezeichnung von Vorgängen, die von einem Zeitpunkt der Vergangenheit aus gesehen noch nicht geschehen waren

Future Perfect in the Past
Zeitform zur Bezeichnung von Vorgängen, die von einem Zeitpunkt der Vergangenheit aus gesehen zu einem Zeitpunkt in der Zukunft abgeschlossen sein werden

G

Gattungsname (common noun)
Substantiv, mit dem eine Gattung von Lebewesen oder Dingen bezeichnet wird; *Appellativum*

Gegenstandswort
vgl. Konkretum

Gegenwart
vgl. Präsens

Gegen(satz)wort
vgl. Antonym

Genitiv (genitive)
der zweite der vier Kasus; *wessen-Fall*

Genitivobjekt (genitive object)
Satzteil, der im Genitiv steht

Genus (gender)
das grammatische Geschlecht eines Substantivs, Artikels, Adjektivs oder Pronomens

Gerund (gerund)
Verbform, mit der ein Vorgang ausgedrückt wird, der parallel zu einem anderen abläuft

Geschlecht
vgl. Genus

Geschlechtswort
vgl. Artikel

Gliedsatz
Nebensatz

Grundform
vgl. Infinitiv

Grundstufe
vgl. Positiv

Grundzahl (cardinal number)
eins, zwei, drei, dreißig, hundert etc; *Kardinalzahl*

H

Hauptsatz (main/principal clause)
übergeordneter Teilsatz in einem Satzgefüge, der alleine stehen kann

Hauptwort
vgl. Substantiv

Hilfsverb (auxiliary verb)
Verb, das zur Bildung der zusammengesetzten Zeiten und des Passivs gebraucht wird *(haben, sein, werden;* to be, to have, to do)

Homonym (homonym)
gleich lautendes Wort

I

Imperativ (imperative)
Verbform, die eine Aufforderung, einen Befehl ausdrückt; *Befehlsform*

Imperfekt
vgl. Präteritum

Indefinitpronomen (indefi-

nite pronoun)
Pronomen, das eine unbestimmte Person, Sache bezeichnet; *unbestimmtes Fürwort*

Indikativ (indicative)
Modus, der einen Vorgang, Zustand als tatsächlich darstellt; *Wirklichkeitsform*

Indirekte Rede (indirect/reported speech)
Aussagen einer Person A werden durch eine Person B an eine dritte Person C weitergegeben

Indirektes Objekt (indirect object)
Satzglied, das im Englischen mit to zum Verb tritt und im Deutschen im Dativ steht

Infinitiv (infinitive)
Grund-, Nennform des Verbs

Interjektion (interjection)
Ausrufewort

Interrogativpronomen (interrogative pronoun)
Pronomen, das Fragesätze einleitet; *Fragefürwort*

Intonationsfrage (intonated question)
Frage, in der die Satzmelodie am Satzende nach oben geht

intransitiv (intransitive)
Verben, die kein Objekt nach sich ziehen

Inversionsfrage
Frage, bei der das Subjekt hinter das Prädikat tritt

Irrealis der Gegenwart (unreal present)
die Erfüllung der Bedingung ist unwahrscheinlich

Irrealis der Vergangenheit (unreal past)
die Bedingung bleibt unerfüllt

K

Kardinalzahl (cardinal number)
Grundzahl

Kasus (case)
der Fall, in dem ein deklinierbares Wort steht (Nominativ, Genitiv, Dativ und Akkusativ)

Kausalsatz (causative clause)
Nebensatz, der den Grund, die Ursache ausdrückt

Kollektivum (collective noun)
vgl. Sammelname

Komparation (comparison)
Steigerung (eines Adjektivs oder Adverbs)

Komparativ (comparative)
Steigerungsform eines Adjektivs oder Adverbs, die den ungleichen (höheren) Grad ausdrückt

Kompositum (compound word)
zusammengesetztes Wort

Konditional (conditional)
drückt eine Bedingung aus

Konditionalsatz (conditional clause, if-clause)
Nebensatz, der eine Voraussetzung, Bedingung ausdrückt; *Bedingungssatz*

Kongruenz (agreement)
Übereinstimmung von Satzgliedern in Person, Numerus, Genus und Kasus

Konjugation (conjugation)
Abwandlung der Grundform von Verben; *Beugung*

Konjunktion (conjunction)
Wort, das zur Verbindung von zwei Satzteilen dient; *Bindewort*

Konjunktion, adversative (adversative conjunction)
Konjunktion, die den Gegensatz ausdrückt

Konjunktion, anreihende (copulative conjunction)
Konjunktion zur Verbindung zweier Sätze oder Satzteile

Konjunktion beiordnende (coordinating conjunction)
Konjunktion, die gleichartige Sätze verbindet

Konjunktion finale (final conjunction)
Konjunktion, die eine Absicht, einen Zweck ausdrückt

Konjunktion, kausale (causative conjunction)
Konjunktion, die den

Fachausdrücke

Grund, die Ursache angibt

Konjunktion, konsekutive (consecutive conjunction)
Konjunktion, die die Folge, die Wirkung ausdrückt

Konjunktion, konzessive (concessive conjunction)
Konjunktion, die eine Einräumung, ein Zugeständnis ausdrückt

Konjunktion, konditionale (conditional conjunction)
Konjunktion, die die Bedingung ausdrückt

Konjunktion, modale (modal conjunction)
Konjunktion, die die Begleitumstände, Mittel bezeichnet

Konjunktion, nebenordnende (coordinating conjunction)
Konjunktion, die gleichartige Sätze verbindet (Hauptsatz mit Hauptsatz)

Konjunktion, temporale (temporal conjunction)
Konjunktion, die einen Zeitpunkt, Zeitraum angibt

Konjunktion, unterordnende (subordinating conjunction)
Konjunktion, die Nebensätze einleitet

Konjunktion, vergleichende (comparative conjunction)
Konjunktion, die einen Vergleich ausdrückt

Konjunktiv (subjunctive)
Modus, der einen Vorgang als nicht wirklich darstellt; *Möglichkeitsform*

Konkretum (concrete noun)
Substantiv, mit dem etwas Gegenständliches bezeichnet wird; *Gegenstandswort*

Konsekutivsatz (consecutive clause)
Nebensatz, der die Folge, die Wirkung ausdrückt

Konsonant (consonant)
alle Laute (Buchstaben) (b, c, d etc.) außer den Vokalen; *Mitlaut*

Konzessivsatz (concessive clause)
Nebensatz, der eine Einräumung ausdrückt

L

Leideform
vgl. Passiv

Lehnwort
ein aus einer anderen Sprache «entlehntes» Wort

M

männlich
vgl. maskulin

maskulin (masculine)
das männliche der drei Genera; *männliches Geschlecht*

Mehrzahl
vgl. Plural

Mitlaut
vgl. Konsonant

Mittelwort der Gegenwart
vgl. Partizip Präsens

Mittelwort der Vergangenheit
vgl. Partizip Perfekt

modal
die Art und Weise eines Geschehens bezeichnend

Modalsatz
Nebensatz, der die Mittel, Umstände angibt

Modalverb (modal auxiliary verb)
Verb, das den Inhalt eines anderen Verbs abwandelt und mit dem Infinitiv eines anderen Verbs verbunden ist

Modus (mood)
Aussageweise. Zu den Modi zählen *Indikativ, Imperativ, Konditional* und *Konjunktiv*

Möglichkeitsform
vgl. Konjunktiv

N

Nebensatz (subordinate clause)
untergeordneter Teilsatz in einem Satzgefüge, der nicht alleine stehen kann; *Gliedsatz*

Negation (negation)
Verneinung

Nennform
vgl. Infinitiv

Nennwort

Fachausdrücke

vgl. Substantiv

Neutrum (neuter)
das sächliche der drei Genera; *sächliches Geschlecht*

Nomen
vgl. Substantiv

Nominativ (nominative)
der erste der vier Kasus; *wer-Fall*

Numerale (numerals)
vgl. Zahlwort

Numerus (number)
Singular oder Plural eines Verbs, Substantivs; *(An)Zahl*

O

Objekt (object)
Satzglied, das im Genitiv, Dativ oder Akkusativ steht

Objekt, direktes (direct object)
vgl. direktes Objekt

Objekt, indirektes (indirect object)
vgl. indirektes Objekt

Objekt, präpositionales (prepositional object)
Objekt mit einer Präposition

Objektfall
vgl. common case

Objektsatz (object clause)
Nebensatz anstelle eines Objekts

Ordinalzahl
vgl. Ordnungszahl

Ordinary Form
vgl. simple form

Ordnungszahl (ordinal number)
der erste, der zweite, der dritte etc.; *Ordinalzahl*

P

Partizip (participle)
infinite Verbform, die keine Angaben über Person, Numerus, Modus und Tempus enthält

Partizip Präsens
Partizip, das im Deutschen auf *-end* endet *(z. B. gehend)*; *Mittelwort der Gegenwart*

Partizip Perfekt
abgewandelte Form des Vollverbs, das zur Bildung der zusammengesetzten Zeiten benötigt wird *(gegangen, gesessen)*; *Mittelwort der Vergangenheit*

Passiv (passive voice)
im Passiv wird eine Handlung nicht selbst vom Subjekt ausgeführt (vgl. Aktiv); *Leideform*

Passiv, unpersönliches (impersonal passive)
Passiv, das im Deutschen mit dem grammatischen, unpersönlichen Subjekt *es* und im Englischen mit *it* gebildet wird

Past participle
Verbform, das zur Bildung der zusammengesetzten Zeiten und des Passivs dient

Past perfect
Zeitform, die Vorgänge der Vorvergangenheit bezeichnet

Past tense
Zeitform, die völlig abgeschlossene Vorgänge der Vergangenheit bezeichnet

Perfekt
Zeitform, das den Vollzug, Abschluss eines Vorgangs ausdrückt; *Vorgegenwart, vollendete Gegenwart*

Perfect participle
Verbform anstelle von adverbialen Nebensätzen zum Ausdruck, dass ein Vorgang vor einem anderen stattfand

Personalform
vgl. Finitum

Personalpronomen (personal pronoun)
Pronomen, das eine Person bezeichnet; *persönliches Fürwort*

Personenobjekt (personal object)
das Objekt ist eine Person

Personensubjekt (personal subject)
das Subjekt ist eine Person

Plural (plural)
Mehrzahl eines Wortes
(vgl. Singular)

Fachausdrücke

Plusquamperfekt
Tempus, das den Vollzug, Abschluss eines Vorgangs ausdrückt, bevor eine andere Handlung ausgeführt, abgeschlossen ist; *Vorvergangenheit*

Positiv (positive)
Vergleichsform des Adjektivs oder Adverbs zum Ausdruck des gleichen Grades; *Grundstufe*

Possessive case
bezeichnet den Besitzer; *Besitzfall* (vgl. common case)

Possessivpronomen (possessive pronoun)
Pronomen, das ein Besitzverhältnis bezeichnet; *besitzanzeigendes Fürwort*

Prädikat (predicate)
Verb des Satzes. Es kann aus dem Vollverb oder aus dem Hilfs- und Vollverb bestehen; *Satzaussage*

Präfix (prefix)
Vorsilbe

Present participle
Verbform zur Bildung der continuous form

Present tense
Zeitform, die die Gegenwart bezeichnet

Present perfect
Zeitform zur Bezeichnung von Vorgängen, die von der Vergangenheit bis in die Gegenwart reichen

Progressive form
vgl. continuous form

Präposition (preposition)
bezeichnet die Beziehung, das Verhältnis zwischen Personen, Dingen; *Verhältniswort*

Präsens
Tempus, das den Ablauf eines Vorgangs in der Gegenwart ausdrückt; *Gegenwart*

Präteritum
Tempus, das ausdrückt, dass ein Vorgang abgeschlossen, beendet ist; *1. Vergangenheit*

Pronomen (pronoun)
Begleiter oder Stellvertreter des Substantivs; *Fürwort*

Pronomen, attributives (attributive pronoun)
Pronomen, das nicht ohne Substantiv stehen kann

Pronomen, besitzanzeigendes
vgl. Possessivpronomen

Pronomen, bestimmendes
vgl. Determinativpronomen

Pronomen, bezügliches
vgl. Relativpronomen

Pronomen, fragendes
vgl. Interrogativpronomen

Pronomen, hinweisendes
vgl. Demonstrativpronomen

Pronomen, persönliches
vgl. Personalpronomen

Pronomen, rückbezügliches
vgl. Reflexivpronomen

Pronomen, substantivisches (substantival pronoun)
Pronomen, das ohne Substantiv stehen kann

Pronomen, unbestimmtes
vgl. Indefinitpronomen

R

Realis (real present)
Bedingungssatz, der eine erfüllbare Bedingung ausdrückt

Reflexivpronomen (reflexive pronoun)
Pronomen, das dieselbe Person wie das Subjekt bezeichnet; *rückbezügliches Fürwort*

Relativpronomen (relative pronoun)
Pronomen, das sich auf ein vorausgehendes Substantiv bezieht; *bezügliches Fürwort*

Relativsatz (relative clause)
Nebensatz, der durch ein Relativpronomen eingeleitet wird

Relativsatz, ausmalender (non-defining relative clause)
Relativsatz, der zum Verständnis des Satzes nicht notwendig ist

Relativsatz, notwendiger (defining relative clause)

Fachausdrücke

Relativsatz, der zum Verständnis des Satzes notwendig ist

Reziprokpronomen (reciprocal pronoun)
Pronomen, das die Gegenseitigkeit, Wechselseitigkeit ausdrückt

S

Sachobjekt
Subjekt, das ein Objekt ist

Sachsubjekt
Subjekt, das eine Sache ist

sächlich
vgl. neutrum

Sammelname
Substantiv, das eine Gruppe gleichartiger Lebewesen und Dinge bezeichnet

Satzaussage
vgl. Prädikat

Satzfrage
vgl. Entscheidungsfrage

Satzgefüge (compound sentence)
Satz, der aus mindestens einem Hauptsatz und einem Nebensatz besteht

Sein-Passiv
vgl. Zustandspassiv

Selbstlaut
vgl. Vokal

Semantik (semantics)
Bedeutungslehre

Semasiologie (semasiology)
Wortbedeutungslehre

Semiotik (semiotics)
allgemeine Zeichenlehre

Simple form
Verbform, die keinen Verlauf ausdrückt (ordinary form); vgl. progressive form

Singular (singular)
Einzahl (vgl. Plural)

Steigerung
vgl. Komparation

Stoffname (substantial noun)
Masse- und Materialbezeichnung

Subjekt (subject)
Satzglied im Nominativ, das eine Handlung ausführt (wer tut etwas?)

Subjekt, grammatisches, unbestimmtes (grammatical subject)
Subjekt, das keine Person bezeichnet (es; it)

Subjektfall
vgl. common case

Subjektsatz (subject clause)
Nebensatz anstelle eines Subjekts

Substantiv (noun)
Wort, das ein Lebewesen, eine Pflanze oder einen Gegenstand bezeichnet; Nomen, Nenn-, Ding-, Hauptwort

Substantiv, abgeleitetes (derivative noun)
von einer anderen Wortart (z. B. Verb, Adjektiv etc.) abgeleitetes Substantiv

Substantiv, abgewandeltes (modified noun)
durch ein Suffix oder Präfix abgewandeltes Substantiv

Suffix (suffix)
Nachsilbe

Superlativ (superlative)
Steigerungsform des Adjektivs oder Adverbs, die den höchsten Grad ausdrückt

Synonym (synonym)
(annähernde) Bedeutungsgleichheit von Wörtern

Syntax (syntax)
(Lehre vom) Satzbau

T

Tatform
vgl. Aktiv

Tätigkeitsform
vgl. Aktiv

Tätigkeitswort
vgl. Verb

Temporalsatz (temporal clause)
Nebensatz, der die Zeit ausdrückt

Tempus (Plural: Tempora) (tense)
Zeit(form)

transitiv (transitive)
Verb, das ein direktes Objekt nach sich zieht

Tunwort

Fachausdrücke

vgl. Verb

U

Umlaut
bezeichnet die Vokale
ä, ö, ü

Umstandsbestimmung
vgl. adverbiale Bestimmung

Umstandswort
vgl. Adverb

Ursubstantiv (original noun)
nicht durch ein Suffix oder Präfix abgewandeltes Substantiv

V

Verb (verb)
bezeichnet einen Zustand oder Vorgang, eine Tätigkeit oder Handlung; *Zeit-, Tätigkeits-, Tunwort*

Verb, faktitives (factitive verb)
Verben, die sonst ohne Objekt stehen, können auch mit einem direkten Objekt stehen

Verb, finites (finite verb)
Verbform mit Zeitangabe

Verb, infinites (infinite verb)
Verbform ohne Zeitangabe

Verb, intransitives (intransitive verb)
Verb ohne Objektergänzung

Verb, kausatives (causative verb)
Verben, die sonst ohne Objekt stehen, können auch mit einen direkten Objekt stehen

Verb, reflexives (reflexive verb)
Verb mit einem Reflexivpronomen

Verb, reziprokes (reciprocal verb)
Verb, dessen Pronomen ein wechselseitiges Verhältnis ausdrückt *(einander; gegenseitig)*

Verb, transitives (transitive verb)
Verb mit einem direkten Objekt

Verb, unpersönliches (impersonal verb)
Verb, das nur in der 3. Person Singular verwendet werden kann

Vergangenheit
vgl. Präteritum

Verhältniswort
vgl. Präposition

Verlaufsform
vgl. continuous form

Vervielfältigungszahlwort (multiplying number)
Zahlwort, das angibt, wie oft etwas vorhanden ist

Vokal (vowel)
Laut (Buchstabe) für dessen Aussprache kein anderer Buchstabe benötigt wird. Vokale sind *a, e, i, o* und *u*; *Selbstlaut* (vgl. Mitlaut)

Vollverb (full verb)
Verb, das das Prädikat alleine, ohne Hilfsverb bilden kann

Vorgangspassiv
Passiv, das eine Handlung, einen Vorgang ausdrückt und mit *werden* gebildet wird; *werden-Passiv*

Vorgegenwart
vgl. Perfekt

Vorvergangenheit
vgl. Plusquamperfekt

W

Wemfall
vgl. Dativ

Wenfall
vgl. Akkusativ

Werden-Passiv
vgl. Vorgangspassiv

Werfall
vgl. Nominativ

Wes(sen)fall
vgl. Genitiv

Wiederholungszahlwort
vgl. Vervielfältigungszahlwort

Wiewort
vgl. Adjektiv

Wirklichkeitsform
vgl. Indikativ

Z

Zahladjektiv (numeral adjective)
Adjektiv, das eine Zahl bezeichnet; *Zahlwort*

Zahlwort
Wort, das eine Zahl bezeichnet

Fachausdrücke

Zeichensetzung
vgl. Interpunktion

Zeit, einfache (non-compound tense)
ohne Hilfsverb gebildete Zeit

Zeit, zusammengesetzte (compound tense)
mit einem Hilfsverb gebildete Zeit

Zeitwort
vgl. Verb

Zukunft
vgl. Futur

Zukunft, unvollendete
vgl. Futur I

Zukunft, vollendete
vgl. Futur II

Zustandspassiv
Passiv, das einen Zustand ausdrückt und mit *sein* gebildet wird; *sein-Passiv*

Lösungen

Lösungen

Lösungen zu den Übungen auf Seite 48 – 51

Übung 1

> 3. Pers. Sg. im pres. t. + -s, Hilfsverb in der 3. Pers. Sg. im pres. perf. ist has

	Infinitive	Present Tense	Past Tense	Present Perfect	Past Perfect
1.	to have	he has	he had	he has had	he had had
2.	to be	I am	I was	I have been	I had been
3.	to do	he does	he did	he has done	he had done
4.	to help	he helps	he helped	he has helped	he had helped
5.	to love	he loves	he loved	he has loved	he had loved
6.	to stop	he stops	he stopped	he has stopped	he had stopped
7.	to cry	he cries	he cried	he has cried	he had cried
8.	to die	he dies	he died	he has died	he had died
9.	to put	he puts	he put	he has put	he had put
10.	to hear	he hears	he heard	he has heard	he had heard
11.	to mean	I mean	I meant	I have meant	I had meant
12.	to meet	he meets	he met	he has met	he had met
13.	to keep	I keep	I kept	I have kept	I had kept
14.	to get	he gets	he got	he has got	he had got
15.	to forget	he forgets	he forgot	he has forgotten	he had forgotten
16.	to sit	he sits	he sat	he has sat	he had sat
17.	to say	he says	he said	he has said	he had said
18.	to begin	he begins	he began	he has begun	he had begun
19.	to run	he runs	he ran	he has run	he had run
20.	to make	he makes	he made	he has made	he had made

> pres. t. (he puts) und past t. (he put) nicht verwechseln

Lösungen

	Future I	Future II	Con. I	Con. II	Cont. Form
	he will have	he will have had	he would have	he would have had	having
	I will be	I will have been	I would be	I would have been	being
	he will do	he will have done	he would do	he would have done	doing
	he will help	he will have helped	he would help	he would have helped	helping
	he will love	he will have loved	he would love	he would have loved	loving
	he will stop	he will have stopped	he would stop	he would have stopped	stopping
	he will cry	he will have cried	he would cry	he would have cried	crying
	he will die	he will have died	he would die	he would have died	dying
	he will put	he will have put	he would put	he would have put	putting
	he will hear	he will have heard	he would hear	he would have heard	hearing
	I will mean	I will have meant	I would mean	I would have meant	meaning
	he will meet	he will have met	he would meet	he would have met	meeting
	I will keep	I will have kept	I would keep	I would have kept	keeping
	he will get	he will have got	he would get	he would have got	getting
	he will forget	he will have forgotten	he would forget	he would have forgotten	forgetting
	he will sit	he will have sat	he would sit	he would have sat	sitting
	he will say	he will have said	he would say	he would have said	saying
	he will begin	he will have begun	he would begin	he would have begun	beginning
	he will run	he will have run	he would run	he would have run	running
	he will make	he will have made	he would make	he would have made	making

! Besonderheiten in den Verbformen sind auch bei den folgenden Übungen blau gedruckt

Lösungen

Infinitive	Present Tense	Past Tense	Present Perfect	Past Perfect
21. to come	he comes	he came	he has come	he had come
22. to find	he finds	he found	he has found	he had found
23. to think	you think	you thought	you have thought	you had thought
24. to buy	he buys	he bought	he has bought	he had bought
25. to take	he takes	he took	he has taken	he had taken
26. to stand	I stand	I stood	I have stood	I had stood
27. to write	he writes	he wrote	he has written	he had written
28. to speak	he speaks	he spoke	he has spoken	he had spoken
29. to tell	he tells	he told	he has told	he had told
30. to eat	he eats	he ate	he has eaten	he had eaten
31. to show	we show	we showed	we have shown	we had shown
32. to know	he knows	he knew	he has known	he had known
33. to see	he sees	he saw	he has seen	he had seen
34. to go	he goes	he went	he has gone	he had gone
35. to lie	he lies	he lied	he has lied	he had lied
36. to lay	I lay	I laid	I have laid	I had laid
37. to fall	he falls	he fell	he has fallen	he had fallen
38. to choose	he chooses	he chose	he has chosen	he had chosen
39. to lose	he loses	he lost	he has lost	he had lost

Lösungen

Future I	Future II	Con. I	Con. II	Cont. Form
he will come	he will have come	he would come	he would have come	coming
he will find	he will have found	he would find	he would have found	finding
you will think	you will have thought	you would think	you would have thought	thinking
he will buy	he will have bought	he would buy	he would have bought	buying
he will take	he will have taken	he would take	he would have taken	taking
I will stand	I will have stood	I would stand	I would have stood	standing
he will write	he will have written	he would write	he would have written	writing
he will speak	he will have spoken	he would speak	he would have spoken	speaking
he will tell	he will have told	he would tell	he would have told	telling
he will eat	he will have eaten	he would eat	he would have eaten	eating
we will show	we will have shown	we would show	we would have shown	showing
he will know	he will have known	he would know	he would have known	knowing
he will see	he will have seen	he would see	he would have seen	seeing
he will go	he will have gone	he would go	he would have gone	going
he will lie	he will have lied	he would lie	he would have lied	lying
I will lay	I will have laid	I would lay	I would have laid	laying
he will fall	he will have fallen	he would fall	he would have fallen	falling
he will choose	he will have chosen	he would choose	he would have chosen	choosing
he will lose	he will have lost	he would lose	he would have lost	losing

Lösungen

Lösungen zu den Übungen auf Seite 58 – 62

Übung 1

1. does not/doesn't like 2. Don't do 3. didn't explain 4. do not/don't think 5. did not/didn't have 6. did not/didn't do 7. does not/doesn't make 8. did not/didn't obey 9. Do not/don't say 10. did not/didn't send

> did bzw. didn't muss mit dem Infinitiv stehen, also send nicht sent

Übung 2

1. had not/hadn't left 2. has not/hasn't forgotten 3. has not/hasn't had 4. am not/'m not allowed 5. am not/'m not fond of 6. would not/wouldn't like 7. could not/couldn't remember 8. had not/hadn't waited 9. may not have been 10. were not/weren't

Übung 3

1. do not/don't show 2. do not/don't seem 3. has not/hasn't been solved 4. are not/aren't doing 5. are not/aren't allowed 6. have not/haven't been 7. were not/weren't 8. cannot/can't tell 9. could not/couldn't hear 10. might not/mightn't be

Übung 4

1. Do drivers have to give 2. Do drivers have to have 3. Did he do it 4. Did he get 5. Does he know 6. Did he really have 7. Did he really say 8. Did he send 9. Did she get 10. Does she want 11. Does the translation do 12. Did they have 13. Did they receive 14. Does this little bag have to be weighed 15. Does your brother like

> did bzw. didn't muss mit dem Infinitiv stehen, also send nicht sent

Übung 5

1. Had he been 2. Is he getting on 3. Was he 4. Was he wanted 5. Would he do 6. Shall I make 7. Has it stopped 8. Is it necessary 9. Had Linda gone 10. Is she hurt 11. Would that be 12. Has the new rocket been tested sufficiently 13. Were they 14. Can we go 15. Shall we have

Übung 6

1. Did Columbus discover 2. Has he asked 3. Might he have had 4. Was Mike's business 5. Hadn't she been 6. Have the gang been caught 7. Hasn't/has the matter yet been put 8. Hasn't/has the present owner got 9. Didn't they pay/did they pay 10. Do they serve

Übung 7

1. What did Bob do 2. Who discovered 3. How did he do 4. Who gave 5. Whom did he suspect 6. When does he usually get up 7. What irritated her 8. Who left 9. Who married Mr W. 10. Which of the boys broke

Übung 8

> Präpositionen müssen erhalten bleiben

1. Who must be sent for 2. Where can he get 3. What had he been arrested for 4. Why has he come back 5. When was he born 6. What was he doing 7. What was he promising 8. Where will he go 9. What is she accusing him of 10. What will Sheila be having

Lösungen

Übung 9

1. What has been made 2. When does he do 3. Who has to be blamed 4. What made her realize 5. What does mother need 6. What do people have to have 7. How could she have acted 8. Who helps him 9. Who has got 10. Where did she ask him to come

> Fragewort what gilt als 3. Pers. Sing., daher steht has und nicht have

Lösungen zu den Übungen auf Seite 83 – 85

Übung 1

1. Can 2. can/could 3. to be able to 4. could 5. be able to 6. could 7. cannot 8. could 9. could 10. cannot 11. could 12. can 13. could 14. being able 15. be able

> auf would (Modalverb) folgt der Infinitiv (to be able to) ohne to
> auf hurt (past t.), folgt could, auf hurts (pres. t.) folgt can
> cannot wird zusammengeschrieben

Übung 2

1. could 2. can 3. are allowed/permitted to 4. can/may 5. are not allowed/permitted to 6. may 7. could/might 8. cannot 9. may/might 10. could/might

Übung 3

1. Do drivers have to 2. have to/had to 3. has to 4. need 5. must 6. must/have to 7. must/has to 8. must 9. must 10. need

Übung 4

1. should/ought to 2. ought to/should 3. are supposed to 4. should/ought to 5. should/ought not be spoken 6. should 7. should 8. are supposed to 9. should 10. are supposed to

> verneintes ought ohne to

Übung 5

1. are you supposed to 2. was supposed to/was to 3. should 4. wants us to 5. want me to 6. should 7. want you to 8. should, are to 9. is to 10. were to

Lösungen zu den Übungen auf Seite 90 – 91

Übung 1

1. myself, themselves 2. yourself/yourselves 3. himself 4. herself 5. ourselves 6. itself 7. itself 8. himself 9. himself 10. oneself

Übung 2

1. everybody 2. ourselves 3. himself 4. your face 5. this criminal 6. themselves 7. the tigers 8. yourself 9. yourself 10. messages 11. her 12. themselves 13. - 14. yourself 15. himself 16. his next letter 17. the dish 18. yourselves 19. you 20. myself

Lösungen

Übung 3

1. imagine 2. care for 3. remember 4. wondered 5. has changed 6. complains of 7. join 8. looking forward to 9. rely on 10. afford

Lösungen zu den Übungen auf Seite 97 – 98

Übung 1

1. to 2. - 3. to 4. - 5. - 6. - 7. to 8. - 9. to 10. to 11. - 12. to 13. - 14. - 15. to 16. - 17. - 18. - 19. to 20. to 21. to 22. - 23. - 24. to 25. to

Lösungen zu den Übungen auf Seite 110 – 114

Übung 1

> 3. Pers. Sing. endet auf -s bzw. -es nach -ch, -sh

1. cries 2. plays 3. lies 4. catches 5. wash 6. possesses 7. reaches 8. enjoys 9. distinguishes 10. establishes

Übung 2

1. enjoyed 2. hated 3. burst 4. sent 5. buried 6. played 7. read [red] 8. controlled 9. studied 10. obeyed, possessed

Übung 3

> has in der 3. Pers. Sing. nicht have

1. has dropped 2. has hit 3. has built 4. have tried 5. have died 6. has had 7. has slipped 8. have put 9. has developed 10. have sprung

Übung 4

1. had liked 2. had stopped 3. had travelled (BE), had traveled (AE) 4. had happened 5. had hurt 6. had made 7. had seen 8. had stayed 9. had forgotten 10. had got

Übung 5

1. will teach 2. will continue 3. will produce 4. will let 5. will give 6. will live 7. will prove 8. will admit 9. will suffer 10. will catch

Übung 6

1. will have finished 2. will have disappeared 3. will have forgotten 4. will have chosen 5. will have heard

Übung 7

1. have known 2. have never changed 3. spent 4. left 5. have not/haven't replied 6. prepared 7. has changed, arrived 8. made 9. have been married 10. ruled, learnt/learned

Übung 8

1. came, had left 2. had met, was 3. had named, could 4. burst, had told 5. gave, had happened 6. put, had stuck 7. did not/didn't know, had made 8. had just finished, found, had forgotten 9. had moved, had 10. heard, had had

Übung 9

1. Are you coming 2. am 3. is playing 4. am flying 5. will make 6. will enjoy 7. will like 8. will come, will believe 9. is leaving 10. will move/are going to move

Lösungen zu den Übungen auf Seite 119 – 122

Übung 1

1. is carrying 2. are saying 3. are lying 4. is blaming 5. is slipping 6. is happening 7. is obeying 8. is living 9. is getting 10. is running

Übung 2

1. was staying 2. were dying 3. was lying 4. was listening 5. were riding 6. was breathing 7. was playing 8. were fitting 9. was stirring up 10. was getting

Übung 3

1. has been writing 2. have been taking place 3. have been rising 4. has been promoting 5. have been sitting

Übung 4

1. had been going 2. had been knitting 3. had been worrying 4. had been tapping 5. had been lying

Übung 5

1. was rising, were getting 2. jumped, tried 3. worked 4. was staying 5. stayed 6. were playing, were sitting, were drinking 7. asked, tried 8. led, was playing 9. left, returned 10. are talking 11. was waiting 12. heard, changed 13. were having, was talking 14. felt, tried 15. reached, was lying, sat up 16. are talking 17. continued 18. sank, revived 19. were lit 20. was steering, were going, was looking

Übung 6

1. is repairing 2. am flying 3. was walking 4. has been sleeping 5. has been speaking 6. did not know, had been looking 7. loves, loves 8. married, started 9. is growing 10. have been doing

Lösungen zu den Übungen auf Seite 130 – 136

Übung 1

Lösungen

> Partizip von bear (tragen) endet auf -e

1. is occupied 2. is laid out 3. is estimated. 4. is put 5. are sent 6. are required 7. are bound 8. are built 9. are born 10. are borne

Übung 2

> news ist Singular, daher was

1. were destroyed 2. was promised 3. was admitted 4. was hit 5. was shot 6. was hurt 7. was left 8. was she taken, was taken 9. was worked out thoroughly and carefully, was judged 10. was received

Übung 3

> Subjekt ist financial position, daher has

1. have been carried 2. has been said 3. have been admitted 4. has been improved 5. have been built 6. has been told 7. have been spent 8. has been divided 9. has often been accompanied 10. have been used

Übung 4

1. had been served 2. had been done 3. had been invented, had been built 4. had been destroyed 5. had been sent 6. had been seen 7. had been emptied 8. had been conferred 9. had been taken 10. had been committed

Übung 5

1. will be carried out 2. will be proposed 3. will be held 4. will be hurt 5. will be required 6. will be sent 7. will be given 8. will be met 9. will be made 10. will be cut off

Übung 6

1. is being built 2. is being taught 3. is being urbanized 4. is being driven 5. is being spoken

Übung 7

1. was being tossed 2. was being said 3. was being looked for 4. were being brought 5. was being waited for

Übung 8

1. The trainer's orders were obeyed by the whole team without any protest 2. Concerts are regularly given by several first-class orchestras in London 3. He will be taken there by the afternoon train on Wednesday 4. The Justices of the Peace are advised by Clerks on points of law 5. New industrial estates were planned around the city. 6. Susan was told to come too, and she was the first to arrive. 7. Everything will be done (by us) to make your flight comfortable 8. The table had been set on the terrace for three. 9. Radioactive pollutants will be found on the earth's surface for generations. 10. She will be joined by her sister. 11. Great efforts are being made (by us) to ensure that poor people are helped 12. Do not enter the studio, a play for today's programme is being filmed (by us). 13. Bob had the feeling that he was being followed (by somebody). 14. If I hadn't fled and changed my name, I would have been put into prison (by them). 15. You will be met by a friend there.

Lösungen

Übung 9

1. The letter was addressed to Mr Harrison. 2. I was recommended another doctor. 3. Here vagabonds are offered warm food and dry beds. 4. On Christmas Day, 1066, William the Conqueror was crowned King of England in Westminster Abbey. 5. There you will be given all the instructions you need. 6. He is allowed five pounds pocket money a week. 7. The event was announced to everybody. 8. He was considered a prudent man. 9. She was granted a small pension. 10. George Washington was made the first President of the United States of America. 11. A reward was promised to anyone who would write a good article for the school magazine. 12. He was saved a lot of trouble. 13. We shall be asked several questions. 14. He was shown all the books. 15. He will be appointed director general. 16. The computer was explained to us by a top-level expert. 17. At the airport duty-free cigarettes can be bought by passengers and during the flight the may be served dinner or a snack by the attendants. 18. At today's press conference at the Yard the journalists were handed photographs of the stolen paintings. 19. I hope he will be spared this ordeal. 20. In general the Bachelor's degree is given to students who pass examinations at the end of three or four years of study.

Übung 10

1. This question has been dealt with by an expert. 2. He has not been heard of since. 3. He has always been laughed at. 4. He was listened to with pleasure. 5. When Mrs Brown came home from hospital, she found that the cat had been looked after. 6. He was looked upon as a wise man. 7. The solution was arrived at by chance. 8. People have often been discriminated against because of race, religion, or colour. 9. Has any decision been come to? 10. Nothing seems to have been disarranged and the drawers have not been interfered with. 11. My hat has been sat on. 12. The bed has been slept in. 13. They forgot their quarrels on seeing that their rights were infringed upon. 14. Amongst all this terrible poverty there were a few big beautiful houses which were lived in by rich men. 15. Oxford abounds in beauty, but it is a hidden beauty that must be sought for.

Präpositionen müssen erhalten bleiben

nobody im Aktiv wird im Passiv durch ein verneintes Verb ausgedrückt

Übung 11

1. More than 800 million people speak English. 2. Bob checked in at the hotel Miramare which some Americans had recommended to him. 3. They closed that part of the road for resurfacing. 4. They have carried through several reforms in recent years. 5. He had run away at seventeen but they had brought him back. 6. I will finish my business in a few hours. 7. They gave him another 1,500 dollars. 8. They had dealt with the matter long ago. 9. You needn't look after boys and girls of 16 all the time. 10. We use disposable dishware for everyday occasions. 11. A judge presides over the court, but a jury makes the decision on guilt or innocence. 12. They warned the public of the dangers of drinking. 13. Somebody is following us. 14. They were doing something. 15. Some women with small children would like to work, if somebody could care for the children during the mothers' working hours. 16. They hoped that the Health Service would improve health in general. 17. It is a shame that they should have treated him like that. 18. They are turning the simple tasks over to the machines. 19. What are they doing about the situation? 20. I don't want you to see me off.

Lösungen zu den Übungen auf Seite 148 – 157

Lösungen

Übung 1

1. was 2. needed 3. didn't/did not need 4. made, were 5. was going 6. swore, was 7. were to integrate 8. were to 9. happened, wanted 10. did not/didn't use, liked

Übung 2

1. hadn't/had not done 2. had been 3. had not/hadn't been 4. had still been 5. had had 6. had died 7. had been, had seen, had given 8. had had 9. had taken, 10. had understood

Übung 3

1. had just left 2. had torn 3. had been 4. had not/hadn't found 5. had been 6. had been 7. had been given 8. had had 9. had just been requested 10. had done

Übung 4

1. had guaranteed 2. had been collected 3. had been 4. had been 5. had been killed 6. had failed 7. had seen 8. had been led astray 9. had been 10. had beaten

Übung 5

1. would be 2. would make 3. wouldn't/would not drink 4. would never end 5. would have come 6. wouldn't/would not like 7. would like 8. would be 9. would have 10. would have

Übung 6

1. couldn't find 2. couldn't do 3. might be 4. might have 5. ought to 6. might be 7. must be 8. should be 9. had to 10. were to, would be

Übung 7

1. I/we 2. he/they 3. you 4. you 5. he/they 6. we/I 7. he/they 8. he/they 9. I/we/you 10. we 11. he/they 12. you 13. they 14. they/he 15. you

Übung 8

1. that day 2. the day before/the previous day 3. two days before 4. the next/following day 5. the following week 6. the week before/the previous week 7. before 8. then 9. there 10. there, that night, then

Übung 9

1. I said that I thought he was wrong. 2. He said that Andrew Johnson was innocent. 3. You said that she didn't admit anything. 4. They said that this would have only negative consequences. 5. The Speaker said that it was time to go on to the next question. 6. The doctors said that he had been dead at least twelve hours. 7. We said that the burglar had entered the garden from the back. 8. He said that there had been no risk of an accident. 9. The captain said that it had been no use arguing with the angry crew. 10. They said that they would arrange to have a conference to settle the matter. 11. He told us that he would receive the

Lösungen

Burtons on Sunday out of doors and give them tea in the garden. 12. He said that between them these two moves would lay a basis for future cooperation. 13. They said that man's lot could not be further improved by more material progress. 14. She said that there should be a redistribution of the male and female roles in society. 15. I said that before taking a decision he ought to make thorough enquiries.

Übung 10

1. I wanted to ask you whether/if you had got any razor blades. 2. He asked whether/if I could bring Carol over for a drink around five o'clock. 3. Our teacher asked us whether/if we would like to form a pen-club. 4. I wondered whether/if he would make it. 5. I wondered whether/if I should ever have time to see London. 6. I wondered whether/if you would like to come to our house and see the President from our balcony. 7. The Clerk read the indictment and asked the prisoner whether/if he was guilty or not guilty. 8. A group of scientists put their heads together to decide whether/if animals thought/think or not. 9. He wondered whether/if he would ever get married. 10. He wondered whether/if there was a microphone hidden nearb<. 11. I wondered whether/if there was anything I had left undone. 12. My wife asked me whether/if I had happened to see her passport lying about. 13. At the end of every debate the Speaker put the question whether/if we/they would accept the motion that had been debated or not. 14. The Government decided to put to the people the question whether/if Britain should remain within the E.C. or not. 15. The shop keeper asked whether/if there was anything he could do for me.

Übung 11

1. I wondered why Mike hadn't turned up yet. 2. I wondered how often the old lady left her house. 3. I wondered why he didn't come. 4. I wondered what Gerald and Caroline were doing. 5. I wondered whose dog this was. 6. He wondered what they had done to the woman in the yard. 7. The king wondered what he might give the queen for her birthday. 8. They asked what people had done with their leisure before there had been television. 9. Now that he has been in America for three years, I asked him what his first impression had been. 10. The theft made him ask again what happened to stolen paintings. 11. She used to ask herself how a teacher should try to gain the positive interest of unco-operative pupils. 12. The police were wondering where the hell he went to. 13. As he was watching a gang of workmen putting in long pipes, he began to wonder what this was all about. 14. I wondered why he had had that idea. 15. I was always asking him how he spent his time.

past tense von spend lautet spent

Übung 12

1. He demanded that I/we/they/he/you write neatly. 2. He suggested that I try the examination again. 3. The officer demanded that I/we/they/he/you lower the flag. 4. They were told to lie on the grass and not to look up at any cost. 5. They told me to go to the information desk. 6. I told them not to forget to lock the door. 7. His wife told him not to drive too fast. 8. His mother told them not to be greedy. 9. My father said that we should go up to the restaurant to have a good look at the planes taking off. 10. I told him not to worry about having failed.

Lösungen

Lösungen zu den Übungen auf Seite 162 – 164

Übung 1

1. will kill 2. will have 3. will not/won't be found 4. will you do 5. pulls 6. does not/doesn't behave 7. rains 8. can't/cannot 9. can 10. does not/doesn't like 11. will soon be able to 12. will be 13. will be 14. will be 15. will not/won't answer

Übung 2

1. left 2. called 3. were 4. had 5. did not/didn't mention 6. would come 7. would be 8. stung 9. could 10. stayed 11. were 12. were not/weren't given 13. would not/wouldn't be used 14. would be likely to 15. had

Übung 3

1. would have run away or caught 2. would not/wouldn't have gone back 3. had not/hadn't tried 4. had not/hadn't carried 5. had not/hadn't hit 6. had not/hadn't held 7. would Mr Palmer have taken 8. would have been 9. would have had 10. would have had 11. had bought 12. had been 13. could have moved 14. would he have said 15. would most certainly have died

Übung 4

1. rains, will be 2. will be, do not/don't cease 3. would like, could be cared for 4. would you choose, were 5. had not/hadn't gone back, would not/wouldn't have caught 6. had known, would never have taken 7. will be exhausted, are preserved 8. continue, will add 9. were, would spend 10. is to, will have to be

Lösungen zu den Übungen auf Seite 178 – 182

Übung 1

1. to 2. - 3. - 4. - 5. - 6. - 7. - 8. - 9. - 10. - 11. - 12. to 13. - 14. - 15. -, to

Übung 2

1. The suitcase is too heavy (for me) to carry. 2. The coffee is too hot (for me) to drink. 3. He was quick to follow their advice. 4. I think you were right to tell us. 5. You are very kind not to tell him. 6. She was naughty to pull the kitten's tail. 7. The opportunity is too favourable (for us) to miss. 8. He is sure to succeed. 9. He racked his brain for something sensible to say. 10. The text is too difficult (for me) to understand.

Übung 3

1. I want you to say something. 2. Would you prefer me to help you. 3. Peter wants you to go home now. 4. He wanted me to leave in the morning. 5. The unemployment rate was over 12.5 % this spring. We hope to reduce it to 11 % in the autumn. 6. People think Mr Templeton to have been a very cautious man all his life. 7. I should hate you to have to ask him a favour. 8. The natives of these islands are

said to be cannibals. 9. She was believed to have lied. 10. She bought a small camera to take pictures with. 11. He hasn't got a chair to sit on. 12. There's a table to write on.13. This is a depressing message to send to you and I regret it. 14. Mrs Miller was the first to discover the broken window. 15. Peter was the next to arrive at the bottom of the hill. 16. Peter was the only one to return to the hotel. 17. It was the best thing to do. 18. She didn't really mind having no friends to play with. 19. He is not an easy man to get along with. 20. I have nine TV channels to choose from, but I usually watch sport. 21. The millionth guestworker to enter the country was given an honorary welcome in front of the press. 22. To the American, whose country is so huge, a few hundred miles are no impediment to speak of. 23. Without TV people would not know what to do in their spare time.

Übung 4

1. to be handled 2. to be kept 3. to be impressed 4. to be divided 5. to be trusted 6. to be seen 7. to be put off 8. to be taken account of 9. to be doubted 10. to be called

Übung 5

1. to be disturbed 2. to have 3. to notice 4. to make 5. to be found 6. to be watered 7. to come 8. to be blamed 9. to get 10. to go

Übung 6

1. to have got 2. to have known 3. to have left 4. to have lost 5. To have made 6. to have seen 7. to have done 8. to have heard 9. to have had 10. to have survived

Übung 7

1. to have been deprived 2. to have been disarranged 3. To have been educated 4. to have been founded 5. to have been visited

Übung 8

1. to displease, ich bedaure, Ihr Missfallen zu erregen, mein Herr; to have displeased; ich bedaure, Ihr Missfallen erregt zu haben, mein Herr. 2. to grow, die Sonne schien heißer zu werden; to have grown, die Sonne schien heißer geworden zu sein. 3. to keep, ich bedaure, Sie warten zu lassen, to have kept, ich bedaure, Sie warten gelassen zu haben. 4. to lose, wir scheinen etwas zu verlieren; to have lost, wir scheinen etwas verloren zu haben. 5. to say, sie sollte das nicht sagen; to have said, sie hätte das nicht sagen sollen. 6. to see, ich würde es gern sehen; to have seen, ich hätte es gern gesehen. 7. to trust, wir sollten ihm vertrauen, to have trusted, wir hätten ihm vertrauen sollen. 8. to understand, ich gab vor sie nicht zu verstehen, to have understood, ich gab vor, sie nicht verstanden zu haben. 9. to do, sie scheinen die Arbeit ziemlich gut zu machen, to have done, sie scheinen die Arbeit ziemlich gut gemacht zu haben. 10. to have, die Eltern waren froh ihr Kind gesund zurückzubekommen; to have had, die Eltern waren froh ihr Kind gesund zurückbekommen zu haben

Lösungen

Lösungen zu den Übungen auf Seite 189 – 193

Übung 1

1. doing 2. laughing 3. washing up 4. travelling, flying 5. going 6. being 7. asking 8. seeing 9. laughing 10. waiting 11. trying 12. getting 13. settling 14. propelling 15. convincing

Übung 2

1. After defeating/having defeated the Norwegians at Stamford Bridge 2. before going to court 3. in spite of feeling bad 4. from sitting in the sun 5. In spite of having a cold 6. In spite of trusting you 7. for stealing 8. for being disobedient 9. instead of standing there criticising 10. without making friends again

Übung 3

1. knitting/to knit 2. learning/to learn 3. interfering/to interfere 4. working/to work 5. staying/to stay 6. leaving/to leave 7. to post 8. going 9. to say 10. crying 11. reading/to read 12. watching, attending 13. watering 14. asking 15. objecting

Übung 4

1. you/your coming 2. me/my eating 3. you/your going 4. me/my leaving 5. you/your returning 6. her mother being 7. you/your interrupting 8. him/his posting 9. you/your smoking 10. you/your being

Übung 5

1. being misunderstood 2. being seen 3. being stared at 4. being treated 5. being discovered 6. being welcomed 7. being captured, being recaptured 8. being followed 9. being known 10. being laughed at

Übung 6

1. answering 2. laughing 3. swimming 4. being deceived 5. speaking 6. being appointed 7. seeing 8. being bound 9. being erased 10. being overheard

Übung 7

1. having done 2. having eaten 3. having left 4. having saved 5. having seen 6. having studied 7. having failed 8. having given up 9. Having appointed 10. having known

Übung 8

1. having been elected 2. having been recognized 3. having been robbed 4. having been sentenced

Übung 9

1. troubling/having troubled 2. reading/having read 3. having seen 4. finding 5. reaching/

Lösungen

having reached 6. trying/having tried 7. having/havin had 8. accepting/having accepted 9. speaking to 10. sending

Lösungen zu den Übungen auf Seite 200 – 203

Übung 1

1. whistling 2. sitting 3. running down 4. encouraging 5. lying 6. saying 7. listening 8. twisting 9. watching 10. starving

Übung 2

1. while watching TV 2. Although being rich 3. hurrying along 4. while attending a theatre in Washington 5. When entering the house 6. living in the fifty biggest metropolitan areas 7. Coming home 8. While packing a suitcase 9. Looking up 10. While waiting in the rain

Übung 3

1. depressed 2. injured 3. lost 4. relieved 5. occupied 6. petrified 7. seated 8. discouraged 9. pleased 10. rejected

Übung 4

1. as practised in England today 2. If posted at once 3. When focused to a sharp point at very close range 4. as if turned to stone 5. Determined to earn her own living 6. when compelled 7. founded by William the Conqueror 8. bought for 25 dollars from the Indians in 1626 9. compared with the other dangers 10. Unless forced to return

Übung 5

1. talking 2. hunched 3. exciting 4. pleased. 5. disappointed 6. inviting 7. excited 8. depressed. 9. depressing 10. increased, decreased

Übung 6

1. Having worked 2. Having lost 3. Having finished 4. If having your car repaired 5. Having been betrayed (passive voice)

Übung 7

1. being done 2. being said 3. being waited for 4. being watched 5. being taken down

Übung 8

1. watching 2. singing 3. running 4. being looked at 5. having

Lösungen

Übung 9

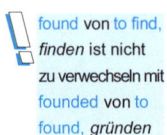

(Randnotiz: found von to find, finden ist nicht zu verwechseln mit founded von to found, gründen)

1. having been found 2. having been founded 3. having been settled 4. Having been bitten 5. Having been brought up

Lösungen zu den Übungen auf Seite 206 – 208

Übung 1

1. had my hair cut 2. has the windows cleaned 3. am having my car washed 4. had had my car washed 5. will have my car washed 6. has had her hair dyed 7. have our house redecorated 8. must have another picture taken 9. have to have your name entered 10. may have his eyes tested

Übung 2

1. let me hear 2. had let her cigarette go out 3. let me have 4. don't let him get away 5. will let you do 6. Has your father ever let you drive 7. would let her know 8. would not have let him go home alone 9. to let her go 10. let oneself worry

Übung 3

(Randnotiz: 3. Pers. Sing. im pres. t. erhält ein -s)

1. made the children get up 2. make Simon come back 3. makes the students think 4. made Consul Carrington write 5. would make you laugh

Übung 4

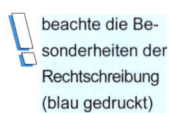

(Randnotiz: beachte die Besonderheiten der Rechtschreibung (blau gedruckt))

1. leave everything lying about 2. left me wondering 3. left them discussing 4. Leave them playing 5. Had Ben kept her waiting

Übung 5

1. allow him to go 2. allow her to lead 3. would allow him to talk 4. allow him to call 5. allow local communities to impose

Übung 6

1. have not had my car washed 2. was having my car washed 3. Let me show 4. leave the wounded soldiers lie 5. let our hair grow 6. had strong castles built 7. did you have your hair cut 8. will let me know 9. Don't let the dog run free 10. Don't let the others see

Lösungen zu den Übungen auf Seite 224 – 227

Übung 1

1. -/The, - 2. The, the, the 3. - 4. The 5. - 6. -, the 7. -, - 8. - 9. the, the 10. - 11. -, - 12. an 13. the, the 14. an 15. an 16. the 17. - 18. the 19. - 20. the, the

Lösungen

Übung 2

1. The/- 2. The, the 3. The 4. -, -, - 5. -, - 6. The 7. -, the 8. the, -, -, - 9. the, - 10. -, -, -, -, -, - 11. - 12. the 13. an 14. the 15. - 16. - 17. the, -, -, -, -, the 18. -, -, -, the 19. -, -, - 20. -

Übung 3

1. - 2. The 3. -/the 4. -/the 5. - 6. the 7. - 8. - 9. - 10. - 11. the 12. - 13. the, the 14. - 15. -/the

Übung 4

1. the 2. the 3. the 4. my 5. your 6. the 7. their 8. the 9. its 10. his, his

Lösungen zu den Übungen auf Seite 229

Übung 1

1. close a friend 2. good a dish 3. half an hour 4. important a question 5. quite a relief 6. terrible a prospect 7. twice a week 8. quite a possibility 9. small a reward 10. twice the acreage

Lösungen zu den Übungen auf Seite 237

Übung 1

1. its/her 2. its/her 3. it 4. his 5. her 6. He 7. it, it 8. he 9. she 10. its/her 11. its/her 12. its 13. it 14. its 15. his

Lösungen zu den Übungen auf Seite 250 – 251

Übung 1

1. boxes 2. buffaloes 3. churches 4. crises 5. difficulties 6. journeys 7. lives 8. roofs 9. studios 10. successes 11. wishes 12. ties 13. taxes 14. ghettos 15. axes

Besonderheiten der Rechtschreibung, S. 30, 386

Übung 2

1. is/are 2. is 3. are 4. are 5. is 6. is 7. is 8. are 9. are 10. is 11. are/is 12. are 13. is 14. are 15. is

Lösungen zu den Übungen auf Seite 257 – 258

Übung 1

Lösungen

1. children's 2. Jenny's 3. father's 4. St. James'/St. James's 5. parents' 6. boys' 7. women's 8. Mrs Stevens'/Mrs Stevens's 9. gentlemen's 10. Smith's

Übung 2

1. bottle of wine 2. hundred pounds 3. Mrs Stevens's husband 4. chairman of the House of Commons 5. Britain's universities 6. City of Boston 7. St Paul's 8. River Thine, River Thames 9. father 10. baker's 11. Woolworth's 12. a hundred years, Australia's chief customer 13. everybody's family secrets 14. Empress of India 15. three months' period

Lösungen zu den Übungen auf Seite 264

Übung 1

1. cheaper, easier 2. paler 3. more difficult 4. bigger, larger, noisier, madder, more fascinating 5. poorer or richer 6. more massive, bigger 7. earlier 8. more varied 9. quieter 10. simplest, least

Lösungen zu den Übungen auf Seite 266

Übung 1

1. one 2. one, one 3. one 4. - 5. - 6. - 7. one 8. -/one 9. - 10. one

Lösungen zu den Übungen auf Seite 270

Übung 1

1. than 2. as 3. as 4. like 5. like 6. than 7. than 8. as, as 9. as, as 10. as 11. as 12. as, as 13. as 14. as 15. as, as

Lösungen zu den Übungen auf Seite 273

Übung 1

1. angrily 2. attentively 3. carefully 4. coolly 5. cruelly 6. dryly 7. duely 8. dully 9. extremely 10. fully 11. gaily 12. surely 13. terribly 14. truly 15. luckily 16. palely 17. pratically 18. radically 19. shyly 20. usually

Lösungen zu den Übungen auf Seite 277

Übung 1

1. more precisely 2. later 3. closer, closer 4. faster 5. better/best 6. lower 7. more often 8. more efficiently, more accurately 9. longer 10. harder 11. least 12. louder 13. higher 14. sooner 15. more acutely

Lösungen

Lösungen zu den Übungen auf Seite 283 – 285

Übung 1

1. spoke absently 2. apparently wants to spend 3. answered calmly 4. cautiously followed 5. can certainly be 6. are not directly concerned 7. was just breaking 8. calmly took off 9. is to be handled carefully 10. was thoroughly and carefully worked out

Übung 2

1. normally only go to the doctor 2. clearly just 3. clearly enough 4. certainly big enough 5. had only arrived on January sixth 6. carefully horizontal 7. an awfully bad 8. absolutely unreasonable 9. barely wide enough 10. only 50 cents left

vor Vokal wird
a zu an

Übung 3

1. Apparently no one ... 2. Carefully he folded ... 3. Eventually they reached ...
4. Finally a little girl ... 5. Regularly visiting ... 6. Instantly a warm wave ...
7. Curiously people ... 8. Yesterday I met ..., I met your sister yesterday. 9. Finally most people ... 10. Of course we wanted ...

Übung 4

1. ... listening attentively 2. ... will eventually drop 3. Frequently corporations merge ... 4. It is certainly nice .. 5. ... the badly injured people 6. Abruptly he turned ... 7. ... drastically reduced others. 8. ... briefly washed, hurriedly brushed his teeth, and quickly changed his shirt. 9. Actually it was ... 10. We do not hope greatly, but, still we hope

Lösungen zu den Übungen auf Seite 289

Übung 1

1. quiet 2. close 3. early 4. attentive 5. angrily 6. close 7. badly 8. least 9. little 10. completely 11. lately 12. late 13. clear 14. clearly 15. pretty 16. pretty 17. hard 18. hardly 19. highly 20. fairly

Lösungen zu den Übungen auf Seite 304

Übung 1

1. It was 2. there came 3. so 4. It was 5. there was, there were 6. there was 7. It was 8. so 9. There were 10. It was

Lösungen zu den Übungen auf Seite 307

Übung 1

1. him 2. myself/I 3. him 4. him 5. himself 6. himself 7. himself 8. myself 9. herself

Lösungen

10. herself 11. himself 12. himself 13. himself 14. himself 15. myself

Lösungen zu den Übungen auf Seite 309

Übung 1

1. one another 2. each other 3. one another 4. each other 5. each other
6. one another 7. one another 8. each other 9. one another's 10. each other
11. one another 12. one another 13. one another's 14. each other 15. one another

> possessive case

Lösungen zu den Übungen auf Seite 312 – 313

Übung 1

1. his 2. mine 3. her 4. his 5. my 6. their 7. her 8. yours 9. my 10. his/hers
11. your 12. theirs 13. Your 14. His 15. his

> Eigennamen werden groß-geschrieben

Übung 2

1. that car of his 2. some village acquaintances of his 3. I hoped that that visit of mine 4. friends of yours 5. a friend of yours 6. is mine 7. is yours 8. a countryman of his 9. this interest of yours 10. This friend of yours

Lösungen zu den Übungen auf Seite 317

Übung 1

1. this 2. those 3. these 4. those 5. that 6. those 7. that 8. those 9. that 10. this

Lösungen zu den Übungen auf Seite 321 – 322

Übung 1

1. that of 2. the one 3. the one 4. the ones 5. the one 6. that of 7. that of, that of 8. that of 9. those of 10. that of

Übung 2

1. the one who 2. He who 3. he who 4. he who 5. those who 6. those who 7. those which 8. those which 9. He who 10. those who

Übung 3

1. those people who 2. The countries which 3. The man who 4. The noise which 5. The pupils who

Lösungen zu den Übungen auf Seite 327 – 328

Lösungen

Übung 1

1. whom 2. whom 3. whom 4. who 5. whom 6. whom 7. who 8. whom 9. whom 10. whom

Übung 2

1. that 2. that 3. who 4. whom 5. that 6. who 7. whom 8. whom 9. which 10. that

Übung 3

1. of which 2. of which 3. of which 4. whose 5. whose 6. whose 7. whose 8. whose 9. whose 10. whose

Lösungen zu den Übungen auf Seite 332 – 334

Übung 1

1. Who told you that? 2. Who/whom are you calling? 3. Whom/who do you believe? 4. Whom/who do you blame? 5. Whose hat do you want? 6. Who are you going to share your room with?/With whom are you going to share your room? 7. Whose job is it to make plans for houses? 8. Who is going to look after your children? 9. Who helps you with your homework? 10. Who/whom did she marry? 11. Who was she talking to?/To whom was she talking? 12. Who does this black bag belong to?/To whom does this black bag belong? 13. Who might have asked the following question? 14. Who/whom does the inspector suspect? 15. Whose socks are these? 16. Who/whom did they begin to help? 17. Whose fault was this? 18. Who were you making fun of?/Of whom were you making fun? 19. Who/whom was he shielding? 20. Who/whom would you call the father of railroading?

man beachte den Gebrauch von to do Präpositionen müssen erhalten bleiben

Übung 2

1. What 2. What 3. What 4. Which 5. What 6. What 7. Which 8. Which 9. What 10. What 11. Which 12. What 13. Which 14. Which 15. What 16. What 17. What 18. What 19. What 20. Which

Übung 3

1. How 2. How 3. How/what 4. What 5. How 6. What 7. What/how 8. How 9. How 10. How/what 11. What/how 12. How 13. What 14. How 15. How/what 16. What 17. What 18. How 19. What 20. How

Lösungen zu den Übungen auf Seite 346 – 351

Übung 1

1. any 2. any 3. any (anything) 4. any 5. any 6. some 7. some 8. any 9. any 10. any 11. any 12. any (anyone) 13. any 14. any 15. some 16. some 17. some 18. some (someone) 19. some (something) 20. some

Lösungen

Übung 2

1. every 2. each 3. every 4. every 5. each 6. every 7. Every 8. Every 9. each, each 10. every

Übung 3

1. the whole 2. the whole 3. all 4. all 5. all 6. all 7. all 8. all/the whole 9. the whole/a whole 10. all 11. all 12. all 13. a whole 14. The whole 15. a whole

Übung 4

1. many 2. much 3. much 4. much 5. many 6. much 7. much 8. Much 9. many 10. much 11. much 12. many 13. much 14. many 15. much 16. many 17. Much 18. much 19. much 20. much

Übung 5

1. few 2. few 3. little 4. few 5. little 6. little 7. Few 8. few 9. little 10. little 11. few 12. few 13. little 14. little 15. few

Übung 6

1. no 2. none 3. nobody 4. no, no 5. Nobody 6. Nobody 7. none 8. no 9. Nobody 10. Nobody

Übung 7

1. Neither 2. Either 3. Either 4. neither 5. Neither 6. Neither 7. either 8. either 9. either 10. either

Lösungen zu den Übungen auf Seite 359 – 361

Übung 1

1. at 2. at 3. for/after/before 4. in 5. in/out 6. into 7. with 8. on 9. on 10. for

Übung 2

1. with 2. on 3. for 4. in 5. for. 6. on 7. after 8. for 9. in 10. up 11. up 12. on/off 13. off 14. for 15. up 16. in 17. for 18. for 19. of 20. into 21. out 22. of 23. in 24. up 25. on

Übung 3

1. in 2. in 3. about 4. on 5. in 6. on/about 7. of 8. of 9. of 10. of 11. on 12. of 13. in 14. in 15. for

Übung 4

1. with 2. over/about 3. with 4. with 5. for 6. with 7. from/to 8. at 9. in 10. for 11. for 12. of 13. for 14. at 15. of

Lösungen zu den Übungen auf Seite 377 – 378

Übung 1

1. does he 2. did he 3. was he 4. will he 5. isn't he 6. can I, didn't we 7. do I 8. didn't I 9. will I 10. aren't I 11. aren't I 12. couldn't they 13. don't they 14. did they 15. do they 16. didn't he 17. doesn't he 18. don't you 19. haven't they 20. hasn't he 21. does he 22. has he 23. isn't he 24. is he 25. hadn't we 26. have we 27. won't we 28. won't we 29. are we 30. aren't we 31. can't you 32. do you 33. didn't you 34. don't you 35. weren't you 36. were you 37. were you 38. won't you 39. aren't you 40. won't you

verneinter question tag von am I heißt aren't I

INDEX

A

a, 209
a billion, 290
a billionth, 292
a hundred thousand, 290
a hundred, 290
a hundredth, 292
a million, 290
a thousand millions, 290
a thousand millionth, 292
a thousand, 290
abgeleitetes Adverb, 271
abgeleitetes Substantiv, 232
abgewandeltes Substantiv, 232
Abkürzungen, 9
aboard, 356
about, 356
above, 356
abstract noun, 231
Abstrakta, 231
accentuation, 11
according to, 356
across, 356
active voice, 123
adjective with a prop-word, 265
adjective, 259
Adjektiv mit einem Stützwort, 265
Adjektiv, 259
Adjektiv, attributives, 259
Adjektiv, prädikatives, 259
Adjektiv, Steigerung, 260
Adjektiv, Stellung, 267
Adverb oder Adjektiv, 286
adverb of degree, 271
adverb of frequency, 271
adverb of manner, 271
adverb of place, 271
adverb of time, 271
adverb or adjective, 286
Adverb, 271
adverb, 271
Adverb, abgeleitetes, 271
Adverb, Steigerung, 274
Adverb, Stellung, 278
Adverb, ursprüngliches, 271
adverbial clause, 381
adverbial element, 94, 363
adverbiale Bestimmung, 94, 363

Adverbialsatz, 381
adversative conjunction, 354
adversative Konjunktion, 354
affirmative clause of statement, 364
after, 352, 356
against, 356
agreement of verb and subject, 99
Akkusativ, 362
Aktiv, 123
all, 339
all the, 269
along, 356
Alphabet, 10
alphabet, 10
als, 286
also, 354
although, 353
American spelling, 390
amerikanische Schreibweise, 390
amid, 356
amidst, 356
among, 356
amongst, 356
an, 209
and, 354
Anführungszeichen, 395
another, 341
anreihende Konjunktion, 354
any, 335
Appellativa, 231
around, 356
article, 209
Artikel, 209
Artikel, bestimmter, 209
Artikel, Stellung, 228
Artikel, unbestimmter, 209
as ... as, 268, 354
as if, 354
as long as, 352
as often as, 352
as soon as, 352
as though, 354
as well as, 354
as, 268, 352, 353, 354
at, 356
attributive adjective, 259
attributive clause, 382
attributive pronoun, 298

attributives Adjektiv, 259
attributives Determinativpronomen, 320
attributives Interrogativpronomen, 329
attributives Possessivpronomen, 311
attributives Pronomen, 298
Attributsatz, 382
Aufforderungssatz, 379
ausmalender Relativsatz, 383
Ausrufesatz, 380
Ausrufewort, 380
Ausrufezeichen, 395
Aussagesatz, 364
Aussagesatz, bejahter, 364
Aussagesatz, verneinter, 368
Aussprache, 13
auxiliary verb, 27, 52

B

be able to, 65
be allowed to, 65, 67, 74
be going to, 77, 79
be in the habit of, 77
be likely to, 67
be permitted to, 65, 67, 74, 76
be supposed to, 73, 74
be to, 74, 79
be willing to, 79
be, 52
because, 353
because of, 356
Bedingungssatz, 158
Befehlsform, 167
before, 352, 356
Begriffswort, 231
behind, 356
Beifügung + of, 252
beiordnende Konjunktion, 352
bejahter Aussagesatz, 364
below, 356
beneath, 356
beside, 356
besides, 356
besitzanzeigendes Fürwort, 310

Besitzfall, 252
Besonderheiten bei der Schreibung, 384
bestimmendes Fürwort, 318
bestimmter Artikel, 209
Bestimmung, adverbiale, 94, 363
Betonung, 11
between, 356
Beugung, 29
beyond, 357
bezügliches Fürwort, 323
billion, 290
billionth, 292
Bindestrich, 395
Bindewort, 352
both, 344
both and, 354
britische Schreibweise, 390
British spelling, 390
Bruch, gemeiner, 294
Bruchzahlen, 294
but, 354, 357
by, 357
by-agent, 123

C

can, 28, 65
capital letters, 384
cardinal number, 290
causative clause, 381
causative conjunction, 352
causative verb, 92
cipher, 291
clause, 362
clause of statement, 364
collective noun, 231
colon, 395
comma, 392
common case, 252
common noun, 231
comparative conjunction, 354
comparative, 260, 274
comparison, 260, 268, 274
complement, 92
compound noun, 232
compound sentence, 362
compound tense, 103
concessive clause, 382

concessive conjunction, 353
concrete noun, 231
conditional, 158
conditional clause, 158, 382
conditional conjunction, 353
conjugation, 29
conjunction, 352
consecutive clause, 382
consecutive conjunction, 353
consonant, 20
continuous form, 115
continuous infinitive, 168
contractions, 40
coordinating conjunction, 352
copulative conjunction, 354
could, 28, 65

D

dare, 28, 82
dash, 397
date, 296
Dativ, 362
Datum, 296
decimal fraction, 294
defining relative clause, 382
definite article, 209
demonstrative adjective, 314
demonstrative pronoun, 314
Demonstrativpronomen, 314
Demonstrativpronomen, substantivisches, 318
derivative adverb, 271
derivative noun, 232
despite, 357
determinative adjective, 320
determinative pronoun, 318
Determinativpronomen, 318
Determinativpronomen, attributives, 320

Dezimalbruch, 294
Dingwort, 231
direct interrogative clause, 373
direct object, 92
direkte Frage, 373
direktes Objekt, 92
do, 54
Doppelpunkt, 395
double, 295
down, 357
during, 357

E

each, 338
each other, 28, 87, 308
ebenso ... wie, 268
Eigenname, 231
Eigenschaftswort, 259
eight, 290
eight hundred, 290
eight hundredth, 292
eighteen, 290
eighteenth, 292
eighth, 292
eightieth, 292
eighty, 290
einander, 87, 308
einfache Zeit, 103
Einzahl, 209
either, 343
either or, 354
eleven, 290
eleventh, 292
Entscheidungsfrage, 373
Ergänzung, prädikative, 94, 363
Ergänzungen zum Verb, 92
erlebte Rede, 137
Ersatzverben, 63
Ersatzverb von can, 65
Ersatzverb von could, 65
Ersatzverb von may, 67
Ersatzverb von might, 67
Ersatzverb von must, 71
Ersatzverb von need, 71
Ersatzverb von ought to, 73
Ersatzverb von shall, 73

Ersatzverb von should, 73
Ersatzverb von used to, 79
Ersatzverb von will, 79
Ersatzverb von would, 79
es, 301
even if, 353
every, 338
except, 357
exclamation mark, 395
exclamatory clause, 380

F

Fachausdrücke, 407
factitive verb, 92
faktitives Verb, 92
feminin, 233
few, 341
fifteen, 290
fifteenth, 292
fifth, 292
fiftieth, 292
fifty, 290
final clause, 381
final conjunction, 352
finale Konjunktion, 352
Finalsatz, 381
finite verb, 27
finite Verbform, 27
first, 292
five, 290
five hundred, 290
five hundredth, 292
-fold, 295
for, 353, 354, 357
fortieth, 292
forty, 290
four, 290
four hundred, 290
four hundredth, 292
fourteen, 290
fourteenth, 292
fourth, 292
fractional number, 294
Frage mit Fragewort, 374
Frage, direkte, 373
Frage, indirekte, 374
Fragefürwort, 329
Fragesatz, 373
Fragezeichen, 395
from, 357
full stop, 392
full verb, 27

Fürwort, besitzanzeigendes, 310
Fürwort, bestimmendes, 318
Fürwort, bezügliches, 323
Fürwort, hinweisendes, 314
Fürwort, persönliches, 299
Fürwort, rückbezügliches, 305
Fürwort, unbestimmtes, 335
future continuous, 108
future in the past, 107
future perfect in the past, 107
future perfect, 107
future tense, 106

G

Gattungsname, 231
Gedankenstrich, 397
gegenseitig, 87
Gegenstandswort, 231
Gegenwart, 103
gemeiner Bruch, 294
gender of the noun, 233
Genitiv, 362
Genus, 233
germanische Steigerung, 260, 262, 274, 276
gerund, 183
Geschlecht des Substantivs, 233
Geschlecht, 209
Geschlechtswort, 209
gleicher Grad, 260, 274
going to, 106
Grad, gleicher, 260, 274
Grad, höchster, 260, 274
Grad, ungleicher, 260, 274
Großschreibung, 384
Grundform, 168
Grundstufe, 260, 274
Grundzahlen, 290

H

hardly when, 352
Hauptsatz, 362
Hauptwort, 231
have got to, 71
have the habit of, 77

have, 52
have to, 71
he, 299
he who, 318
her, 299, 311
hers, 310
herself, 305
Hilfsverb, 27, 52
him, 299
himself, 305
hinweisendes Fürwort, 314
hiphen, 395
his, 310, 311
höchster Grad, 260, 274
how, 329
however, 323, 353, 354
hundred, 290
hundredth, 292

I

I, 199
if, 353
if-clause, 158
Imperativ, 167
imperative, 167
imperative clause, 379
impersonal passive, 124
in, 357
in case, 352, 353
in front of, 357
in order that, 352
in that, 353
indefinite article, 209
indefinite pronoun, 335
Indefinitpronomen, 335
Index, 445
indicative, 165
Indikativ, 144, 165
indirect interrogative clause, 374
indirect object, 93
indirekte Frage, 374
indirekte Rede, 137
indirektes Objekt, 93
infinite verb, 27
infinite Verbform, 27
Infinitiv, 168
Infinitiv des Passivs, 125
infinitive, 168
Inhaltsverzeichnis, 5
inside, 357
intend to, 79

interior monologue, 137
interjection word, 380
Interpunktion, 392
interrogative adjective, 329
interrogative clause, 373
interrogative pronoun, 329
Interrogativpronomen, 329
Interrogativpronomen, attributives, 329
Interrogativpronomen, substantivisches, 329
into, 357
intonated question, 373
Intonationsfrage, 373
intransitive verb, 27
intransitives Verb, 27
Inversion des Subjekts, 373
inversion question, 337
Inversionsfrage, 373
Irrealis der Gegenwart, 159
Irrealis der Vergangenheit, 159
it, 299
its, 311
its own, 310
itself, 305

J

je ... desto, 268

K

kausale Konjunktion, 352
Kausalsatz, 381
kausatives Verb, 92
Kleinschreibung, 384
Kollektiva, 231
Komma, 392
Komparativ, 260, 274
Konditional, 158
konditionale Konjunktion, 353
Konditionalsatz, 158, 382
Konjugation, 29
Konjugation passiver Formen, 128
Konjugation reflexiver Verben, 88

Konjugation regelmäßiger Verben, 36
Konjugation unregelmäßiger Verben, 38
Konjugation von to be, 34
Konjugation von to have, 32
Konjunktion, 352
Konjunktion, adversative, 354
Konjunktion, anreihende, 354
Konjunktion, beiordnende, 352
Konjunktion, finale, 352
Konjunktion, kausale, 352
Konjunktion, konditionale, 353
Konjunktion, konsektuve, 353
Konjunktion, konzessive, 353
Konjunktion, modale, 353
Konjunktion, nebenordnende, 352
Konjunktion, temporale, 352
Konjunktion, unterordnende, 352
Konjunktion, vergleichende, 354
Konjunktiv, 144
Konkreta, 231
konsekutive Konjunktion, 53
Konsekutivsatz, 382
Konsonant, 20
konzessive Konjunktion, 353
Konzessivsatz, 382
Kurzformen, 40
Kurzfrage, 376

L

lassen, 204
Leideform, 123
lest, 352
let, 74
level stress, 12
like, 268, 354
likewise, 354

little, 341
Lösungen, 419

M

main clause, 362
männlich, 209, 233
many, 339
mark of exclamation, 395
mark of interrogation, 395
maskulin, 233
may, 28, 67
me, 299
mean to, 79
Mehrzahl, 209, 238
might, 28, 67
million, 290
millionth, 292
mine, 310, 311
Mitlaut, 20
modal auxiliary verb, 28, 63
modal conjunction, 353
modale Konjunktion, 353
Modalverb, 28, 63
modified noun, 232
Modus, 165
mood, 165
much, 339
multiplying number, 295
must, 28, 71
my, 311
myself, 305

N

Nachsilbe, 402
near, 357
nebenordnende Konjunktion, 352
Nebensatz, 362, 381
need, 28, 71
negative clause of statement, 368
neither, 343
neither nor, 354
Nennwort, 231
neutrum, 233
nicht notwendiger Relativsatz, 383
nil, 291
nine, 290

nine hundred, 290
nine hundredth, 292
nineteen, 290
nineteenth, 292
ninth, 292
ninetieth, 292
ninety, 290
no, 342
no one, 342
no sooner than, 352
nobody, 342
Nomen, 231
nominative clause, 381
non-compound tense, 103
non-defining relative clause, 383
none, 342
nor, 354
not as as, 354
not eiher, 354
not only but also, 354
not so as, 354
note of exclamation, 395
note of interrogation, 395
notwendiger Relativsatz, 382
notwithstanding that, 353
nought, 291
noun, 231
now, 352
number of the noun, 238
Numerus des Substantivs, 238

O

o, 291
object, 362
objective clause, 381
Objekt, 362
Objekt, direktes, 92
Objekt, indirektes, 93
Objekt, persönliches, 93
Objekt, präpositionales, 363
Objekt, präpositionales, 94
Objektfall, 252
Objektpronomen, 300
Objektsatz, 381
of, 357
of which, 323
off, 357
on, 357
on condition (that), 353

one another, 28, 87, 308
one billion, 290
one hundred, 290
one hundred thousandth, 292
one hundredth, 292
one million, 290
one millionth, 292
one thousand, 290
one thousandth, 292
one, 265, 290, 344
oneself, 305
or, 354
ordinal number, 292
ordinary form, 115
Ordnungszahlen, 292
original adverb, 271
original noun, 231
other, 341
ought to, 28, 73
our, 311
ours, 310
ourselves, 305
out, 357
outside, 357
over, 357

P

participle, 194
Partizip, 194
Passiv, 123
Passiv, unpersönliches, 124
passive infinitive, 125
passive voice, 123
past, 357
past participle, 194
past perfect subjunctive, 166
past perfect, 105
past subjunctive, 166
past tense continuous, 109
past tense, 103
past unreality, 159
per, 357
perfect continuous infinitive, 169
perfect gerund, 183
perfect infinitive, 168
perfect participle, 194
period, 392
peronal pronoun, 299

Personalpronomen, 299
persönliches Fürwort, 299
persönliches Objekt, 93
Plural, 209, 238
Pluralbildung zusammengesetzter Substantive, 249
position of the article, 228
position of the adjective, 267
position of the adverb, 278
Positiv, 260, 274
positive, 260, 274
possessive adjective, 311
possessive case, 252
possessive pronoun, 310
Possessivpronomen, 310
Possessivpronomen, attributives, 311
Possessivpronomen, substantivisches, 310
Prädikat, 362
prädikative Ergänzung, 94, 363
prädikatives Adjektiv, 259
Präfix, 400
Präposition, 356
präpositionales Objekt, 94, 363
predicate, 362
predicative adjective, 259
predicative complement, 94, 363
prefix, 400
preposition, 356
prepositional object, 94
present continuous infinitive, 168
present gerund, 183
present infinitive, 168
present participle, 194
present perfect continuous, 103
present perfect, 103
present subjunctive, 165
present tense continuous, 108
present tense simple, 103
present tense, 103
principal clause, 362

principal forms, 41
progressive form, 115
Pronomen, 298
Pronomen der Gegenseitigkeit, 308
Pronomen der Wechselseitigkeit, 308
Pronomen, attributives, 298
Pronomen, substantivisches, 298
pronoun, 298
pronunciation, 13
proper noun, 231
prop-word, 265
provided that, 353
punctuation, 392
Punkt, 392

Q

quadruple, 295
question mark, 395
question tag, 376
question with a question word, 374
quotation mark, 395

R

real present, 159
Realis, 159
Rechtschreibung, 384
reciprocal pronoun, 308
reciprocal verb, 28, 87
Rede, erlebte, 137
Rede, indirekte, 137
reflexive pronoun, 305
reflexive verb 28, 86
reflexives Verb, 28, 86
Reflexivpronomen, 305
relative clause, 382
relative pronoun, 323
Relativpronomen, 323
Relativsatz, 382
Relativsatz, ausmalender, 383
Relativsatz, nicht notwendiger, 383
Relativsatz, notwendiger, 382
repetition of the article, 230
reported speech, 137

reziprokes Verb, 28, 87
Reziprokpronomen 308
romanische Steigerung, 260, 262, 274, 276
round, 357
rückbezügliches Fürwort, 305

S

sächlich, 209, 233
Sammelnahme, 231
Satz, 362
Satzaussage, 362
Satzgefüge, 362
Satzgegenstand, 362
scarcely when, 352
second, 292
seeing that, 353
sein-Passiv, 124
Selbstlaut, 13
seven, 290
seven hundred, 290
seven hundredth, 292
seventeen, 290
seventeenth, 292
seventh, 292
seventieth, 292
seventy, 290
shall, 28, 73
she, 299
she who, 318
should, 28, 73
Silbentrennung, 398
simple, 295
simple form, 115
since, 352, 353, 357
single, 295
Singular, 209
six, 290
six hundred, 290
six hundredth, 292
sixteen, 290
sixteenth, 292
sixth, 292
sixtieth, 292
sixty, 290
small letters, 384
so ... as, 268
so ... wie, 268
so that, 352, 353
so, 302, 353
some, 335
Stammformen, 41

Steigerung des Adjektivs, 260
Steigerung des Adverbs, 274
Steigerung, germanische, 260, 262, 274, 276
Steigerung, romanische, 260, 262, 274, 276
Steigerung, unregelmäßige, 263, 276
Stellung des Adjektivs, 267
Stellung des Adverbs, 278
Stellung des Artikels, 228
Stoffname, 231
Stützwort, 265
subject, 362
Subjekt, 362
Subjektpronomen, 299
Subjektsatz, 381
subjunctive, 165
subordinate clause, 362, 381
subordinating conjunction, 352
substantial noun, 231
Substantiv, 231
Substantiv, abgeleitetes, 232
Substantiv, abgewandeltes, 232
Substantiv, Geschlecht, 233
Substantiv, Numerus, 238
Substantiv, zusammengesetztes, 232
substantival pronoun, 298
substantivisches Demonstrativpronomen, 318
substantivisches Interrogativpronomen, 329
substantivisches Possessivpronomen, 311
substantivisches Pronomen, 298
substitutionary narration, 137
such, 314
such that, 353
Suffix, 402
suffix, 402
Superlativ, 260, 274
superlative, 260, 274
supposing that, 353

syllabification, 398
syllable division, 398

T

Tatform, 123
Tätigkeitsform, 123
Tätigkeitswort, 27
temporal clause, 381
temporal conjunction, 352
temporale Konjunktion, 352
Temporalsatz, 381
ten, 290
ten thousand, 290
ten thousandth, 292
tense, 103
tenth, 292
than, 268, 354
that, 314, 320, 323, 352, 353
that of, 318
that which, 318, 320
that who, 320
the, 209, 320
the ... the, 268
the one, 318
the one which, 318
the one who, 318
the ones, 318
the ones which, 318
the ones who, 318
the two, 344
the which, 320
the who, 320
thee, 299
their, 311
theirs, 310
them, 299
themselves, 305
there, 302
therefore, 353
these, 314
they, 299
they who, 318
thine, 310, 311
third, 292
thirteen, 290
thirteenth, 292
thirtieth, 292
thirty, 290
this, 314
those, 314

those of, 318
those which, 318, 320
those who, 318, 320
thou, 299
though, 352
thousand, 290
thousandth, 292
three, 290
three hundred, 290
three hundredth, 292
through, 357
throughout, 358
thy, 311
till, 352, 358
time, 296
-times, 295
to, 358
toward, 358
towards, 358
transitive verb, 27, 92
transitives Verb, 27, 92
treble, 295
triple, 295
Tunwort, 27
twelfth, 292
twelve, 290
twentieth, 292
twenty, 290
twice, 295
two, 290
two hundred, 290
two hundredth, 292

U

Übereinstimmung von Verb und Subjekt, 99
Übungen zu den Ergänzungen zum Verb, 97
Übungen zu den Hilfsverben, 58
Übungen zu den Modalverben, 83
Übungen zu den Partizipien, 200
Übungen zu den question tags, 377
Übungen zu den reflexiven Verben, 90
Übungen zu den Zeiten, 110
Übungen zu Fragesätzen, 59

Übungen zum Adverb und Adjektiv, 289
Übungen zum Artikel, 224
Übungen zum common und possessive case des Substantivs, 257
Übungen zum Demonstrativpronomen, 317
Übungen zum Determinativpronomen, 321
Übungen zum deutschen *lassen,* 206
Übungen zum gerund, 189
Übungen zum Geschlecht des Substantivs, 237
Übungen zum Indefinitpronomen, 346
Übungen zum Infinitiv, 178
Übungen zum Interrogativpronomen, 332
Übungen zum Konditional, 162
Übungen zum Numerus des Substantivs, 2509
Übungen zum Passiv, 130
Übungen zum Personalpronomen, 304
Übungen zum Possessivpronomen, 312
Übungen zum Reflexivpronomen, 307
Übungen zum Relativpronomen, 327
Übungen zum Reziprokpronomen, 309
Übungen zum Stützwort des Adjektivs, 266
Übungen zum Vergleich des Adjektivs, 270
Übungen zur Bildung des Adverbs, 273
Übungen zur indirekten Rede, 148
Übungen zur Konjugation 48
Übungen zur Präposition, 359
Übungen zur simple und continuous form, 119
Übungen zur Steigerung des Adjektivs, 264
Übungen zur Steigerung des Adverbs, 277

Übungen zur Stellung des Adverbs, 283
Übungen zur Stellung des Artikels, 229
Übungen zur Verneinung, 58
Uhrzeit, 296
Umschreibung mit to do, 54
umso, 269
Umstandsbestimmung, 363
Umstandsbestimmung, 94
Umstandswort, 271
Umwandlung aktiver Sätze in passive Sätze, 126
unbestimmter Artikel, 209
unbestimmtes Fürwort, 335
under, 358
ungleicher Grad, 260, 274
unless, 353
unpersönliches Passiv, 124
unreal present, 159
unregelmäßig gesteigerte Adjektive, 263
unregelmäßig gesteigerte Adverbien, 276
unterordnende Konjunktion, 352
until, 352, 358
up, 358
upon, 358
ursprüngliches Adverb, 271
Ursubstantiv, 231
us, 299
used to, 28, 79

V

veranlassen, 204
verb and its complements, 92
Verb und seine Ergänzungen, 92
Verb, 27
verb, 27
Verb, faktitives, 92
Verb, intransitives, 27
Verb, kausatives, 92

Verb, reflexives, 28, 86
Verb, reziprokes, 28, 87
Verb, transitives, 27, 92
Verbform, finite, 27
Verbform, infinite, 27
Verbformen und Verbarten, 27
Vergangenheit, 103
Vergleich, 268
vergleichende Konjunktion, 354
Verhältniswort, 356
Verlaufsform, 115
verneinter Aussagesatz, 368
Vervielfältigungszahlwort, 295
via, 358
Vokal, 13
Vollverb, 27
Vorgangspassiv, 124
Vorsilbe, 400
Vorsubjekt, 302
Vorvergangenheit, 105
vowel, 13
vulgar fraction, 294

W

want s.o. to do s.th., 74
want to, 79
we, 299
weiblich, 209, 233
wem-Fall, 362
wen-Fall, 362
werden-Passiv, 124
wessen-Fall, 362
what, 318, 323, 329
whatever, 323
when, 323, 329, 352
whenever, 232
where, 323, 329
whereas, 354
wherever, 323
which, 318, 323, 329
whichever, 323
while, 352, 354
whilst, 352, 354
who, 318, 323, 329
whoever, 323
whole, 339
whom, 323, 329

whose, 320, 323, 329
why, 329
wie, 268
Wiederholung des Artikels, 230
Wiewort, 259
will, 28, 77, 79
wish to, 79
with, 354, 358
within, 358
without, 354, 358
would, 28, 79

Y

ye, 299
yes-/no-question, 373
yet, 354
you, 299
your, 311
yours, 310
yourself, 305
yourselves, 305

Z

Zahlwort, 290
Zeichensetzung, 392
Zeit, 103
Zeit, einfache, 103
Zeit, zusammengesetzte, 103
Zeitenfolge im Bedingungssatz, 159
Zeitenfolge in der indirekten Rede, 144
Zeitwort, 27
zero, 290, 291
Zukunft, 106
zulassen, 204
zusammengesetzte Zeit, 103
zusammengesetztes Substantiv, 232
Zustandspassiv, 124